History of the
Idea of Progress

HISTORY OF
THE IDEA
OF
PROGRESS

Robert Nisbet

Basic Books, Inc., Publishers *New York*

The author gratefully acknowledges permission to reprint excerpts from the following:

"It is Almost the Year Two Thousand" from *The Poetry of Robert Frost* edited by Edward Connery Lathem. Copyright 1942 by Robert Frost. Copyright © 1969 by Holt, Rinehart and Winston. Copyright © 1970 by Lesley Frost Ballantine. Reprinted by permission of Holt, Rinehart and Winston, Publishers.

"Dry Salvages" by T. S. Eliot from *Four Quartets*. Reprinted by permission of Harcourt Brace Jovanovich, Inc.

Library of Congress Cataloging in Publication Data

Nisbet, Robert.
   History of the idea of progress.

   Includes index.
   1. Progress. I. Title.
HM101.N574   1980   303.4   79-1979
ISBN: 0–465–03025–4

To My Wife

CONTENTS

CONTENTS

viii

FOREWORD

READERS who are acquainted with my *Social Change and History* (1969) will recognize in this book intellectual ground that was gone over with a different objective in the earlier one. That book is a critical exploration of modern social theory; its aim, the demonstration through historical as well as analytical arguments of the frailties in reigning theories of change —chiefly functionalism, developmentalism, and evolutionism—in the contemporary social sciences. Treatment of the idea of progress is brief and is subordinated throughout to other, larger interests.

The present work was conceived as a short history of the idea of progress alone. I have tried, within the limits of space, to identify and put in proper perspective the major personages, texts, presuppositions, intellectual climates, and philosophical and ideological uses of the idea during the past twenty-five hundred years. Although the dogma of progress held magisterial status during most of its Western history, it has obviously fallen to a low and sorely beset status in our century. Its future, as I suggest in the final chapter, is cloudy, to say the least. One conclusion, though, may be stated confidently. If the idea of progress does die in the West, so will a great deal else that we have long cherished in this civilization.

Dependence upon the scholarship of others is of necessity great in a book such as this, and although I have made specific reference in the text to all those whose insights and interpretations have been valuable to me, there are a few who must be given special mention here. They are: the late Ludwig Edelstein, whose *The Idea of Progress in Classical Antiquity* was almost indispensable to me in the preparation of the first chapter of this book; Gerhart B. Ladner for his remarkable *Idea of Reform* chiefly, but for his other writings as well, all of which guided me through early Christian thought along paths I should not, in all probability, have found for myself; the late Ernst Kantorowicz, whose *The King's Two Bodies* opens doors to so much more in medieval thought than its title might suggest, including the idea of progress; Marjorie Reeves for her *The Influence of Prophecy in the Later Middle Ages,* which provides us with full and authoritative treatment of that twelfth-century prophet–genius Joachim de Fiore and also traces in detail his influence down into the nineteenth century; there is no other figure whose influence upon the formation of the medieval idea of progress is larger and more fertile than Joachim's; Arthur Lovejoy and George Boas for their rich studies of primitivism and progress in classical and medieval writings, and Lovejoy alone for his *The Great Chain of Being,* one of the masterpieces of twentieth century scholarship. There are, as I have noted, many others whose scholarly investigations and commentaries have been of great value to me, but I believe I have rendered sufficient acknowledgment of them in the text, with two exceptions.

The first is Frederick J. Teggart, for many years a member of the faculty of the University of California, Berkeley. His own fruitful and influential interest in the idea of progress, going back to the early part of this century, led to my interest in the subject. A number of interpretations and emphases in this book differ sometimes sharply from Teggart's, but that fact in no way diminishes my lifelong obligation to one of the profoundest and most original scholars in this century.

Tribute must also be given J. B. Bury for his *Idea of Progress: An Inquiry into its Origins and Growth,* published in London in 1920. The highest compliment to be paid the book is to observe that it has itself become a part of the history of the idea—in short, a classic. It is, however, a deeply flawed classic. Bury (in a tradition that goes back at least to Auguste Comte in the early nineteenth century) denied to both the classical and medieval worlds any real conception of human progress on earth. And, quintessential rationalist and free thinker that he was, he chose to see Christianity as the final great foe to be routed before the idea of progress could emerge in, according to Bury, the late seventeenth century. His positions in those respects as well as others simply cannot be legitimately maintained today, given the great amount of specialized scholarship on classical and medieval thought that has appeared since his book was published. But errors or omissions notwithstanding, Bury's book must be respected both for its content and its widespread influence.

I am grateful to The Rockefeller Foundation, particularly to its Division of Humanities under the directorship of Dr. Joel Colton, for a generous grant-in-aid that helped greatly in the research necessary for the writing of this book. That grant makes it possible to thank Joseph Lawrence and Christopher Kobrak, graduate students at Columbia University during the early phase of the book, for their valuable research assistance. To Columbia

I am indebted for the privilege of serving on its faculty as Albert Schweitzer Professor in the Humanities during the years 1974–78. This book was begun and largely completed during those years, and it cannot therefore be separated from the stimulating and rewarding atmosphere of Morningside Heights.

The book was completed during my tenure as resident scholar at The American Enterprise Institute for Public Policy Research, in Washington, D.C., and I take this opportunity to thank the William J. Baroodys, Sr. and Jr., for their perception of the book's subject as falling within public policy research. It is impossible for me to imagine a more congenial setting for research and writing.

Finally, I take pleasure in thanking Martin Kessler, Midge Decter, Maureen Bischoff, and others at Basic Books for their wise counsel and unfailing assistance in converting manuscript into book during this past year.

Part I

The Genesis and
Development of the
Idea of Progress

Introduction

It is Almost the Year Two Thousand

To start the world of old
We had one age of gold
Not labored out of mines,
And some say there are signs,
The second such has come,
The true Millennium,
The final golden glow
To end it. And if so
(and science ought to know)
We may well raise our heads
From weeding garden beds
And annotating books
To watch this end de luxe.

ROBERT FROST

A S the year 2000 comes closer, there is certain to be a widening and quickening of interest—scientific, scholarly, intellectual, and popular—not only in the year itself, given its chiliastic overtone, but also in the whole question of human progress. What, it will be—is now being—asked, may be expected of the year, as far as the West is concerned? Does a Golden Age lie ahead; or, as the result of degeneration, an Age of Darkness? And how will progress or regress be assessed, by what criteria? What *is* progress: basically moral and spiritual, with *absence* of material wealth a better indicator than abundance? There are those in the past as well as in the West today who have so argued. Or is progress inextricably related to the skills and insights proceeding from accumulation of knowledge, as a long line of philosophers commencing with Xenophanes and Protagoras in ancient Greece have insisted? Throughout most of Western history, the Middle Ages included, respect for reason, knowledge, and science was so high that it was almost inevitable that criteria of human progress would be drawn from these values. It is different, however, in the twentieth century. The revolt against rationalism and science, the cultivation of irrationalism in a variety of forms, religious and secular, and the astonishing growth of subjectivism, of preoccupation with one's own self and its pleasures—all of this is different in scale at least from anything the West has before known. Will the historic idea of progress be driven entirely from the intellectual field by the massed forces of pessimism: belief in cycles of civilization, with our own Western civilization even now hastening toward the bottom of the downswing?

It is not the purpose of this book to seek direct answers to any of these obsessing questions, although I like to think that some light will be thrown on the questions by pursuit of the actual aim of the book, which is that of providing a straightforward history of the idea of progress, from the Greeks to our own day. For more than twenty-five hundred years philosophers, scientists, historians and theologians have been occupied in varying degrees of intensity by this idea—and, of course, its opposite: degeneration or cyclical recurrence, although from Hesiod and possibly Homer on, the faith in progress has been, as I show in the chapters of this book, the dominant faith. We live, it has often been said, under the spell of ideas, good or bad, true or false. We may think we are responding directly to events and changes in the histories of institutions, but we aren't; we are responding to these events and changes as they are made real or assimilable to us by ideas already in our heads.

No single idea has been more important than, perhaps as important as, the idea of progress in Western civilization for nearly three thousand years. Other ideas will come to mind, properly: liberty, justice, equality, community, and so forth. I do not derogate from one of them. But this must be stressed: throughout most of Western history, the substratum of even these ideas has been a philosophy of history that lends past, present, and future to their importance. Nothing gives greater importance or credibility to a moral or political value than belief that it is more than something cherished or to be cherished; that it is an essential element of historical movement from past through present to future. Such a value can then be transposed from the merely desirable to the historically necessary.

Simply stated, *the idea of progress holds that mankind has advanced in the past—from some aboriginal condition of primitiveness, barbarism, or even nullity—is now advancing, and will continue to advance through the foreseeable future.* In J. B. Bury's apt phrase, the idea of progress is a synthesis of the past and a prophecy of the future. It is inseparable from a sense of time flowing in unilinear fashion. Arthur O. Lovejoy, in his *Primitivism and Related Ideas in Antiquity,* writes that the idea represents "an appraisal both of the historic process in general and of the predominant trend which is manifested in it." The consequence of this awareness of historical process, Lovejoy continues, is widespread belief in "a tendency inherent in nature or man to pass through a regular sequence of stages of development in the past, the present and the future, the latter stages being —with perhaps occasional retardations or regressions—superior to the earlier." To which it is necessary to add only that most often this idea also contains assumptions as to the continuity, the gradualness, the naturalness, even the inexorability, of these stages of development. The idea must not be thought the companion of mere caprice or accident; it must be thought a part of the very scheme of things in universe and society. Advance from the inferior to the superior must seem as real and certain as anything in the laws of nature.

But what does "advance" or passage from "inferior to superior" mean in substantive terms? We shall find from the Greeks down to the twentieth century two closely related though distinguishable propositions. First slow, gradual, and cumulative improvement in *knowledge,* the kind of knowledge embodied in the arts and sciences, in the manifold ways man has for coping with the problems presented by nature or by the sheer efforts of human beings to live with one another in groups. From Hesiod and, more vividly, Protagoras, through such Romans as Lucretius and Seneca, through St. Augustine and his descendants all the way to the seventeenth-century Puritans and beyond, down to the great prophets of progress in the nineteenth and twentieth centuries, such as Saint-Simon, Comte, Hegel, Marx, and Herbert Spencer, we find a rarely interrupted conviction that the very nature of knowledge—objective knowledge such as that in science and technology—is to advance, to improve, to become more perfect.

The second major proposition or strand of thought we find in the history of the idea of progress centers upon man's moral or spiritual condition on earth, his happiness, his freedom from torments of nature and society, and above all his serenity or tranquillity. The goal of progress or advancement is mankind's eventual achievement, *on earth,* of these spiritual and moral virtues, thus leading toward ever-greater perfection of human nature. There have been in the past, there are now, there always will be, no doubt, those who believe that the two propositions just stated have an inverse relationship to one another. That is, achievement of spiritual bliss and moral perfection demands, as its condition, *not* achievement or increase of knowledge

—of world and man—but repudiation of such knowledge. To know is to sin, or lay the foundations of sin. The Greeks had their legend of Pandora's box to make the point that all the moral evils on earth had had their origin in Pandora's unconquerable desire to know the contents of the chest she had been forbidden to open. When she did open the chest, out flew the insects of avarice, cupidity, cruelty, exploitativeness, conflict, and others. More famous, the Jews had their Garden, an originally innocent Adam and Eve, and then, also through insatiable desire to know, the Fall. There hasn't been an age since in Western history in which some variant of this view of the inverse relation between happiness and knowledge hasn't had currency. In his *A Study of History,* the late A. J. Toynbee argues that so close is the correlation between technological advancement and moral decline that the appearance of the former may be used as the ground of accurate forecasting of the latter.

But old and recurrent as this conception is, it is by no means, and never has been in any age, universally held by intellectuals. There were indeed classical and Christian minds convinced of a primal golden age followed by degeneration. But, as we shall see there were from the beginning Greeks and Romans who believed the very opposite, that the beginning was wretchedness, that salvation lay in the *increase* of knowledge. So have there been such minds in the Christian, the medieval, and above all in the modern epoch.

Quite obviously, so sweeping a proposition as the idea of progress as just described cannot be empirically or logically verified. One may say, precisely and verifiably enough, that the art of medicine or the art of war has advanced, given our perfectly objective ways of noting the means toward the long-held end or purpose in each art: saving or healing life; destroying one's enemies as effectively and lastingly as possible. Plainly, penicillin is, and can be proved to be, superior to old-fashioned remedies—blood-letting or leeching, for example. And modern artillery is superior to cross-bows and boiling pitch.

Matters become more complicated, though, even within either of these specialized, technical domains, when we ask what the overall *effects* are— environmental, social, moral, demographic, spiritual, and so forth—of even the kind of progress we see in the art of medicine. One need only think of the present burgeoning, fast-spreading area of thought known as medical ethics, including the right to die with dignity amid all the technological achievements by which the dying can be held indefinitely in that suspended state, to be reminded of the extent to which even the oldest of ethical issues can become activated by technological success in medicine.

And, of course, matters become almost hopelessly complicated and conflicting when we try to speak of progress (or regress) in reference to "humanity," "mankind," or "civilization." And yet these inherent complications, conflicts, and paradoxes notwithstanding, many very wise and eminent philosophers, scientists, historians, and statesmen *have* spoken of progress in these terms. To call the roll is to summon up such names as Protagoras, Plato, Aristotle, Lucretius, Seneca, St. Augustine, Jean Bodin, Isaac Newton, Robert Boyle, Joseph Priestley, Comte, Hegel, Darwin, Marx, Herbert Spencer, and in America, a line that commenced with Cotton Mather and Jonathan Edwards, and included Jefferson, John Adams, Franklin, and very nearly every major thinker and statesman in the United States who succeeded the Founding Fathers. These are but a few of the West's light and leading for whom the progress of mankind, especially in the arts and sciences, was as real and as certain as any law in physical science.

The point is not that any of these believers in progress ever thought empirical validation likely or even possible when the referent was as abstract and vast as humanity or civilization. The point is that for these believers there was no more necessity for empirical proof of universal progress than there was for a geometrical proposition—or, if one was religious, for a commandment or other injunction in the Bible. Call it axiom or dogma: the fact is, no matter how meaningless the idea may have come to seem to intellectuals in this second half of the twentieth century, the idea was as self-evident as anything in Euclid for immense numbers of scholars and scientists in Western history down through the early twentieth century.

Nor can we overlook the masses. From at least the early nineteenth century until a few decades ago, belief in the progress of mankind, with Western civilization in the vanguard, was virtually a universal religion on both sides of the Atlantic. And whatever its parlous state today in the West, there is considerable reason to believe that this is one of the hardiest of Western ideas or values to take root in Eastern Europe—the Soviet Union preeminently—and much of Asia.

True, even in very modern times there have been profoundly convinced skeptics and disbelievers. We shall come to some of these in a closing section of this book, but for the moment it will suffice to name Tocqueville, Burckhardt, Nietzsche, Schopenhauer, Max Weber, Sorel, W. R. Inge, and Spengler as among those—a small minority in their day, to be sure, but the direct source of the intellectual-literary malaise now so widespread among us in the West—who could not bring themselves to believe that the condition of the West as they perceived it reflected progress. But as previously noted, such skeptics duly acknowledged, the overwhelming majority of the greatest minds in Western history are oriented toward the dogma of progress.

Not, as we shall observe, that this dogma has always had salutary effect. For the most part, it *has* been a benign intellectual influence—inseparable, as I have come to believe, from the crucial motivations, impulses, desires, and incentives which have been behind the extraordinary accomplishments of Western civilization, perched upon what is no more than a tiny promontory of Eurasia. The history of all that is greatest in the West—religion, science, reason, freedom, equality, justice, philosophy, the arts, and so on —is grounded deeply in the belief that what one does in one's own time is at once tribute to the greatness and indispensability of the past, and confidence in an ever more golden future.

But, as I say, the record is not always a clean one for the consequences of belief in progress. Faith in the advance of mankind, stage by stage, to some still unfulfilled end or goal can be, and has been, united with faiths most of us in the West find repugnant and hateful. The kind of absolute military-political power we find in twentieth-century totalitarianisms, left and right, has behind it a philosophy of inexorable progress. So does the kind of racism that flourished in the nineteenth and early twentieth centuries: to a man the Gobineaus, Houston Stewart Chamberlains, and Madison Grants were believers in progress, or at least in its possibility and seeking its cause —which they found in race.

But, corruptions of the idea of progress understood—and the two I have just mentioned do not exhaust the number—I remain convinced that this idea has done more good over a twenty-five hundred-year period, led to more creativeness in more spheres, and given more strength to human hope and to individual desire for improvement than any other single idea in Western history. One may say that what is ultimately crucial, the will to advance or improve, lies in the individual alone, that an unverifiable, paradoxical, cosmic dogma is not needed. The individual's own drives and aspirations will suffice to effect progress, and therefore so comprehensive and abstract a proposition as the Western idea of progress is expendable.

I do not agree. The springs of human action, will, and ambition lie for the most part in beliefs about universe, world, society, and man which defy rational calculations and differ greatly from physio-psychological instincts. These springs lie in what we call dogmas. That word comes from Greek roots with the literal meaning of "seems-good." As Tocqueville wrote, "No society can prosper; no society can exist" without dogma. For the individual also "dogmatic belief is not less indispensable to him in order to live alone." It was Cardinal Newman who wrote: "Men will die for a dogma

Introduction

who will not even stir for a conclusion." The idea of the slow, gradual, inexorable progress of mankind to higher status in knowledge, culture, and moral estate is a dogma, precisely the kind that Tocqueville and Newman had in mind.

Everything now suggests, however, that Western faith in the dogma of progress is waning rapidly in all levels and spheres in this final part of the twentieth century. The reasons, as I attempt to show in the final chapter, have much less to do with the unprecedented world wars, the totalitarianisms, the economic depressions, and other major political, military, and economic afflictions which are peculiar to the twentieth century than they do with the fateful if less dramatic erosion of all the fundamental intellectual and spiritual premises upon which the idea of progress has rested throughout its long history.

Perhaps I exaggerate. But I cannot help but think we shall know shortly whether civilization in any form and substance comparable to what we have known during most of the preceding twenty-five hundred years in the West is possible without the supporting faith in progress that has existed along with this civilization. Our problem in this final part of the twentieth century is compounded by the fact that the dogma of progress is today strong in the official philosophies or religions of those nations which are the most formidable threats to Western culture and its historical moral and spiritual values —one more instance of the capacity for Western skills and values to be exported, corrupted, and then turned against the very West that gave them birth.

Chapter 1

The Classical World

Is the idea of progress to be found in classical Greek and Roman thought: the idea that mankind has slowly, gradually, and continuously advanced from an original condition of cultural deprivation, ignorance, and insecurity to constantly higher levels of civilization, and that such advancement will, with only occasional setbacks, continue through the present into the future? The answer to this question is an emphatic yes, as the contents of this chapter will make evident.

It would be disingenuous, however, to omit reference here to the long-held, contrary view of this subject, one with a great deal more currency than the one I have just stated. From at least the time of Auguste Comte, whose volumes on Positive Philosophy published in the 1830s made the "law of progress" the very foundation stone of his view of civilization, the judgement has prevailed that the ancients knew nothing of the idea of the continuous progress of mankind from past to future. So learned a mind as Walter Bagehot wrote in 1872: "The ancients had no conception of progress; they did not so much reject the idea; they did not even entertain the idea." J. B. Bury, in his *Idea of Progress*, also denied the existence of the idea of progress in Greek and Roman thought (and in Christian thought as well) on the grounds, first, that their philosophers lacked awareness of a long historical past within which progress could be discerned; second, that they were victims of their own belief in a theory of historical degeneration (with the story of mankind perceived as one long decline from an original golden age); and, third, that Greek and Roman philosophers were generally committed to an envisagement of human history as endlessly and recurrently cyclical, thus making any thought of linear advancement through the ages quite impossible.

Bury's assessment of the matter—which, as noted, only echoes the assessments of Auguste Comte and a large number of other nineteenth-century philosophers, scientists, and historians—remains to this moment a part of the conventional wisdom regarding the classical world. Thus John Baillie, in his learned *The Belief in Progress*, finds the faint beginnings of the idea of progress not earlier than the beginning of Christianity. F. M. Cornford argues in his *The Unwritten Philosophy* that a conception of progress could not possibly have existed in Greece—so deeply and widely held was the idea of historical degeneration. The erudite W. R. Inge, Dean of St. Paul's in London, in his Romanes Lecture—delivered in 1920, the year Bury's book was published—declared that this "pernicious superstition" was the spawn of modernity, with not a trace of it to be found in either classical or Christian thought. R. G. Collingwood's *Idea of History* does not allow the ancient Greeks even a true sense of time and history, much less a conception of progress. And Hannah Arendt, who was so perceptive of the nature of the idea of progress and its capacity for evil as well as good, denies flatly that "such a thing as the progress of mankind [existed] prior to the seventeenth century."

Weighty testimony indeed. But the truth, I believe, lies in the opposite corner. Through the specialized scholarship of such eminent classicists as Ludwig Edelstein, M. I. Finley, W. K. C. Guthrie, and Eric R. Dodds—not to ignore earlier studies by Frederick J. Teggart, Arthur O. Lovejoy, and George Boas—we have come to see that the Greeks and Romans, contrary to conventional interpretation, *did* have a distinct awareness of a long past, *did* see a measured progression of the arts and sciences and of man's estate on earth, and *did* on occasion refer to a future in which civilization would have gone well beyond what it was in their own time. In the late sixth century, Xenophanes wrote: "The gods did not reveal to men all things from the beginning, but men through their own search find in the course of time that which is better." Ludwig Edelstein, who regards Xenophanes' words as the first statement in Western history of the idea of progress, assures us that Xenophanes meant his generalization to apply to the future as well as to the past and present.

M. I. Finley, in his *The World of Odysseus*, suggests that a recognition of the advancement of mankind through the centuries may be found even in Homer. The dread Cyclopes were seen by Odysseus as devoid of all culture, even agriculture ("they neither plant anything nor till," Homer writes); but they were also seen as examples of what the Greeks themselves had once been, so far as culture was concerned. Behind the account of the Cyclopes, Finley writes, lies "a distinct view of social evolution. In primitive times, the poet seems to be suggesting, man lived in a state of permanent struggle and war to the death against the outsider. Then the gods intervened, and through their precepts, their *themis*, a new ideal was set before man, . . ." An ideal, Finley concludes, that would go a long way toward generating the actual progress the Greeks experienced down through the great fifth century B.C.

By the time we come to the fifth century B.C. awareness of and fascination with the idea of progress were relatively widespread. At the very beginning of that century Protagoras set forth his view that the history of man had been and would remain a progressive history. "By the classical period of Greek thought," writes W. K. C. Guthrie, "the idea of a past Golden Age had been very widely replaced by the view of man's early condition as 'brutish' and 'disorderly.'" These words—especially "brutish" or "animallike" are repeated as an echo by a number of writers. In this chapter we shall see abundant evidence of Greek and Roman belief in the progress of mankind through the ages as expressed in Hesiod, Protagoras, Aeschylus, Sophocles, Plato, Aristotle, Epicurus, Zeno, Lucretius, and Seneca. As Protagoras put it: "In the course of time" or in Plato's words, "little by little," and *pedetemtim progredientes,* or "step-by-step" in Lucretius' statement of the matter.

I am not arguing that the perspective of progress is the entire story of classical belief. There were those who were convinced that degeneration rather than progress was the true picture of man's history, that a golden age had once existed, with all subsequent history one of decline and decay. Some of the writers we shall be concerned with in this chapter were able to hold to concepts of progress *and* of degeneration. None of this is to be denied. But it might be noted that we do find in our own century contrasting views of progress and decline, even theories of recurrent cycles. The point is not that the Greeks and Romans were unaware of the phenomena of degeneration, that they were without any belief whatever in a primordial golden age: it is that along with these beliefs existed beliefs in the progress of man from the remote past through the present, even to the distant future. Preoccupation with the future may not have been the same obsession among classical thinkers as it was among philosophers of the seventeenth and eighteenth centuries, but, as Edelstein has demonstrated in detail, belief in progress extending into the distant future is to be found throughout the entire period that stretches from Xenophanes at the end of the sixth century B.C. to Seneca in the first century A.D.—belief for which the words of Seneca are entirely apposite: "The time will come when mental acumen and prolonged study will bring to light what now is hidden. . . . the time will come when our successors will wonder how we could have been ignorant of things so obvious." We shall commence our story with Hesiod, who was second only to Homer in his appeal to not only the Greek philosophers but to countless other European thinkers down to the beginning of the modern age.

Hesiod

Any account of belief in progress among the ancient Greeks must begin with this extraordinary and so often misunderstood Boeotian farmer-philosopher of the late eighth century B.C. Almost invariably he is cast in the lineaments of pessimism (which to be sure he was not wholly lacking in) and of unqualified belief in degeneration from past to present and in the hopelessness of the future. But there is another, truer, and far more fertile Hesiod than the conventional one, and we shall be concerned here with him. For he is the real source of the Greek belief in progress, through history and reform.

His *Theogony* is cosmic in scope, a history of the formation of earth, sky, ocean (each likened unto a god or goddess), and of the convulsive couplings of gods and goddesses and the resulting births of new ones, which kept the universe for so long in a condition of war and other torment that makes Hobbes's state of nature seem mild by comparison. "Verily, at first Chaos came to be," Hesiod tells us—but then shortly after, Earth and then, indispensably, Eros or Love (in the *Symposium* Socrates, three centuries after Hesiod, would pay tribute to Hesiod's vital introduction of Love). Afterward Heaven appeared on the scene, to lie with Earth in one of the most cataclysmic embraces known in all literature, thus giving birth to Cronus who in turn sired, and came from jealousy to hate, Zeus. The great and ultimate achievement of Zeus, Hesiod declares, is the creation, but only after frenetic battles with the feared Titans and his theft of their awesome thunderbolts, of order and stability in the world. No one reading *The Theogony* could possibly deny Hesiod, or so it seems to me, a very real sense of both the passage of very long periods of time and of the progressive amelioration of the world in which humanity was to come into existence.

But for all the interest that *The Theogony* generates with its rich sexual and parturitional imagery, its episodes of terroristic war, mutilation, destruction, and final outcome of good, it is Hesiod's *Works and Days* we are obliged to turn to, at least for purposes of our narrative. This is the work, written, it is judged, after the *Theogony*, that makes it possible for one commentator to declare Hesiod the first in the European tradition to use poetry for purposes of instruction: moral, religious, yes, but also political, social, and economic. In many ways, the book is a miscellany. We get from it extremely practical advice on the tilling of the soil and the proper harvesting of crops, on the proper ways to conduct business relationships, on the condition of justice in Hesiod's time (appalling!), and on a great many other matters rooted in past, present, and also, by implication or adjuration, the future.

Among the book's bequests to posterity are two which have had immense influence in Western thought: Hesiod's telling of the myth of the successive, metallic ages: the golden, silver, bronze, and iron (with an age of heroes intercalated between the third and fourth); and second, the myth of Prometheus and his stealing of fire from Mt. Olympus to give to mankind, thus generating mankind's capacity to move from primordial deprivation and fear to eventual civilization. There is a third myth, that of Pandora and her forbidden opening of the chest, thus inflicting upon man miseries not before known, which might be termed the genesis of male chauvinism in Western thought. I shall pass over it as it is not as closely related to our subject as the other two are.

Let us begin with the myth of the ages. The idea of a succession of ages over a long time span is by no means original with Hesiod or the Greeks. Other, much older literatures in the world, Egyptian and Babylonian included, make reference to these ages in one context or other. There is indeed, as has often been pointed out, a certain degree of archaeological sophistication in them. Irrespective of moral and spiritual implication, the succession from gold to iron has some correspondence with the actual historical succession of cultures in early times in the prehistory of Europe. Use of gold for ornamental purposes undoubtedly preceded use of silver, certainly of bronze and iron.

But Hesiod's employment of the metallic ages is indubitably set in spiritual and moral contexts. It is important, however, to observe that Hesiod, in *Works and Days*, does not refer to *ages* as such, but to races. Thus in his telling it was the "golden race" that the gods first created. This race, we learn, was characterized on the one hand by ignorance of the practical arts, and on the other by moral probity, peacefulness, and, in general, happiness. This race existed in the time of Cronus, predecessor to Zeus, and eventually they were removed, hidden in the earth. Following them is the "silver race," "in no way like the first, in body or mind." Such indeed was their wickedness, their fondness for war and other kinds of strife, that

Zeus, by now supreme, put them out of existence. Then Zeus created a third race, one of bronze. What this race of men cherished above all things was martial combat. They were hardhearted but nevertheless impressive in their pursuit of valor. Their armor, housing, and implements, were all made of bronze; iron had not yet come into being. This bronze race, Hesiod writes, destroyed themselves through unending warfare and went down without name or any other identity to Hades. Zeus then created a fourth race, of "hero-men"—also skilled in the arts of war, brave and bold in battles at Thebes and Troy, and, unlike their predecessor race, aware of and respectful to justice. Eventually they too disappeared, many by death in battle, but others, by Zeus's own providence, permitted to live eternally, in happiness and moral probity, on the Isles of the Blest. Last of all comes the "iron race," of which Hesiod himself was a member. He has much to say about the toil, the torment, the injustice, the cruel deprivations to which his own race is subjected. Hence the famous words: "Would that I lived not among the fifth race of men, but had died before or been born afterward."

Clearly, there is basis for the conventional interpretation of the myth of the ages: that of a cycle of degeneration beginning with the golden race and culminating in the iron; a cycle that would repeat itself endlessly, thus giving foundation to Hesiod's wish that he had been born earlier—among men of gold, say, at the beginning of his own cycle, or later at the beginning of the new cycle, also golden. There is basis for this reading of the myth, and I am frank in saying that until three or four years ago I so read it myself.

I do no longer. Careful reading of the myth itself and a placing of it in conjunction with other themes of Hesiod's work suggests something rather different. In the first place, the sequence given us by Hesiod is by no means one of unrelieved worsening of the lot of mankind. There is no doubt that for Hesiod the first of the races, the golden race, was indeed a pure and happy one, devoid though it was of the skills and arts which would in time increase man's material comforts. But the very next race created (there is no implication in Hesiod of any genetic descent of the races) is not a second best in any sense. It comes close to being the very converse of the first. The bronze race that is third in order of time is markedly *better* than its silver predecessor and the next succeeding race, that of "hero-men," is better yet. This, as noted, is the race that acquitted itself so valiantly that those not killed in war were settled by Zeus in the Isles of the Blest.

Nor, to come now to the real point, is the iron race as monolithically evil as conventional interpretation would have it. Moreover, this race is far from being committed by Zeus to early extinction because of its injustices and immoralities. True, Hesiod tells us that Zeus will destroy this race, but that declaration ends with the words "when they come to have gray hair on their temples at birth," a fate Hesiod does not seem to believe to be exactly imminent. His comment, taken in larger context, is much like our own "until hell freezes over," a reference of unlikelihood, not of serious expectation. And consider the following passage from *Works and Days*. It appears after one of Hesiod's several condemnations of those who fail to observe justice and thus cause much unhappiness.

But to those who give straight judgment to strangers and to the men of the land, and not aside from what is just, their city flourishes, and the people prosper in it. Peace, the nurse of children, is abroad in their land, and all-seeing Zeus never decrees cruel war against them. Neither famine nor disaster ever haunt men who do true justice; but light-heartedly they tend the fields which are their care. The earth bears them victual in plenty, and on the mountans the oak bears acorns upon the top and bees in the midst. The wooly sheep are laden with fleeces; their women bear children like parents. They flourish continually with good things, and do not travel on ships, for the grain-giving earth bears them fruit."

This is no golden age of the past that Hesiod is writing about, but rather the kind of life that all of his own race may anticipate provided they clean up current injustices and commit themselves to lives of rectitude. It is, only too clearly, progressive reform that Hesiod is holding up to us, reform that can make life for this contemporary iron race of men not only endurable but desirable. The eminent Berkeley classicist, the late George M. Calhoun, a half-century ago reached this assessment of Hesiod in his book, *The Growth of Criminal Law in Ancient Greece:*

One cannot read far in the *Works and Days* without perceiving that here is the genesis of our political literature. For the first time an author addresses himself consciously and deliberately to the social and political problems of his day. He presents a vigorous arraignment of things as they are, and also a program of reform, founded upon the twofold gospel of industry in the individual and justice in those who rule the state. Bitter as is the poet's sense of personal injury, it is almost lost, as he progresses with his theme, in righteous indignation against the greater social wrong of which his own experience is but a single instance.

Let us go back again to the famous lines in which he laments the hardships and injustices of his own age: "For now, verily, is a race of iron. Never do men rest from toil and hardship, nor from suffering by night, and sore cares shall the gods lay upon them. *Howbeit, even for these shall good be mingled with evil."* (Italics added) Any dispassionate reading of that final line suggests no doomsayer at all, but instead a mind that can see and foresee the good that comes from discipline, hard work, and honesty.

Why would Hesiod be as admonitory to his brother Perses as he is in the following lines, if only inexorable decline and destruction were seen by Hesiod to lie ahead?

To you, Perses, I speak with good intent . . . . Long and steep is the way thereto, and it is rough work at the first, but when one has reached the top, easy is it thereafter despite its hardness . . . . Both gods and men are wroth with a man who lives in idleness, for in nature he is like the stingless drones who waste the labor of the bees, eating without working; but let it be your care to order your work properly, that in the right season your barns may be full. Through work men grow rich in flocks and substance and working they are much loved by the immortals. Work is no disgrace; it is idleness that is a disgrace.

Those are the words not of a believer in relentless, unremitting decline and in eventual extinction of a race, but of a believer, instead, in a philosophy of life and work not very different from what in modern history is termed the Protestant Ethic, the kind of advice that we find in *Poor Richard's Almanack*. There is hope, indeed faith, in Hesiod's words of warning to his brother—at, of course, a price. But the price is no more than hard work and honesty in personal dealings.

At the beginning I spoke of two myths in Hesiod which have had a great deal of impact in Western thought, starting with the Greeks themselves. We have just examined the first. The second is the myth of Prometheus. In Hesiod's telling of this myth, the original condition of mankind was one of great material want, of unhappiness and fear. It was Prometheus, braving the wrath and terrible punishment of Zeus, who out of pity for this wretched condition of mankind brought fire, thus generating the advance mankind would subsequently make to civilization. It is a myth, clearly, in the direction of progress, man's progress from want to plenty. Nor is *Works and Days* the only text of its age in which this contrast between a bad past and a good present is set forth. In the *Hymn to Hephaestus* there is a contrast between the "old men [who] used to dwell in caves in the mountains like wild beasts" (like the Cyclops of Homer's telling), and men of today who, thanks to the bequest by Hephaestus of crafts and arts to men, "easily live a peaceful life in their own houses all the year round."

Hesiod's myth of Prometheus would become one of the very building blocks of the Greek idea of progress; nowhere more vividly than in the great fifth century B.C. where we find its serious use in the writings of Aeschylus, Protagoras, Plato, and many others. Prometheus was rivalled in Attic affection and gratitude only by Demeter, goddess of the grain, who also had a heroic role in every Athenian telling of mankind's liberation from want and fear. (By comparison, the outcome for Hesiod's other myth of the original condition of man—that of Pandora, of the Woman and the Chest, with its implication that everyone was happy until Zeus put a woman on earth to make men miserable—was ignoble. So little was the credence given it that it became a mere staple of comedy in later Greek writing.)

In summary, Hesiod—the Hesiod who was to have such a profound effect upon philosophers from Xenophanes through Socrates, Plato and Aristotle, all the way to Hellenistic philosophers such as Epicurus and Zeno and to the Romans—was not one who seems to have given much thought to a golden age of the past or to a future irremediably and inexorably degenerate. With justice made universal in the human community through calculated and unremitting social reform and through individual hard work, there was a benign future to anticipate. The careful reading of *Works and Days* reveals a mind strikingly like that which would be extolled by Protestants, especially Puritans, many hundreds of years later. Hesiod was a believer in progress and in the effect man himself, through the abolition of strife, through the universalization of justice, and through hard work, would have in bringing about a progressive future. What Teggart writes seems to me authoritative:

> Hesiod set before men the first idea of human progress: the idea that the good life is attainable; that this attainment is dependent upon the thought and activity of men themselves; that the essential requisite is the actuation of the members of the community by a common regard for justice.

We shall see in the ensuing pages the steady expansion of Hesiod's vision of a progressive, rather than a degenerative, mankind—an expansion that lights up the pages of some of Greece's greatest artists and philosophers.

Aeschylus

Nowhere in Greek literature did Hesiod's myth of Promethus and the giving of fire and thus the means of civilization to mankind make its appearance more magnificently and eloquently than in Aeschylus's *Prometheus Bound.* Aeschylus' life spanned the formation of the Athenian *polis* just before the great fifth century B.C. began, the epochal wars fought between the Greeks and the Persians (in which Aeschylus himself fought bravely and effectively), and the subsequent eruption of economic wealth, political power, and cultural genius that made Athens for nearly a century the greatest city in antiquity. It would be a long time before Europe came even close to the artistic, literary, and philosophical efflorescence of the age in which Aeschylus lived.

It is easy to imagine the pride Athenians took in their culture. E. R. Dodds observes in one of his essays that there is usually a correlation between the actual, perceived *experience* of progress and the *belief* in mankind's progress. Small wonder, then, are the contrasts made by Athenians with respect to themselves and other, contemporaneous peoples, and to past ages. Small wonder too is the presence in the dramas of Aeschylus, Sophocles, and others of a faith that what the Athenians wrought would be built upon and improved in the future.

It is in Aeschylus' *Prometheus Bound* that we can see most clearly faith in progress, and conviction that in all major respects the life of man is better today than at any point in the past. Prometheus was of course a favorite god among all Greeks. He epitomized the spirit of revolt against fettering tradition, of man's accomplishment through his own efforts of a better and freer society. No one in Greek literature so successfully conveys the grandness of liberation from primal ignorance and fear and the achievement of the kind of civilization, material and spiritual, which the Athenians cherished, as does Aeschylus' Prometheus. W. K. C. Guthrie of Cambridge University gives us some interesting insight into the very word "Prometheus," in his *In the Beginning*. He states, "Prometheus is an ancient and fully personalized mythological character, prominent already in Hesiod, yet his name is one of transparent meaning. It is a regularly-formed Greek word, and means Forethinker (or perhaps Forethought in the abstract)." This fact, Guthrie continues, is emphasized early in Aeschylus' play "when Zeus's minion taunts the fettered Titan on the inappropriateness of this name: 'Falsely do the gods call thee Forethinker' (Forethought?), for thou are thyself in need of a forethinker (or 'of forethought')."

Prometheus' crime in the eyes of Zeus was of course that of having lifted mankind from its primal degradation and misery to a level where man might seek to rival the gods. He is punished accordingly, for all eternity. But Prometheus does not accept his dreadful fate without seeking to justify what he has done. His brief for himself is one of literature's most famous passages.

But harken to the miseries that afflicted mankind—how they were witless and I made them to have sense and be endowed with reason . . . .
First of all, though they had eyes to see, they saw to no avail; they had ears but understood not; but, like to shapes in dreams, throughout their length of days,

without purpose they wrought all things in confusion. Knowledge had they neither of houses built of bricks and turned to face the sun, nor yet of work in wood; but dwelt beneath the ground like swarming ants, in sunless caves. . . .

Not only did Prometheus bring man into full use of intelligence, but he either endowed human beings with, or spurred them to discover for themselves, mathematics, the alphabet, and written language, with the knowledge that made possible the use of beasts of burden in agriculture and commerce, and ships for crossing the seas. Nor was this all. "Hear but the rest and thou shalt wonder the more at the arts and resources I devised": medicines with which to heal the sick or infirm, food, drink, and luxuries that man could not possibly have dreamed of had not Prometheus taken a hand. And then the culminating words: "Hear the sum of the whole matter in the compass of one brief word—every art possessed by man comes from Prometheus."

Or from *forethought!* Aeschylus was the writer of tragedies, yes, in which gods, demigods, and mortals utter their matchless lines. But Aeschylus was also the philosopher—he could not have been other—keenly interested in what it was that had allowed human beings to progress from initial savagery to the kind of culture that, in his mind, Athens so resplendently exemplified. Again Professor Guthrie gives us clarifying insight:

How hard it is to enter fully into the minds of men to whom personification comes so naturally as it did to the Greeks! If the spirit of Forethought—Prometheus—is not a living, divine person, suffering torments for having defied the tyranny of Zeus, the whole tragedy has no importance. Yet I find it difficult to believe that in writing this speech Aeschylus had no thought of the meaning of the word, no consciousness that he was really describing a technical revolution brought about historically by human ingenuity alone.

Aeschylus was by no means alone among dramatists in his celebration of human progress, in his stark contrasting of primitive ignorance, squalor, and mental torment with the combination of technology, arts and sciences, material luxuries, and political greatness contained in the present. There is the famous chorus in Sophocles' *Antigone* with its most celebrated line: "Many a wonder lives and moves, but the wonder of all is man." From this Sophocles moves, as had Aeschylus before him, to a recounting of all the achievements by which mankind had progressed from past into present. It is man, not the gods, whom Sophocles lauds in such lines as "Wise utterance and wind-swift thought, and city-moulding mind," "Full of resource, without device, he meets no coming time," "Inventive beyond wildest hope, endowed with boundless skill," and so on.

Nor were the dramatists simply hailing progress from past to present.

As Ludwig Edelstein points out in his *The Idea of Progress in Classical Antiquity,* Aeschylus' Prometheus is careful to say that men will learn many arts in the future. And in Sophocles' ode to the inventive genius of man there are the words: "with plans for all things, planless in nothing, *he awaits the future."* (Italics added) In truth, as Edelstein shows us in such richly documented detail, Greek religion as well as the drama that sprang from religious rites was steeped in conviction that the remote past had been the very opposite of any golden age, that the present was superior to the past, and that hope in future was assuredly present even if not always as explicit as in Sophocles' ode.

When, Edelstein observes, the Athenians in 418 B.C. invited all the Greeks to send offerings and sacrifices to the goddess Demeter (by all odds the Athenians's favorite), "their plea was most probably based on the claim that Eleusis was the cradle of agriculture and therefore of all civilized life," in the future as in the present. Nor can we afford to forget the spirit behind the words of Xenophanes—so often to be quoted by later Greek writers— already cited in this chapter: "The gods did not reveal to men all things in the beginning, but, in the course of time, by searching, they came to find better." In that sentence are to be seen more than mere hints of, first, teleology—design for the future left unrevealed at the outset; of human ingenuity behind the "searching" for the better; and very important, the notion of measured progress *through time:* all of these vital in the shaping of the Western idea of progress.

Protagoras

Protagoras was the first and greatest of the Sophists, so far as we know, and did much to give Greek philosophy a moral as well as physical dimension. To be sure, many of the concepts basic to Sophist and then Socratic and post-Socratic moral and political philosophy are really only adaptations of ideas present, as we have seen, in Hesiod and also, as the classicist John Linton Myres pointed out many years ago in an epochal study, in the pre-Socratic physical philosophers—Anaximander, Empedocles, above all Heraclitus among them. Not only is the idea of progressive development, of growth and evolution, to be found among these physical philosophers but also an interest in social and political matters—the consequence, Myres suggests, of the actual political careers many of them had or had had prior to their turning to cosmic problems.

Still, it is only fair to think of Protagoras as the first systematic social and moral philosopher among the Greeks. Socrates (as cited by Plato) believed him to be. Protagoras' most famous utterance is, of course: "Man is the measure of all things." What is less well remembered is that immediately following this line—indeed, continuing its thought—are the words: . . . "of things that are, that they are; of things that are not; that they are not. . . . All matter is in a state of flux [the Heraclitean heritage]. A fluctuating thing may retain its shape, however, because matter is essentially the sum of all the seemings it has for any and all persons." And finally: "As for the gods, I have no way of knowing either that they exist or that they do not exist, of what form they are. For the obstacles to that sort of knowledge are many, including the obscurity of the matter and the brevity of human life."

These surviving fragments of Protagoras' thought are but anticipatory. For his full conception of mankind's progress, we must go to Plato's dialogue *Protagoras*. There is no reason whatever to believe that Plato did other than set down as accurately as he could the actual, stated views of Protagoras. The respect for Protagoras is evident throughout, and the detail that is provided of Athenian political and intellectual life gives a high degree of support to the view that it is in fact Protagoras, and not Plato speaking his own views through the personage of Protagoras, who comes to the fore.

"The Sophist's art," Protagoras tells us, "is an ancient one"—that is, the search for knowledge, for the truth, as contrasted with conventional myth or legend. But in earlier times, as with Homer and Hesiod and their contemporaries, it was necessary to cover true objective with the veil of poetry or religion, the better to escape the odium that might have attended the quest for truth and reality. It is different, though, in his day, Protagoras declares. "I admit to being a Sophist and an educator, and I consider this a better precaution than the other—admission rather than denial."

The context of Protagoras' delineation of human progress is his discussion with Socrates of the nature of virtue and of the extent to which it can be learned by human beings through experience. It is precisely at this point that Protagoras asks and receives his hosts' permission "to tell you a story." The "story" is nothing less than a condensed account of the development of mankind, from cultureless primitivism all the way to the civilization the Greeks knew and loved.

In the beginning, according to Protagoras there were gods but no mortal creatures. The latter were formed by the gods from within the earth out of a mixture of earth and fire, and "the substances which are compounded from earth and fire." The first of mortal beings were subhuman: animals, birds, fishes, and so forth, and these spread out on earth in accordance with the differential of strengths and weaknesses among them. The small were given speed for their protection, others were granted strength alone. "Thus he [Epimetheus, who assisted Prometheus] made his whole distribution on a principle of compensation, being careful by these devices that no species should be destroyed."

All the while, Protagoras continues, man alone was left uncared for: "Epithemeus was not a particularly clever person." And when Prometheus came to inspect the work entrusted to his assistant, he was shocked to discover man still "naked, unshod, unbedded and unarmed." Being compassionate, Prometheus stole from Hephaestus and Athena both the gift of skills in the arts and also fire. "Through this gift man had the means of life . . . "

What follows is Protagoras' detailed account of progress in culture, in the arts and sciences, from a state of nature in which by reason of constant strife men almost destroyed themselves completely. Soon, with the help in the very beginning of the gods, they "invented houses and clothes and shoes and bedding and got food from the earth." They also created altars in shrines as the means of rendering thanks to the gods who had brought them out of their initial wretchedness. Protagoras relates that language, too, came early, "articulate speech and names."

Thus provided for, they lived at first in scattered groups; there were no cities. Consequently they were devoured by wild beasts, since they were in every respect the weaker, and their technical skill, though a sufficient aid to their nurture, did not extend to making war on the beasts. They sought therefore to save themselves by coming together and founding fortified cities, but when they gathered in communities, they injured one another for want of political skill, and so scattered again and continued to be devoured.

At this point Protagoras tells us that Zeus, fearing the total destruction of the human race, sent Hermes "to impart to men the qualities of respect for others and a sense of justice, so as to bring order into our cities and create a bond of friendship and union." Protagoras is insistent that justice lies at the foundations of civil society. Thus when Hermes asked Zeus if he should distribute these values equally among men, Zeus answered: "To all, let all have their share. There could never be cities if only a few shared in these virtues, as in the arts."

Protagoras' story is brief, but in his few paragraphs are to be found all the essential elements of a panorama of progressive development, elements which Plato in *The Laws* and *The Statesman* expanded upon considerably, as did other Greeks. True, Protagoras invokes the aid of the gods in his saga of mankind's progress, but let us become accustomed now to that practice. Through ancient (even Lucretian), medieval, and a great deal of modern thought to this very day, the divine is frequently invoked, no matter how much emphasis is placed on mankind's native endowments.

It is no wonder that Protagoras was treated with such respect by Socrates, Plato, and others in the gathering described in this dialogue. Protagoras was elderly at the time, Socrates' fame as a mind and debater was very high, and Plato makes us see that Protagoras was somewhat reluctant to engage the eminent (and younger) Socrates in debate. But it is one of the joys of this dialogue, as W. K. C. Guthrie points out in the introduction to his translation, that Protagoras is shown several times as having the better of Socrates in discussion, and Plato obviously disports himself with both charm and humor, gently baiting now one, now the other of the two great philosophers. The pleasure taken by all present is evident; there are spoken thanks for the pleasure of "listening to wise men." Plato's respect for Protagoras throughout is unqualified.

Apart from Protagoras, the Sophists generally have been given a bad press by historians of Greek thought—largely the result of Plato's frequently uncharitable treatment of some of them. But there is much more in common between the Sophists, the abler ones at least, and those who like Plato made Socrates their hero, than we are wont to acknowledge. The Sophists, well before Socrates, advocated the use of knowledge and reason in matters of government and public policy. If they—like Socrates—could seem on occasion to be flouting the verities of Athens, it was chiefly because so many of them had traveled widely, observed carefully, and sought to infuse in Athens, which they cherished, some of the better laws, customs, and conventions which they had encountered. Most of the Sophists believed as ardently as the philosophes of the French eighteenth century that given the irrefutable fact of the progress of the arts and sciences over the ages, no reason existed why educated minds drawing from the yield of this progress should not consciously and deliberately improve things for the benefit of posterity.

We need only read some of the plays of Aristophanes, a kind of pre-Burkean conservative in political philosophy, to see through his caricatures and lampoonings the actuality of an Athens well populated by intellectuals committed to belief in progress and to the kind of improvement upon historical progress that could be effected through reason.

Thucydides

How conventional among Greeks a sense of advancement from a remote past was can be inferred easily enough from the opening pages of Thucydides's *History of the Peloponnesian War*. The primary purpose of the book is of course that of setting down in exact detail the personages, acts, and events which figured most prominently in the war between Athens and Sparta. Himself a participant in the war for a time, Thucydides decided early that this war "was certainly the greatest movement that ever happened among the Greeks, and some part of the barbarians, and extending, as one may say, even to most nations of the world." Having so decided, Thucydides thought it his duty to leave a record of the war for posterity. His work, he tells us, "is composed as a possession forever," not as a mere literary ornament for the present. "Now, for hearing it recited, perhaps the unfabulous character of my work will appear less agreeable: but as many as shall wish to see the truth of what both *has* happened and *will* hereafter happen again, according to human nature—the same or pretty nearly so— for such to think it useful will be sufficient".

Nearly all of the book is taken up with the military and political events following 431 b.c., but as noted above, Thucydides thought it important to deal briefly at least with the past out of which Athens and the Hellenes had come. It is evident, he writes, "that what is now called Hellas, was not of old inhabited in a settled manner; but that formerly there were frequent removals . . ." Moreover, the level of culture was very low. "For as there was no traffic, and they did not mix with one another without fear, either by sea or land; and they each so used what they had as but barely to live on, without having any superfluity of riches . . . they were not strong either in greatness of cities or other resources."

Adding to the insecurity and deprivation of early times among the Greeks was the practice of piracy as described by Thucydides:

For the Grecians in old time, and of the barbarians both those on the continent who lived near the sea, and all who inhabited islands, after they began to cross over more commonly to one another in ships, turned to piracy . . . as this employment did not yet involve any disgrace, but rather brought with even somewhat of glory.

We learn that in most ancient times the Greeks "robbed one another on the continent" and "the whole of Greece used to wear arms, owing to their habitations being unprotected and their communication with each other insecure; and they passed their ordinary life with weapons like the barbarians."

How, we may ask, does Thucydides come by his descriptions of what life had been like so far back in Greece's past? By the same means anthropologists came by theirs in the nineteenth century—through use of what in that century would be called "The Comparative Method," that is, the employment of contemporaneous primitive or barbaric peoples as extant examples of what Western civilization itself had been like in primordial times. Such peoples were likened to "our living ancestors." Still another method used by anthropologists and proto-anthropologists of the eighteenth and nineteenth centuries was that of seizing upon persistences or survivals of the old within the confines of modern Western civilization. In rituals, games, and other pursuits which had no apparent function in contemporary life beyond simple recreation, it was possible to discern actions and beliefs which once had been part and parcel of Western culture but were now simply so many survivals of the primitive past.

Thucydides, it is interesting to see, uses precisely the same kinds of observation to validate his thesis that the Greeks were not always as they were culturally and politically in his day, but once lived in primitive want and barbarism. Thus, defending his view that piracy had once been practiced by Greeks, he writes: "This is shown by some that dwell on the continent even at the present day, with whom it is an honor to perform this cleverly;" he follows the same method with respect to his assertion that early Greeks engaged in direct robbery, arguing that "to this day many parts of Greece live after the old fashion." So, among distant and unprogressive peoples in Thucydides' own time "the fashion of wearing arms has continued." And until fairly recently, he continues, the elderly, slow to change, wore their hair and dressed in a manner that had once been strictly associated with the carrying and use of arms—survivals of what had once been common but has now become outmoded and archaic. And just as among "some of the barbarians, and especially those of Asia, prizes for boxing and wrestling are given, and they wear girdles when they contend for them," so once in the dim past did Greeks themselves play in this fashion. "And in many other respects," Thucydides concludes, "one might show that the ancient Greeks lived in a manner similar to the barbarians of the present age."

The point of this anthropological reconstruction of the Greek past is, of course, to make plain not simply the superiority of present culture among the Athenians but also the emergence of this superiority from a primitive past. Before coming to the great events starting in 431 B.C., in short, it was felt necessary by Thucydides to describe, however briefly, Athenian progress.

In still another respect Thucydides contributed to Greek—and post-classical—treatment of progress. This has to do with his mode of presenting historical data, the structure of his work. This structure is narrative, unilinear, and chronological, a presentation of past and present that would become and remain to this day the conventional practice of historians. There is beginning, middle and end (though Thucydides did not give his own work an end—the consequence of exile and death). For Thucydides the referent of this unilinear temporal progression was the war between Athens and Sparta. But for a long, still unended line of successors the referent would be anything from a single people to the whole of mankind—fitted precisely into the kind of linear time frame that Thucydides fashioned.

Plato

Is there to be found a clear perspective of human progress over long vistas of time in the works of this most important and influential of all classical thinkers? The answer is a firm yes. But we must be prepared for the onslaughts of all those readers of Plato who find in him nothing but adoration of the unchanging, the timeless, and the perfect. And in almost equal number are the interpretations which make of Plato a simple-minded reactionary, a mind bent solely on returning Greek society to a tribal Golden Age. Legion are the columns of those for whom the thought of any idea of change, development, and progress in Plato is anathema. Only the heavenly world of perfect forms is the real world; all else is but appearance.

But such a characterization does great injustice to a mind made richly aware, through travels and keen observation of political and social changes at home, of the empirical order of "appearance"; richly aware and also profoundly analytical and critical of this order. As F. M. Cornford has emphasized in his *Plato's Cosmology*, there were for Plato, as there were and would be for so many other philosophers, *two* orders of reality: that of the essentially religious or mystical, the timeless, eternal, and perfect; and that of the material, the social, economic, and political, the order in which we are obliged to live our days. For Plato this order is, as Cornford tells us, dynamic, always changing.

Plato's best account of progress is in *The Laws*, written late in life and embodying all that we have every reason to regard as his maturest wisdom. Book 3 is Plato's essay, or dialogue, on the development of mankind and the progress of man's institutions over a very long period of time. As was true of Protagoras' treatment of the matter, Plato's is set in the perspective of accounting for, and analyzing, virtue—without doubt the greatest single occupation of the Greek philosophical mind. And just as Protagoras a century or more before had offered a developmental-progressive account, so does Plato in *The Laws.*

At the beginning we are offered the prospect of a human development involving "thousands and thousands of cities" which has taken place over "an immense and incredible time." Fluctuation in time is considered axiomatic. Good cities may become bad ones; bad ones, good. All kinds of legends are recognized as dealing with the problem of origins, and for Plato's characters it suffices to stipulate that at some point very far back in time a great catastrophe, no doubt a flood, has wiped out whatever had previously existed in the way of civilization. Only a few survivors escaped —very probably "mountain shepherds" high enough to remain clear of the devastating waters—to become the primitive beginners of a long new development of mankind.

As would literally hundreds of successors down to our own age, Plato stresses the extreme primitivism of the beginning, the almost total lack of those arts and possessions which bespeak civilization. This cultureless, knowledgeless beginning lasted for "untold thousands of years." To be sure, there were compensations. The very absence of institutions, skills, metals, money, and political and social complexity threw men back upon themselves, as gradually the number of human beings increased.

For one thing, men's loneliness made them sociable and friendly; for another, there could be no quarreling over the means of subsistence. Except perhaps in some instances at the very first, they were not stinted for flocks and herds . . . there was no shortage of milk or meat, and besides they could supply themselves with plenty of excellent viands by hunting . . . . Thus they were not extremely poor, for the reason I have assigned, and so were not set at variance by the stress of penury; rich they could never become in the absence of gold and silver which was then their case. No, a society in which neither riches nor poverty is a member regularly produces sterling characters, as it has no place for violence and wrong, nor yet for rivalry and envy. Thus they were good men, partly for this reason, and partly from their proverbial simplicity . . . .

It is evident from the foregoing that more than a little of Greek primitivism has entered into Plato's thinking. The equation of cultural simplicity and moral innocence and purity is, as I have iterated, far from being the whole story of Greek thinking in these matters. It is nevertheless a powerful theme in Western thought—from the Greeks and Romans through the Renaissance, and from the eighteenth century with its cult of exoticism and worship of the "noble savage" down to the vast and growing romantic-ecological literature at this moment in the West. It would be extraordinary if it were not reflected in some of Plato's anthropological reconstructions.

But, moral ruminations notwithstanding, it *is* developmental reconstruction. There is the premise of an original condition of homogeneous simplicity, of absence of the central arts of civilization, and of "modern" forms of social and political organization. In the beginning, Plato tells us, human beings were organized solely into kinship units in which only "the oldest members rule." "The rest follow them, and form one flock, like so many birds, and are thus under patriarchal control, the most justifiable of all types of royalty."

But there is constant growth in time. The kinship units themselves "are in the process of growth from the smaller and most primitive." In time, "each group comes accordingly . . . into the larger settlement with special laws of its own, and prepared to imprint its own preferences upon its children, and their children after them."

Such is, for Plato, the first great stage of social development. The next is coalescence of kinship groups. Now, Plato remarks, for the first time, "we find ourselves insensibly embarked on the beginnings of legislation." Gradually the heads of the kinship components form themselves into assemblies "and get themselves the name of legislator." Other developments, of a cultural and technological as well as political character, follow in course. Bear in mind that the purpose of this anthropological-developmental discourse is explanation of the eventual appearance of the city-state, the kind of state the Greeks brought to fullness. For Plato, as for any other Greek, explanations were best when they were cast in the terms of growth, of unfolding of qualities contained in a primal seed.

"We have inspected a first, a second and a third community succeeding one another in order of foundation *through a vast period of time,* and now, at last, we come, in the fourth place [stage of progress] to the founding of the city—or, as you may prefer to say, a nation, which persists to this day as it was founded." (Italics added)

Central to all of this is the long period of time necessarily involved, and the gradualness of development. Hence Plato's "doubtless the change was not made all in a moment, but *little by little,* during a long period of time." (Italics added) Well travelled, he could cite lots of peoples and cultures for illustrations of successive stages.

But one profoundly important aspect of Plato's discussion must be mentioned before we continue with the classical idea of progress. This is the *function* of Plato's digression into the progressive advancement of mankind. Why, in a very practical work on statecraft, are we given a reconstruction of the past? The answer is simple: only when a statesman knows the general course of development of mankind, only when he knows the true course from the countless departures from the true course, will he be able to rule or make laws wisely and justly. For all Greeks—and Plato, his doctrine of eternal forms notwithstanding, was no exception—reality lay in growth; and wisdom or understanding lay in appreciation of growth. The greatest mistakes, Plato writes, have been made by rulers, legislators, and also businessmen who have imagined that some great creation of government or commerce was perfect in itself and would have worked perfectly if only individuals had been found qualified to administer it.

"This, Clinias and Megillus, is the charge I bring against the so-called statesmen and legislators of both past and present, and I bring it in hope that examination into its causes will disclose the very different course which ought to have been taken."

The course which ought to have been taken! Over and over in the history of the idea of progress we shall find that refrain, as it affects political and economic and social matters, echoed and reechoed. What else were minds as unlike as Adam Smith and J. J. Rousseau interested in, in the late eighteenth century in their *Wealth of Nations* and second Discourse respectively, but discovery of "the very different course which ought to have been taken" by rulers and legislators? And just as Smith and Rousseau wrote in at least the implied hope that political leaders would read them and take their counsel seriously, so of course did Plato. To suppose that Plato was unconcerned with the future, with the possibility that his wisdom would or might be used to betterment of man, is to suppose nonsense. His cosmology, with its great concentric cycles of time, may have led to belief in some ultimate extinction, or temporary extinction of human institutions, but there is no evidence that Plato had other than a reasonably long human future in mind when he created his political dialogues.

Let it not be imagined that the developmental account of mankind's progress I have just described in *The Laws* is something unique or exceptional in Plato. There is, after all, *The Protagoras* which we have already considered, and which assuredly would not be among Plato's works if he had not admired that great Sophist. But there is also *The Statesman,* one of the finest of all Plato's dialogues and, what with the luster of *The Republic,* a rather sadly underregarded work. Here Plato introduces us to a "stranger from Elea" who begins his account of human progress with the appearance of a new race on earth countless ages ago.

Once the new race was in existence, the process of advancement commenced. As in *The Laws,* Plato posits an initial stage of simplicity in matters of knowledge. "Men lacked all tools and all crafts in the early years. The earth no longer supplied their food spontaneously and they did not yet know how to win it for themselves; in the absence of necessity they had never been made to learn this." It was in the first instance the gifts from the gods—fire from Prometheus, the crafts from Hephaestus—that led to the beginning of the long ascent of man. But from then on, the responsibility for cultural advancement, for continuing progress in the arts and crafts, was man's alone.

Precisely as in *The Laws,* there is purpose and function in Plato's rendering of the advancement of mankind out of primeval ignorance. It is to illustrate the fact that the mission of "the statesman" is one thing in an early period of man's development, and something else in a later period. In short, the art of government must be tempered to the stage of development of a people—a conclusion that has, it must be admitted, a strikingly modern flavor. Once, long ago, there was necessity for "violent control," for "the tyrant's art." But true statesmanship in our time, Plato writes, at our advanced state of civilization, calls for "free acceptance" of the governed.

There is not space here, nor need, for that matter, to contrast in any detail the kind of analysis we are given in *The Statesman* with what Plato had set forth many years before in *The Republic*. This, though, can be said confidently. Whereas the youthful Plato took delight in designing what was to him the most perfect state, *eutopia* in the highest degree, a faithful representation of the idea of the state that lay timelessly in heaven, and disdained the uses of any material, comparative or historical, which would divert attention from political perfection, the older Plato, in *The Laws* and *The Statesman,* has a substantially different perspective—one that invoked comparative, historical data.

On the basis of Plato's works there is not one Plato but several.* Belief in a heavenly repository of unchanging, timeless, and perfect forms of things was no more likely to blind Plato to the actual empirical world than belief in God and Christian revelation blinded Newton and other devoutly religious scientists of the modern world to the actualities and principles of the natural world. There is, Plato no doubt believed to the end, a supernatural world in which nothing but perfect ideas exist, but there is also the world that we live in, that our ancestors lived in, and, most important, that our descendants will live in—a world of change and progress.

It is also possible to challenge the fact of Plato's belief in human progress

*This includes the fascinating, tantalizing Plato-as-philosopher in the famous Letter 7, the Plato who comes close to renouncing all that he had earlier written as being inconsistent with his true beliefs.

by adducing his belief also in cycles—great, long-range cycles of time and concentrically located smaller, short-range cycles. Beyond doubt Plato along with other though by no means all Greek thinkers believed in cycles of one kind or other, cycles which necessarily imply eventual degeneration and destruction. (I cannot understand the claimed inability of certain contemporary classical scholars—most recently Jacquelin De Romilly, in her *Rise and Fall of States According to Greek Authors*—to discover *any* cyclicality in Greek and Roman thinking.) The cycle (*pace* Plato, Aristotle, and others) is certainly not the whole story in Greco-Roman scientific and historical thinking, but it is demonstrably *a* story. Even in cyclical thinking, though, the point should not be lost that what eventually is to become decline and fall commences as genesis and progress. But this is merely parenthetical. All that is important here is that in the contextual presence of whatever amount of cyclical thought there may have been in classical antiquity, there was also a solid and fertile substance of belief in linear progress —from remote past to distant future.

Aristotle

I shall be brief here simply because however widely different Plato and his student Aristotle became in their philosophies, much of what it has just been possible to write on Plato's envisagement of progress holds substantially for Aristotle. In his *Generation and Decay,* Aristotle states emphatically that *natural* change, especially in the organic world, is cyclical or "circular." But not everything falls into this category. Aristotle tells us that in other realms the cycle is not necessary. There is the phenomenon of regress alone; there can also be the phenomenon of progress alone.

Aristotle was fascinated by cultural progress. What else but political progress is his depiction in his *Politics* of the development of the political state from the family through the village and then confederations of villages? And although there is not to be found in Aristotle, as there is in Plato, any sustained account of the development of the whole of mankind, we find frequent references to elements or aspects of this development. As Ludwig Edelstein stresses: "Aristotle carefully considers the way in which the arts and sciences are established and perfected." We learn from him the great importance of invention or, rather, the inventor who starts a whole process of historical improvement. But Aristotle in keeping with his belief in advancement over time also insists that great as the original act of invention is, those who are responsible for later inventions are superior. Here in short is an early version of what would be known in the seventeenth century in Europe as the "quarrel between the ancients and moderns." Aristotle sides with the moderns.

There is an almost contemporary ring in the following passage, cited by Edelstein from Aristotle's *Metaphysics*: "No one is able to attain the truth adequately, while on the other hand we do not collectively fail; but each one says something true about the nature of things, and while individually we contribute little or nothing to the truth, by all of us together, a considerable amount is amassed." For Aristotle, Edelstein continues, "Civilization is the work neither of god nor of heroes, half-human, half-divine, but of men cooperating throughout history, helping one another and bound to one another like the links of a chain." The following passage from Aristotle is illuminating, and the first or one of the first of what would prove to be a long line of uses of its rhetorical figure from the Greco-Roman to the contemporary Western world.

> Those who are now renowned have taken over as if in a relay race (from hand to hand, relieving one another) from many many predecessors who on their part progress, and thus have themselves made possible progress.

Aristotle believed, as had Plato, that the human race is eternal, and although individual societies and civilizations may rise and fall, mankind as a whole is advantaged. He tells us in the *Politics* that as changes in the arts and sciences have so evidently been valuable to men, changes in political ways should always be considered in this light.

> If politics is an art, change must be necessary in this as in any other art. The need for improvement is shown by the fact that old customs are exceedingly simple and barbarous [the very point, be it noticed, that Thucydides had made in the first pages of his *History of the Peloponnesian War*] . . . . The remains of ancient laws which have come down to us are quite absurd . . . men in general desire the good, and not merely what their fathers had . . . the primeval inhabitants, whether born of the earth or the survivors of some destruction, may be supposed to have been no better than ordinary foolish people among ourselves . . . and it would be ridiculous to rest content with their notions. Even when laws have been written down, they ought not always to be remain unaltered.

Precisely as would any eighteenth- and nineteenth-century social reformer, Aristotle gives linkage to the very old and the obsolete, not hesitating to liken the antique in institutions with the sentiments of the very foolish among us. Those such as Locke and his followers and including the Founding Fathers in America who prided themselves upon their knowledge of

Aristotle the statesman knew very well indeed that in Aristotle could be found ample justification even for revolutions of the sort represented in England by the year 1688 and in America by 1776.

In any event, the supposition, so widely repeated in even the best of modern and contemporary interpretations of Greek political thought, that time and change were regarded as enemies, that reality lay in the permanent and unchanging, and that everything must be seen as dictated by Fate —that supposition should be laid to rest forever.

Hellenistic Civilization

I follow convention here in giving the date 323 B.C. (the death of Alexander) as the beginning, and 30 B.C. (the establishment of the Roman Empire, which of course included Greece) as the end of this civilization. Except in histories of science and technology, Hellenistic culture is commonly dealt with in the somber tones of decline, decadence, and philosophical retreat from the world. We are not as used to treatments of its philosophy, or a substantial part at least, cast in terms of optimism, faith in the continuing advance of human thought, and man's capacity for effecting improvements of political and moral nature in his scene. And yet, as a good deal of analysis of this age reveals, there is much more in common between the philosophy of this age and that of the sixth and fifth centuries B.C., the so-called golden age of Greek rationalism, than we are often likely to think.

True, there was the philosophy of Cynicism, with its exaltation of the simple and natural and its implied contempt for the cultural (especially material) achievements of man. Pyrrhonism was built in large degree around skepticism toward the results of reason, toward any ascription of progress in civilization. Peripateticism, though not without respect for advances in the arts and sciences, looked nostalgically to the simpler past. And undoubtedly, given the efforts of Alexander after he reached and conquered Persia to unite the East and West—quite literally, as in the marriages he ordered between Greeks and Persians—and to make certain that ideas and beliefs resident in the East would make their way West, and vice versa, there were many exotic beliefs current in Greece during the Hellenistic age, beliefs which would have been repulsed in the Athens of Pericles.

But, this much accepted, there is still a very large, other story to tell about Hellenistic culture. Sir Gilbert Murray and those of like mind attempt to convey the impression that antirationalism and pessimism were the essence of the age, with consequences which in the long run would reflect a collective "failure of nerve," invite mystical and occult faiths from the East which had their very roots in repudiation of reason and material progress, and prepare the ground for eventual rise and diffusion of Christianity. Despite this conventional view emphasizing Hellenistic rejections of man's earthly state, and celebrations of the afterlife and of the kinds of faith and ritual which alone could prepare men for this afterlife, a great deal of rationalism and science and belief in material progress are to be found in the period.

The Hellenistic period after all is, as Pericles' Athens emphatically was not, the age of extraordinary discoveries in physical science and of mechanical inventions which profoundly altered the character of men's day-to-day lives. Gregory Vlastos in his recent *Plato's Universe* puts the matter authoritatively so far as *Hellenic* philosophy is concerned: it cannot be properly referred to as containing science, as we and later Greeks might understand the word, but it did arrive at "the conception of the cosmos that is *presupposed* by natural science and by its practice." It is in *Hellenistic* Greece that natural science and engineering made their appearance and in so doing produced a tradition in the West that might, as during two or three centuries following the breakdown of the Roman Empire in the West, flicker, become almost extinguished, but would be once again robust by the twelfth century in Europe and would have, even earlier, as Lynn White has emphasized in his *Medieval Technology and Social Change,* at least something to do with those early medieval inventions which changed not only the character of argiculture but European life as a whole.

It is easy to imagine that the Greece of Eratosthenes and Archimedes, to name but two of the greater scientists, would have room in it for philosophers still able to believe in reason and knowledge and still able to recognize the long ascent from primeval darkness to civilization, as had Protagoras, Aeschylus, Plato, and Aristotle, and as able to resist the lure of either archaism or primitivism.

Epicurus was one of these. Zeno, founder of Stoicism, was another. Edelstein writes of the former: "Epicurus in his analysis of the development of civilization certainly followed the earlier progressivist view and even refashioned it boldly with additions of his own." Thus Epicurus distinguishes between subhuman creatures whom nature had prepared to live and cope through instinct, and human beings whose very weakness against natural forces led them to the construction of artificial aids. He is quoted by Edelstein to the effect that human nature "was taught and constrained to do many things of every kind merely by circumstance; and later on, reasoning elaborated what had been suggested by nature and made further inventions, in some matters quickly and in others slowly at some epochs and time (making great advances) and lesser again at others."

Zeno, founder of Stoicism, the philosophical rival of Epicureanism, declared that the appearance of man through divine intervention coincided exactly with the age of arts and crafts on earth. Not for Zeno any Golden Age of the distant past. It was man himself who, with the help of providence, to be sure, made the earth suitably habitable and suitably endowed with the material needs for the good life to make possible that preoccupation with morality and with moral improvement which for Zeno was the mark of the truly wise and virtuous man. If for the Stoics there was virtue in keeping material and sensuous pleasures at relatively a low level of importance and in stressing the kind of pleasure that is attainable only by acts of genuine moral dedication, it certainly cannot be said of the Stoics that they turned a blind eye to the material arts. And however distinctively they may have defined reason, there is still a continuity to be seen between the Stoics and their predecessor Plato.

"On the whole," writes Edelstein, "early Hellenistic philosophy expressed less enthusiasm for the ideal of progress than did its classical counterpart." Edelstein also notes, however, that there is no sure way of knowing how far into the public mind even this tempered progressivism reached. Certainly there were those such as Dicaearchus and Aratus who lamented the decline from mankind's initial golden age of happiness that sprang in their view from the imposition of practical knowledge and affluence upon pristine purity of morality. But the evidence suggests that throughout the Hellenistic period the major thinkers, with the Roman Lucretius the last and the greatest of them, retained the faith in knowledge and the conviction in the progress of knowledge—and thus of human welfare—that began with Hesiod and Xenophanes and flourished so vigorously in the fifth and fourth centuries B.C. What Arnaldo Momigliano has written on a closely related aspect of Greek thought in this period is helpful:

The fact is that the Greek wise men always operated within the *polis,* always accepted its gods and very seldom rejected its conventional morality. If we exclude the Cynics, whom nobody except themselves considered wise, the Greek image of wisdom was a higher form of civic virtue. Where religious sanction was sought (the Pythagoreans and Socrates did), it did not challenge recognized rites or sanctuaries. Socrates was notoriously approved of by Delphi: he even accepted condemnation in accordance with an ordinary law of his own city. The traditions of the Seven Wise Men, which were given coherence in the fifth century B.C., insist on the down-to-earth, albeit slightly eccentric, contents of their teaching.

The faith in intellectual and cultural progress that we find among the Greeks could not have existed apart from the foundations which Professor Momigliano describes. Of course there were variations throughout, in the fifth as well as in the second and first centuries B.C. But on the whole, as the philosophies of Epicurus and Zeno make clear enough, faith in knowledge, in wisdom, and in the capacity of man to better both himself and his society remained strong.

Lucretius

Certainly this faith was strong enough to captivate the Roman Lucretius, whose great *On the Nature of Things* may be seen not only as the triumphant culmination of the Hellenistic age, but, if we are more interested in the future, as a work unique, I believe, in all antiquity for its anticipations of theories as modern as Darwin's natural selection. Lucretius is one of the three greatest of Latin poets, and if Virgil and Catullus are no doubt destined for continuing appeal on the intrinsic merits of their command of sheer poetry, quite apart from knowledge of life and history, it cannot be denied that Lucretius is *the* poet-philosopher, *the* poet-scientist among all Romans and will remain so for as long as classical reading continues. He is also the philosopher *non pareil,* among Romans, of human progress. What had been built up from Hesiod to Epicurus in this respect receives its most complete and most eloquent statement in Lucretius's work.

He was, as the early pages of his master-work make clear, learned in the Greek corpus, and his commentary as well as criticism reflect full understanding of the doctrines of the Greeks back to Heraclitus, Empedocles, Anaxagoras, and others. Clearly, it was Democritus's vision of atoms in the void that had a most profound effect upon Lucretius, at least in early sections of his work. But it is Epicurus, who combined atom-philosophy with so much else of not merely physical but psychological and sociological character, whom Lucretius most admired. Not least among the reasons for this is Lucretius's appreciation of the fact that Epicurus, without necessarily consigning all gods to oblivion, created a system of thought that did not require recourse to gods for explanation of physical and human processes.

Unless one wishes to term Lucretius' passionate, profound adoration of nature a religion (and no one can protest the assertion that Lucretius' great work at least served a religious function in its adjuration to abandon fear of death, take comfort in the natural and the rational, and seek the tranquillity and serenity of mind possible for human beings), there is no way of finding in his work the slightest intimation of what conventionally passes for religion. At the very beginning of his poem Lucretius speaks of religion as "our foe," a use of the mind that has been responsible "again and again" for "deeds sinful and unholy." Lucretius, for all we know, may have tolerated, if not subscribed to, at least a few benign and compassionate forms of religious faith, but for the whole stock of what he refers to as "superstitions," he had nothing but hate and contempt. Too often, he writes, have these beliefs been responsible for man's worst torments of spirit. Given Lucretius' bitter declamations on religion, and the sheer power of his poetry on man and mankind, it is easy enough to understand the virulence of later, Christian attacks on Lucretius, however often the Fathers may have borrowed from his insight and imagery. St. Jerome went so far as to judge Lucretius insane and, in the end, a suicide, unable to live with his own doctrines. Alas, little is known about Lucretius' life, and there is no absolutely certain way of giving the lie to St. Jerome. But anyone who reads *On the Nature of Things* with an open mind cannot but be struck by the overriding tranquillity, the serenity and repose of the mind behind this evolutionary epic.

There is indeed in it, as Lucretius' greatest translator Cyril Bailey and also the historian Charles N. Cochrane have noticed, a profoundly religious quality all its own. His poem must have had and must have been designed to have a reassuring effect upon the Romans of his day. Rome of the late second and early part of the first century was a deeply tormented society, divided politically into warring groups, economically distressed, subjected to revolts which once would have seemed impossible, and subject to a series of treasonous acts. It is understandable that faith in old gods would weaken and disappear, especially in the sacred city itself. Old beliefs were challenged by new ones. There were the faiths and cults imported from the East, attracting followers just as the cult of Christ would in the next century, especially in the cities. But there had to be a great many educated, morally upright Romans who, although weakening in the beliefs of their fathers, could not bring themselves to accept doctrines so closely associated, as many were, with repugnant rites and sacrifices. For these Romans, or many of them, Lucretius' poem with its own distinctive form of the "good news" must have brought solace as well as sheer intellectual and reading pleasure. Lucretius had no more liking than they did for the political corruption, visible moral decay, consecrated skepticisms and cynicisms, and outright, often pornographic, floutings of sacred tradition in even the most sanctified of temples. So evil and intellectually bankrupt an age deserved a restorative, renewing testament to goodness and reason. It is easy to imagine that Lucretius believed this, and believed that his long poem might serve in this capacity. What Charles N. Cochrane has written in *Christianity and Classical Culture* is enlightening:

> His object, indeed, was to show how that anarchy might be overcome; and if, in a sense, he speaks the language of revolt, it was with no intention of feeding the

devouring flames of revolutionary passion, but rather to establish a new principle of understanding and control. That principle was reason . . .

Let knowledge and reason banish or at least allay the insecurities and terrors which religion was no longer capable of restraining or assuaging—assuming, from the point of view of the committed rationalist, it ever had been in fact capable. Hence the Lucretian appeal at the beginning of his book to Venus "the life-giver" for help in making his words of "lasting loveliness" in order that "the wild works of warfare may be lulled to sleep over all seas and lands." And what is the message that Lucretius offers? Nothing less than an evolutionary panorama of the formation of world, man, and society, one starting with "the first-beginnings of things, from which nature creates all things, and increases and fosters them, and into which nature too dissolves them again at their perishing . . . ." Not, really, until the late eighteenth century or beginning of the nineteenth will we again encounter a work—such, for example, as Erasmus Darwin's brilliant and learned *Zoonomia*—in which sheer naturalism is combined so fruitfully with poetry, in which developmentalism is made into the law of life. Such is the case with Lucretius' striking poem of science.

The Lucretian account of the beginnings of the universe through the chance collisions and conformations of atoms—through *chance,* be it noted well, "not by design" as Lucretius is careful to insist—details all the successive motions and processes, each begot naturally of a preceding one, which eventually brought the world and its inhabiting beings into existence. Suffice it to say that for Lucretius the whole enormous process of development required an immensity of duration, and that the very essence of the process lay in an infinity of "natural experiments," with some forms of life found inadequate and thus doomed to infertility and eventual extinction, and other forms capable of generating new, higher species. There is more than a hint of what Darwin, nearly two thousand years later, would call "natural selection" and, following his admired contemporary Herbert Spencer, "Survival of the Fittest." Such, Lucretius writes, is the controlling necessity of experiment and adaptation, of ability of a species to survive in its environment: some species are bound to disappear, just as others remain and propagate. What counts is differential reproduction.

For we see that many happenings must be united for things, that they may be able to beget and propagate their races; first that they may have food, and then a way whereby birth-giving seeds may pass through their frames, and issue from their slackened limbs . . . . And it must needs be that many races of living things then perished and could not beget and propagate their offspring. For whatever animals you see feeding on the breath of life, either their craft or bravery, aye or their swiftness has protected and preserved their kind from the beginning of their being. And many there are, which by their usefulness are commended to us, and so abide, trusted to our tutelage.

But our primary concern here is not with Lucretius as biological evolutionist or atomic scientist; it is with Lucretius as portrayer of the cultural progress of mankind. For this extraordinary burst of speculation and knowledge we turn to the famous fifth book of *On the Nature of Things.* Not until the late eighteenth century at very earliest will we find again in Western writing so detailed, so measured, so aptly sequenced a picture of the origin and progress of the human arts and sciences.

Lucretius begins with the condition of human beings in their very earliest state of existence, as this might be recovered through the uses of reason and informed speculation. He stresses the original hardiness of the human body and mind, and the aboriginal cunning and ability to invent weapons as the means by which human beings could defend themselves against larger, much more powerful beasts, reptiles, and birds then on earth. We learn too of the ease with which human beings lived long and healthy lives off "oaks laden with acorns" and "the arbute berries" which were then, Lucretius informs us, larger and richer than in his own time. There was no community of any kind in the beginning; human beings roamed and ate and slept at individual will, mating when desire drove them but without the bond of recognized kinship. True, men were often killed by other, larger and fiercer beasts, but, Lucretius says, "never were thousands of men led beneath the standards and done to death in a single day, nor did the stormy waters dash ships and men upon the rocks." It is essentially the image of mankind's primal state that Rousseau will offer in his second *Discourse.*

So is the careful account of man's emergence from this primitive condition. Gradually, huts were contrived as protection from the elements, skins were adapted to human use for clothing, fire was utilized and protected, "and woman yoked with man," retiring to a single dwelling place where "the laws of marriage" were gradually learnt, and the family became a reality. Soon families joined with families. "Neighbors began eagerly to form friendship with one another, not to hurt or be hurt" and "with cries and gestures they taught by broken words that 'tis right for all men to have pity on the weak."

Language slowly, haltingly, came into existence. Lucretius is as careful to dismiss the possibility that language was *invented* by any single individual or group of individuals at a given point in time as he is any thought that language was a gift by the gods. Culture heroes play as infinitesimal a role in the Lucretian scheme of development of culture as do gods. Lucretius offers us the theory that language evolved very slowly out of the instinctive cries human beings share with animals and also (in anticipation of a great deal of what was to be found in nineteenth-century philology) out of the "experiments" with sounds, especially those of children, which were the natural outcome of man's interaction with man, the animal world, and the universe.

He takes nothing away from the influence in earliest times of "those who excelled in understanding and were strong in mind," one more instance of Lucretius's utilization of natural selection as a mechanism of change. These were the individuals who showed their fellows "more and more how to change their former life and livelihood for new habits and fire." But such strong minds and imaginations were as natural to human development as were weaker ones—in no respect creatures of divinity or undue endowment of qualities altogether lacking in others.

Not that the early development of society was one of undiluted happiness. Property soon came into existence, gold was discovered, "which easily robbed the strong and beautiful of honor; for, for the most part, however strong men are born, however beautiful their body, they follow the lead of the richer man." Here Lucretius cannot forgo the temptation to philosophize: "Yet if a man would steer his life by true reasoning, it is great riches to a man to live thriftily with calm mind, for never can he lack for little." Kings gradually made their appearance, to rule with power and majesty, but monarchy was followed by anarchy, absolute government trampled "beneath the feet of the mob." There ensued a stage during which all things "would pass to the utmost dregs of disorder, when every man sought for himself the power and the headship." But this phase too disappeared in time, followed by the beginnings of genuine government and law, with settled principles existing where once only arbitrary, monarchical power had prevailed.

Lucretius gives much attention to the origin and development of religion. Himself devoid, as we have noted, of belief in gods, and grateful to those philosophers such as Epicurus who had liberated men's minds from thralldom to religion, Lucretius is bound to offer a naturalistic explanation of the beginnings of human belief in deities and divine forces. He allows for the probability that earliest men contrived "glorious shapes of gods with waking minds," that is, fantatasies and delusions, but ones to which men were prone to assign external reality. Dreams also were involved, with the sometimes extraordinary objects of dreams converted by the awakened, conscious mind into real things. There were also of course the "workings of the sky" and "the diverse seasons of the year come round," and for these primitive man had no reasons to assign, and hence took further refuge in belief in the supernatural.

Thus they placed the abodes and quarters of the gods in the sky, because through the sky night and the moon are seen to roll on their way, moon, day and night, and the stern signs of night, and the torches of heaven that rove through the night, and the flying flames, clouds, sunlight, rain, snow, winds, lightning, hail, and the rapid roar and the mighty murmurings of heaven's threats.

Again Lucretius interposes homily: If only men had not been driven by fear of the unknown to accept the existence of gods, from what unhappinesses they and all their issue would have been spared. How much better to observe the turbulences as well as the tranquillities of nature with calm, reasoning mind. And yet, this said, Lucretius again explains how understandable it was that earliest man, in his fears of the unknown, would gradually bring gods and other supernatural essences into his belief.

He speculates on the appearance in civilization of the precious metals. These were no doubt exposed in parts of the world which had been cracked or fissured by devastating forest fires caused by lightning, or else by torrential floods or earthquakes. Inevitably men would come to notice these metals. "And when they saw they afterwards hardened and shining on the ground with brilliant hue, they picked them up, charmed by their smooth, bright beauty . . . ." In due time it would occur to men that through utilization of the same fire that had brought metals into sight on frequent occasion, the metals could be shaped and given designs which would be perpetuated and ever improved upon.

It is not possible to describe Lucretian developmentalism, with its numerous details and illustrations in its entirety. Suffice it to offer the following paragraph, the very last in the fifth book which appears after he has given account of the rise of the fine arts including music, of navigation, and of comforts earliest man could not have dreamed of.

Ships and tilling of the land, walls, laws, weapons, roads, dress, and all things of this kind, all the prizes, and the luxuries of life, one and all, songs and pictures, and the polishing of quaintly-wrought statues, practice and therewith the experiences of the eager mind taught them *little by little*, as they went forward step by step (pedetemtim progredientes). So, little by little, time brings out each several thing into view, and reason raises it up into the coasts of light. For they saw one thing after another grow clear in their mind, until by their arts they reached the topmost pinnacle.* "(Italics added)

My stress on that passage is richly merited, for not only is it the first in all literature to utilize the word *progredientes,* from which our own word "progress" derives, but it also is a passage that in content, meaning, and

*Plato's phrase, it will be recalled; also, with only slightest alteration, the still earlier Xenophanes'.

orientation could be inserted aptly into literally dozens of works on the progress of mankind written in the eighteenth and well into the nineteenth century. Everything essential is there: the naturalness of the process (for example, autonomy from divine cause or intervention); the stress upon human insight and ingenuity; the insistence upon the gradual, slow, and cumulative character of the process; and at the very end, the reference to "topmost pinnacle." Not until Turgot's discourses of 1750 and Rousseau's second Discourse will we encounter such a passage, indeed such a chapter, as this from Lucretius in the first century B.C.

Nor, be it stressed, is Lucretius without expectations for the future. Consider the following passage, found early in the fifth book:

> But indeed, I trow, our whole world is in its youth, and quite new is the nature of the firmament, nor long ago did it receive its first beginnings. Wherefore even now certain arts are being perfected, even now are growing; much new has been added to ships, but a while ago musicians gave birth to tuneful melodies. Again, this nature of things, this philosophy, is but lately discovered, and I myself was found the very first of all who could turn it into the speech of my country.

Such a passage, as must be obvious, could hardly have been written by anyone who, in J. B. Bury's words on Lucretius, "did not look forward to a steady and continuous process of further amelioration in the future," who, also in Bury's words, thought his "own philosophy the final word on the universe," and whose ideas were a "philosophy of resignation . . . thoroughly pessimistic and therefore incompatible with the idea of Progress."

Seneca

There are as many anomalies and contradictions in Seneca's view of the history of mankind, past, present and future, as there are in his personal career and his moral and political writings in general. He was eloquent in his praise of liberty, justice, and fraternity, but he seems to have found no difficulty in serving as prime minister to Nero during the worst of his violations of public morality. As Cochrane has written: "[Seneca] attacked 'superstition' but recommended the worship of the political gods 'both as a matter of form' and as expedient 'for binding the masses to civil society'. . . . Finally, while keeping his eye on the main chance, he argued volubly that the business of philosophy is to teach men 'to despise life'."

Much more important from our point of view are the inconsistencies in Seneca's philosophy of history. As I shall indicate in a moment, there are without any question some striking affirmations of the progress of man on earth, from farthest past to the most distant future. But it would be incomplete and deceptive if we did not take into account historical and evolutionary views of a decidedly different character. In a number of places Seneca refers to the destructive effects progress in knowledge has had on the human bond, for example, in the intensification and diffusion of the technology of warfare. He writes of the pervading moral decay in Rome, of man's having lived "under better auspices" in his early history on earth, and of man's having been long ago "without knowledge of crimes." And, as Edelstein notes, Seneca can contemplate the annihilation of the world and everything on it with seeming unconcern even though he occasionally thought that this destruction was not far ahead in time.

But in the history of ideas it is not the overall consistency of thought in a philosopher that governs the extent to which his ideas exert long run influence, least of all which ideas. And if it must be said that Seneca was indeed —at least some of the time—a primitivist and regressivist with allied beliefs in some kind of primal golden age, it must also be said that there are some eloquent and even profound observations in his writings on the reality of progress in science and other forms of knowledge and on the benign results to humanity of such progress. And according to some Senecan scholars there is good reason to believe that Seneca became almost a complete progressivist in his mature, later years, showing little interest in the antiprogressivist views of his earlier writings.

He is lavish in his praise of "human ingenuity," the real source, he tells us, of the greater accomplishments in the history of civilization. He catalogues some of the major achievements of mankind through the ages, and writes: "It was man's ingenuity, not his wisdom that discovered all these devices." The most useful of inventions have come from the "nimble and the keen," not the "great and exhalted." The interventions of the latter have occasionally been required, but in the areas which are fundamental—agriculture and weaving are among those Seneca most often cities—it was the simple people, those who, unlike the wealthy and powerful, had the most to gain, who brought about advances. Thus, when Seneca describes wondrous inventions and refinements of his time, he writes:

> Reason did indeed devise all these things, but it was not right reason. It was man, but not the wise man, that discovered them; just as they invented ships, in which we cross rivers and seas—ships fitted with sails for the purpose of catching the force of the winds, ships with rudders added at the stern in order to turn the course of the vessel's course in one direction or another. The model followed was the fish, which steers itself by its tail . . .

Who, he concludes, but simple people in daily contact with fishes and fishing would, therefore, come up with such an invention?

Not, of course, that Seneca was hostile to wisdom and philosophy. "But wisdom's course is toward the state of happiness; thither she guides us, thither she opens the way for us." For there must first be the establishment of, over long periods of time, the kind of material setting in which alone wisdom and men of wisdom can be afforded.

As with Hesiod, much too much has been made of Seneca's invoking of a primal golden age. We get a better appreciation of his real views on primitive people from the following:

> Justice was unknown to them, unknown prudence, unknown also self-control and bravery; but their rude life possessed certain qualities *akin* to all these virtues. Virtue [true virtue] is not vouchsafed to a soul unless that soul has been *trained and taught,* and by unremitting practice brought to perfection . . . and even in the best of men, before you refine them by instruction, there is but the stuff of virtue, *not virtue itself.*

There is in Seneca a great deal of developmentalist thought and of change conceived as an unfolding, a conversion of potentiality into actuality over a stretch of time. He is Aristotelian.

> Whether the world is a soul, or a body under the government of nature, like trees and crops, it embraces in its constitution all that it is destined to experience actively or passively from its beginnings right on to its end; *it resembles a human being,* all whose capacities are wrapped up in the embryo before birth. (Italics added)

Over and over during the next nineteen-hundred years Seneca's analogy between mankind's growth of knowledge and the growth of a single human being will be employed by philosophers of progress. We shall find St. Augustine using it; it is the very basis of the victory claimed by the Moderns over the Ancients in the Battle of Books that took place in the seventeenth century; and Auguste Comte, positivist and founder of sociology, made it the pivot of his own "law" of progress. Nor is the analogy lacking in our own day, as we shall see.

Seneca makes explicit his conviction that the kind of growth of knowledge that has taken place over a very long past will continue indefinitely on into the future. "Many discoveries are reserved for *the ages still to be,* when our memory shall have perished. The world is a poor affair if it do not contain matter for investigation for the whole world in every age." (Italics added) And again:

> I marvel at wisdom as I marvel at the world itself which, no matter how often I contemplate it, seems always new. I revere the discoveries of wisdom and its discoverers. It pleases me to approach the subject as a legacy left to me by many men. For me they have gathered up, for me they have labored. May an even greater legacy be left by myself to posterity. Much remains to do; much will remain; and no one born

45

after thousands of centuries will be deprived of the chance of adding something . . . (Italics added)

True, Seneca placed himself on record as believing that at some future time the earth and everything on it would be destroyed by catastrophe. But the passage just quoted doesn't allow us to believe that Seneca thought such destruction lay immediately ahead. He could write: "All that long forbearance of fortune has produced, all that has been reared to eminence, all that is famous, and all that is beautiful, great thrones, great nations, all will descend into one abyss and will be overthrown in one hour." But so, it might be emphasized here, are there intimations of *eventual* ending of the world in the writings of philosophers and scientists of the nineteenth and twentieth centuries who are unambiguous in declaration of commitment to progress past, present, and future.

We can do no better than conclude this section and chapter with a wise assessment of Seneca by Ludwig Edelstein regarding all that is implied by Seneca's thought:

For Seneca, then, the ideal of progress was an expression of the highest aspirations of man and mankind, and in explaining it and defining its scope he argued very much in the manner of the thinkers in the eighteenth century who were preoccupied by the same ideal. If Condorcet, whose manifesto inaugurated modern progressivisms, takes "advance in knowledge as the clue to the march of the human race," if for him "the history of civilization is the history of enlightenment," the same is true of Seneca; and with slight changes of language one could say of the latter as has been said of the former that "he insists on the indissoluble union between intellectual progress and that of liberty, virtue, and the respect for natural rights, and on the effects of science on the destruction of prejudice. . . ."

I trust that enough has been cited and demonstrated in the preceding pages of this chapter to put to rest in readers' minds the long held fallacy that the Greeks and Romans were not only without vision of progress in the arts and sciences, but were hopelessly enmired in a pessimism that could see nothing but decline and degradation in the passage of time. From Hesiod to Seneca we find, *first,* respect, even reverence, for knowledge—practical knowledge, the kind that gives protection, comfort, and well-being to mankind; *second,* a clear conception of the acquisition of this knowledge by man through his own abilities, helped on occasion by the gods, yes, but nevertheless in the long run by man's own efforts; *third,* recognition that such acquisition has taken place cumulatively over a period of time—"in the course of time," as Xenophanes stated it early on, "little by little," in Plato's phrasing, and "step by step," in Lucretius' words, written half a millennium after those of Xenophanes.

Chapter 2

The Early Christians

W HAT classical pagan thinkers began, classical Christian thinkers continued—continued and also added to in ways which would give to the idea of progress a large and devoted following in the West and a sheer power that the idea could not otherwise have acquired. The Greeks contributed the seminal conception of the natural growth in time of knowledge, and accordingly the natural advance of the human condition. This emphasis upon knowledge, upon the arts and sciences, is, as we shall see, very much a part of the Christian philosophy of history; it became such indeed in the Age of the Church Fathers.

But the Christian philosophers, starting with Eusebius and Tertullian and reaching masterful and lasting expression in St. Augustine, endowed the idea of progress with new attributes which were bound to give it a spiritual force unknown to their pagan predecessors. I refer to such attributes as the vision of the unity of all mankind, the role of historical necessity, the image of progress as the unfolding through long ages of a design present from the very beginning of man's history, and far from least, a confidence in the future that would become steadily greater and also more *this*-worldly in orientation as compared with *next*-worldly. To these attributes one other must be added: the emphasis upon the gradual, cumulative, *spiritual* perfection of mankind, an immanent process that would in time culminate in a golden age of happiness on earth, a millennium with the returned Christ as ruler.

There are of course two vital sources of Christianity as a world religion and a philosophy of history. The first is Jewish. From the Jews the Christians obtained the conception of history as sacred, as divinely guided and therefore *necessary*. Also from the Jews, and particularly from the strong currents of Jewish millenarianism which were flowing both before and after the advent of the Christian religion, came the belief in a golden age on earth in the future, a belief set forth in the Book of Revelation in the New Testament and to be found in varying degrees of intensity throughout the history of Christianity—never more effectively, so far as the idea of progress is concerned, than in the Puritan seventeenth century.

The other source of Christianity is Greek. The Jewish followers of and missionaries for Christ were obliged to learn Greek if they were to be able to communicate the Good News. And in learning the language they also learned ideas: such Greek ideas as natural growth, of change conceived of as the unfolding of potentiality into actuality, of fixed stages of the advancement of knowledge and mankind, and of the divine value that could be placed upon this advancement.

Fundamentally, Christianity and its conception of progress are results, then, of Christian fusing of Jewish and Greek concepts. We see the fusion in St. Paul. He compared the growth of the Church to the growth of a single individual human being, a comparison that would never disappear from Western thought, that would be used and reused in a great diversity of contexts. Such growth of Christianity and of the human being was for St. Paul both natural and necessary. It not only sprang from the very nature of things, as the Greeks conceived nature, but it was, as the Jews had declared of themselves and their history, necessary because of divine will. And just as the human body has a multiplicity and variety of organs all functionally related, so, St. Paul declared, has the Church—to be seen in its offices, sanctuaries, prophets, missionaries, teachers, and communicants. As the individual undergoes a pre-designed history from infancy to old age, so does the Church. Only as something developing in time, as something destined to be universal in scope, can the Church be understood. St. Paul's contemplation of time is, with only occasional significant exception, optimistic and progressive. The pessimism inherent in the Christian epic must not be undervalued, but more often what we find undervalued by modern historians is not the pessimism but the *optimism* in Christianity from the very beginning. Marjorie Reeves, in her *The Influence of Prophecy in the Later Middle Ages,* has this to say about both qualities:

> From its birth Christian thought held within it both a pessimistic and an optimistic expectation concerning history: its end could be conceived either as a mounting

crescendo of evil or as the Millennium, a Messianic Age of Gold . . . . The hope in a future Age of Gold finds its origin in the concept of the Jewish Messianic Age, when a Holy People was expected to reign in Palestine in an era of peace, justice, and plenty, in which the earth would flower in unheard-of abundance . . . [T]he Messianic age is conceived *as within history, not beyond it.* (Italics added)

Nothing in the entire history of the idea of progress is more important than, indeed if as important as, this incorporation by Christianity, from earliest times, of Jewish millennarianism. For, given its universalist cast from St. Paul on, Christianity could and did widen this millenarianism to encompass the whole of mankind. Moreover, the mere idea of a future age of gold on earth, to last a thousand (perhaps many thousands of) years, and of mankind advancing continuously and inexorably toward this golden age, was bound to diminish the importance somewhat of the transhistorical, the next-worldly, vein of thought in Christianity and to give stimulus to concern with the things and happenings of this world.

The distinguished religious historian Gerhart B. Ladner has put the matter in authoritative terms:

All the great *social* concepts of Christianity, be it the Kingdom of God or the Communion of Saints, the Church, or the City of God, were conceived *as immanent in this world,* as struggling and time-bound, and, at the same time, as transcendent, as invisible, as triumphant, as eternal in the world to come. There was, then, a Church as the community of the faithful on earth and a Church as the congregation of the heavenly city consisting of its citizens, that is to say, the saints and the angels. It is one of the great paradoxes of Christianity that such a concept as the Church can appear under these two aspects and nevertheless be ultimately one. (Italics added)

There is a great deal of Greek ontology and epistemology in the paradox Professor Ladner describes. The spirit of Plato was, as we know well, powerful in the thinking of the early Fathers, and nowhere more evidently, even resplendently, than in St. Augustine. But there was also a great deal of Roman thought and life at work in the formation of Christianity. Andre Grabar in his *Christian Iconography* writes that by the year 200, the earliest, he tells us, in which Christian art may be said to exist in public form, everything about this art save only theme or subject is Greco-Roman in the extreme—reflected in technique, form, uses of color, and so on. Something of the same may properly be said of Christian doctrine, Christian philosophy of history, and practical Christian politics of this time. Christianity, although Jewish at the core, was affected by, directed and oriented toward, Roman life. The real relation between Roman polity, culture, and thought on the one hand and Christianity on the other is one more instance of the genuine continuity that is evidenced during the centuries leading up to and following the fall of Rome as the Western capital of the Empire. The invading barbarians have been used too often and too much to give emphasis to *discontinuity*. We need only read Peter Brown's *The World of Classical Antiquity* to see how large was the measure of Greco-Roman swallowing up of the barbarians and their culture—and also of a great deal of Christian practice. Brown writes:

A city, its habits and associations, changes slowly. In seventh-century Rome, the members of the clerical oligarchy of the city still proceeded to their churches as the consuls had proceeded in the early sixth century—greeted by candles, scattering largess to the populace, wearing the silken slippers of a senator. The Lateran Palace was so called because it was thought 'good Latin' was still spoken there. In their great basilicas, the popes continued to pray for the *Roman libertas*. The idea that Western society had to recognize the predominance of a sharply defined, clerical elite, as the emperors had once recognized the special status of members of the Roman Senate, was the basic assumption behind the rhetoric and ceremonial of the medieval papacy: like the last warm glow of evening, the late Roman senator's love of *Roma aeterna* had come to rest on the solemn facade of papal Rome.

And, as Brown goes on to stress:

A Roman senator could write as if he still lived in the days of Augustus, and wake up, as many did at the end of the fifth century A.D., to realize that there was no longer a Roman emperor in Italy. Again, a Christian bishop might welcome the disasters of the barbarian invasions, as if they had turned men irrevocably from earthly civilization to the Heavenly Jerusalem, yet he will do this in a Latin or Greek unselfconsciously modelled on the ancient classics; and he will betray attitudes that mark him out as a man still firmly rooted in eight hundred years of Mediterranean life.

If, then, we are to understand Christian thought, and specifically Christian philosophy of history with its powerful currents of progressivism, we must abandon all thought of Christian intellectuals as forming an enclave, as renouncing all contact with Greco-Roman ideas, interests, hopes, and expectations. Different though the Christians were from the pagans in religious belief, there was a large and important area of political and historical belief that Christians and pagans and, in a relatively short time, the assimilated barbarians, occupied in common. And although belief in an eternal heaven for the saved, one that would follow destruction of this world, was a strong belief in Christian minds—as it has been right down to our own day —it was not so strong as to obliterate all interest in the things of this world.

Christian Worldliness

To comprehend the interest that the things of this world could generate in the minds of early Christians we need only turn to some of the works of the Church Fathers. From the time (at latest) of Tertullian and Eusebius there is a manifest acceptance of, and respect for, Greco-Roman worldly values. We are accustomed to the image of the early Christian with eyes turned only upward, beseechingly, to heaven and to Christ. We would do well to think somewhat less of this image than one of the Christian with eyes turned sharply to the ongoing spectacle of Roman life, its rewards, incentives, and motivations as well as its pitfalls and torments—in brief, to the worldly rather than the supernatural. And this concern with the worldly, with worldly achievement and reform past and present, is very much a part of the Christian statement of human progress.

Although our prime exhibit in this section is St. Augustine's *The City of God,* it is interesting to cite briefly two of his illustrious predecessors, Tertullian and Eusebius.

Tertullian was the foremost defender of Christianity in his day, from the time of his conversion (he was the son of a Roman centurion, possessed of a thorough education in Greek and Latin philosophy, history and literature), ca. 155, until his death, ca. 230. We think of him instantly as the author of "It is certain because it is impossible" and are consequently prone to emphasize the miraculous and the mystical in this thought. But there is a good deal else in Tertullian, including high respect for human and especially Roman achievements of a cultural character. Charles N. Cochrane, in his *Christianity and Classical Culture,* brings this side of Tertullian vividly to our attention. Two centuries before *The City of God* was written, we find Tertullian engaged, as Cochrane observes, in defending Christianity against charges that it was this religion that began the erosion of *Romanitas,* and generated the military, political, and economic problems with which Romans were forced to live. Tertullian's reply to these charges is in the rhetoric of history; all of man's history on earth, he argues, has been characterized by destruction, followed, however, by new and higher levels of civilization. As for Christian repudiation of the Romans' ancestors, he declares in resounding fashion:

> In your clothing, your food, your habits, finally even in your language, you have repudiated your ancestors. You are always praising antiquity, but you renew your life from day to day.
> Consider whether the general accusation you bring against us, namely, that we have discarded ancestral custom, may not be levelled equally against yourselves . . . .

If you look at the world as a whole, you cannot doubt that it has grown progressively more cultivated and populated *(cultior de die et instructior pristino)*. Every territory is now accessible, every territory explored, every territory opened to commerce. The most delightful farmsteads have obliterated areas formerly waste, plough-land has subdued the woods, domestic cattle have put to flight the wild beast, barren sands have become fertile, rocks are reduced to soil, swamps are drained, the number of cities today exceeds the number of isolated huts in former times, islands no longer inspire fear nor crags terror: everywhere people, everywhere organized communities, everywhere human life . . . .

Nor is that passage to be seen as something fanciful, without philosophical foundation in Tertullian's thought. He tells us that change, mutation, and development are fundamental to the world and life in it. The law of motion, he declares, is to be found manifest in the movements of celestial bodies, in the solar year, the phases of the moon, the alternation of day and night, of storm and calm, and so forth. The earth as a whole has changed dramatically. Once it was covered by waters, a fact demonstrated, Tertullian asserts, by the presence of sea shells on mountain tops. The law of physical mutation applies to both animals and human beings, both of which have, since primeval times, spread themselves all over the earth.

There is more than a hint of Malthusianism in the following comment. Tertullian is seeking to prove that the advance of human arts has been such that a population larger than that of early times is creating problems of population pressure:

Most convincing as evidence of populousness, we men have actually become a burden to the earth, the fruits of nature hardly suffice to sustain us, there is a general pressure of scarcity giving rise to complaints, since the earth can no longer support us. Need we be astonished that plague and famine, warfare and earthquake come to be regarded as remedies, serving, as it were, to trim and prune the superfluity of population.

Nor was this champion of the Faith without appreciation of what had been accomplished, and even as he wrote being accomplished, through reforms:

What reforms has this age not witnessed! Think of the cities which the threefold virtue of our present sovereignty has built, augmented, or restored, God bestowing his blessing on so many Augusti as on one! The censuses they have taken! The peoples they have driven back! The classes of society they have honored! The barbarians they have kept in check! In very truth, this empire has become the garden of the world.

That there were indeed crises forming which the Romans would not succeed in meeting, as the history of the third century would make only too clear, serves in present context only to give emphasis to the progressive character of Tertullian's mind. He was not the first, nor would he be the last, to trumpet on the very eve of severe depression and accumulating military defeat the happiness of man and the greatness of his achievements. Nothing of what I have just cited from Tertullian can take away from the centrality of the divine, the spiritual, and the eternal in his writings and teachings. But the important point is that even in a mind as God- and Christ-driven as Tertullian's, the Greco-Roman foundations are plain to be seen—foundations which included not merely awareness of, but hope for, the secular world.

Eusebius (whose notable *Ecclesiastical History* was first completed ca. 303), the major figure in the generation following that of Tertullian as far as Christian theology is concerned, has been referred to by Cochrane as "the first of a long succession of ecclesiastical politicians to pass across the European stage." Never mind the passion that went into his Christian belief; there was enough left to serve Rome and his admired Constantine very well indeed. It was he who sat to the right of the imperial throne during the historic sessions of the Nicene Council, and we have every right to believe that what was uppermost in Eusebius's mind was no invisible, eternal church, but the very visible and increasingly worldly church which he served brilliantly as Bishop of Caesarea.

Robert Hanning, in his *The Vision of History in Early Britain,* after declaring that in his judgment no universal principle of progressive development can be found in Eusebius's writing, adds: "Yet his views on Rome and its meaning in providence are certainly developmental or progressive." Hanning continues:

To Eusebius, Constantine is more than just a liberator of Christianity; he is also the imperial hero who accomplishes the pacification and unification of the empire after a period of intense civil strife. As Eusebius pondered the climax of the twin crises of church and empire, he formulated for the first time his conception of the empire's place in God's providential scheme for history and for the church in history; that is, he admitted the principle of development or progress into his Christian historiography.

Constantine, Hanning observes, becomes for Eusebius "the last of the patriarchs," the new Abraham, in whom the promise made to Abraham is literally fulfilled; the Roman Empire of which Constantine is head becomes the definitive force of providence in history, and promises to the Christian the prospect of an ever triumphant and ever improving society. . . ."

Virgil, three centuries earlier in his paean to Augustus and a new golden age, hardly exceeded, in theme at least, what Eusebius could say of his own emperor, Constantine: "The God of all, the supreme governor of the whole universe, by His own will appointed Constantine, the descendant of so renowned a parent, to be prince and sovereign. . . ." What is overriding in Eusebius's approach to Christianity and his beloved Rome is his ingenious weaving of the two together through institutional strands. He saw the two as profoundly interdependent, each attaining ever higher levels of meaning and authority through association with the other. In Eusebius's mind there was little doubt, as Cochrane stresses, that the age of Constantine promised on this earth a "universal and perpetual peace," the ancient Roman dream expressed in *Pax Romana* but now brought through Christianity's success to a much higher level of ideal and reality alike. Christianity, by its extermination of local, particular, and necessarily competitive idols, aided Rome in its establishment of political unity and peace, but through the benevolence of a divinely planned progress Rome, through its empire, furnished Christianity with the ground needed for ecclesiastical expansion and development.

But let us turn now to the *pièce de résistance,* St. Augustine's passages on material progress in Book 22 of *The City of God.* These could as well have been written by a Sophocles or Lucretius or, for that matter, by a Condorcet or Godwin in the eighteenth century. Augustine too is fascinated by the fecundity and diffusion of the human race over the earth and refers as any Greek would have to "the marvellous power by which seed is produced, and which seems to be as it were inwrought and inwoven in the human body." He likens the growth and development of mankind to a "river" or "torrent" that has carried man's virtues as well as his vices down through time. God is of course the author or architect of it all, but He gave human beings as well as animals "a congenital capacity to propagate their kind, not imposing on them any necessity to do so."

Immanent developmentalism is as vivid in this section of Augustine's work as in any Heraclitean or Aristotelian text. For Augustine it is not enough to make of God the Creator, the Being who brought the world and mankind into existence fullgrown. It is the Greek strain in Augustine that causes him to put God in a developmental, progressive light. He "causes the seed to develop, and to evolve from certain secret and invisible folds into the visible forms of beauty which we see." And it is the Greek strain that is responsible in the two or three pages following Augustine's celebration of fecundity and growth in the organic kingdom for a paean to the wonders of secular culture, of the arts and sciences, that is without parallel in scope and intensity until we come to the late-Middle Ages and early-modern era. Consider the following:

For over and above those arts which are called virtues, and which teach us how we may spend our life well, and attain to endless happiness—arts which are given to the children of the promise and the kingdom by the sole grace of God which is in Christ—has not the genius of man invented and applied countless astonishing arts, partly the result of necessity, partly the result of exuberant invention, so that this vigor of mind, which is so active in the discovery not merely of the superfluous but even of dangerous and destructive things, betokens an inexhaustible wealth in the nature which can invent, learn, or employ such arts.

This is a truly extraordinary passage in a work whose author has been declared innumerable times to be oblivious to the things of this world. Observe some of the words: "genius of man," "invented," "the result of necessity," "exuberant invention," and so forth. Consider now, in the same section, St. Augustine's tribute to man's own achievements on earth, from distant past to present. It begins with the words: "What wonderful—one might say stupefying—advances has human industry made in the arts of weaving and building, of agriculture and navigation." There follows an unqualified, even joyous, admiration for all the painting, sculpture, and pottery done through the ages, for the drama and its skilled performers, for all the ingenious contrivances by which wild beasts have been caught and either tamed or killed, and for the luscious foods which have been concocted. "To provoke appetite and please the palate, what a variety of seasonings have been created!" There is equal admiration for all the diverse languages man has brought into being, for the science of numbers, for explorations of nature—"with what sagacity have the movements and connections of the stars been discovered! Who could tell the thought that has been spent upon nature?"—and for the grand systems of philosophy and history, even in their errors not the less testaments to man's greatness and power of reason.

Nor is St. Augustine without esthetic appreciation of man himself, his physical and psychological endowments. He is not stooping toward the earth like the animals, "but his bodily form, erect, looking heavenwards, admonishes him to mind the things that are above." There is the "nimbleness" of man's tongue and hands, making him fit to speak and write. There is a functional quality to St. Augustine's esthetics of the human body. "Assuredly no part of the body has been created for the sake of utility that does not also contribute something to its beauty." He expresses the hope that the intricate relationships of nerve, muscle, vein, and all the internal organs, now still insufficiently understood, will in time be better known. As a religious man of his time, Augustine is necessarily ambivalent with respect to the kinds of operations necessary to such inquiry. He speaks of "the cruel zeal for science" that leads certain anatomists to dissect bodies of the dead, even of "sick persons who have died under their knives," but at the same time he makes evident his fascination with what has been learned and his hope that in time some one will be "audacious" enough to make the required analyses of body and mind which will explain for us the "concord, or, as the Greeks call it, 'harmony', of the whole body outside and in . . . ."

No less rapturous are St. Augustine's comments on the world of nature: "Shall I speak of the manifold and various loveliness of sky, and earth, and sea; of the plentiful supply of and wonderful qualities of the light; of sun, moon, and stars; of the shade of trees; of the colors and perfume of flowers, of the multitude of birds . . . ?" He tells us how remarkable are the works of ants and bees, "astonishing us more than the huge bodies of whales," and how magnificent is the sea, in force but also in beauty. "Is it not delightful to look at it in storm, and experience the soothing complacency which it inspires, by suggesting that we ourselves are not tossed and shipwrecked?" (Whether Augustine knew it, that sentence is almost word for word the opening lines of Lucretius Book 2, *On the Nature of Things;* indeed the style and content of this whole Augustinian passage relate significantly to Lucretius's great poem.) Further commentary and citation are unnecessary. But in all truth, neither earlier nor later in Western thought do we find words more expressive—indeed lyrical—of the greatness of man and his works, of the beauties of man and nature, than those given us by St. Augustine in a large number of writings. For Augustine, to be sure, God's will and infinite devotion to man underlay human greatness and beauty. The latter was not possible without the incessant force of the former. But the history of much Western social and political thought is one not so much of changing Augustinian-Christian perspectives, nor even of adding to them. It consists instead in the removal, especially in the modern West, of theistic assumptions which for an Augustine were utterly vital to progress and perfection but which in a day of looser logic, such as the eighteenth century, could seem expendable, the perspectives themselves self-supporting.

The Spirit of Social Reform

One of the seemingly ineradicable fallacies about Christianity is that it is interested solely in the spiritual and is governed primarily by faith in the next and eternal world. It is not in our time and it was not in the time of the Church Fathers. The doctrines of the fifth-century Pelagius give us an important clue to the extent to which Christians, in whatever number, were interested in the achievement of perfection in this life, on this earth; and such perfection, although for Pelagius primarily an individual quest, could easily be given social and political contexts. True, Pelagius is known to us as heretic—chiefly as the result of St. Augustine's numerous assaults upon the Pelagian doctrine of perfection to be achieved through man's own free will in this world. But as John Passmore has shown us in his thoughtful study of the whole concept of perfectibility in Western thought, Christianity has known tension throughout its history between Augustinian belief in dual predestination and Pelagian (authorship however concealed) faith in the power of each individual and of each age of society to reform, renovate, and redeem itself *now;* not to have to endure all earthly immoralities and wickednesses, with perfection to be attained only in the next world. How deeply Pelagian ideas entered Augustine's mind may be inferred not only from the extraordinary intensity of Augustinian analysis and condemnation of these ideas, but also from the degree to which they in one way or another, like the ideas of his renounced Manichaeism, tinctured his later views of moral and social reform in this world.

Gerhart B. Ladner in his magisterial *The Idea of Reform: Its Impact on Christian Thought and Action in the Age of the Fathers* has given us what is by all odds the most detailed and illuminating account of early Christian preoccupation with reformation and advancement of their own society. Ladner writes:

> In modern times the term and idea of reform are applied to the renewal and intended improvement of many things, more often however of social entities and institutions than of individuals. The origins of the Christian idea of reform on the contrary are related to the core of evangelical and Pauline doctrine on the human person: to the experience of its newness in Christ . . . . And yet, in spite of the personal, individual character of the Christian idea of reform it became effective as a *supra-individual force* at a relatively early date . . . (Italics added)

Down until the nineteenth century—indeed very often during that century and also our own—the idea of reform, whether directed toward individual or social order, almost invariably carried with it the message of *return, renewal,* or *recovery.* Even the vision of revolution, as Melvin Lasky has stressed valuably, was based—when used metaphorically, extricated from its prevailingly astronomical contexts in the sixteenth and seventeenth centuries—upon the idea of a turning or revolving of things back to their pristine condition. Much reformism of the eighteenth and nineteenth centuries springs directly from a vision, religious or secular, of a past endowed more deeply than the present with virtues and therefore to be regained through direct action.

Similarly, the early Christian ideas of *reformatio, renovatio, restauratio,* and *regeneratio*—with their implications of spiritual, but also, repeatedly, of material, political, and social improvement—were anchored in the psychology of renewal, a psychology that, as I have just noted, would remain powerful during all subsequent centuries in the West. Such terms, Ladner tells us, were used by Gregory the Great when he proposed manumission of slaves; Gregory specifically refers to the original liberty men enjoyed. A similar premise lies behind Alcuin's hope that a *renewal* of wisdom and knowledge had begun under Charlemagne. In the twelfth century St. Bernard of Clairvaux speaks of the entry into monastic life as a reformation; indeed, a Cistercian monk of the turn of the century dealt with the whole history of monasticism as one of successive reforms of this world.

"In that age," Ladner writes, "the individual and monastic realizations of the idea of reform had already begun to expand into a new conception of reform of the Church and of Christian society."

Rightly and illuminatingly does Professor Ladner emphasize the monastic movement, from its inception in the West, as being just as much a movement of reform of this world as one of the individual's reform of himself. To see the Benedictine, Cistercian, and Franciscan orders, among so many others, as mere retreats from this world, havens in which dedicated men would seek to prepare themselves for this world's imminent end and for ascension to the next, eternal world is insufficient, to say the very least. A sizable body of scholarship exists to point out how continuous the line of technological invention is from early monastic life to modern times.

But our interest here is not so much in the monasteries as in the vein of thought, present from earliest times in Greco-Roman Christianity, which many other Christians in addition to the monks drew heavily from. This vein of thought was grounded in the things of this world which needed improvement, among them agricultural practices, the keeping of accurate records for the benefit of posterity, the measurement of time, the preparation of new, more durable and also more beautiful books, and a host of other things which could never have assumed the importance they did in Christian-monastic life had there been serious expectation of an early ending of life on this earth.

It is St. Augustine's relation to all of this, however, with which I am chiefly concerned. The germs of monasticism lie deep in Augustinian writ, as Ladner has stressed. Monasticism of the Western, communal type exemplified for Augustine the deeply important *social* character of Christianity. He "sharply reasserts," Ladner writes, "his firm resolve not to tolerate in his Church any cleric who does not truly lead the 'social life' (*vitam nostram socialem*) . . . ." It is a matter of record that St. Augustine's interest in "the social life" went well beyond Christianity as such. It included an abiding interest in matters political and economic in this world. His admiration for the Roman state and its history is nearly boundless, and he actually suggests that it had developed under God's eye in the interest of providing the ideal, far-flung political organization within which Christianity could best be nurtured and diffused to the largest number of people.

But important to the history of the idea of progress as Augustinian and other early-Christian interest in social reform is, there are still other aspects of St. Augustine's thought which proved to be more influential, more shaping and directing, than this interest. I refer to his ecumenical vision, the contemplation of the human race in its entirety as the basis of Christianity; to his interest in the flow of time, in epochs and ages—that is, divisions of time—; to his doctrine of historical necessity; and far from least, the exciting vision of conflict as a dynamic in history, in his view the conflict between the two cities.

The Unity of Mankind

In its commonest form in the modern world, the idea of progress has for its referent not often a particular people or nation, but rather the whole of what we think of as humanity or mankind. The major philosophers of progress were—and to the degree that they exist in our time still are—addressing themselves to, formulating principles or laws for, the whole of humanity. That any given people, empire, nation, or state tends in time to lose the powers which were instrumental in its rise, to decline and even perish—all of this was well understood by Condorcet, Comte, Spencer, and the others who constructed their systems of human progress in the eighteenth and ninteenth centuries. What was of infinitely greater importance to them was that, irrespective of what might happen to a single people on earth, the progress of mankind as a whole was ensured. Before the light of any one great culture was extinguished, it would be reflected to some other new and burgeoning people which would then occupy the vanguard of humanity's advance in time.

It is Christianity that most systematically and consecratedly set forth the idea of humanity and, more important, the *unity* of humanity. As we have seen, the Greeks and Romans were well aware of other peoples on earth, peoples as far distant as the Chinese. And the reference to "man" was, of course, frequent in the classical treatments of progress. We need recall only Protagoras' "man is the measure of all things" and Sophocles' ode to the wonders effected by man on earth. But neither this nor an awareness of a great multiplicity of peoples and cultures on earth is the same thing as a rooted conception of humanity or mankind existing in its own right, unified and also possessed of a capacity to develop and to progress over a long period of time. This conception is peculiar to Western civilization, and is not to be found prior to about 200 A.D. It was then that Christian theologians, eager to promote the theme of the Church's universality and its availability to all human beings irrespective of family, local, ethnic, or cultural origin, and to advance the idea of God's suzerainty over *all* the peoples on earth, found themselves going increasingly beyond Roman civilization in their writings, going to—mankind!

It is in St. Augustine's *The City of God* that this idea of the universal social bond, of a unified humanity, attained its richest and most powerful expression. God created only one man, Augustine tells us, "not certainly that he might be a solitary, bereft of all society, but that by this means the unity of society and the bond of concord might be more effectually commended to him, men being bound together not only by similarity of nature but by family affection." God took care, Augustine continues, to avoid creating woman directly and separately, "but created her out of the man, that the human race might derive from one man."

It is of passing interest to note the anthropological attention Augustine gives to the inevitable problems of kinship relation and potential incest following this kind of creation—one man alone, from whose body woman was made, and this in the interests of the complete unity of all mankind. Incest in the beginning once Adam and Eve bore children was inevitable, Augustine tells us, and must therefore be pronounced good. In the beginning there was no alternative to men taking their sisters for wives. But this did not, could not, last long, Augustine argues. For, by the time of the third generation, the situation was markedly different. Grandchildren were able to choose not sisters or brothers for mates, but cousins. Had men instead chosen their sisters, as was proper and necessary for the second generation, the whole structure, hierarchy, and authority of kinship would have been threatened. Were brothers to marry sisters, "one man would be in that case father and father-in-law, and uncle to his own children . . . and his wife would be mother, aunt, and mother-in-law to them." It was therefore vital from a very early time that prohibitions of incest be established—not, be it noted, because of anything intrinsically debasing about the sexual union of brother and sister (*that* had been rendered pure, as it were, by such union among the children of Adam and Eve), but because of the confusion which would be thrust into social relationships. Augustine tells us that failure to prohibit sexual unions among those closely related by birth would have "loosened the social bond."

One final note on the Augustinian theory of incest and the tabu necessary to incest. He might have given responsibility for the sudden rise of incest tabu to a direct act of God; for there is never any doubt that for

Augustine the presence of God is constant in time and space. But we learn that the prohibition of incest came about as the result of human action—of "custom, with a finer morality." Custom, Augustine notes, "has very great power either to attract or to shock human feeling."

Custom, tradition, use and wont all have played a large role in what Augustine refers to as "the education of the human race" over a long period of time. He sees the progress of mankind, the material progress we have already found to shine so brilliantly in his account, as akin to a long process of cumulative education in a single human being.

"The education of the human race, represented by the people of God, has advanced, like that of an individual, through certain epochs or, as it were, ages, so that it might gradually rise from earthly to heavenly things, and from the visible to the invisible."

There is the flavor of Xenophanes and his late sixth century B.C. words on progress in Augustine's statement. Xenophanes, as we saw, put the matter thus: "The gods did not reveal to men all things from the beginning, but men through their own search find in the course of time that which is better." Deeply dependent though Augustine's theology was upon the Old Testament, with its themes of God the Creator and God the-Ever-Intervening-Mover, there is nonetheless the overriding influence of Greek ideas of growth, cumulative advancement, and intellectual progress in his words: *the education of the human race.* That phrase would remain a popular one in Western writing; in the eighteenth-century Lessing wrote a small but influential book bearing the phrase as its very title, a book that makes substantial use of Augustine's thesis for its content. Even more important, though, is the Augustinian analogy between the human race and a hypothetical individual living and educating himself over a long period of time. The analogy has recurrent philosophical appearances from Augustine on, and at no time more visibly than in the secular thought of the seventeenth, eighteenth, and even the nineteenth centuries, though it is extremely doubtful that such employers of the phrase as Fontenelle, Perrault, Turgot, Condorcet, and Comte ever had the faintest suspicion that it was the product of St. Augustine's mind.

The Flow of Time

The same mind that conceived the unity of mankind conceived also a single, unified, linear flow of time that was made to encompass everything that had happened to mankind in the past and that would continue to encompass it in the future—however short the future might be. Time was an almost obsessive concept for Augustine. In his *Confessions* he asks, "For what is time?" He answers: "If no one ask me, I know; if I wish to explain it to him who asks, I know not. Yet I say with confidence, that I know that if nothing passed away, there would not be past time; and if nothing were coming, there would not be future time; and if neither were, there would not be present time."

What is most striking in Augustine's reflections on time, however, is his awareness that what we think of as "past" and "future" are in reality but constructions within the present.

> . . . What is manifest and clear is, that neither are there future nor past things. Nor is it fitly said, "There are three times, past, present, and future"; . . . it might more fitly be said, "There are three times; a present of things past, a present of things present, and a present of things future."

But despite this acute realization of the subjective and present-rooted nature of time, Augustine is nevertheless capable of dealing with the categories of past, present, and future as though they are as objective and real as anything else in the universe. He is, above all, concerned with establishing the unilinear flow of time, a flow that accompanies—indeed, is the context of—"the education of the human race." Thus, in Book 12 of *The City of God* we are informed in unambiguous terms that time is a creation of God and therefore as real as any of God's other creations. ". . . He caused time to have a beginning; and man whom He had previously made, He made *in time,* not from a new and sudden resolution, but by his unchangeable and eternal design."

Time, then, is real, it is objective, and it is linear in nature. For Augustine, grounded as he is in history as recorded in the Old Testament, time is also finite. He is contemptuous of those who treat time in terms of eternity or who insist, as did the Manichaeans, that vastly greater length to the past must be given than was allowed by the authors of the Old Testament. For Augustine, working from the computations made earlier by Eusebius, 6,000 years intervene between Creation and the present. For the critics of this view of time, Augustine has these words:

> If it offends them that the time that has elapsed since the creation of man is so short, and his years so few according to our authorities, let them take this into consideration, that nothing that has a limit is long, and that all the ages of time being finite, are very little, or indeed nothing at all, when compared to the interminable eternity.

Suppose, he asks, we gave six hundred or six hundred thousand years to the past, or six hundred, or six hundred thousand times those years, "the same question could still be put, Why was he [man] not made before?" It is easy for us (as indeed it was for more than a few of Augustine's contemporaries among philosophers) to treat as mere biblical literalism Augustine's defense of his six thousand years, but it has to be admitted, I think, that the questions he hurls back at the skeptics of his day have a polemical power and relevance even in our time, for with very different bases in evidence and vastly greater periods of time, the introduction of time—measured times— into the evolutionary picture continues to vex and exasperate us.

In his desire to demonstrate the linear-flow character of time, Augustine singles out the theory of recurrent cycles for attack and censure. Here, as has more than once been suggested by students of Augustine, he is setting up a straw figure. Augustine is but caricaturing what actually existed among Greek philosophers in the way of belief in temporal cycles when he writes scornfully of "those philosophers" who declare that an endless succession of cycles must be assumed, with each cycle repeating exactly every event, act, and personage of its predecessor: ". . . as if, for example, the philosopher Plato, having taught in the . . . Academy, so, numberless ages before . . . this same Plato, and the same school, and the same disciples, existed, and so also are to be repeated during the countless cycles that are yet to be." There were, as we have seen, some Greeks and Romans who thought in terms of great cycles of time, but I know of none who ever argued that within such cycles there is detailed repetition of specific events and persons. But Augustine was concerned here, we may infer, less with descriptive fact than with intent to knock over every possible objection that might be entered against his vision of finite and linear time.

The dimension of *irreversible* time, too, has great and strategic importance in his whole conception of the human race advancing to ever greater perfection. To suppose that we could, if we chose, go back to some earlier condition of mankind, or through inspiration project ourselves now to a condition that is not yet meant for us in our development is, from Augustine's point of view, as great a fallacy as to suppose that an individual human being can will himself back to infancy or forward to old age. The point for Augustine is that time is inseparable from development, from the kind of step by step advancement that we have seen to lie in the idea of progress from its Greek beginnings. The greatest single change that Augustine made in the sacred history he took over from the Jews, in the Old Testament, is his substitution of the Greek perspective of *growth*, of things constantly realizing their true, full identities through an unfolding of what in the first instance was but potentiality, for a perspective that was ordered, patterned succession rather than development of an aboriginal design. Augustine is as eloquent and passionate as any author of the Old Testament in his deference to God, who made all things and all things possible. But

Augustine's God is a being who sets seeds into motion, into growth. "He willed to make in time," Augustine says, "and this without changing his design and will."

Epochs and Stages

If, as Augustine argued, there is in fact a unitary mankind advancing through time, then it follows that this advancement may be described in terms of successive, emergent stages—just as the development of an individual human being may be so described, whether we use specifically dated periods in this being's life or have recourse to such terms as "infancy," "adolescence," "maturity," and the like, in which case actual dates are more or less irrelevant. The Greeks, as we have seen, were familiar with the concept of man advancing over a long period from lower to higher levels of existence. But it is difficult, if possible at all, to find in either Greek philosophical or historical writing the distinct idea of measured stages or epochs. Aristotle, in his *Politics,* gives us the panorama of the *polis* moving slowly from its origin in the family through federations of families and then through villages and their federations to the kind of political entity he lived within. But there is no effort in Aristotle or anyone else, even Polybius, to *fuse* the developmental and the historically episodic.

This is precisely what we find Augustine attempting: a rendering of "the education of the human race" into the "epochs, or as it were, ages" which characterize human advancement, but a rendering that would be put in the terms of actual, historical peoples of the past and, boldest of all, in the terms of more or less exactly dated periods of history. We may say, correctly, that no such fusion, such compressing, of the actual plurality of history and time into a unitary series is possible. For Augustine, however, the premise of a single, unified mankind, created in and through Adam and advancing in accordance with an immanent design, made the actual multiplicity and particularity of recorded history a matter of mere appearance. Reality for Augustine lay in the unitary human race and its progress toward fulfillment of all that was good in its being. And whether or not true stages and epochs of human history set in linear series are possible, the most striking part of Augustine's performance is the extent to which it entered permanently into Western consideration of time, history, and development. When Bossuet wrote his *Discourse on Universal History* in the last part of the seventeenth century, he was consciously following the pattern set by Augustine—following and, with highest respect, updating it, bringing it into accord with what scholarship had revealed long after Augustine's death. And, when Turgot wrote his immensely significant essay *On Universal History* in the mid-eighteenth century, he acknowledged Bossuet's work as his point of departure yet chose to relegate divinity to a distant background and to expunge dated epochs of time in favor of undated, developmental stages. More than any other eighteenth-century figure, Turgot initiated the modern statement of the idea of progress. Different as his perspective is from that of St. Augustine, it is hardly comprehensible apart from the long series of works on ages, epochs, and stages that Augustine's work generated in the continuing study of the history of "mankind."

St. Augustine is liberal and free moving in his division of human history. Thus, we find him, in different sections of *The City of God,* using a two-, three-, and also a six-stage scheme, the latter with implication of a seventh stage that would be the bridge from the historical to the transhistorical. The twofold division of history is nothing more than "before Christ" and "after Christ." This is hardly more, obviously, than glorification of Christ that began almost immediately in the Christian religion. More interesting, and pagan in root, is his differentiation of mankind's "youth," "manhood," and "old age," in which he seeks to compress the events and changes from the time of Adam all the way to the Rome he believed to be in process of eventual destruction.

It is, however, the sixfold division that gives Augustine his pristine place in Western philosophy of history. The first epoch reaches from Adam to Noah, with mankind occupied primarily by satisfaction of basic material needs; the second stretches from Noah to Abraham, and it is during this epoch, Augustine tells us, that the rise and proliferation of languages and identifiable peoples took place; the third age, beginning with Abraham, represents the liberation of mankind from "youth" and entrance into "maturity," and concludes with David; the fourth epoch goes from David to the Babylonian Captivity; the fifth goes from the Captivity to the appearance of Christ; and a sixth age begins with Christ and continues to a time that Augustine refuses to try to predict. All he says is: "The sixth is now passing, and cannot be measured by any number of generations, as it has been said, 'It is not for you to know the times, which the Father hath put in His own power.'"

It is interesting to note that Augustine, in his *De Genesi contra Manichaeos,* which is his earliest treatment of the problems posed by the Book of Genesis and was written in reply to the taunts and criticisms of the Manichaeans, who refused to give much credence to the Book of Genesis, employs, as Ladner points out, physiological-developmental terms for his six stages—set forth, as we have just seen, in historico-chronological fashion in *The City of God.* The terms he uses in the earlier work for the successive stages are: *infantia, pueritia, adolescentia, juventus, senoris aetas,* and *senectus.* The influence of the Greek idea of organic development is obvious.

We are, however, given in *The City of God* promise of more than the six stages. At the very end of the book, he takes note of a seventh age on earth. ". . . suffice it to say that the seventh shall be our Sabbath, which shall be brought to a close, not by an evening, but by the Lord's day, as an eighth and eternal day, consecrated by the resurrection of Christ and prefiguring the eternal repose not only of the spirit but also of the body."

It may not be altogether clear and certain just what St. Augustine had in mind in his fleeting reference to a seventh, penultimate epoch ahead. I myself am disposed to the belief that he meant it as prophecy of a future millennium, a kind of golden age, on earth. After all, he refers to this seventh stage as "our Sabbath which shall be brought to a close, not by an evening but by the Lord's day . . ." Clearly it is not the epoch of mankind's final destination, for that is described by Augustine as the *eighth* epoch, that which shall be eternal and begin only after this world has been brought to end. What else could the seventh epoch be but the kind of earthly millennium that a few centuries later Joachim de Fiore would announce with such lasting effect, the kind that the Puritans of the seventeenth century, in England and America, were so obsessed by?

But, although this is my interpretation of the reference to the seventh age, I concede that the case is far from closed. For, in Section 7 of Book 20, Augustine dissociates himself from those who go "by the name of Millenarians." But that is hardly definitive. For, he tells us that his chief objection to this group is their preoccupation with the "immoderate carnal banquets" which adorn the millennium. And he goes on to say that this opinion [on an imminent millennium as promised by the Book of Revelation] "would not be objectionable if it were believed that the joys of the saints in that Sabbath shall be spiritual . . ."

There is also the fascinating passage in Section 30 of Book 20 in which Augustine sets forth his judgment of what the final succession of events will be prior to the end of this world. Among them are the conversion of the Jews, a reign by the Antichrist, the second coming of Christ, the judgment by Christ ("Christ shall judge"), the separation of the good and evil, and the burning and "renewal" of the world ("the world shall be burned and renewed"). St. Augustine finishes this passage by saying: "All these things, we believe, shall come to pass; but how, or in what order, human understanding cannot perfectly teach us but only the experience of the events themselves. My opinion, however, is that they will happen in the order in which I have related them."

There are scholars, Norman Cohn and Marjorie Reeves among them, who flatly declare Augustine a non- or antimillennialist. For Reeves, the great significance of Joachim de Fiore in the twelfth century was his repudiation of Augustine's teaching on the matter and his affirmation of a millennium, an age of spiritual perfection on earth.

However, I do not think the case for Augustine's anti-millennialism is quite as clear as others make it to be. When we look at the specific events Augustine predicts will take place, and "in the order in which I have related them," when we recall that even in the paragraph in which he criticizes the so-called Millenarians it is because of their emphasis upon the material and carnal rather than the spiritual, and when we reflect upon Augustine's specific prediction of a seventh age, still ahead, which will *precede* the eighth and final, the eternal age, we cannot help but suppose that—seemingly contradictory passages in Augustine notwithstanding—there are grounds for belief that Augustine foresaw a progressive, fulfilling, and blissful period ahead, *on earth,* for humanity—prior to entry of the blessed into heaven.

Irrespective of the full and exact position St. Augustine may have taken on the millennium, we know that Christians, from at least the second century on, included fanatical millennialists. There were the Montanists, at first a purely local group in Phrygia. From the year 177, one of a large number of Roman persecutions of Christians, Montanism became a very widespread movement. The central tenet was belief that Christ would return shortly and a New Jerusalem would manifest itself in Phrygia. That tenet, however, was modified in time by spreading Montanist belief that the New Jerusalem would appear elsewhere, possibly in Rome, possibly throughout a whole, vast territory. It is worth emphasizing that the great Tertullian himself became a Montanist.

The point, in sum, is that from earliest times Christianity contained a millennialism sharply distinct from belief in the heavenly hereafter. This millennialism would come and go, at least in its extreme manifestations, but we cannot appreciate the origins of the modern, secular idea of progress in the eighteenth century and after apart from such millennialist revivals in Christianity as that of the Puritans in the seventeenth century, a revival which was itself driven in some degree by persistence of Joachimite millennialist ideas dating from the twenfth century.

I have mentioned the second-century Montanists. But F. H. Brabant in his too little known *Time and Eternity in Christian Thought* takes Christian belief in the millennium back to the first century. Even then, Christians, drawing from still earlier Jewish belief in a millennium dominated by the Messiah, "feeling," Brabant writes, "that the earth is unfit for God's Kingdom, suppose a temporary Messianic Age on earth followed by the Day of Judgment and the coming of the heavenly Kingdom." Moreover, and perhaps most important, Brabant shows us in considerable detail how unwise it is to give exact duration to either the millennium or to any other age leading up to the eternal Kingdom. Thus, whereas in the books of Esdras "the Messianic Kingdom only lasts 400 years," in another of the Old Testament apocrypha, Baruch, "the principate (of the Messiah) will stand for ever, until the world of corruption is at an end"; and in the Sybilline Oracles "the Messianic Kingdom stands 'for all ages.'" As Brabant concludes, the Greek *Aion* (age) as found in the Septaguint, used alike by Hellenistic Jews and Greek-speaking Christians including St. Paul and many after him, is a very flexible concept, by itself standing for no definite length of time. Never, writes Brabant, "in the New Testament are the words Aion and Aionian used of limited periods of time." The very word millennium, or the concept at any rate, "first occurs in the Slavonic book of Enoch, which dates from A.D. 1 to 50 . . . arose from a combination of Gen. ii.2 ('God rested on the seventh day') with Ps. xc.4 ('A thousand years in Thy sight are but as yesterday'); 'six millennia of toil were to be succeeded by a millennium of rest'."

Through the fertile mixture of pre- and post-Christian Jewish millenarian thought and Greek metaphysical and scientific ideas, Christianity had a well-developed millennialist doctrine by the second century, one that presented a picture of a future earthly paradise in the richest colors, of a heaven come down to the earth. No other element of Christian thought has had as profound and far-reaching effect upon the entire world, not merely the West, as has its millennialist vision. We should be hard put to account for the social utopias of the Saint-Simonians, Comtists, and especially the Marxists (with their uniquely dread contributions to the twentieth-century political landscape) were there not a long and powerful tradition of Christian millennialist utopianism which could be, in some degree, secularized, with its apocalytic intensity left undiminished.

Necessity

What gave special impact to theories of progress in the modern period, especially the nineteenth century, was the solid conviction of such minds as Saint-Simon, Comte, Fourier, Spencer, and Marx (yes, current exegesis notwithstanding, Marx!) that the progress they described in past and present and prophesied for the future was in no way the result of what Spencer scornfully referred to as "accident," of either the fortuitous on the one hand or the calculated, planned, and willed (by human beings of humanitarian proclivity) on the other. What led each of these minds and their many contemporaries to suppose that their laws of progress were elements of the social *science* they believed themselves to be constructing was the quality of necessity—the same kind of necessity that physicists found in Newton's laws of motion in the *Principia* and that biologists found, or would find, in Darwin's theory of natural selection and the filiation of species.

But the idea of necessity as it applies to human history, and above all to the future, is scarcely the product of science as we know it in such disciplines as chemistry and physics. In all truth, the idea of necessity is the product of nothing exclusively rational at all. It also is the child of religion— especially Augustinian Christianity. It is a concept born of the fusion of Jewish sacred history and Greek interest in natural growth. True, the history we find in the Old Testament was regarded by the Jews as "necessary" in the sense that God had willed every bit of this history. But St. Augustine, proceeding from the Greek metaphysics of growth, added to Jewish faith in divine governance a view of necessity that was teleological. He took over Jewish and Greek concepts and united them in a linear perspective in time that is at once, sacred, natural, and necessary: necessary first because, in Augustine's words, "the whole plenitude of the human race was embraced in the first man," and second because of "the creation of the human race in time . . . without any new design or change of purpose on God's part." In other words, the progress of mankind springs from the potentiality of this progress in the seed-Adam, from whom the whole human race sprang, and from the fact that nothing, not even a change of God's mind, could remove the design of progress, once established, from its natural-necessary course. In simple formula: telic growth plus the unchangeable design of Providence equals necessity. Augustine can hardly be called a deist in the modern sense of the word, much less a scientific determinist of the nineteenth century. For him, God is an ever-present reality. But, this accepted, there is a continuous line from the Augustinian view just stated and the thought of those in the seventeenth and eighteenth centuries for whom God was essentially but a Prime Mover and thereafter content to allow his laws of nature work themselves out, and those of the nineteenth century who, with or without belief in any God whatever, saw nature and society operating through unchangeable laws of order and development.

It is this fixity of belief in history as a necessary process that allows Augustine to wax contemptuous of ideas of fate, chance, and the merely fortuitous. His celebrated treatment of "the will and necessity" early in *The City of God* is indicative of his every word on the subject. He is critical of the Stoics, who in the interest of rescuing something from divine necessity ascribed to man a will free of this necessity, free to decide and to do as it wishes. Augustine fully accepts free will as an ineradicable part of the nature of man. Indeed, he holds such will in highest respect: ". . . if we will, it *is*; if we will not, it *is* not—for we should not will if we were unwilling."

But, the Stoics to the contrary, necessity still reigns, Augustine insists.

[If we define] necessity to be that according to which we say that it is necessary that anything be of such or such a nature, or be done in such and such a manner, I know not why we should have any dread of that necessity taking away the freedom of our will. For we do not put the life of God or the foreknowledge of God under necessity if we should say that it is necessary that God should live forever, and foreknow all things; as neither is His power diminished when we say that He cannot die or fall into error—for this is in such a way impossible to Him, that if it were possible for Him, he would be of less power.

God, then, being by nature totally of free will and being also the author of mankind and of the design which mankind (and also God) would never deviate from, took care *to make necessary* in man's nature a freedom of will that is subject only to the free will of God himself, certainly not to any other beings or forces in the universe.

Our wills, therefore, *exist* as *wills,* and do themselves whatever we do by willing, and which would not be done if we were unwilling. But when anyone suffers anything, being unwilling, by the will of another, even in that case will retains its essential validity—we do not mean the will of the party who inflicts the suffering, for we resolve it into the power of God . . . Therefore whatsoever a man suffers, contrary to his own will, he ought not to attribute it to the will of men, or of angels, or of any created spirit, rather to His will who gives power to wills . . .

There is, thus, for Augustine a will in every human being that is indeed free, that permits him to will good or evil, truth or falsity, and to be responsible for his own acts. But this will, free though it is in the context of the individual's own concrete life, is nevertheless a part of God's sovereign will and has been shaped by His foreknowledge. The individual wills freely, but what he wills is, and must be, tempered by the necessity that binds all things to world and God.

I do not suggest that Augustine's resolution of this famous problem of free will and necessity is a successful one (but whose resolution of the problem ever has been or is?), but it has to be said that in his treatment lie all the essential elements of successive discussions down to the present day. Merely substitute "nature" or "environment" or "history" for Augustine's God and His suzerainty and foreknowledge, and we have in the words just cited a remarkable prototype of the kind of discourse on the problem that has been a persisting part of Western philosophy down to the present day. (Current discussions of "praxis" by Marxists have a distinct flavor of Augustinianism, with God replaced by, say, "phase of historical development" and free will by "individual volition.") With every reason, Western philosophy can be declared a series of footnotes on St. Augustine—praise the late A. N. Whitehead chose to bestow on Plato.

Augustine uses "necessity" in still another sense, one with a very modern ring. Cochrane brings this sense out in lucid fashion. He is referring to Augustine's conception of discrete historical events and actions: each is unique in its way, and can be made to seem but an accident, the result of fortune. But Augustine is as opposed to use of this concept here as he was in his treatment of free will and necessity. "What we call the fortuitous," Augustine writes, "is nothing but that, the reason and the cause of which is concealed from our view." The seeming caprice of history, the randomness of events, does not mean, Augustine enjoins upon us, that chance does in fact govern, or that there has been intervention by some erratic extraterrestrial force. Events and actions, all of them, are related—among themselves in time and to environing contexts. Needless to say, such rescue of human events from the category of the fortuitous or the irrational and their placement within a web of historical law or necessity would become secular-scientific dogma in the nineteenth century. For Augustine this law or necessity on earth is but the objectification of God. But the Comtes and Marxes of the nineteenth century would find no difficulty in jettisoning God here or anywhere else for that matter.

There is still one more sense in which Augustine uses the idea of necessity, a sense closely related to that implicit in his view of all history as a "tissue of births and deaths." Inasmuch as there has been an iron connection in time between persons, acts, events, and settings, with each of these in unbreakable relation to the other, it follows that the time and place each human being or each act or event is actually found in is the *only possible* time and place. As Cochrane notes, the idea that any individual, however gifted, could be "out of his age" is repugnant to Augustine. We thus have no right as historians to invest the people of one age with the attributes of people of another age.

Conflict-as-Mechanism

We cannot conclude consideration of Augustine's philosophy of progress without treatment of his doctrine of "the two cities," the City of God and the City of Man, and, above all, the abiding, relentless, and crucial conflict between them—a conflict that began almost with the human race and that will continue until the City of God eventually triumphs. The notion of conflict as a motor cause of change and development is of course a very old one in Western thought, going back to the pre-Socratics, especially Heraclitus. It is also very obviously a modern idea, one that the writings of Hegel and Marx did a great deal to popularize in the nineteenth century and to catapult into twentieth-century social thought. The idea of the dialectic, whether in its Greek form, drawn from rhetoric, or in the form Hegel and Marx gave it, is only a variation of the more fundamental idea of conflict as necessary to generate development. Whether the conflict is among members of a species, as with Darwin, between classes, as with Marx, or among manifestations of the Spirit, as with Hegel, is of less concern than the emphasis upon conflict as an indispensable process.

Augustinian historical thought is incomprehensible apart from the idea of conflict. Just as "creation" becomes for Augustine a protracted process of unfolding, of developing what lay potential or latent from the beginning, so does conflict become the all-important, immanent, efficient cause of this development. In the first human being, Augustine writes, "there was laid the foundation, not indeed evidently, but in God's foreknowledge, of these two cities or societies, so far as regards the human race . . . ."

> This race we have distributed into two parts, the one consisting of those who live according to man, the other of those who live according to God. And these we mystically call the two cities, or the two communities of men, of which the one is predestined to reign eternally with God, and the other to suffer eternal punishment with the devil.

Augustine makes it clear that the entire human race—the earth with all its diverse peoples—falls under the two categories of cities or communities:

> And thus it has come to pass that though there are very many and great nations all over the earth, whose rites and customs, speech, arms and dress, are distinguished by marked differences, yet there are no more than two kinds of human society, which we may justly call the two cities . . . The one consists of those who wish to live after the flesh, the other those who wish to live after the spirit.

What is crucial so far as the dynamical quality of Augustine's philosophy of history is involved is conflict or struggle between the two cities. Only thus is advancement effected:

> All mankind fell from God in Adam. And just as Adam's soul was divided against itself by sin, so all men were divided against one another by selfishness. The envy of Cain, which would have been impossible in Eden, bred murder in a world where each self-centered individual had become his own little god, his own judge and standard of good and evil, falsity and truth.

The difference between the two cities in Augustine's mind is, as Thomas Merton has observed, a difference between two loves. Those brought together in the City of God are unified by common love of God and of one another *in* God, whereas those who fall within the other city are preoccupied by self and thus indifferent to God. What Augustine himself wrote was: "These two cities were made by two loves: the earthly city by the love of self unto the contempt of God, and the heavenly city by the love of God unto comtempt of self."

The theme of conflict, however, is not restricted by Augustine to the struggle between the two cities. He stresses the conflict that exists *within* the earthly city, the city of man. This city, he writes, "is often divided against itself by litigations, wars, quarrels, and such victories as are either life-destroying or short-lived. For each part of it that arms against another part of it seeks to triumph over the nations itself in bondage to vice."

Conflict is endemic in the human race, and will always be until the heavenly city is attained once and for all, simply because

"the founder of the earthly city was a fratricide. Overcome with envy, he slew his brother, a citizen of the eternal city, and a sojourner on earth. So that we cannot be surprised that this first specimen, or, as the Greeks say, archetype of crime, should long afterwards, find a corresponding crime at the foundation of that city which was destined to reign over so many nations, and be the head of this earthly city of which we speak."

The End and the Beginning

We come now to what is in many respects St. Augustine's greatest single legacy to the medieval and modern worlds, whether for good or bad. I refer to his fateful union of the idea of necessary destruction on the one hand with the idea of redemption on the other. From Augustine on, with only occasional lapses, there has been in the West a tradition preoccupied by the attainment of the perfect society, whether on this earth or in the next world. The condition of this attainment is a necessary period of suffering, torment, fire, and destruction. The modern linkage of destructive, coercive, terroristic revolution and the promise of utopia at the end is but a secularization (or rhetorical modification) of a cognate linkage to be seen throughout the Middle Ages and the Reformation, one that goes directly back to Augustine's *The City of God*—though we should not omit here mention of the

Book of Revelation which exerted such powerful influence upon the minds of Augustine and other Christian chiliasts both in Augustine's day and later.

It is in Book 20, Section 16, titled "Of the New Heaven and the New Earth," that we find the core of the tradition of thought and action I have just described. This core is destruction, pure and simple. For how can the good, the ideal, be achieved unless all that is corruptive and noxious be exterminated? No reader here needs to be told how modern that idea is. But it is also Christian-medieval—and Augustinian. He quotes the Book of Revelation: And I saw a new heaven and a new earth; for the first heaven and the first earth have passed away; and there is no more sea." Further, and still quoting from Revelation, Augustine gives us the momentous words: "I saw One sitting on the throne, from whose face heaven and earth fled."

Augustine adds:

For as soon as those who are not written in the book of life have been judged and cast into eternal fire . . . then shall the figure of this world pass away in a conflagration of universal fire, as once before the world was flooded with a deluge of universal water. And by this universal conflagration, the qualities of the corruptible elements which suited our corruptible bodies shall utterly perish, and our substance shall receive such qualities as shall, by a wonderful transmutation, harmonize with our immortal bodies so that, as the world itself is renewed to some better thing, it is fitly accomodated to men, themselves renewed in their flesh to some better thing.

Never mind that Augustine's eschatology was largely a complex matter, to say the least. Who can reasonably doubt the magnetic attraction such words as those in the final part of the quoted passage would have later for those, beginning possibly with Joachim de Fiore in the twelfth century, for whom the *renovatio mundi*—in theory preparatory to the advent of divine eternity—would become an ever more dazzling thing in itself?

Turn to Augustine's own passages on the felicity that lies ahead for the saved, passages which conclude his book. It is hard not to be struck by the calculated intrusion of purely secular values and rewards into what for Augustine is the postmundane, the posthistorical. For Augustine, there will be beauty of body:

For all those parts of the bodily harmony which are distributed through the whole body, within and without, and of which I have just been saying that they at present elude our observation, shall then be discerned; and, along with the other great and marvellous discoveries which shall then kindle rational minds in praise of the great Artificer, there shall be the enjoyment of a beauty which appeals to the reason. What power of movement such bodies shall possess, I have not the audacity rashly to define, as I have not the ability to conceive. Nevertheless I will say that in any case, both in motion and at rest, they shall be, as in their appearance, seemly . . . .

But there is more in Augustine's utopian musings to suggest the degree to which earthly aspirations or longings or ideals had set the theme of his discourse on heaven. He is fascinated by honor, as would be many a utopian of the secular tradition. "True honor shall be there, for it shall be denied to none who is worthy, nor yielded to any unworthy; neither shall any unworthy person so much as sue for it, for none but the worthy shall be there." So will there be that most sought after of all goals on earth: peace. "True peace shall be there, where no one shall suffer opposition either from himself or any other." What else, asks Augustine, could God have meant in Leviticus (xxvi, 12) when He said "I will be your God, and ye shall be my people"? Only, and here we turn to Augustine's words, "I shall be your satisfaction, I shall be all that men honorably desire—life, health, nourishment, and plenty, and glory, and honor and peace, and all good things." Certainly, we are bound to conclude, there is a highly mundane, even carnal, cast to Augustine's vision of the good life. As noted above, he had publicly renounced millenarianism on the ground that it promised "carnal" as well as spiritual rewards to the faithful. But no reader of the final paragraphs of *The City of God* can conclude other than that Augustine's rendering of the "spiritual" delights of the heavenly hereafter has a decidedly earthly, human flavor. A great deal of subsequent Western utopianism, reaching indeed all the way down to Marx and his followers in the nineteenth and early twentieth centuries, can be found in embryonic form in the following passage:

But who can conceive, not to say describe, what degrees of honor and glory shall be awarded to the various degrees of merit? Yet it cannot be doubted that there shall be degrees. And in that blessed city there shall be this great blessing, that no inferior shall envy any superior, as now the archangels are not envied by the angels, because no one will wish to be what he has not received, though bound in strictest concord with him who has received; as in the body the finger does not seek to be the eye, though both members are harmoniously included in the complete structure of the body. And thus, along with his gift, greater or less, each shall receive this further gift of contentment to desire no more than he has.

In that passage is to be found Augustine's effort at resolution of a number of the problems which would occupy the minds of utopians in the eighteenth and nineteenth centuries: social rank, equality, envy, the relation between need and ability, merit and reward, and the like. So too does Augustine give evidence of his preoccupation with the seeming contradiction of free will as it would exist in a heavenly society where human beings would enjoy freedom of will in the fullest and the purest form even though evil had been destroyed, and temptation could not exist:

> Neither are we to suppose that because sin shall have no power to delight them, free will must be withdrawn. It will, on the contrary, be all the more truly free, because set free from delight in sinning to take unfailing delight in not sinning . . . . Are we to say that God himself is not free because He cannot sin? In that city, then, there shall be free will, one in all the citizens, and indivisible in each, delivered from all ill, filled with all good, enjoying indefeasibly the delights of eternal joys, oblivious of sins, oblivious of sufferings, and yet not so oblivious of its deliverance as to be ungrateful to its Deliverer.

L'Envoi

In Augustine, especially in his *The City of God,* all of the really vital, essential elements of the Western idea of progress are present: mankind or the human race; the unfolding, cumulative advancement of mankind, materially and spiritually through time; a single time frame into which all the civilizations, cultures, and peoples which have ever existed on earth, or now exist, can be compressed; the idea of time as a unilinear flow; the conception of stages and epochs, each reflected by some historic civilization or group of civilizations or a level of cultural development; the conception of social reform rooted in historical awareness; the belief in the necessary character of history and in the inevitability of some future end or objective; the idea of conflict of cities, nations, and classes as the motor spring of the historical process; and finally, the raptured picture of the future, set by Augustine in the psychological, cultural, and economic terms which would remain the essential terms of nearly all utopias in later centuries: affluence, security, equity, freedom, and tranquillity. And justice!

Chapter 3

Medieval Currents

BY the beginning of the thirteenth century, the Christian idea of progress was in full bloom. Both of the strands I have identified as crucial to the European conception of human progress—awareness of steady, cumulative advancement of culture from remote past to distant future and, along with this awareness, belief in a golden age of morality and spirituality ahead, in the future, on this earth—are highly visible in the writings of the twelfth and thirteenth centuries.

Like the earlier periods in which consciousness of progress of the arts and sciences flourished in Greece and Rome the age formed by the twelfth and thirteenth centuries was one of striking innovation and intellectual boldness in the material and secular spheres as well as the religious. Many a thirteenth-century philosopher, artist, or technologist must have looked about him and felt the same sense of progress at hand and of progress yet to be that Protagoras, Aristotle, Lucretius, and Seneca felt.

The time has long since passed when the Middle Ages can be placed by historians, as it was for so long placed, almost exclusively in the category of theology and of contemplation of the spiritual and the supernatural with but a minimum of thought given to this world. Largely as a consequence of the scholarship of this century—ongoing scholarship that continues to provoke ever-new revelations, we have come to know well that the High Middle Ages must be ranked among the very greatest ages in world history so far as intellectual and cultural achievement is concerned. This holds for science and technology quite as much as for art and humanistic scholarship.

Nor is the age I speak of a sudden mutation, a flowering without genuine roots. We have also learned how relatively bright those preceding centuries were, centuries which for so long had been labelled the Dark Ages. Thus the tenth century is found by the art historian, Lord Clark, to be one of remarkable achievement in the arts. He comments on this in his now famous *Civilization*.

The amount of art is astonishing. The princely patrons like Lothar and Charles the Bald commissioned quantities of manuscripts with jewelled book covers, and sent them as gifts to their fellow rulers or to important ecclesiastics. An age when beautiful things could be valued as instruments of persuasion could not have been wholly barbarous.

And an equally eminent historian of art, Meyer Schapiro, tells us in his recent *Romanesque Art*, that we do not have to wait for the so-called Renaissance of the fifteenth century to find *secular* art of highest quality. By the eleventh and twelfth centuries, Schapiro writes,

. . . there had emerged in Western Europe within church art a new sphere of artistic creation without religious content and imbued with values of spontaneity, individual fantasy, delight in color and movement, and the expression of feeling that anticipate modern art. This new art, on the margins of religious work, was accompanied by a conscious taste of the spectators for the beauty of workmanship, materials, and artistic devices apart from religious meanings.

And as the late Helen Waddell has shown us in two separate volumes of translations of Latin lyrics in the Middle Ages, some of them as early as the eighth and ninth centuries, there was a significant amount of poetry written that was far from being restricted to religious themes. In Helen Waddell's beautiful renderings of the medieval poetic imagination, we find much about nature and its glories as revealed in landscape, much about the beauties of love between man and woman, about the depths of individuality and self-awareness, much that is expressive of the enchantment that could seize the minds of individuals as they contemplated this world. Of course there was a great deal of poetry with strong Christian content (so was there in the nineteenth century!), but it is gross caricature of the people of the age to deny them keen interest in the things of nature and society around them.

So was there ardent attention given to technology and science, as Lynn White, contemporary representative of a tradition of scholarship that began with Pierre Duhem, has made vividly clear in a long succession of studies. White notes that iron came to have highest importance in Carolingian times, with abundant and diverse use made of the ore. It was a period in which among other major inventions the all-important iron axe and plow came into existence in a degree of excellence and efficiency unknown in classical times. It was the new mode of plowing, made possible by the early-medieval perfection of the iron instrument, that brought into existence a field system of cultivation—with the nucleated community widely if not universally connected—that lasted for many centuries well into the modern era.

As Lynn White demonstrates, it is the thirteenth century and not the fifteenth or sixteenth century that in fact "produced the 'invention of invention,'" thus marking the true "moment of crisis in mankind's relation to the natural environment." Man and nature, White continues, are now two things, "and man is the master." As to compatibility between Christianity and science, White writes: "Robert Grosseteste, Roger Bacon, and Theodoric of Freiburg produced startlingly sophisticated work on the optics of the rainbow. From the thirteenth century onward, up to and including Leibniz and Newton, every major scientist, in effect, explained his motivations in religious terms." The long-held belief that medieval man was uninterested in nature or its reshaping is pure absurdity. In his recent fascinating *The Medieval Machine: The Industrial Revolution of the Middle Ages,* the French social historian Jean Gimpel shows conclusively that the period running from the tenth to the start of the fourteenth century is "one of the great inventive eras of mankind." Moreover, industrial dynamism was accompanied by "psychological dynamism," Gimpel writes, something that not only extended itself into many areas of thought and work but is the real beginning of those forces which, after a period of relative decline in the fourteenth and fifteenth centuries, flowered in the seventeenth and eighteenth centuries, the period commonly characterized, as *the* beginning of the modern work ethic and also of *the* industrial or mechanical revolution.

Nor can it properly be said that scholars in the Middle Ages were devoid of awareness of the immensity of the extraterrestrial universe. Ptolemy, after all, centuries before had declared the earth but a mere dot in comparison with the stellar universe. Arthur Lovejoy, in his *Great Chain of Being,* cites Maimonides in this matter: "And if the earth is thus no bigger than a point relatively to the sphere of the fixed stars, what must be the ratio of the human species to the created universe as a whole?" Lovejoy gives us the following statement from Roger Bacon:

The least of the visible stars is greater than the earth . . . According to Ptolemy a fixed star, because of the magnitude of the heaven, does not complete its circuit in less than thirty-six thousand years, though it moves with incredible velocity. But it is possible to walk around the earth in three years.

The truth or error of such computations is of no significance here. What is alone important is the implicit refutation of conceptions still prevalent today which declare that medieval man's world was a small one, limited to this earth. As Lovejoy properly observes, the magnitudes in medieval astronomy and cosmography may be small by comparison with the hundreds of millions of light years astronomers work with today, but they nevertheless reflect a heightened and expanded consciousness we are too seldom likely to acknowledge.

Just as medieval thought had a large place in it for an immense universe, so did it have a place, at opposite extreme, for the individual. Despite the conventional view that during the Middle Ages the individual was subordinated to corporate and communal groups, it is hard to imagine any period as rich in innovation—artistic, architectural, technological, economic, and philosophical—as the medieval age without imagining that a very distinct sense of the individual and of individuality existed also. What we generally ascribe to the Renaissance, the Renaissance of Michelet and Burckhardt, in the way of "discovery of the world and man" might better be ascribed to the twelfth and thirteenth centuries. As Colin Morris has concluded in his *The Discovery of the Individual: 1050–1200*:

> The discovery of the individual was one of the most important cultural developments in the years between 1050 and 1200. It was not confined to any one group of thinkers. Its central features may be found in many different circles: a concern with self-discovery; an interest in relations between people, and in the role of the individual within society . . . "Know thyself" was one of the most frequently quoted injunctions.

Morris is far from alone among contemporary medievalists in his insistence upon the reality, the *perceived* reality, of the individual in medieval consciousness. Sylvia Thrupp has shown us the variety of economic and commercial contexts in which individuals operated with a great deal of the autonomy and enterprise we are likely to associate with later periods in European history. Walter Ullman in his *The Individual in Medieval Society* has done much the same with respect to the political and legal realms in the Middle Ages. Nor, as the following statement by Etienne Gilson shows, was there any lack of awareness of the *physical* aspects of the individual.

> One of the surprises in store for the historian of Christian thought lies in its insistence on the value, dignity and perpetuity of the human body. The Christian conception of man is almost universally taken to be a more or less thoroughgoing spiritualism . . . . But to the no small scandal of a goodly number of historians and philosophers the contrary turns out to be the fact. St. Bonaventura, St. Thomas Aquinas, Duns Scotus, I will even say St. Francis of Assisi himself—one and all

were men who looked benignly on matter, respected their bodies, extolled its dignity, and would never have wished a separate destiny for body and soul.

Reference once more to Helen Waddell's two volumes of translation of medieval poetry—going back as far as the ninth century and coming down to the fourteenth century—is apposite. In a great many of these poems there is not only the awareness of nature and its beauties that I previously commented on, but awareness too of the individual, of individual beauty, and of the distinctiveness of individual identity. Pure romance is also to be found in the poems. Some of them, in style and theme, could be transplanted to some anthology of modern romantic poetry, and there would be few if any readers aware of any anachronism.

In sum, all of the essential attributes of culture were present in the Middle Ages so far as proper context of belief in human progress on earth was concerned. There was—how, amid all the activity of the age could there *not* have been?—consciousness of change and innovation taking place everywhere in western Europe; there was vivid awareness of the Greek and Roman past. As one historian has put it well, whereas the aim of the Renaissance (in Italy at least) was imitation of Graeco-Roman luminaries, the aim in the Middle Ages was that of absorbing their ideas and then building on them. Finally, despite the apparently ineradicable myth, even among professional historians, of single-minded concentration upon the spiritual and the hereafter, there was the deepest and widest interest in the economic, political, and social matters which concern life on earth. To which I add the words—*future* life on earth. Roger Bacon in the thirteenth century foretold a future that would be shaped by science in large measure, one in which ships would operate without sails or oars, in which vehicles would move at high speed on land, and without animals to draw them, in which even "flying machines" would cross the skies. And Roger Bacon was far from being alone in such forecasts of the future.

Progress and History

Medieval interest in both historical writing and human progress has deep roots in the works done by St. Augustine and some of his followers. Having shown the central place occupied in Christian creed by the material and spiritual progress of mankind, Augustine saw to it that historian-apprentices among his following would continue his work: refine, develop, extend in time, and above all disseminate the philosophy of history he had begun. Two of these apprentice-historians in Augustine's century are especially interesting, and their works had a good deal to do with the continuity through the Dark Ages and early Middle Ages of what first Eusebius and then St. Augustine had commenced. The first is Prosper of Aquitania—a direct disciple of Augustine—and the second, John Scotus.

As George Boas stresses in his *Primitivism and Related Ideas in the Middle Ages,* there is the full flavor of progressive development in the writings of both men. Prosper likened the whole of mankind's history to the unfolding of life in the organic world. Prosper writes:

> [There is not] a single uninterrupted advance, nor is there one measure. For the works and gifts of grace are varied in many ways . . . For just as in the seeds of grasses and trees, which earth brings forth, there is no one species, nor one genus in them all . . . so too the seeds of God's gifts and of the plant of virtue are not produced in the whole field of the human heart at once, because it is to be in the future, nor is maturity easily found in a seed, nor perfection in a beginning.

The essence of Prosper's argument is of course to be found throughout his master's *The City of God,* but Prosper, in accord with Augustine's wishes, substantially enlarged the historiography.

The second of the two followers, John Scotus, also placed human history in the context of a necessary unfolding, over a long period of time, of virtue. In Scotus we find too a clear division of human history into three great stages, a temporal triad that, as we shall see repeatedly, was to become a permanent part of the European developmentalist tradition of thought, first in religious, then in secular terms. John Scotus declares that history may be divided into three great epochs: the first is that of the Law (the Old Testament); the second that of the Spirit (the New Testament); and a third that which "will be celebrated in the future life, in which there will be no symbols, no obscurity of metaphor, but the clearest truth as a whole." In all probability, Scotus has the next world in mind when he refers to "future life," but it is well to remember that St. Augustine had hinted at a Seventh Age, one foretold in *Revelation,* one in which human beings would find complete happiness on this earth. And, by the time we reach Joachim there is no doubt whatever that life on this earth forms the substance of the third stage.

Such renderings of history may be seen in a continuous line from Augustine's century. It was Augustine who put still another of his followers, Orosius, to work on a universal history: *Historia Contra Paganos.* Christian in orientation of course, this book is constructed nevertheless from what had to be intensive research in the records of Greco-Roman and other histories. Here too the history of mankind is set forth in successive, cumulative stages or epochs. In the seventh century Isidore, Bishop of Seville, wrote his *Chronicle,* also a universal history based upon the works of predecessors, but with much in the way of both thought and data added.

Otto of Freising's *On Two Cities,* written in the twelfth century, is in direct line of those I have mentioned, but it marks a significant advancement so far as effort at historical accuracy is concerned—investigation of lay as well as religious documents and conscientious utilization of them in the narrative—and also in its relatively sophisticated use of the ideas of causation and connection. Nancy F. Partner, in her *Serious Entertainments: The Writing of History in Twelfth Century England,* has pointed out how rare and small are the uses of causation by the chroniclers of the age. Events and actions are set forth in serial and episodic form, of course, but little if any effort is made to supply linkage through appeal to motive, other event, or context. Even more striking is Partner's observation: "The peculiarity of medieval histories is not that they are so thoroughly Christian but that they are so little so, and that those particularly Christian elements in them are so often perfunctory and odd." That is one more illustration, I cannot refrain from noting here, of the large, long undervalued, secular content of medieval thought and writing.

But if chroniclers gave little attention to God and to mechanisms of causality, Otto was not among them. Like his revered St. Augustine Otto sees world history as developing and unfolding in accord with a divine plan from which God never diverged. Otto brings universal history down to the year 1146, later extended to 1209 by a fellow monk. As in Augustine, conflict as Prime Mover plays a large part and Otto is much more exact in his identification of epochs in history.

The Prologue to the third book of Otto's *Two Cities* is highly instructive with respect to his belief in progress. God, of course, began it all, but what he began was the course of human advancement that would require long periods of time for attainment of fullness and perfection. His evocations of mankind's primitive beginnings are suggestive of those we found in Lucretius. Otto refers to the debased and tormented lives of the earliest inhabitants of the earth: men "devoid of reason, incapable of receiving the truth, unacquainted with justice and with laws . . ." Not for them any golden age with degeneration to follow. Otto writes:

Then as this age gradually grew and made progress—partly through the association of men dwelling together, partly through the putting together of their wisdom for the purpose of establishing laws, and partly through the agency of wisdom and of the teachings of philosophers . . . the minds of men were suited to grasp more lofty precepts about right living.

Each of Otto's two cities—the city of Evil and the city of Christ—undergoes a three-stage development. The city of Evil has a first stage that is described as wretched; a second stage that is still worse, and a third worse still. "On the other hand," Otto assures us, "the first condition of that other company (the people of the city of Christ) is abject; the second prosperous; and the third perfect."

The eighth and concluding book of *The Two Cities* suggests very strongly that man may look forward to a golden age of happiness and of civilized pursuits in the future, one of uncertain duration, but a reality nevertheless that will precede any destruction of this world and advent of the eternal. "Accordingly it is not through destruction of the substance but by a change in the form that there will be a new heaven and a new earth, fittingly prepared by a new beauty and by new bodies for new use, purified by the removal of every inequality." As we shall see at the end of this chapter, another religious figure in the twelfth century put the matter with even greater assuredness and far more prophetic passion.

A contemporary of Otto, Anselm of Havelberg wrote strongly to the effect that spiritual progress was the essence of Christian doctrine. As John Mundy has written of Anselm:

Although he believed that men were living in the last of three ages, that initiated by Christ's coming, there was progress within that age. Seven seals or periods were delineated, of which men were then in the fourth, and, in spite of persecutions, each age was one of fulfillment through which the Church moved on its upward course.

Anselm declared it normal that an unchanging God should allow the Church to change in time, progressively,

. . . because it is necessary that, according to the progression of time, the signs of spiritual grace should increase and increasingly declare the truth. Thus, together with the desire, the knowledge of truth will grow in the course of time, and so first there have been published good things, then better, and lastly the very best.

This spirit of progression in time, progression that is slow but continuous and certain, remained strong throughout the next, the thirteenth, century. In his widely-read *Breviloquim*, St. Bonaventura wrote:

God could have brought all this [the world and the life on it] about in a single instant. He chose instead to act through time, and step by step, and this for three reasons. First there was to be a distinct and clear manifestation of power, wisdom and goodness; second there was to be a fitting correspondence between the days or times and the operations; third, the succession of days was *to prefigure all future ages*, in the same way as, at creation, the seeds of all future beings were planted. So the distinction of the future times—explained above when we spoke of the seven ages of history—stemmed, as if from seeds, from the distinction of the seven days.

The interest in sacred historical progression that we find in the twelfth and thirteenth centuries has as one of its major contexts the immense efflorescence of historiography generally. G. C. Coulton (no candle burner to the Middle Ages!) refers to a "veritable renaissance" in the eleventh century. In her recent, fully documented, and detailed *Historical Writing in Medieval England* Antonia Grandsen has admirably described the abundance, the variety, and the individual distinctiveness of this historical writing. There is scarcely a sphere of human existence that is without reflection in this writing, including the political, economic, geographical, literary, and architectural. What we can learn about the true breadth and diversity of medieval man's earthly interests from Helen Waddell's poetic translations is fully matched by Antonia Grandsen's detailed coverage of historical writing during the same period.

Even by twentieth-century standards of historical scholarship the writings of the High Middle Ages can be judged very favorably. The care, imagination, objectivity, and diligence with which Matthew Paris (admittedly one of the greatest historians, if not the greatest in his day) went about his studies, his faithful examination of abbey charters and muniments, town and guild charters, papal communications, and letters from interested correspondents from abroad all suggests a pride of historical construction that had fitting place among the impressive creations of the age in art, architecture, physical science, technology, and town planning, among other spheres. In the next century Froissart, much in the spirit of Thucydides, was inspired to study, interpret, and record the great events of the wars which long afterward would be known as the Hundred Years' War. Not always meticulous about his details, too ready at times to sacrifice fact to historical drama, his chronicle nevertheless brings an age to life with a brilliance rare in any period.

Inevitably, given the mass of historical writing during the period, there would be philosophical concern with the meaning of history, its purpose, its eventual outcome. And overwhelmingly this philosophical appraisal of the historical process was expressed in the rhetoric of progress. What Etienne Gilson in his Gifford Lectures *The Spirit of Medieval Philosophy* tells us is highly instructive on this point. It was natural, Gilson writes, for medieval thinkers to be deeply aware of progress extending well into the future. The pessimism and gloom of the Middle Ages have been greatly exaggerated. There is a spirit of optimism in the very greatest of twelfth- and thirteenth-century works that would be hard to equal in even the eighteenth century. Christian medieval thinkers, writes Gilson,

. . . would naturally come to conceive, with St. Augustine and Pascal, that the entire human race, whose life resembles that of a single man, passes from Adam till the end of the world through a series of successive states, grows old in regular sequence, laying up meanwhile a store of natural and supernatural knowledge until it shall attain the perfect age, which shall be that of its future glory.

Future *earthly* glory is understood, we might add. Gilson continues:

So, if we are to conceive it as the Middle Ages conceived it, must we represent the history of mankind. It is no history of continuous decadence, since, on the contrary, it affirms a regular collective progress of humanity as such . . . it affirms that progress tends toward its [humanity's] perfection . . . the history of a progress oriented towards a definite term.

Dwarfs and Giants

There is a figure of speech, a metaphor, in the Middle Ages that expresses admirably the sense of relationship medieval thinkers had with those of the past. So too does it express the medieval esteem for knowledge and for men of knowledge. Bernard of Chartres gave the metaphor pithy expression: "We are dwarfs standing on the shoulders of giants." Whether as has often been stated the phrase was actually coined by Bernard (some have given the credit to Roger of Blois) and then conveyed by his pupils to John of Salisbury for renowned use in his *Metalogicus,* is of no great importance here. I am more interested in the meaning, and also the popularity, of the metaphor.

There are some students who have drawn from it simply the conviction that in self-deprecatory fashion, medieval scholars considered themselves dwarfs by comparison with the great minds, pagan and Christian, who had existed before them. In this light, the metaphor might be accepted as evidence for the proposition that the medieval mind saw degeneration—giants down to dwarfs—rather than progress as the movement of history.

But I do not think this inference from the metaphor can be sustained, either on intrinsic or circumstantial evidence. Consider the immense popularity of the quest for knowledge in the time of Bernard and of John of Salisbury, and for that matter the extraordinary esteem in which each of these men was held by contemporaries—and why may we not assume by themselves, given their accomplishments and honors? The image suggests not only scholars' respect for the works of predecessors but also the sense of a certain kind of superiority that comes from being able—simply by virtue of earlier, great, far-reaching discoveries by the Platos, Aristotles, and Augustines—to see what a Plato himself had not been able to see. "On the shoulders of giants . . ." Does this not almost instantly convey the scholar's capacity to see farther, that is, to know more than did his predecessors, illustrious though many of them were—even though by comparision with the long procession of mighty intellects before him he might properly see himself as a dwarf?

My belief that this was the medieval sense of the figure of speech is buttressed by the presence in medieval thought of that other, related metaphor, the one Augustine borrowed from some of his predecessors and applied to the whole of the human race. I refer to the comparison Augustine made between the progress of knowledge of mankind as a whole and the education of a single individual who might be imagined living throughout all human time. Augustine's phrase "the education of the human race" was as I noted in the preceding chapter destined to survive for a great many centuries—indeed, to be utilized down into our own century as a means of graphically conveying the measured, cumulative, slow, step-by-step nature of the progress of mankind's knowledge. The Augustinian comparison is richly abundant in the lay literature of the seventeenth and eighteenth centuries on progress. It held high place in the Moderns's arguments during the Quarrel in the seventeenth century with advocates of the Ancients. Later Condorcet and Comte made strategic use of it.

The metaphor of the dwarf standing on the shoulders of giants had a comparable subsequent fate. We learn that it was well-known in the Renaissance, appearing in Montaigne and Burton. Bacon made use of it, and there is an extended statement of it in Pascal's influential *Fragment of a Treatise on Vacuum.* So did Isaac Newton employ it. The metaphor in fact became a prized possession of the scientists of the seventeenth century in their efforts to define themselves and their works. It has made its way just as Augustine's "single individual living through all ages" has into our own day. It may be doubted, however, that very many who have used the figure since the Renaissance have had any notion of its origin.

But the important point is not the metaphor itself and its history; it is rather the metaphor's symbolization of medieval belief in and recognition of the cumulative increase of knowledge through the ages, secular knowledge foremost. As John Mundy has written in his impressive study of the thought of the High Middle Ages, "resigned passivity did not find universal favor." Thomas Aquinas, Mundy writes, "asserted that man's successive generations ever better comprehended both the speculative and the practical sciences, a conviction received with especial sympathy by those intellectuals whose bent was practical or technical." (Mundy cites the lawyer Rolandino Passaggeri, covering the subject of legal contracts in 1265):

> And because it is true that those who are more recent are more perspicacious and because our age brings with it new and more subtle *mores* in matters contractual as in other things, it is fitting that, ancient rites being omitted . . . we should imitate the character *(forma)* of our age in the dispositions and modes of contracts, just as we do in other things, and we should employ the customs of our own time in order that the quality of our life should be improved.

How charming to realize that even back in the thirteenth century thought was given to "the quality of life." Parallel can be extended by the thought of environmental reclamation and improvement by literally thousands of monasteries over Western Europe.

No one expressed better this interest in the cumulative advancement of knowledge through time than the remarkable Roger Bacon in the thirteenth century. We are all aware of his striking mechanical inventions and his work in optics and other areas of physics. We may not be so aware of his interest in improving, through direct reform, laws, regulations, and customs, especially those which affected scholarship and science in the universities and out. He gave a great deal of his time to the betterment of education at all levels. What he wrote in his *Opus Majus* along this line bears quoting here:

> And because individuals, cities, and whole regions can be changed for the better . . . life should be prolonged as much as necessary, all things should be managed functionally, and even greater things can be done than are mentioned in this book, not only in the natural sciences, but also in the moral sciences, as is evident in Moses and Aristotle.

The Reform of Time

Prior to about the twelfth century time was generally held to be something inseparable from God, since it had been created by Him. So St. Augustine had declared, though as we have seen this linking of time and God did not keep Augustine from giving to time the linear, flowing, cumulative, progressing character that it would retain to our own day. Beginning in the late twelfth century and reaching full momentum in the thirteenth, there took place what can only be referred to as a reform in time—its measurement, its place in life, and its conceived nature. Jacques Le Goff in his *Pour un autre Moyen Age* (the contents of which deal with much more than time) has brilliantly illuminated the kinds of secular pressure and stimulation which led to philosophical reassessment of time and its function. What Le Goff refers to as the change from "medieval to a modern social psychology of time" involved the extrication, so to speak, of time from its purely divine and religious context and the fusing of time with the burgeoning economic, social, and cultural activities of the thirteenth century. Apart from accurate and also respectful reckoning of time in lay matters, it was simply not possible to develop such vital areas of finance and business as interest, lending, commercial contracts, and investment. Time became secularized or, better, "rationalized" during this period. This did not mean an alienation of the merchant and banker from the Church and God. As Le Goff suggests, even if the Church was obliged by secular pressures to yield its suzerainty over time, the businessman could still treat the religious perspective of time as "the other horizon of his existence." Like his Calvinist successors of the seventeenth century, the medieval merchant could live satisfactorily in two worlds so far as time was concerned.

Ernst Kantorowicz in *The King's Two Bodies,* also brings out the great importance of the reform of time which took place in this age.

> . . . [A] new approach to Time and a new conception of the nature of Time must be considered not only as a philosophical but also as an historical factor of great moment. The new valuation of Time, which then broke to the surface, actually became one of the most powerful agencies by which Western thought, at the end of the Middle Ages, was transformed and energized; and apparently it still holds sway with unabated vigor over modern thought. After all . . . the optimistic philosophy of unlimited progress which the generations before the two World Wars saw fit to cherish, had its roots and premises in those intellectual changes which stirred the thirteenth century . . .

As Kantorowicz and other interpreters of the Middle Ages make clear, it is by no means certain that the reformulation of the nature and significance of time would have taken place—emerging pressures from business and finance notwithstanding—had it not been for the Averröistic presentation of Aristotle. Averröes, Spanish-Arabian, touched by, indeed participant in, the Islamic cultural efflorescence, had very strong influence indeed upon Jewish and Christian philosophy in the West. Averröes's commentaries upon Aristotle were almost immediately seized upon by scholars and philosophers, and there came into existence a group of (mostly young) "extremists" whose laudation of the Averroistic Aristotle gave the official spokesmen of the Church much to think of and worry about. A long list of *errores condemnati* followed the Church's effort to stem the Averroistic turbulence in philosophical and theological circles.

The Church, rallying to its Augustinian commitment with respect to time, did all within its power to halt the spread of doctrines, Averroistic-Aristotelian in origin, which declared the earth eternal and motion, change, and development timeless processes. No less alarmed was the Church by other Averroist "errors," particularly those which stated or strongly hinted that there will be no resurrection of the dead, that there is not such a thing as a "first man" or a "last man" on earth, and that there will always be a human race, with generations rising and falling within linear time without end. But opposition notwithstanding, the new, reformed conception of time, man, and history spread widely in intellectual circles. As Kantorowicz writes:

> Time was infinite, a continuum of successive moments rolling forth perpetually from endlessness to endlessness. *Tempus,* the limited span of terrestrial Time, thereby lost its ephemeral frailty and limitation, and its character also changed morally: Time no longer appeared predominantly as the symbol of paucity, of Death; Time, to the Averroists, became a vivifying element, a symbol of endless duration, of Life.

Kantorowicz, like Jacques Le Goff, points to the almost immediately perceived practical consequences of the new contemplation of time. "The factor of Time . . . started to permeate . . . the daily technique of public, financial, and legal administration." Thus, whereas taxation in the past had not been tied to fixed periods of time, but rather to notable events which broke the routine of life, now there arose and quickly spread the idea of annual taxation "dependent not upon an event but upon Time." The ideas of the inalienability of the royal demesne and of an impersonal fisc "which never dies," although certainly rooted in use, wont, and custom, nevertheless acquired fresh force from the new, radical philosophy of time.

In sum, the conception of an indefinite if not infinite time, well known to the Greeks but not to the early Christians who worked strictly from the Old Testament and the message contained in the New Testament, received in the High Middle Ages the statement that would be accepted as axiomatic by more and more thinkers after the end of the Middle Ages. Quoting once more from Kantorowicz: "It [time] gained, through its connection with ideas of religious and scientific progress, an ethical value when one recognized that 'the daughter of time was Truth.' "

Not least among the benefits to the idea of progress accruing from the revised conception of time in the thirteenth century was the renewed vigor we find in the all-important concepts of plenitude, fecundity, and continuity —applied to the world and humanity and all that humanity governs.

Plenitude and Continuity

Fundamental to both the medieval and the modern ideas of progress are the assumptions first of plenitude and second, continuity. By the first is meant the existence in this world of everything, whether actual and in full realization of itself or potential with realization yet to be, that is necessary to the goodness and the capacity for perfection of mankind. From the second, the idea of continuity, springs the equally important proposition that each condition or state of whatever it is we are interested in contains within it the seeds of the next and higher state or condition. Also contained in the idea of continuity is the assumption that between the very lowest of organisms on earth and the very highest manifestation of being—whether man or, above him, angels and Almighty God—there is what Arthur Lovejoy has called in his notable book of the same title "the great chain of being."

It was Plato, as Lovejoy emphasizes, who transmitted to European philosophy "the vast assumption" that there is plenitude in "the World of Becoming," that everything necessary to perfection is either present or exists *in potentia.* Lovejoy writes: "The concept of Self-Sufficing Perfection, by a bold logical inversion, was—without losing any of its original implications—converted into the concept of a Self-Transcending Fecundity." Or, as Plato put the matter in the *Timaeus,* since he who created and set in motion all things was himself perfect and therefore without envy, "he desired that everything should be so far as possible like himself." Plato goes on: "This, then, we shall be wholly right in accepting from wise men as being above all the sovereign originating principle of Becoming and of the cosmos." For Plato, as Lovejoy emphasizes, the Absolute would not be what it is "if it gave rise to anything less than a complete world in which the 'model,' i.e., the totality of ideal Forms is translated into concrete realities." In brief, for Plato, the principle of plenitude required "that every possible, every imaginable, place in the universe be filled"—either by the already-accomplished or by the self-accomplishing. The idea of plenitude, with its corollaries of self-transcending and self-perfecting fecundity, is one of the most powerful as well as persisting ideas in all of European thought. We shall see it in Leibniz and Spinoza, in the writings of the eighteenth-century evolutionary biologists, and far from least, albeit in different statement, in Darwin's *Origin of the Species.*

Closely connected to this idea is another, more nearly an Aristotelian than Platonic idea. Aristotle wrote: "Things are said to be continuous whenever there is one and the same limit of both wherein they overlap and which they possess in common." Lovejoy is entirely correct in his assertion that Aristotle "is responsible for the introduction of the principle of continuity into natural history." In his *History of Animals* Aristotle tells us that nature "passes so gradually from the inanimate to the animate that their continuity renders the boundary between them indistinguishable; and there is a middle ground that belongs to both orders."

Lovejoy writes:

The result [of the ideas of plenitude and continuity] was the conception of the plan and structure of the world which, through the Middle Ages and down to the late eighteenth century, many philosophers, many men of science, and, indeed, most educated men were to accept without question—the conception of the universe as a "Great Chain of Being composed . . . of an infinite number of links ranging in hierarchical order from the meagerest kind of existents, which barely escape nonexistence, through 'every possible grade' up to the *ens perfectissimum* . . .

Lovejoy writes "down to the late eighteenth century." But in all truth, these same principles of plenitude and continuity are to be seen vividly expressed in the writings of such nineteenth-century notables as Auguste Comte, Karl Marx, Charles Darwin, and Herbert Spencer. Darwin was so committed to these principles that in *The Origin of the Species* he not only argues in their behalf on the basis of his field observations but, when the geological evidence fails to attest to either principle, credits this failure to what he calls "the imperfections of the geological record."

Both ideas were ascendant in the High Middle Ages. In the twelfth century Abelard sought to give prominence to the ideas of sufficient reason and plenitude, as these could be inferred from conviction of the inherent goodness of God. Long before Leibniz, Abelard reached the conclusion that in the light of God's power and of the reality of plenitude this had to be the best of all *possible* worlds. We must inquire, writes Abelard, "whether it was possible for God to make more things or better things than he has in fact made." And he answers by reference to Plato:

Hence is that most true argument of Plato's, whereby he proves that God could not in any wise have made a better world than he has made . . . . Whatever is generated is generated by some necessary cause, for nothing comes into being except there be some due cause and reason antecedent to it.

From all of this, Lovejoy notes, comes that argument for optimism of the sort which "was to become so universally familiar in the seventeenth and eighteenth centuries; the goodness of this best of possible worlds consists, not in the absence of evils, but rather in their presence." That argument, as we shall have occasion to stress, was to be vital to the rationalist arguments in the eighteenth and nineteenth centuries for evolutionary progress.

Just as the idea of plenitude and fecundity held sway in the Middle Ages, so did the doctrine of continuity. Thomas Aquinas in the thirteenth century writes of "the wonderful linkage of things," citing Albertus Magnus who had declared that "nature does not pass from extreme to extreme except through fine gradations." Like Aristotle, Aquinas points to the continuity that may be seen among organisms, from the simplest to man himself. And he goes beyond Aristotle in pointing to the continuity of the physical and the spiritual "classes." He writes:

Man has in equal degree the characters of both classes, since it [man's constitution] attains to the lowest member of the class above bodies, namely the human soul, which is at the bottom of the series of intellectual beings—and is said therefore to be the horizon and boundary line of things corporeal and incorporeal.

Every thing acts for a good, Aquinas argues. "And if the action consist in the transformation of external matter, clearly the mover intends to induce some perfection into the thing moved, toward which perfection the movable also tends, *if the movement be natural.*" (Italics added) The Greek element in that last phrase will not be missed. For attainment of perfection to be not merely divine in nature but also "natural" says a good deal about Aquinas's philosophical roots. He is Greek to the very essence in the following aphorism: "Therefore every natural agent tends to that which is best; and much more evidently is this so with the intellectual agent."

Earthly Paradises

We are still so dominated by the myth that medieval thought was lost in contemplation of the heavenly hereafter and in despair of or disdain for the things of this world that it can come as something of a shock to realize how avid was medieval interest in earthly paradises: those believed to lie in remote but reachable parts of the earth and those believed to lie ahead in time for all mankind.

As to the first—contemporary, actual paradises—George Boas writes in his *Primitivism and Related Ideas in the Middle Ages:*

The twelfth century is the great age of legendary voyages to the Earthly Paradise. Sometimes the legends are written with didactic purpose and are cast in the form of visions, but at other times the didactic intention is not emphasized. The accounts had a certain added power because the Earthly Paradise was supposed to be physically existent, and also because a number of reports of wonderful countries, given in apocalytic terms, were believed in full seriousness.

The best known early-medieval accounts of Earthly Paradise are those by Hugo of Saint Victor, Prester John, and Henry Saltrey, the last the author of *The Purgatory of Saint Patrick,* a work that in one version or another delighted its readers and listeners for a long time after its initial appearance. Every effort seems to have been made by the composers of these tales to make their proffered earthly paradises as realistic as possible, not only in substance but in terms of actual discovery and access. It is in this light that Boas writes:

The Atlantic continued to be held a sea of wonderful islands approaching the marvellousness of the Earthly Paradise, until the period of explorations was over. In fact, so strong was this belief that the very explorers began to describe the lands which they had found in legendary terms. The most dramatic case of this is to be found in the reports of Columbus. In his Narrative of the Third Voyage, he points out that the site of Earthly Paradise must lie near the stem of the pear-shaped earth.

Medieval appetite for the exotic on earth was fed by more than legend. There were, for example, the fascinating accounts of the famous Polo family, Niccolo, Maffeo, and Marco, who could combine chronicles of actual visits to settings as far off as China with rhetorical images of the paradisiacal. Just as there is a continuous line from the medieval travelers to the explorers of the sixteenth century, so is there equally a continuous line from medieval chronicles of travel and discovery to, say, Hakluyt's *Voyages* of the same century. And both lines reflect throughout the spell of Earthly Paradise.

But from our point of view here, the more interesting and also influential earthly paradise is that which is set in time, prophesied for the future, on earth. By all odds the most powerful of prophecies in the Middle Ages of a future earthly paradise is that of Joachim de Fiore, who lived and wrote in the twelfth century. Although this extraordinary mind was to be condemned at the Lateran Council of 1215, it is worth noting that earlier three popes had given encouragement to Joachim in his inspired account of what had happened and what would happen to mankind. And despite repeated declarations and charges of heresy, his doctrine exerted immense power in his lifetime and continued to exert power, albeit less grandly, for centuries after his death. As Marjorie Reeves, whose *The Influence of Prophecy in the Later Middle Ages* is the most complete and authoritative study of Joachim, writes:

A prophet foretells the future; he can also create it. For the historian the history of prophecy contains the delicate problem of the interplay between word and action.

Are prophecies fulfilled because of their far-seeing diagnosis or because of the response they evoke in action? The historical significance of Joachim lies in the dynamic quality of certain key ideas which he proclaimed. They worked underground in the following centuries, from time to time springing to new life in a group or individual. Their vital quality arose from the fact that they worked in the imagination, moving to hope and so to action; thus their impact was emotional rather than intellectual.

I would prefer to say *as well as* intellectual. For, as Marjorie Reeves herself stresses (as have such other historians as Karl Löwith, Frank Manuel, Norman Cohn, and Melvin Lasky), the intellectual content, quite apart from the spirit of prophecy in which this content is contained, was to make its way, albeit interruptedly and through more or less subterranean channels, through all of the centuries succeeding Joachim's twelfth down to the nineteenth. In the eighteenth century Lessing referred to Joachim with high respect; indeed, he employed a considerable part of Joachim's view of historical time. And in the nineteenth century Auguste Comte, founder of Positivism, preeminent expositor of the *science* of progress, cited him also. Probably the latest full and genuinely fruitful period of Joachim's influence on European thought was that of the Puritan Revolution in England in the seventeenth century; we shall come to that later on. What Marjorie Reeves writes is sufficiently instructive at this point: "From the thirteenth to the sixteenth century, and even beyond, there were those who fastened on this conception of future spiritual orders and found in it the understanding of their own mission in the world."

Joachim is generally and no doubt properly regarded as the first to make the triadic division of history the framework of his conception of the golden age yet to come on earth. His first great stage in human history is characterized by what he calls "the ascendancy of the flesh," with all its imperious drives holding man's consciousness down to the material level, with but the rarest of exceptions. This first age lasted until the appearance of Christ. In the second stage of history, "men lived between the flesh and the spirit," as Joachim describes it. Originating with the first appearance of Christ, the second age has continued to our own day, according to Joachim, and its ending will not occur without a period of extreme agitation of society— violence, terror, fear, and suffering. Only through such pains and torments will it be possible for mankind to be cleansed and made ready for the third and greatest of ages, that of the spirit, when human beings (all Christians, of course, but also, we are assured by Joachim in one place, the rest of humanity too, the Jews included, who by then will have been converted) become "contemplatives," living lives entirely through mind. The Age of Contemplatives will be nothing less, Joachim writes, than heaven descending on earth. The Trinity is never far from Joachim's thinking; it may indeed be said that his philosophy of history springs from his lifelong desire to understand the Trinity and to demonstrate the ways in which human history on earth may be seen as an expression, a "temporalizing," of the Trinity. As Marjorie Reeves writes:

> Joachim . . . founded his interpretation of history upon a belief that it reflected the nature of the Godhead, sometimes in the twofold relationship of Father and Son, sometimes in the threefold relationship of Father, Son, and the Holy Spirit . . . Joachim's spiritual longing to approach the mystery of the Triune God was part and parcel of his Scriptural and historical studies.

Joachim is clearly fascinated by his proclaimed third age, and spends much energy finding figures of speech which will give the age concrete exemplification: birds which will fly upward to the heavens, the brilliance of the sun, the abundance of wealth, the joyful feeding in the pastures of the Scriptures, and so on. He even offers the bold prospect of the disappearance of the clergy prior to the advent of the third age. On this ground, among others, as might be expected, he was found guilty of extreme heresy in the following century and condemned.

Joachim, himself a monk, was profoundly influenced by the monastic-communal ideal in Christianity—just as four centuries later Sir Thomas More, whose *Utopia* was so largely shaped indeed by More's admiration of the best in the English monastic tradition, would be. All human beings, Joachim predicted, would live during the third great age in communal fashion in the name of charity and in the unity of a dedicated sharing of all things. Only once, Reeves points out, does Joachim ever offer poverty, as an element of this spiritualized, communal life. He is far more interested in depicting his age in the rhetoric of fullness and abundance. Despite Joachim's focusing on the spiritual and on the contemplative life, he does not remove this from the earth. The whole point, the potentially revolutionary point of Joachim's message is that, as before noted, heaven will come to earth. Without doubt it was this gospel of spiritual happiness and perfection to be achieved in this rather than the next world that most captivated followers and readers. As George Boas writes:

> For we find throughout Europe in the early thirteenth century not only doctrines of three dispensations like that of Joachim, but also the rise of mystical groups of men and women who look to a reign of love and believe in the apostolic life. They also hold to the idea, in general, that each individual is as sure a source of religious truth as is the hierarchy, thus nullifying the need of a priesthood . . . They popularized the idea that history might move from worse to better, which was essential if we were to believe in progress; they also popularized the idea of individual interpreta-

tion of religious truths, which was essential if Protestantism in some of its forms was to survive.

In all of this, Joachimism could and did play a significant role even if Joachim himself might well have drawn back from explicit statement of such ideas. We need look no further for reasons justifying the accusations and condemnations which came in the next century from Thomas Aquinas, St. Bonaventura and others, and also, as I have noted, the Lateran Council. That Joachim refrained from any participation in movements of the sort just described—as would Rousseau in the eighteenth century with respect to, say, peasant or worker uprisings or any other kind of direct social action, apart only from his advice to governments—does not minimize the revolutionary potential of his writing and the electric effect it would have on others.

What gave extra revolutionary implication to his doctrine was Joachim's confident belief that the present, that is, the second age of history, was alive with evil and torment. Moreover, things will become worse before the advent of the third age. All the more important, therefore, as Melvin Lasky points out in his *Utopia and Revolution* with respect to Joachim and the groups inspired by his ideas, is the mission of the small group of the genuinely faithful. Earthly deliverance will not come easily. There are strong implications in Joachim that realization of the "inevitable" requires the active participation of those who are the heart and mind of resistance to present forces of corruption and evil. The present period must be seen as one of transition, characterized and to be continuedly characterized by struggle, violence, and warfare between the opposed forces of good and evil. Only when this period is terminated will the third age of communal plenty and concord begin to manifest itself. "To each," Joachim writes, "will be given in such manner that he will rejoice less on his own account than because his neighbor has received something. He will count a thing less as his own than as given to others through him."

If this has a peculiarly modern ring so far as utopian ideas and revolutionary action are concerned, we must not forget its Augustinian roots. St. Augustine's rendering of the heavenly city that must finally triumph, it will be recalled, is rich in this-world imagery—of gold and silver, of endless abundance of everything, of harmony, liberty, and justice. There is really nothing extraordinary in the fact that Augustinian heavenly rapture would in time be converted into rapture that had this earth, not heaven, as its object.

Well before the dawn of the modern era, the implications of Joachimism toward direct action in political and social matters were seen—by Dante, among others. As Melvin Lasky argues in his *Utopia and Revolution,* there are unmistakable evidences of Joachimite influence on Dante's political mind. He may not have been the first of medieval figures to recommend direct action toward the hastening of paradise on earth, but he is without question the first towering literary mind in this respect. The following passages, cited by Lasky, are telling:

Since the present subject is political—indeed the source and principle of all just governments—and anything political lies within our power, it is obvious that the matter in hand is not primarily directed towards speculation but towards action. Again, since in practical affairs the ultimate end is the principle and cause of all that has been done . . . it follows that the formulation of the means is derived from the end in view.

When the root of this monstrous perversion [of existing government and society] is extracted, the prickly branches will wither on the trunk.

To your sorrow you will see your palaces . . . fallen under the battering-ram or consumed by fire. You will see your populace, now a raging mob, disorganized, divided against itself, part for, part against you, soon united against you . . . You will see with remorse your churches, now thronged everyday by crowds of your ladies, pillaged, and your children doomed to pay for their fathers' sins in bewilderment and ignorance.

Awake, therefore, all of you, and rise.

It is in Dante's *De Monarchia,* which for understandable reasons the Pope ordered burned in the square at Bologna, Dante's high birth and literary eminence notwithstanding, that we find his progressive-utopian plan for a better polity on this earth, one that has more than a few likenesses to that which Joachim had foretold. There is no mistaking Dante's complete disillusionment with papal government as it extended into lay affairs, nor is there any mistaking his preference for a powerful, messianically inspired *lay* ruler to destroy the old and corrupt and hasten the new. Dante's admiration for Emperor Henry VII, crowned in Rome in 1312, was high enough to make him think of this emperor in the terms of earthly redemption.

As we have seen, Joachim foresaw (heretically) the time when the clergy and all other visible accoutrements of ecclesiastical authority would no longer be needed since society would be composed of free, pure, righteous contemplatives in no need of external authority. Norman Cohn, in his *The Pursuit of the Millennium,* has strongly emphasized the significance of this vision. In Joachim's interpretation, Christ no longer stands at the center of history, and the Christian revelation is of only limited and temporary validity. Hence the ever-rising, ever more thrilling dream of post-Christian society. We see this in a wing of the Franciscan Order. Professor Cohn writes:

These men—the Franciscan Spirituals—formed a minority party, at first within the Order, later outside it. By the middle of the century they had disinterred Joachim's prophecies (which hitherto had attracted little attention) and were editing them and producing commentaries upon them. They were also forging prophecies which they successfully fathered upon Joachim and which became far better known and more influential than Joachim's own writings. In these works the Spirituals adapted the Joachite eschatology in such a way that they themselves could be seen as the new order which, replacing the Church of Rome, was to lead mankind into the Age of the Spirit.

Then fatefully and in full keeping with the tenor of Spiritualist interpretation of Joachim came the search for a new messiah, one in lay-secular trappings, wielding earthly power but qualified nevertheless to guide mankind through the final days of terror in the second stage and into the blissful existence of the third age, the age of the Spirit. Many were the potential candidates for this messianic role in the eyes of those whose imaginations were inflamed by Joachimite prophecy. I have already mentioned the fascination that Henry VII had for so powerful and learned a mind as Dante. Even earlier, however, there had been the cult of Frederick II. When his forebear Frederick I (Barbarossa) had died in 1190 there were almost immediately prophecies, we learn, of a later Frederick who would become an eschatological savior, the emperor to preside over the glorious entry into the age of the Spirit. Cohn continues:

"When, thirty years later, the imperial crown was bestowed on Frederick II . . . these prophecies were confidently applied to him. So for the first time the image of the Emperor of the Last Days was attached to the actual ruler of the territorial complex, centering on Germany but embracing also Burgundy and most of Italy . . . ."

As Cohn stresses, there was a great deal about Frederick II to encourage messianic expectations. Learned, brilliant of mind, handsome, fearless in battle, both feared and respected, he was every inch what we term today a charismatic figure. Even his notable licentiousness and cruelty seem to have attracted rather than repelled. Nor was there lacking evidence of greatness in his actions. After all, in participation in a crusade in 1229 he had been able to recapture Jerusalem and declare himself king of that city. Finally, and perhaps most important of all, Frederick seems to have believed deeply in his messianic role. The extravagant writings of his intellectual courtiers concerning Frederick's spiritual and cosmic powers and his capacity for transcending the ordinary mortal dimension of life seem to have induced no skepticism about him in the intellectual and lay mind. The cult of Frederick II would last a long time.

There were still other, equally remarkable consequences of Joachim's prophetic writings. I mentioned above the impression left upon fifteenth- and sixteenth-century navigators' minds of the medieval legends of remote earthly paradises, real paradises, waiting only to be discovered. Columbus, as we saw, was one of those convinced at first, as he wrote in his journal, that he had rediscovered the Garden of Eden. Lasky writes: "When Columbus crossed the ocean sea to find an *otro mundo,* an Other World, he was convinced . . . that he had rediscovered the Garden of Eden." But then, sick and troubled in the Indies, Lasky goes on, Columbus turned his attention to the prediction of Joachim that a redeemer would come from Spain to rebuild Jerusalem, to inaugurate the third age on earth. "Columbus presented himself," Lasky writes, "as a millennial messenger, echoing the apocalyptic tones of Joachim deFiore (whom he had cited in his *Book of Prophecies,* written just before his last voyage to America)."

It was the Joachimite prophecies and themes that the Franciscans had in mind when they went from Spain to Mexico in the 1520s. As the historian J. H. Elliott has written:

> These first missionaries to mainland America saw themselves as divine agents in a providential unfolding of history, in which the conversion of all mankind would be the prelude to the end of the world. This projection of the millenarian hopes of Renaissance Europe onto sixteenth century America meant that the empire of Montezuma was overthrown, and New Spain conquered and settled in a climate of expectation which itself did much to shape the future course of Mexico's development. The extraordinary sequence of events, leading to the surrender of Montezuma and the collapse of the Aztecs before Cortes's handful of soldiers, cried out for explanation both by the conquerors and the conquered.

Such is the power of an idea, or complex of ideas. What fascinating irony that the explanation proffered following the Aztec surrender, thousands of miles from and several centuries from the Europe of Joachim, should have been couched essentially in the terms of a medieval Franciscan monk's threefold pattern of the history of mankind culminating in a *renovatio mundi.*

It was not, in sum, the oft-heralded rationalism of the Renaissance that affected the expansion of European geographical consciousness, that provided motivational forces for the voyages and discoveries of the fifteenth and sixteenth centuries, as much as it was those deeper currents of thought in a still dominant Christianity which sprang from the medieval-Christian conception of progress with its millennialism, its varied utopias, and its powerful, driving sense of the importance of understanding and also improving upon this world in preparation for life in the next. What we commonly give to Renaissance might better go to ideas of progress and renovation which are quintessentially medieval.

Chapter 4

The Renaissance:

Some Cross-Currents

So FAR as the idea of progress is concerned, any chapter on the Renaissance must bear comparison with the chapter that Dr. Johnson called to friends' attention—one in a book titled *The Natural History of Iceland.* Johnson declared that he committed the entire chapter to memory inasmuch as it consisted of but a single sentence: "There are no snakes to be met with throughout the whole island."

Nor are there any ideas of progress to be met with throughout the whole Renaissance—a hallowed word I use with reference to a pattern of thought rather than to any sharply identifiable period of time. The beginnings of this pattern are to be seen during what the historian Johan Huizinga has so well called "the waning of the Middle Ages," the late fourteenth and the fifteenth centuries. The high point of this pattern of thought is no doubt the sixteenth century, but extensions of theme and style can be found in the first part of the seventeenth century.

The concept of a "renaissance" at the end of the medieval era is, to say the least, a flawed one. As noted in Chapter 3, scholarship beginning with Pierre Duhem and continuing to the present moment has made it solidly evident that medieval culture was rich in those qualities attributed to the culture of France and Italy in the fifteenth century by Michelet and Burckhardt in their momentous volumes published in the nineteenth century.

These we have tended almost universally to deny to the Middle Ages and to ascribe to some "rebirth" of ancient Graeco-Roman ideas and virtues, thus making possible, as the myth goes, the termination, once and for all, of medieval thought and the advent of modernity. Even today this myth can be found stated with cultist intensity by Renaissancists, though one can never know in advance which particular element of modernity—"civic humanism", "subjectivist individuality," or something else equally boneless—will be featured.

But flawed or not, the concept of a fecund renaissance appearing in the fifteenth century would appear to be an ineradicable part of both Western historiography and Western popular consciousness. For how many minds the following paraphrase of Alexander Pope on Newton must not ring with dogmatic certitude!

> Europe and Europe's mind lay hid in night;
> God said, "Renascence be!," and all was light.

But this has to be said: even if no "rebirth" ever actually took place in the fifteenth and sixteenth centuries, a *birth* most certainly did. I refer to the beginning of a line of intellectuals—in the Italian humanists of the fifteenth century—that continues to this day in which the flouting of tradition, the spirit of counterculture, and the exaltation of the wayward or dissident are the high water marks.

I have said that the idea of progress, as we have seen it from Xenophanes to Joachim, is not to be found in the Renaissance. This is not to imply, however, that Renaissance minds were unconcerned with cultural superiority and inferiority or that they did not take pride in their own age as it compared with much earlier ages, even those of ancient Greece and Rome. Consider the following statement of the fifteenth century Italian humanist Ficino; he is referring to his own city of Florence:

> For this golden century, as it were, has brought back to light the liberal arts, which were all but extinguished: grammar, poetry, oratory, painting, sculpture, architecture, music, the chanting of songs to the Orphic lyre, and all this in Florence.

In light of what we know today about the abundance of all these intellectual and artistic riches in the Middle Ages, one's mind is boggled by Ficino's words "all but extinguished." But the phrase tells us a good deal, all the same, and offers us one reason why the idea of progress could not exist, much less flourish, in Renaissance context.

For fundamental to the idea of progress, as we have seen in the three preceding chapters, and shall see in all chapters that follow this one, is the premise of *historical continuity.* Whether in Xenophanes, Plato, Lucretius, St. Augustine, or in Otto of Freising and Joachim of Fiore, the present and future are set deeply in a perceived and fully accepted past—a past that "step by step" or "little by little" becomes the present. As I have already emphasized, respect for and acceptance of the past is absolutely vital to the theory of progress; without a past, conceived as coming down in cultural substance as well as in time to the present, no principles of development, no stages emerging from one another, and no linear projection to the future are possible.

But for the Renaissance mind, any such respect for the past, the *whole* past, was out of the question. Such respect would have entailed respect for the Middle Ages—the Italian humanists referred to the period as the *medium aevum*—a time frame that for them was of at least a thousand years duration. The humanists adored the *ancient* past, to be sure, and it was their wholesale rejection of everything medieval and their passion to imitate what the ancient Greeks and Romans had accomplished that created the foundation for their vaunted golden age in the fifteenth century. Their theory of history was a simple one: the Greeks had brought civilization into being; the Romans added to it. Then, however, came the fall of Rome, caused by the external barbarians sprung from Germany's forests and by the Christians within Rome. The result, in the Renaissance mind, was a thousand years of desuetude, of sterility and drought, and worse, of a vast thicket of ignorance, superstition, preoccupation with the hereafter, and unremitting ecclesiastical tyranny. In the fifteenth and sixteenth centuries, the Renaissance humanists theorized, they were giving rebirth to civilization by dismissing all products of the *medium aevum* and concentrating on the works of the ancient classical world. Granted that the rebirth of true civilization might not last forever, that it too would, in all probability, eventually decay, with yet another period of ignorance and evil to follow, nevertheless, the Renaissance humanists felt that a complete break with the past had been effected at least temporarily, and with this would come the inauguration of another golden age in history.

This theory of history suggests a second reason why the gradual, unfolding, cumulative and continuous, linear theory of progress was foreign to the Renaissance mentality. I refer to the almost total domination of ideas of cyclical recurrence in Renaissance thought. As Frank E. Manuel has written in his *Shapes of Philosophical History,* "The Renaissance writers were directly, almost slavishly, dependent on the cyclical theories that they found in the ancient texts." Say, rather, *some* ancient texts, for, as we saw in the first chapter, cyclical ideas by no means dominated the texts of the Greeks and Romans. But Manuel's point is correct. Renaissance thinkers, from the fifteenth-century humanists in Italy to Francis Bacon, tended overwhelmingly to see history not as something unilinear in its flow, as continuous and cumulative, but as a multiplicity of recurrences, of cyclical ups and downs, all of them the consequence of the fixed elements in human nature: evil and good. It is useful to quote Frank Manuel again:

> When Renaissance writers dwell upon the unchanging character of basic human nature, so that the vicissitudes are merely a consequence of the interplay of human passions, mostly criminal, with fate, the historian's theory becomes a rather banal view of man in perpetual commotion. No concrete shape of philosophical history is discernible in this psychological jungle.

It is not that the humanists and other Renaissance minds were indifferent to the cultural record of the past. In the writings of Manetti and Ficino, to name but two of the fifteenth-century humanists in Italy, there are long passages attesting to the genius of man as represented by great inventions and discoveries in the ancient world. Some of the sections, especially in Ficino, read like paraphrases of St. Augustine's paragraphs (Bk. 22, *The City of God*) which, as we saw, also paid tribute to human genius and its multitude of artistic, scientific and technological works. But there is this difference. In the works of Ficino, Manetti, and the other humanists, there is basically no more than a cataloging of past wonders. In St. Augustine all of these great human achievements are fitted into a perspective of progress that is historically linear, continuous, and cumulative. However, such a perspective was alien to the Renaissance mind.

There are other aspects of Renaissance culture and thought which also constituted an inhospitable setting for any genuine theory of progress. There is, especially in Italy, the intense subjectivism in so much of what was thought and written. This subjectivism goes back, as Charles Trinkhaus has demonstrated in his splendid study of the Italian Renaissance, *In Our Image and Likeness,* to certain elements of St. Augustine's theology, elements which the humanists felt they could use effectively against scholasticism and churchly corporatism in their own age. It is not that the humanists withdrew themselves from the externalities of life—far from it—but in their war on scholasticism and the *structure* of Christianity, they understandably went, as would the Protestants during the Reformation, to the inner nature of man for religious reality, to inner consciousness, awareness, and grace in contrast to the external forms of religion. Throughout the Renaissance, from Petrarch to Descartes (whose famous *Cogito, Ergo Sum* was subjectivism carried to almost revolutionary heights), there is this emphasis upon what lies within the human mind rather than upon those works external to subjective consciousness which are, of course, the fundamental data of any theory of historical progress.

Moreover, there is, as Trinkhaus has also emphasized, an obsession with the nonrational or the irrational in man in much Renaissance writing. "Humanist moralism", Trinkhaus writes, "rather than stressing rationalistic restraint and inhibition of human action, emphasized the dominance of irrational or arational elements in man's psychic make-up." The humanists were also led to stress, as Trinkhaus notes, the ease with which virtue became the very seed of vice. Manetti is cited to this effect:

> And from this so great and so sublime dignity and excellence of man, as though from the very root, envy, pride, indignation, lust for domination and ambition and other perturbations of the soul of this sort not unjustly arise and flow.

In their reaction to medieval scholasticism, which was supremely rationalist and objectivist, the humanists were necessarily carried to place an emphasis upon the emotions, passions, and other nonrational affective states which were scarcely compatible with any theory of progress.

One final aspect of the Renaissance should be mentioned here, one also in utter conflict with the possibility of a theory of human progress: the sway of the occult, of magic, and of fate or fortune. Few people in our day, are likely to think of such profoundly irrational or antirational matters—such as Hermetic doctrine, the Kabbala, Ficino's cult of the sun and his solar magic, or the Magus—in conjunction with the almost universal image of the Renaissance. Contemporary historian Frances Yates has shown, with a wealth of illustration, that occult matters became very much a part of the scientific imagination of Bruno, Copernicus, and, quite possibly, Galileo. In all probability, it was not the strictly scientific or the rational that the Church was primarily concerned with in its responses to these titans, but, rather, the religious and the magical influences which could properly be seen as genuinely inimical to Christian faith.

But there is more. Never in Western history has belief in and fear of witchcraft flourished as it did during the Renaissance. During the Middle Ages the Church bent its efforts toward scotching such belief and fear. But in the period of the Renaissance when Catholic and feudal authority decayed and there was a loss of popular faith in spiritual and moral authority, imaginations of men ran riot. The Devil assumed a shape and proximity never before known in the West. It was only too easy to see in scientific experiments and new ideas, however rationally and empirically grounded, the works of the Devil and his witches.

Given the decline of traditional authority and doctrine, and rising fascination with the occult, it was only natural that there would spring up, as it had in the post-Alexandrian world of ancient Greece, a conviction that fate or fortune, not reason and probity, is the ultimate determiner of history and of man's lot on earth. How could one be seriously interested in the rational principles—divine or secular in foundation—which underlay ancient and medieval belief in the advancement of man when ideas of luck, chance, and accident flourished in an age of crumbling faith in reason and morality?

In the remainder of this chapter, I have chosen to profile a half-dozen notable minds as illustrations of some of the varied facets of the Renaissance. No one of them held by any means to all of these facets, but each in his way offers evidence of how difficult it would have been (*was,* as we shall see in the treatment of the late sixteenth-century philosopher Bodin in chapter 5) to sustain faith in history conceived as the march of humanity through all time toward the better and better, the faith that was so powerful in the ancient and medieval worlds and that would become powerful again in the modern world.

Machiavelli

Machiavelli sees in history nothing but ups and downs, cyclical returns *(ricorsi).* Not for this extraordinary mind any belief in long run, irreversible progress for mankind. Men, he writes, are "readier to evil than to good," and the result of this is a fixed oscillation in history between the bad and the good, but with the bad in control more often and over longer periods of time. Fortune is supreme, and Machiavelli devotes the twenty-fifth chapter of *The Prince* to the ultimate dependence of all political rulers, irrespective of their wile or wisdom, on the kindness and indulgence of Fortune. In another of his writings, titled *On Fortune,* he goes more deeply into the subject. Fortune "turns states and kingdoms upside down as she pleases; she deprives the just of the good that she freely gives to the unjust." Moreover "she times events as suits her; she raises us up, she puts us down without pity, without law or right."

Human existence is thus inherently cyclical or oscillatory, the result of Fortune's mercurial character. "That man most luckily forms his plan, among all the persons in Fortuna's palace, who chooses a wheel befitting her wish. . . . because while you are whirled about by the rim of a wheel that for the moment is lucky and good, she is wont to reverse its course in midcircle." Machiavelli concludes his essay with these words: "We see at last that in days gone by, few have been successful, and they have died before their wheel reversed itself or in turning carried them down to the bottom."

Machiavelli was, as we know, fascinated by history, especially histories of states and their rulers. His *History of the Florentine Republic* is basically little more than a medieval annals, but it is saved from being solely that by his speculations on the causes of history. Thus he observes in the fifth book of the *History* that

In their normal variations, countries generally go from order to disorder and then from disorder move back to order, because—since Nature does not allow worldly things to remain fixed—when they come to their utmost perfection and have no further possibility of rising, they must go down. Likewise, when they have gone down and through their defects have reached the lowest depths, they necessarily rise, since they cannot go lower. So always from the good they go down to bad and from bad rise to the good.

Precisely the same conclusion is reached in Machiavelli's *Discourse on the First Ten Books of Titus Livius.* Under the chapter title, "The world as a whole is always the same," he writes:

When I meditate on how these things move, I judge that the world has always gone on in the same way and that there has been as much good as bad, but that this bad and this good have varied from land to land, as anyone understands who knows about those ancient kingdoms which differed from one another because of the difference in their customs, but the world remained the same.

Fortune, chance, fate—these alone have true suzerainty over men's affairs. Any effort to descry a pattern, save that of *ricorsi,* particularly a progressive pattern involving all humanity, from beginning to the present, from the present to the future, did in fact seem, futile and fatuous to Machiavelli.

The same basic beliefs are to be found in the work of Machiavelli's younger contemporary, Francesco Guiccardini. An admired diplomat, administrator, business man, statesman, and historian, he took pains to criticize many of Machiavelli's ideas. But the more he criticized, the more Machiavellian he himself became. He served the Papacy, but detested it, and once wrote that one of his three greatest hopes was for a "world freed from the rascally priests." In his histories of Florence and of Italy he almost outdoes Machiavelli in his cynicism of and contempt for the majority of personages dealt with therein. It is his feeling that men do not change, except superficially. The same situations come around repeatedly, and there is no event to be found that may not be seen to have occurred before. He criticizes Machiavelli for resting conclusions on the experience of Rome alone, but there is no significant difference to be found between Guiccardini's conclusions and Machiavelli's.

Machiavelli at least believed in the ideal superiority of popular government, but Guiccardini held it in disdain. He wrote: "Who speaks of the people speaks of a mad monster full of errors and confusions." His *Ricordi*, a collection of maxims he coined over many years, testifies to his almost complete conviction that while men may naturally be inclined to do the good, the consequences of their actions are far more often than not evil. And this is overwhelmingly the result of the dominance of Fortuna. Skillful and shrewd though Guiccardini was in his political and business dealings, he had the typical Renaissance intellectual's faith that in the end, chance and fate will decide. Although Guiccardini was coldly rational in his statecraft and deeply steeped in the empirical materials of history, he could no more conquer his dependence upon the nonrational and irrational, and upon consultation with those who claimed to foretell fate, than could any other humanist of his time—a time that, especially after the Italian wars of 1494, produced a state of mind in Northern Italy compounded of pessimism, helplessness, and total inability to conceive history as other than a quilt of chance, mischance, error, and the demonic, with no one but Fortuna to look toward. What Sir Walter Raleigh was to write a century later in his uncompleted *History of the World*—"All that the hand of man can make, is either overturned by the hand of man, or at length by standing and continuing consumed"—would have been accepted as no more than the obvious by both Machiavelli and his friend Guiccardini.

Erasmus

This exemplar of learning and high humor brings to the fore qualities decidedly different from any to be found in Machiavelli, but not the less inimical to the kind of thought that goes, and must go, into the theory of human progress. Erasmus, unlike Machiavelli, remained a devoted, though far from uncritical, member and supporter of the Roman Catholic Church. His works included editions of and commentaries on some of the early Church Fathers, particularly Jerome and Athanasius. But such works and continued support of the Church, notwithstanding, there is in Erasmus a pronounced, almost Protestant, turning from religion as institution to religion as internal faith. His essential humanism and Renaissance cast of mind are nicely illustrated by the following passage in his *Education of a Christian Prince:*

But . . . do not think that Christ is found in ceremonies, in doctrines kept after a fashion, and in constitutions of the church. Who is truly Christian? Not he who is baptized or anointed, or who attends church. It is rather the man who has embraced Christ in the innermost feelings of his heart, and who emulates him by his pious deeds.

Noble sentiments indeed. But hardly those of a mind—such as St. Augustine, Otto of Freising, or later, the Bishop Bossuet—in which the primary and decisive attribute of religion is the historic *church* conceived as a constantly developing, unfolding, ever-improving corporate body that alone provides substance and foundation for individual faith. In its way, Erasmus's emphasis upon inner individual grace, upon individual thought as alone productive of good, is as antagonistic to a theory of the progress of mankind as Machiavellian stress upon chance and fortune. For the Western idea of progress rests, as it has from the time of the Greeks, upon the value and reality of things external—institutions, the arts and sciences, in which alone advancement is to be descried. But for Erasmus—as for Luther, whom Erasmus at first respected, then opposed strongly—the essence of Christianity has nothing to do with forms and contents which are susceptible to progressive change in time. It has everything to do with the subjective, the inward, the kind of thought and faith which can never be genuinely expressed by institution or ritual.

He was deeply read in history, particularly in the ancient classical texts, but what he did best with history, including that of his own time, is represented by his brilliant *In Praise of Folly*. Folly is, in Erasmus's rendering, a goddess—we might call her a distant cousin of the Italians' Fortuna—and what Folly loves above all else is the self liberated from convention and ceremony. I am interested only in the fact that for Erasmus, bemused by the goddess Folly, any conception of human progress through the ages is as unlikely as for a mind attuned to Fortuna.

That there might be an "education of the human race," as St. Augustine had declared, one taking place gradually throughout time, would have seemed preposterous to Erasmus. So, presumably, would have the metaphor of the dwarf on the shoulders of a giant. Erasmus admired many of his contemporaries—Sir Thomas More perhaps most greatly—and no doubt respected their works. But so far as the modern thought of his day in general, and even more, medieval thought, was concerned, there was, in Erasmus's assessment, only decline and degeneration to be seen. Nothing since the downfall of classical civilization, not even, we are led to believe, the Scriptures, exceeds the genius of the greatest of the ancients. To suppose any superiority in the moderns on the basis of their possession of the works of the ancients—which would be the argument of the Moderns in the late seventeenth century in the famous Quarrel of the Ancients and Moderns—was, to Erasmus, to suppose nonsense. He writes:

To confess freely among friends, I can't read Cicero on "Old Age," on "Friendship," his "Offices," or his "Tusculan Questions" without kissing the book, without veneration towards that divine soul. And, on the contrary, when I read some of our modern authors, treating of politics, economics and ethics, good God! how cold they are in comparison with these! Nay, how do they seem to be insensible of what they write themselves. So that I had rather lose Scotus and twenty more such as he (fancy twenty subtle doctors!) than one Cicero or Plutarch.

The Greeks and the Romans, the greatest of the Church Fathers, and the philosophers and scholars of the Middle Ages could respect and cherish their forerunners, as did Socrates, Lucretius, St. Augustine, and St. Bonaventura, and still believe in the greatness of their respective presents: each a present that was inseparable from the measured progress of past into present. But for all but a few of the minds of the Renaissance, Erasmus's words were gospel. We ourselves may find an Erasmus, a More, or a Montaigne the equal—at least in the essayist's wit and insight into the foibles of man—of anything of comparable genre in the ancient world. But it is unlikely that Machiavelli, Guiccardini, or Erasmus ever did. Their sense of regress was too overwhelming.

Thomas More

It may be thought there surely breathes a spirit akin to progress in More's *Utopia*. For was not this book More's presentation of not only the good community but the kind of community that could be achieved in the future if men would but give themselves to its attainment? The answer, unfortunately, is largely negative. I shall come back momentarily to that point. First, though, let it be said that even if *Utopia* is More's cherished form of society—one that would constitute progress over the present if but accepted by rulers and people—it in no way reflects what we know as the idea of progress. For, as we have repeatedly seen, the essence of the idea lies in its relation to *historical development* over time: of knowledge, institutions, and morality. There is not a hint of this in More's classic.

What we are given, following an opening devoted to the crimes inflicted by the nobility in England upon the common people, and the unwillingness of any, including the clergy, to intervene, is a detailed account by one Raphael Hythloday of a society he declares he had once chanced upon in a very distant part of the world. It would be gratuitious to describe this society for *Utopia* is one of the most widely read and respected books in

Western literature. It is enough to say that in almost every respect the society described is the opposite, detail for detail, of More's own England. And without question much of what is described would appear to be to More's personal liking. But, and this is the key point here, the title is *utopia* (nowhere), not *eutopia* (the best society), even though we cannot help but feel that a little of the latter lies in the former. The book, whatever else it may be, is a fantasy—set as far from English reality as possible.

Moreover, as the historian J. H. Hexter has so importantly pointed out, by no stretch of imagination can the complex of customs and institutions among the Utopians be thought reflective of More's own highest ideals. Profoundly Catholic Christian that he was, he could hardly have felt any kinship with the bizarre religious beliefs of the Utopians. Most important, their communism of property could only have been repugnant—all else equal—to More, for he believed deeply in private property and in the just profits proceeding from private property. He is too often on record in that respect for any doubt to exist. These are but two of the instances in which Utopian life, as described by More, is at odds with his own cherished and well-recorded convictions.

Why, then, did he—after cataloging the ills and torments of the English people in the first part of *Utopia*—present the form and substance of society he did? Again we turn to Professor Hexter's illuminating analysis which tells us that the practices of the Utopians, including the prohibitions and coercions, were, or could be seen as, repudiations of the pride, the cupidity, the avarice of the English aristocracy. These were the qualities which More had in mind when he limned utopian life, *not* his own personal ideals. As Hexter has emphasized, Sir Thomas was engaged in presenting a society that would best restrain the emanations of pride which he saw in the English aristocracy. Utopia, far from being More's ideal social order, is, in effect, a kind of hair shirt for the nobility of England.

There is one final point to be made about the book that also removes it from possible thought as an ideal design for English, or European, society. When, years after its publication, *Utopia* actually showed signs of being accepted as a model by militant Reformation groups seeking instant, millennialist achievement of goodness on earth, More was prompt in expressing his utter hostility to all such efforts. Melvin Lasky, in his *Utopia and Revolution,* tells us that More went so far as to declare that had it ever entered his mind when he conceived the book that it would someday be used for revolutionary purposes, he would have never written the book at all, or, if the manuscript already existed, he would have had it burned. Repugnant though More found the treatment of peasants under enclosure laws and other depredations upon the common people, and though surely willing to accept moderate and realistic reforms, he would have preferred what existed in England to anything that would come from millennialist-revolutionary zeal.

In sum, the appreciations and laudations of tens of millions of readers notwithstanding, *Utopia* is as far from the idea of progress as was More's beloved friend Erasmus's *In Praise of Folly*. Both are ineffaceable classics, but as far from the history of the subject of this book as any two classics could be.

Francis Bacon

There are, without doubt, occasional expressions in the writing of Bacon which clearly suggest the theory of historical progress. His often-cited observation, in *The Advancement of Learning, Antiquitas saeculi juventus mundi* is evidence enough that Bacon saw, as had innumerable pre-Renaissance thinkers, that we in our day are the true ancients. Those commonly termed so are in reality at the youth of the history of thought: in short, a perception of the substance of what St. Augustine had referred to as the education of the human race. There is also reference to a three-stage history of the West in the aforementioned work: the first stage being that of the Greeks and Romans; the second, the Christian–medieval stage; and the third, only at its beginning, Bacon's own age. But, then, this patterning was a common one even among the Italian humanists, who coined the term *medium aevum* to take care of the gulf between ancient-classical enlightenment and the humanists' own. His essay "The Wisdom of the Ancients" is far from being what its title suggests. It is in fact a kind of diversion, concerned with explaining classical fables, drawing from them what Bacon supposes to have been the actual meanings behind their modes of expression. It is hard to miss the disdain in which he held these meanings or the irony implicit in the title of this long essay.

In truth, Bacon was, so far as the past was concerned, not especially respectful. He was below the level, in this respect, of the earlier Italian humanists for whom the ancient world, at least, was worthy of respect. And Bacon shared fully—despite some unconscious lapses into a formalism that suggests scholasticism—the Renaissance contempt for, hatred of, medieval culture. His essay "Of Superstition" is illustratively rich in medieval concepts and beliefs. Nor, despite the three-stage theory just mentioned, is there in Bacon any genuine sense of history as a lineal flow, an unfolding, a necessary, continuous concatenation of events, ideas, and persons. His "Of Vicissitude of Things" is an essay perfectly reflective of the Renaissance tendency to see history at best as a storehouse of usable anecdotes, at most as a record of the incessant operation of the principle of rise and fall. Bacon has the same appreciation of the role of chance in history that Machiavelli and Guiccardini had.

Far more to the point, though, is the central object of Bacon's philosophical and scholarly works. His object is to demonstrate the utter falsity, at best unreliability, of all that has been said and thought in the past for want of a proper method of inquiry. As everyone knows, Bacon was only too happy to describe this method; it is fundamentally that of empirical observation and, above all, experiment. Bacon seems to have been ignorant of some of the remarkable works in science, including experimental science, which were taking place on the Continent in his time, and it is a matter of record that he regarded with near-repugnance any thought of the union of mathematics and science. But, irrespective of Bacon's own barren career in actual, substantive science, there can be few if any philosophers who have ever argued the *cause* of science with greater eloquence and passion. It is not too much to say that he saw science—that is, the kind of science which would exist if his proposed method were universally adopted—as redemptive gospel, and scientists as appointed prophets and priests.

Bacon's primary, indeed exclusive, mission was that of seeking to demonstrate *first*, as I have noted, the sterility and falsity of all inherited knowledge, and *second*, the wonders to be anticipated in the world if the only true method of scientific inquiry were to be adopted. *To be adopted!* His *Advancement of Learning* has little if any relation to the meaning the title phrase had to ancient and medieval scholars, and would have throughout the modern era. It is not historical advancement over time, but, rather, the impetus, the propulsion, that would be given to knowledge *if* only men banished all the accumulated errors—the *idola*—from their minds and devoted themselves for the first time in history to the proper method for the advancement of knowledge. Although Bacon can refer to "the noble helps and lights which we have by the travails of ancient writers," the sentiment is no more, really, than rhetorical; it does not in any degree match in enthusiasm what may be found in almost any of the Italian humanists. Bacon, a thoroughly educated mind, knew the past, but he saw it in much the same manner as Montaigne, from whom Bacon must have acquired the art of the essay. He saw it as an expanse to graze on, to nibble at, to eat from occasionally, to exhibit for rhetorical and illustrative purposes; *not* as the sacred, indispensable soil that alone makes intelligible the present and any anticipated future.

His most famous, and by all odds, directive work is of course the *Novum Organum*, a truly apposite title for what the book contains. Its most famous sections are those devoted to the "idols of the mind," and here we find in succession the idols of the tribe, the preconceptions and distortions which lie universally in mankind; the idols of the cave, the flaws of perception which spring from the individual human being's biases; the idols of the market place, the confusions and errors resulting primarily from our disposition to mistake words for reality; and the idols of the theatre, erroneous types of thinking which come from easy acceptance of fashionable systems of philosophy.

Only when human beings prove able to liberate themselves from these "idols", Bacon argues, will it be possible for a "new logic," a new scientific method, to take over and make possible, for the first time, man's understanding and then conquest of nature. What is required, obviously, is first of all a complete skepticism of all that has emerged from the past, inasmuch as this heritage is deeply flawed by the idols of the mind which have heretofore dominated human thought. Only then, and with strict use of the method of observation, of experiment, of induction, Bacon argues, will it be possible for there to be an advancement of knowledge.

Of the brilliance, substantive and stylistic, of Bacon's major philosophical works, as well as his essays, there cannot be the slightest question. And there is no doubt that, his own violations of his redemptive method notwithstanding—his metaphysics of "forms" and his scholastic structure of argument, along with other faults previously cited—Bacon's was a mind of brightest luster. His reputation remains so to this day. But there is no more hint of a historical philosophy or theory of progress in Bacon than in any of the other Renaissance minds we have dealt with.

The perfect vessel for Bacon's motives, understanding, and, above all, his contemplation of the future so far as "the advancement of knowledge" is concerned, is his *The New Atlantis*. Like More's *Utopia*, Bacon's society is set in a distant part of the world. Unlike More's work, which, as we noted, is ambiguous in inspiration, Bacon's is as unambiguous as a searchlight. The perfect society may not, and probably will not, ever come into existence, but Bacon tells us exactly what it is: a society governed solely and exclusively by the values of science and by its guardians, the scientists. By today's standards—set by Aldous Huxley in *Brave New World* and then a host of followers—Bacon's work makes for chilling reading. Such is the relentless, omnipresent, unceasing surveillance and control of human life by science. *The New Atlantis* marks the beginning of the long tradition in Western letters where scientists and technologists are seen as redeemers, a tradition that was to be mocked unmercifully by Samuel Butler in the nineteenth century in *Erewhon* and, in our century, more often than not, made the subject of bitter despair. It is a fantasy set in nowhere that Bacon gives us, an augury of at least some degree of nineteenth- and twentieth-century technological reality. But that is all that can be said for it.

There is, however, one respect in which Bacon's philosophy has a linkage with the history of the idea of progress: that is, as Charles Webster has pointed out in his recent, illuminating book, *The Great Instauration,* the avidity with which certain progress-inspired Puritans in seventeenth-century England and America took to his writings. As we shall see in chapter 5, the Puritans—who were the central figures in seventeenth-century revival of millenarianism—had a philosophy of human progress that united past, present, and future into one seamless web that pointed to a golden future on earth, one of a thousand, or perhaps many thousands of years. For these Puritans, nothing was more important in the achievement of this earthly paradise than the unremitting search for knowledge—especially practical, experimental, scientific knowledge. With much reason, therefore, did these millennium-driven Puritans take to a mind—however far in religious belief it was from Puritan tenet—such as Bacon's.

René Descartes

There are really two Descartes, both occupying the same body, but as different in mind as any two unrelated, separate individuals can be. The first is the Descartes of learned and imaginative contributions to mathematics and to such fields of accumulated learning as optics, physiology, and psychology. But this Descartes is best known to the historians of science. The second, and by far more influential, is the Descartes of the *Discourse on Method* and the *Meditations.* The first Descartes could not possibly have existed had it not been for libraries of one kind or other, storehouses of what had been done and what was known in the sciences in which Descartes worked and to which he contributed significantly. It was the second Descartes who urged the destruction of all libraries because of the errors and superstitions they contained and because, by their very existence, they constituted obstacles to the use of the method that Descartes so momentously set forth in his *Discourse* and his *Meditations.*

I have previously referred to Bacon's skepticism and to his insistence upon the necessity of this state of mind until genuine truth, in the form of experimental science, can be drawn upon. But the skepticism Descartes enjoins upon us in his classic works is far more radical than Bacon's, for Descartes's skepticism applies to literally everything, most especially the empirical data which Bacon thought alone real. In other words, Descartes renounced all forms of perceived, external reality in the name of his cherished methodological skepticism, along with, of course, all known systems of thought or ideas in any shape or size. Not without reason has a recent French commentator referred to the Cartesian method as a form of "intellectual terror."

The rules for acquiring knowledge, *real* knowledge—which had never existed, in Descartes' considered judgment—are four. First, never accept anything as true that one cannot "clearly and distinctly" see to be true; that is, in effect, axiomatic. Second, "divide each of the difficulties under examination into as many parts as possible." One must never deal with large propositions in the beginning; everything must be conceptually broken down into the smallest possible intellectual elements. Third, always conduct thoughts in logical order, "beginning with objects that are the simplest and easiest to know and so proceed, gradually, to knowledge of the more complex." Fourth, reason rigorously, as in a geometrical proposition, and make certain at all times that nothing in the way of a logical step has been omitted.

Everyone knows how Descartes himself applied his proffered method: by doubting the existence of everything; by realizing that what alone could not be doubted was the existence of a doubter-thinker, from this subjectively arriving at an axiom and proceeding step-by-step to demonstrate the existence of world, man, and God.

What made Cartesian philosophy revolutionary was Descartes's insistence that his method was available to Everyman, that one need no longer pay homage to scholars and scientists and archives and libraries. The only truth that counts, the only real truth, is that which any normal individual, educated or not, can reach by himself, so long as each of the four steps is followed closely. Just as Luther had, when his doctrines were carried to their logical conclusions, made church and clergy unnecessary—and most certainly, sacraments, liturgies, theology, and, thus, its works—with individual faith directly transmitted to God the sole basis of true religion, so Descartes, through his philosophical method, made everything in the form of extant knowledge—all books, documents, and the like—equally unnecessary; worse, he viewed them as actual, formidable barriers to ascertainment of the truth, the real truth. This was the reasoning behind Descartes's notorious views on all disciplines in which empirical or documentary research was involved. Historians, Descartes sneered, are people who spend a lifetime learning facts about Roman life which every illiterate serving maid in Cicero's time knew well.

There is no need to go further into Cartesianism and its relation to any possible conception of progress in Descartes' mind. Any thought of such belief in Descartes is clearly absurd, given his contempt for, his renunciation of, all that had ever been learned in the past, his conviction that the sole reality worth knowing is that which is reachable only by the individual mind preoccupied by its own precepts and concepts. Descartes condemned all that lies outside us to the realm of mere appearance, or even illusion, and by this he dismissed any thought of a belief in progress that involved necessary growth of knowledge through the past, the present, and into the future, that involved either the arts and sciences or the advancing welfare of mankind. Unlike the Italian humanists two centuries earlier, Descartes could not bring himself to admire even the ancient Greeks and Romans, and such admiration, as we have seen, is close to the core of the Renaissance. But even closer to the core is that belief in the superiority of the subjective imagination over anything that has been inherited from, or that has developed and unfolded from, the past.

A final note is in order on Descartes, if only because of its amusing implications. Descartes, as we have seen, declared that he had first emptied his mind of all that he had ever learned, then took the position of doubting everything, including his own existence, and thus emerged triumphantly with the conclusion that while he might seek to doubt everything, he could not doubt the existence of the doubter-thinker: *Cogito, Ergo sum.*

What Descartes in fact may or may not have known is that he was anticipated in this mode of analysis by none other than St. Augustine, whom Descartes must surely have read during his Jesuit university education. St. Augustine (*The City of God*, XI, 26) declared his own existence, and thus his capacity for perceiving the outer world, although he conceded that others might argue that he had deceived himself in believing in his own existence on earth. To which St. Augustine replies:

I am most certain that I am and that I know and delight in this. . . . I am not at all afraid of the Academicians who say, what if you are deceived? For if I am deceived, I am. For he who is not, cannot be deceived; and if I am deceived, I am.

As is so often the case in history, what a seer, prophet, or philosopher believes to be the result of novel and original inspiration almost invariably turns out to be a remembered insight from some perhaps long-forgotten book or author.

Chapter 5

The Great Renewal

T HE doldrums in which the idea of progress lay during the Renaissance began to disappear amid the gathering winds and currents of doctrine in the Reformation. Whatever else the Reformation may be in historical scholarship, it is one of the major religious awakenings in history. If our minds tend to think first of the Protestant manifestations of this resurgence of Christian commitment, similar manifestations of the Roman Catholic Church should not be left out of our considerations. The great schism led to rich intellectual contributions from Catholic as well as Protestant circles.

Renewal of Christian faith in Europe brought with it the revival of ideas which had been closely connected with Christianity from the time of the Church Fathers through the Middle Ages but which had languished or been driven from the scene during the Renaissance. The idea of progress was prominent among them. Whether in so deeply Catholic a work as the Bishop Bossuet's *Discourse on Universal History* or in the multitude of books and tracts which issued forth from the Puritans in the seventeenth century, it is clear that thinkers recovered their belief in the linear progress of humanity.

We shall be concerned in this chapter with the period stretching roughly from 1560 to 1740, beginning with the seminal ideas of Jean Bodin and concluding with those of the Italian Giambattista Vico. In between, for our purposes, lie the Puritan Revolt and, closely allied to it, the remarkable efflorescence of the arts and sciences in England during the seventeenth century; the Quarrel of the Ancients and Moderns; the burgeoning literature on voyages and discoveries, and its contributions to the theory of progress; and the restoration to European philosophy of the concepts of plenitude and continuity by the great Leibniz.

Jean Bodin

I am aware of the frequent inclusion of this extraordinary figure in the context of the Renaissance. Without doubt Bodin had his share of interests and beliefs we were concerned with in the preceding chapter—among them the idea of cycles, preoccupation with the occult, and, lamentably, deep conviction of the reality of witchcraft.

But this said, and in full recognition of his dates (1530?–96), I believe there are overriding reasons for *not* considering him as primarily and essentially a man of the Renaissance, and considering him instead as a kind of morning star of the philosophy of history, of the belief in human progress, that takes shape in the seventeenth and eighteenth centuries as a part of the great renewal of religious commitment. There is, to begin with, Bodin's obvious respect for medieval institutions and values. In his most famous work, *Six Books on the Commonweale,* published in France in 1576 and translated into the English with immediate and large effect in 1603, Bodin provides us with more than the theory of sovereignty for which he is perhaps most celebrated. This is a work in the philosophy of history also. And it is a mark of Bodin's respect for the traditional, cumulative character of human society's history that in the early part of his *Commonweale* Bodin offers praise for the guilds, monasteries, and fraternities which had grown up during the Middle Ages. Far from detesting them and wishing to be rid of them, Bodin sees them as important layers of membership between individual and political sovereign.

Another quality that separates Bodin from the Renaissance mind is his clear understanding of political power not merely in the hands of a prince but in the *state,* the territorial, sovereign state. Still another important element of conviction in Bodin, at once ancient and medieval, is his absolute insistence upon the patriarchal character of the family, with the father possessed of the kind of power that had inhered in the Roman *patria potestas.* If Bodin has to be seen looking backward to antiquity, he must be seen looking forward, in this respect, to Blackstone's *Commentaries* which had so much to do with securing all patriarchal tendencies in the law and with virtually obliterating female rights and privileges in legal, political, and economic matters.

Next, there is in Bodin a respect for institutional, revealed religion, for the structure as well as content of religion, that is of course largely alien to the Renaissance. His extraordinary, almost timeless *Colloquium of the Seven about the Secrets of the Sublime,* which lay in manuscript (Latin) for close to 300 years and was to be published at last in 1857 but was only very recently translated by Marion Kuntz into English, reveals Bodin as a deeply learned student of comparative religion. The colloquy has representatives of all religions—one each for Roman Catholicism, Lutheranism, Calvinism, Islam, and Judaism, one for all other religions in the world and, finally, one for all sects in the world. Tolerance is the outstanding feature of the colloquy among the seven. And such tolerance is the issue of respect, not cynical disdain, for religion. There must be in the good state complete political acceptance of all religions which do not by their nature seek to prevent tolerance of others. What, we are led to ask, is Bodin's own religious faith? There is no obvious answer, but the best guess seems to be Judaism which, in Bodin's hands, is the embodiment of The Law.

Finally, as an equally impressive mark of the modernity of Bodin's mind there is his advocacy of free trade within a nation and among nations—in the interests of economic justice. Not until we come to the Physiocrats and Adam Smith in the eighteenth century do we find the theory of free trade set forth as clearly and convincingly as we do in Bodin's *Response to a Paradox of Monsieur Malestroict.* All in all, then, Bodin's is a truly remarkable mind. If he were but three-legged we could accurately have one leg in the Middle Ages, another in the Renaissance, and the third in the modern world of thought.

Let us turn to his philosophy of history, as set forth in some degree in *Commonweale,* which had immense effect in the decades following its publication (among its recognized virtues was Bodin's utter hostility to the ideas of Machiavelli), and, more systematically, in his treatise on historical method. The first thing we notice in both works is respect for the past; respect and also desire to show the indispensability of the past so far as understanding of the present is concerned. Bodin stresses the importance of time and its epochs, of causes and processes involved in our understanding of history. Religious, fully respectful of God's role in the unfolding of human progress, he nevertheless interests himself in such phenomena as climate and topography as factors in the advances and declines of single empires and peoples. Not until Montesquieu in the eighteenth century does there appear in Western writing as sophisticated a treatment of political geography as we get in Bodin.

His *Method of Understanding History (Methodus ad facilem historiarum cognitionem)* published in 1566, ten years before the more famous *Commonweale* appeared, is probably the best source for our understanding of Bodin's theory of mankind's progress, though the *Commonweale,* especially in the early parts, and also the colloquy in the *Heptaplomeres,* cannot be excluded.

What Bodin gives us is a panoramic view of the origin and development of human society. He is very critical of the myth of the Golden Age—one more mark of his differentness from so many of the minds of the Renaissance—and tells us that this primal age "if it be compared with ours, would seem iron in nature." The beginnings of humanity are marked by ignorance, terror of the unknown, oppression, and constant insecurity, the result of ignorance of the arts.

And yet it is not the abstract, imaginary "state of nature" Bodin gives us, the condition which would be the point of departure for so much political writing during the two following centuries, and from which, according to this writing, human beings escaped only by a "social contract." Bodin is much more the developmentalist than Hobbes or Locke would be:

> The beginnings of all civil societies are derived from a family, which is (as we say) itself a natural society. . . . But when reason, by God himself ingrafted in us, had made man desirous of the company and society of man, and to participate together both in speech and conversation; the same so wrought, as that proceeding farther from the love of them that were domestic and their own, it extended farther, to take pleasure in the propagation and increase of families. So also families by little and little departing from the first beginning, learned by civil society to imitate the natural society of a family.

Human society, then, has its origin in the kinship group, and development takes the form of formation of other, more diverse, groups and associations which although modelled on the family make possible an ever more variegated existence. It is worth repeating that for Bodin it is utter folly to glorify the beginnings of things. Family notwithstanding, "men were scattered like beasts in the fields and woods and had as much as they could keep by means of force and crime, until gradually they were reclaimed from that ferocity and barbarity to the refinement of customs and the law-abiding society we see about us."

It is progress—unfolding, developing, advancing—and not regress or degeneration that Bodin sees as overridingly characteristic of the human condition from its primitive beginnings. If human affairs "were becoming worse, long ago we should have reached the extreme limit of vices and improbity, whither indeed I think in times gone by they had arrived." He contrasts the manner in which the ancients including the Greeks and Romans dealt with captive peoples—enslaving, torturing, and mutilating them for public enjoyment—with the far more humane condition of all human beings under Christianity. Human sacrifice, he points out, existed widely in the so-called golden age of mankind, whereas we, the moderns, have abolished it altogether.

Turning to knowledge, Bodin is every bit the modern; there is no extravagant, Renaissance-like mooning over the achievements of the Greeks and Romans. Bodin respects them, yes, but he does not worship them:

> Some will say that the ancients were inventors of the arts and to them the glory ought to go. They certainly did discover many things—especially the power of the celestial bodies, the calculated course of many stars, but yet not all, the wonderful trajections of fixed stars and of those called 'planets' . . . [Y]et they left incomplete many of those things which have been completed and handed down to posterity by men of our own time . . . Although nothing is more remarkable in the whole nature of things than the magnet, yet the ancients were not aware of its use, clearly divine, and whereas they lived entirely within the Mediterranean basin, our men, on the other hand, traverse the whole earth every year in frequent voyages and lead colonies into another world, as I might say, in order to open the farthest recesses of India . . . Indeed, in geography, one of the most excellent arts, one may understand how much advance has been made from the fact that information about India which used to seem fabulous to many . . . have been verified by us, as well as the motion of the fixed stars and the trepidation of the great sphere . . . [H]ealthful medicines are daily brought forth . . . I pass over the method of investigating celestial longtitude from equal hours, which could not be calculated by the ancients from the normal to the ecliptic without great error . . . I omit finally countless arts, both handicraft and weaving, with which the life of man has been aided in a remarkable way. Printing alone can easily vie with all the discoveries of the ancients.

Two important points should be made here about Bodin's metholological approach. He is insistent, in the first place, upon the historian's responsibility for using only verified natural causes—climate and geographical terrain are examples he cites—and for utilizing to maximum degree valid documents. He impresses upon the historian that "our system of chronology from the Creation must be taken out of historical documents." And, in the second place, there is no evident concern in Bodin with any future ending of the world. As we shall see, he is well aware of the phenomena of decay and decline in human history, but these are but cycles, with each new cycle on a higher level. But as to any ending of the world: "Not even the angels know—certainly no one of us mortals." So much for doomsday predictions! Above all, the historian must be as calm and objective as possible. He refers to those self-styled historians who forever "contradict themselves, either from zeal or anger or error."

The study of mankind's progress must be made, in sum, through use of reason, through diligent research and investigation, and with wary eye on the foibles of human observation. But of the reality of long-range, human advancement in all spheres, there is not the slightest doubt in Bodin's mind. His words on St. Louis, the king of France are striking:

> . . . what prince of all antiquity can be compared to St. Louis the king? . . . certainly no such devotion of any prince towards God, responsibility to his country, love toward his subjects, and justice to all have been recorded. Not only the virtues of our men are equal to those of the ancients but also the disciplines.

Yet, as I have indicated, Bodin was not blind to the facts of decay at the expense of being aware of development in the great panorama of history. He is as sensitive as Machiavelli to *ricorsi,* but whereas Machiavelli saw history as scarcely more than an endless repetition of things, without overall advancement, Bodin sees the cycles of genesis and decay following one another at a constantly ascending level.

"Literature suffers changes of fortune." In this statement Bodin manifests his awareness of the fact that the arts, as we study them in history, "flourish for a time at a fixed level, then languish in their old age, and finally begin to die and are buried into a lasting oblivion." All of this because of too many wars, too much intellectual decadence brought about by affluence, or because God himself inflicts just punishments on writers as well as others from time to time. Such rise and fall, Bodin goes on, are plainly to be seen in the histories of Greece and Rome (and of other, earlier, or different societies). The Greeks eventually declined, Bodin seems to assert, by virtue of their belief that they and their works were at the highest possible peak of human achievement. The same is true of Rome, where "talented men were so abundant that almost simultaneously they excelled all peoples in warlike glory and in superiority of culture." Yet they too eventually yielded to forces of decay and decline. But fall is followed in the larger history of mankind by rise; decay, by fresh genesis. New cycles come into being. And each later cycle reflects a higher level of achievement than its predecessor:

> So they who say that all things were understood by the ancients err not less than do those who deny them the conquest of many arts. *Nature has countless treasures of knowledge which cannot be exhausted in any one age.*
> Since these things are so and since by some eternal law of nature the path of

change seems to go in a circle, so that vices press upon virtues, ignorance upon knowledge . . . and darkness upon light, they are mistaken who think that the race of men always deteriorates. When old men err in this respect, it is understandable that this should happen to them—that they sigh for the loss of the flower of youth, which of itself breathes joy and cheerfulness . . . . As though, returning from a distant journey, they narrate the golden century—the golden age—to the young men. (Italics added)

But however understandable such nostalgia may be, it is not, Bodin tells us, to be believed. The present is in fact better than the past, and the future will be better than the present. All of this is a part of God's design, the result of forces and causes which, though natural and temporal, are products of God's will. It is true that Bodin does not spend any time specifically on the future; what was there to say unless one were to lapse into idle utopianism? But his utter rejection of any of the doctrines of degeneration which had been cardinal elements of the Renaissance, the high regard he has for his own age in history, and perhaps above all, the profound care he took in writing his great treatise on politics as the means of making government more humane and effective suggest a mind very much attuned to the future. There is also—and this is evident in nearly all of his important works including the *Commonweale, Methodus,* and the *Heptaplomeres*— Bodin's very keen interest in the world at large, in the totality of peoples living on earth in the past as well as in the present. He was an ardent patriot, a member of a group in France that called itself *Les Politiques* and correctly saw the incapacity of any institution other than the sovereign territorial state for maintaining order, given the collapse of unified Christianity. But, patriot, even nationalist though Bodin was, he had a conception of the unity of mankind that is Augustinian, a conception easily wedded to the envisagement of humanity's progress through the ages. There is every reason, in sum, for seeing Bodin—his medievalist and Renaissance traits notwithstanding—as the morning star of the age that would yield the West an interest in—a preoccupation with—history and progress beyond anything known in ancient or medieval times.

The Puritan Revolution

I refer to the political and social revolution, of course, but much more to the intellectual revolution, especially in the arts and sciences, which the Puritans had so much to do with. It is impossible to find any single conjunction more fruitful to the emergence of the modern idea of progress than that between faith in the arts and sciences on the one hand and, on the other, in a millennium ahead which progress in the arts and sciences could only hasten.

Despite the still popular phrase "The Age of Reason," it is far better to conceive of the seventeenth century as the Age of Faith—religious faith. As John Redwood writes in his recent study of the intellectual scene we are now concerned with, "Seventeenth century thought was God-ridden." So it was. Thomas Hobbes and a few others excepted, it is impossible to find any genuinely notable names in the sciences or the arts, in philosophy, or theology, which were not profoundly religious. This includes, as we shall see, even the greatest of the scientists of that day, Isaac Newton. His devout religious faith was no aberration, no indulgence of senescence. It was from boyhood until death the dominant influence upon his life.

Our chief concern here is with Puritan belief and achievement. No doubt with all the extensive and diversified scholarship done during the last several decades on the seventeenth-century Puritans in England, there has been exaggeration. It may well be, as Christopher Hill has recently observed, that the whole debate as to actual Puritan influence on English science, thought, and political action shows signs of becoming tedious. Even so, what is left of Puritanism as simply an intellectual phenomenon after all has been said and done will, without serious question, be impressive.

There is no exaggeration in saying that the rise and spread through intellectual England of Puritanism in the seventeenth century is the preeminent intellectual event of the century. Max Weber was the first but not the last to demonstrate that among other causes for the rise of the capitalist spirit in the modern world Puritanism must be ranked high. Since then, in scores of works, we have been assured too that it was within the Puritan Revolution that the first clear-cut working- and lower-class social radicalism made its appearance in modern Europe. Still others, commencing with Robert K. Merton's pioneering classic of four decades ago, have made incontestably clear how close are the roots of Puritan religious faith and the kind of science we associate with Newton and his contemporaries. This closeness is demonstrably more than coincidence. We have learned how passionately Newton and many another scientific mind, whether Puritan or Royalist, felt about religion and about what they perceived as the necessary linkage between science and religion. And, as Charles Webster has recently shown, even Baconianism was brought into the Puritan fold.

Nor is this all. It is apparent, as it was not but a very few decades ago in the general European histories, that the first great modern political and social revolution is not, as was so long believed, the French at the end of the eighteenth century, but the Puritan in the seventeenth. It may not have begun as a social revolution with capture of governing power its aim (but then neither did the French, later) but it was not long before all of the now-familiar attributes of political, social, and economic revolution were present in Puritan England. Very correctly and properly did the Jacobins in the early 1790s regard the Puritan revolutionists as their direct forebears.

Finally, and most pertinently for our purposes, it can be and has been shown that there is the very closest of intellectual relationships between Puritan millenarianism in the seventeenth century and the efflorescence in the next century of the "Modern" secular idea of progress, which as we shall see has, in the works of such minds as Condorcet, William Godwin, Saint-Simon, and Comte, its own form of millenarianism.

True, not everything important to us was Puritan. We might remember that Dr. Joseph Mede, whose extraordinary prophecies of the millennium made at the very beginning of the seventeenth century had such impact upon later Puritan thinkers, was himself a Cambridge scholar and presumably Anglican (he was also Newton's tutor). And it has been emphasized recently by Quentin Skinner that Gresham College, founded in 1597, one of the most notable centers of experimental work in the sciences in the century, was anything but Puritan. The same holds, Skinner points out, with respect to the Royal College of Physicians, where a great deal of observation and experimentation took place in the areas of physiology and medicine. It was Royalist and hostile toward Puritanism. And, we learn, of the substantial number of scientists at work at Oxford under the inspiration of the great William Harvey, none was Puritan. To the same point it must be stated that of the dozen scientists who formed the working nucleus of the Royal Academy in England, half were outright opponents of Puritanism. Finally, as we shall see in the next section of this chapter, one of the greatest of all expressions of the Christian doctrine of progress was that of the Catholic Bishop Bossuet in his *Discourse on Universal History* published in 1681.

We have acknowledged the non- and anti-Puritan sources of science and philosophy of history, and accepted the possibility of exaggeration or distortion of actual Puritan influence. Still, it remains impossible to do justice to modern thought, scientific and other, without explicit recognition of the large number of Puritans whose combinations of physical science (at the level of Newtonian genius), powerful statements of millenarianism after Joachim and his followers, and consecrated interest in a progressive philosophy of history are among the most fascinating and vital works of the seventeenth century.

Let us turn immediately to the idea of progress as we find it in Puritanism. E. L. Tuveson in his seminal *Millennium and Utopia* puts the matter in these words:

> Gradually the role of Providence was transferred to "natural laws" whereby God was thought to operate . . . Thus it is that "evolution" and "stages of advancement" have come to hold for modern man very much the same significance that "grace" had for his ancestors . . . The notion of history as a process generally moving upward by a series of majestic stages, culminating inevitably in some great, transforming event, which is to solve the dilemmas of society—that is the concept destined to dominate "modern" thought. Its forebears, I believe, are to be found in seventeenth-century apocalytic theorists, not in Renaissance cyclical historiographers.

Tuveson is assuredly correct in his assessment of the force and influence of the Puritan millenarians, and also in his reference to the Renaissance. What is missing, however, as Marjorie Reeves points out in the study of medieval prophecy we have drawn from previously, is reference to the real origins of Puritan apocalytic thinking. These we find, as Reeves documents fully, in persisting currents of Joachimite, twelfth-century prophecy. "One cannot study sixteenth- and seventeenth-century apocalyptists without putting them in the perspective of their medieval ancestry." As she points out, James Maxwell's *Admirable and Notable Prophecies* in 1615 was but one of a number of prophetic works in the century to acknowledge Joachim: "extraordinarily inspired" in Maxwell's words.

I have stressed several times in this book the great importance of recognizing *two* essential elements of progress: the first, introduced by the Greeks, centering on the advancement of the arts and sciences; the second, the product of Augustinian fusion of Jewish millenarianism and the Greek idea of unfolding growth into the Christian philosophy of history, which puts its emphasis upon not knowledge primarily but the spiritual state of bliss that mankind will ascend to prior to the ending of life on earth.

What is so striking about the Puritan conception of progress is that it clearly and firmly *unites* these two strands for the first time in Western history. Progress in the arts and sciences is held to be at once a *sign* of the imminence of the golden age of the spirit on earth and a *cause* of this imminence. Nor will this liason between knowledge and spiritual fulfillment end with the onset of the millennium. Calvin had expressed himself strongly on the proposition that, well before the return of God to this earth and his making of final judgment, there would take place a spread of knowledge throughout the world, one that would bring about the complete unity in Christ of all mankind, the Jews included. "The knowledge of God shall be spread throughout the whole world," prophesied Calvin; "the glory of God shall be known in every part of the world." But Calvin restricted knowledge entirely to sacred knowledge, that of God and his wonders. It is in the seventeenth century that we find Calvin's stress upon sacred knowledge widened to include all knowledge, including that found in the secular arts and sciences.

Nowhere in the century is there to be found more profound faith in the unity of religion and science than in Isaac Newton's works. The time is long gone when Newton's *Principia* can be treated as something separate from the religious and biblical studies with which he occupied himself throughout most of his life. In 1713 he wrote his General Scholium for the second edition of the *Principia;* it includes these words: "This most beautiful system of the Sun, planets, and comets, could only proceed from the counsel and dominion of an intelligent and powerful Being." The historian of science I. Bernard Cohen has emphasized the fact that Newton (and many of his contemporaries and also predecessors of the sixteenth century) sought to demonstrate irrefutably that the Copernican order was "the divine order." Still another student of the history of science, P.M. Rattansi, has written valuably on Newton's relation to the tradition "very much alive in Newton's England, that the millennium would be preceded by a flourishing of the arts and sciences that would bring men nearest to the condition of the prelapsarian Adam." And Frank E. Manuel, in his several brilliant and penetrating studies of Newton, notably in *The Religion of Isaac Newton,* has documented fully Newton's own absolute and unwavering conviction that his laws of motion and his unflagging studies of the biblical prophecies, especially those of Daniel and the Apocalypse, proceeded from exactly the same method. We learn that the products of his final years of biblical study were thought by Newton to be fully the equal of the propositions set forth in the *Principia.* Biblical and other religious investigations were, in Newton's own words—cited by Rattansi—"no idle speculation, no matter of indifferency, but a duty of the highest moment." Newton, of course, was but one of the many in his century who sought to demonstrate on the one hand the necessity of religious devotion to scientific achievement, and on the other, the indispensability of scientific observation and reasoning to a true understanding of the divine order.

The importance of all this to the idea of progress is obviously profound. Fundamental to the idea, as we have seen, is faith in the value of human knowledge, the kind of knowledge that is contained in the sciences and the practical arts, and faith also in the capacity of such knowledge to lift humanity to ever-higher levels of human life. For such an idea to become as deeply implanted in Western consciousness as it has, commencing with the Greeks and Romans and gathering added strength from the Christians, ordinary experience, logic, and reason are not enough. So sweeping a proposition as that which declares progress a *necessity* for mankind can scarcely be supported by the common rules of evidence. Deeper wells of faith are required, and these necessarily lead not so much to conclusion as to *dogma.*

And here is where Puritanism comes into the picture. This religion, more than any other making up Christianity, endowed knowledge—theoretical, practical, above all scientific—with millenarian importance. Only through the cultivation of research into nature and man, the Puritans argued, can the millennium be brought to an early existence on earth. They were not lacking in appreciation of what was going on around them in the sciences. Through the sheer abundance of scientists, of centers and institutes and colleges in which scientists dwelt, and of publication of the results of scientific researches, the millennium was bound to be in the very near future. So thought countless Puritans, as indeed did other religious groups in England, among them Anglicans.

And, as the religiously-intoxicated minds of the seventeenth century in England (and also in New England) were further intoxicated by faith in the arts and sciences, so were they still further intoxicated by confidence in progress as a universal law in mankind's history, a law that would give inevitability to a golden age on earth in the imminent future. When we come to the middle of the seventeenth century and after, God is no longer seen as a remote, separate, directing omnipotence. He becomes understandable, rather, as a kind of *process.* Ernest Tuveson cites the influential Burnet very pertinently to this point:

You ought always to have before your eyes, and always in your designs, the *progress of Providence* in gradually promoting Piety in the world and in illuminating Humankind. (Italics added)

"The progress of Providence!" Burnet's phrase could serve perfectly to epitomize the crucial historical process we are concerned with in this chapter: that by which belief in the Christian God was supplanted in the minds of intellectuals by belief in a certain natural and inexorable pattern of progress. In Burnet's phrase we see God-the-being transposed into God-the-unfolding, God-the-advancing. The faith in the permanence and regularity of natural law which so many historians ascribe to Cartesian sources might better be ascribed to Christian, chiefly Puritan. How easy, really, it would be for Turgot, Condorcet, and others in the next century to let God slip away entirely. The way had been prepared by the type of thinking among Puritans so well represented by Burnet.

Other ages, including the Renaissance and going all the way back at least to the Greeks, had found knowledge in the arts and sciences important, as something to cherish. But the signal contribution of the Puritans in the seventeenth-century in England was to endow the arts and sciences with something a great deal more majestic than mere utilitarian importance: that is, with redemptive value. Just as religion was made the prime justification for unceasing study of nature and man, so was this study made absolutely necessary to the proper enhancement of religion. John Edwards, in 1699, is quoted by Robert Merton thusly: "And why proportionable Improvement in Divine Knowledge and in Moral and Christian Endowments may not be expected, I confess I don't understand. Can there be any Reason why God should not prosper Religion as well as the Arts?" It is impossible not to be struck by the order in which Edwards places religion and the arts. And just before the words cited are these, also from Edwards: "Thus we surpass all the times that have been before us; and it is highly probable that those that succeed, will far surpass these."

There is still another major contribution to the modern idea of progress that is found in a great deal of Puritan philosophical and scientific writing. This has to do with the way or the conditions through which mankind will at last enter into the millennium. As we saw, for Joachim and for a great many of his followers and successors during the next several centuries, attainment of the golden age on earth, Joachim's "Age of Spirit," demanded a heavy price: a period of time in which anarchy would prevail, in which torments would multiply, in which strife of every kind would become dominant. And the millennium, when it did finally come, would come suddenly, precipitately, blindingly. What we find in Puritan writing (not all, by any means, but a great deal, especially that of the great theologians and scientists), however, is the millennium conceived as but a stage, the final earthly stage, of human progress. Evolution, not revolution, is the essence. And this too is a prime ingredient of nineteenth-century theories of progress, along with the spirit of reform and utilitarian emphasis upon the material happiness of mankind.

Richard F. Jones in his *Ancients and Moderns* has suggested that "our modern utilitarianism is the offspring of Bacon begot upon Puritanism." There is every reason to think Professor Jones correct. Religious the seventeenth century assuredly was; but it was the kind of religion, especially among Puritans, that was easily combinable with utilitarianism and reform —social and political reform. It is quite possible that the modern sense of "the public" arose in this rather than the next century. As Jones emphasizes, "the public good" has increasing currency as phrase and thought during the seventeenth century. Human needs, perhaps for the first time since the ancient classical world, take on reality in the minds of philosophers, scientists, and theologians. Man in the seventeenth century, in England at least, becomes social minded. And with this went the spirit of reform; a spirit then, as in later centuries, tightly linked to assumed patterns of natural or Providential progress.

In no respect did the passion for reform-linked-to-progress exceed its orientation to education. Rarely even since has the desire for the razing of the old and the building of the new—in the light of science and reason—been as great as it was in England in the seventeenth century. John Webster, in the beginning a Cambridge scholar and then a member of the parliamentary army, published in 1654 the very proposal indeed for the clearing out of the antique and useless from the universities. In one chapter titled "Customs and Method," Webster rails against the indulgence at the universities of student sloth and waywardness in respect to their studies. He complains that students "never go out by industrious searches and observant experiments, to find out the mysteries contained in nature." Webster attacks the use of Latin instead of English, the ridiculous respect paid to Aristotle and to classical antiquity generally. As Richard Jones writes: "His view of the English language is worthwhile, and suggests the part that science, and Puritanism too, played in depreciating Latin and in recognizing the importance of the mother tongue." Webster writes that the Greeks and Romans had the pride and intelligence to use their own languages, "yet we, neglecting our own, do foolishly admire and entertain that of strangers, which is no less a ridiculous than prejudicial custome."

Hostility to the universities in England was widespread. (Hobbes hated them, and blamed them in substantial degree for the outbreak of the Civil War.) But it was the Puritan attack, of which Webster's book was a signal part, that had far greater force. For what the Puritans desired was the expunging from the universities of all efforts at the inculcation of religion and piety. After all, the Bible was sufficient for all religious ends. Therefore let the universities confine themselves to knowledge in the secular realm, above all the scientific-experimental. In no respect was there greater liaison between Bacon and the Puritans than in the matter of university curriculum. That emphasis upon the practical and utilitarian which we ordinarily associate with nineteenth-century theories of progress flourished in the seventeenth century wherever Puritans spoke out. They recommended the abandonment of divinity and all associated studies; they subordinated classical science to that embodied in direct observation and experiment; they proposed the abolition or at least significant reduction of the humanities in the universities, with such fields as mathematics, chemistry, geography, and outrightly vocational courses to take the place of the study of classical language and literature. With only occasional exception Puritan attitude toward the classical education, so prominent in the Middle Ages, the Renaissance and again in the nineteenth century prior to the fresh wave of reform in the name of utility, was one of unremitting hostility—and in the name of popular progress. Experimental scientists, Bishop Sprat declared, much preferred "the language of artisans, countrymen, and merchants before that of wits and scholars."

I have mentioned the deep interest in progress conceived in terms of sequential stages found among Puritan scientists and theologians. There was a very close relationship between the projects and schemes for the reform of education and social order of the kind so well associated with the names of Glanvil, Hooke, and Boyle and the kind of progressive history that such men as Glanvil and Sprat wrote. Glanvil in his *Plus Ultra: or, the Progress and Advancement of Knowledge since the Days of Aristotle* saw steady progress in science—true science—since the days of the Greeks, and saw this progress setting the stage in his own time for even greater progress in the future: "We must seek and gather, observe and examine, and lay up in bank for the ages that come after." Robert Merton in his study of Puritanism and science cites a contemporary of Glanvil, one Jeremy Shakerly, in these progress-intoxicated words: "And indeed what shall we mortals now despair of? Within what bounds shall our wits be contained?" What bounds indeed, given the burst of scientific achievements taking place all around him and, not to be forgotten, the coming millennium when science and human happiness would be firmly linked, perhaps forever.

The best example, though, of a study of past and present that demonstrates the progress of knowledge is Thomas Sprat's notable *History of the Royal Society* published in 1667. Richard F. Jones writes: "Its importance lies not only in its being the most elaborate and comprehensive defence of the Society and experimental philosophy in this century, but more especially in its constituting an official statement on the matter." But Sprat's work has an importance beyond even that. Its greatest objective is to put the wonderful Royal Society in historical perspective, thus to vindicate historical progress by reference to the Society and to celebrate the Society by declaring it the triumph of historical progress. Baconian though Sprat is in temper, there is a respect for and a reliance upon the evolving processes of history—a sense of the cumulative character of progress—that we do not find in Bacon.

Sprat begins his book with an account of the rise of science in the ancient East and its spread to classical Greece and Rome. Without denying initiative and intelligence in the ancient world, he is careful to note the crippling effects of the classical scientists' aversion to experiment, to using their hands for discovery of truth. Sprat doesn't deny even the philosophers of the Middle Ages acumen and skill in reasoning, but, given scholastic fixation with abstractions and "notions," their ideas could not develop. There was, Sprat tells us, no way by which either the Schoolmen or anyone else could move from their apparatus of thought to actual study of the external world. Whatever continuing place scholastic thought may have, properly, in the schools for the training of young minds, it has no place whatever in an organization such as the Royal Society.

There is not space here to describe even in the terms of Sprat's general historical perspectives the contents of the first part of his book. It is enough to say that throughout, whether dealing with Greeks, medieval minds, or moderns, his touchstone of excellence is, unfailingly, willingness to observe and experiment. He is suspicious, or at least hesitant in his praise, of some of the greatest moderns by virtue of their tendency to turn to grand theory, mathematical or other. For Sprat there is one great form of inquiry alone— that epitomized by the experiment. The past has contributed a great deal, though unevenly, to the present, but the sovereign task of the present, and also the future, is commitment to gathering of data and refining it through modest, tentative conclusions. For the Cartesian type of mind, driven to the discovery of great encompassing laws, Sprat has scant sympathy and much criticism.

The second part of his *History* is given entirely to the Royal Society—its rise, its progress, and the kinds of work which most distinguish it. Sprat lauds what he terms the modesty of the first members, or rather their restraint; not for them, he writes, the framing of all-inclusive laws. Their purpose was to "heap up a mixed mass of experiments, without digesting them into any perfect model . . ." Richard Jones ably paraphrases: "They [the Royal Society experimenters] experimented for data, not for theories, because hastiness in devising the latter seemed to them 'the *Fatal point,* about which so many of the greatest *Wits* of all ages have miscarried' ". And although the experimenters allowed absolute freedom for those seeking to experiment their way to truth, they insisted always upon "the *critical* and *reiterated* scrutiny of those things which are the plain objects of their eyes."

Sprat has no hesitation whatever in seeing the Royal Society, or the kind of work at least contained in it, as the road to the golden future. His words, cited by Professor Jones, are eloquent and optimistic in the extreme.

> . . . by bringing *Philosophy* down again to men's sight and practice, from when it was flown away so high: the *Royal Society* has put it into a condition of standing out, against the invasions of *Time,* or even *Barbarism* itself . . . they [the founders of

the Society] have provided that it cannot hereafter be extinguished, at the loss of a Library, at the overthrowing of a Language, or at the death of some few *Philosophers;* but that men must lose their *eyes* and *hands,* and must leave off desiring to make their *Lives* convenient, or pleasant; before they can be willing to *destroy* it.

The very last part of the *History* is concerned with a still more forthright defense of the experimental road to knowledge, in which Sprat seeks to assuage the fears of those who think such a road might lead to destruction in time of Christian faith, the Church of England, business, commerce, the nobility, gentry, indeed the whole of the English nation. Far from any evil being visited upon the people, what we shall see, Sprat insists, is the opposite. "The beautiful bosom of *Nature* will be exposed to our view . . . we shall enter its Garden and taste of its *Fruits,* and satisfy our selves with its *plenty."*

Melvin Lasky in *Utopia and Revolution* has discerningly brought out the extravagantly utopian cast of Sprat's mind—and also its seeming prescience. Sprat was attracted to the vision of America becoming a power in its own right. ". . . if ever that vast Tract of *Ground* shall come to be more familiar to Europe, either by a free Trade, or by Conquest, or by another *Revolution* in its Civil Affairs, *America* will appear quite a new *Thing* to us." As Lasky suggests, very early on, then, "some kind of American Revolution became part of the utopian dream." Not that Sprat was completely consistent in his several expressions of the kinds of minds which would be required for the continuing progress of science. He writes in one place of the need for "violent and fiery . . . the Impetuous men," on the ground that indispensable and valuable though experiment is, it cannot survive dullards, men without grand vision. On the other hand Sprat can speak of the new scientists' "assurance of eternal quietness and moderation in their experimental programs."

There is, as Lasky tells us, one point in Sprat's discourse that establishes his affinity with those later scholars—beginning with Vico in the early eighteenth century, through Hume and Turgot in the same century, to Maine and Tocqueville in the nineteenth, all the way to Teggart and Toynbee in the twentieth—who see intellectual ferment and advance a function of social and political, even military, disorder. Sprat writes:

The late times of *Civil War,* and *confusion,* to make recompense for their infinite calamities, brought this advantage with them, that they stirred men's minds from long ease, and a lazy rest, and made them *active, industrious* and *inquisitive:* it being the usual benefit that follows upon *Tempests,* and *Thunders* in the *State,* as well as in the sky, that they purify, and clear the *Air,* which they disturb.

Sprat serves as a kind of bridge between the developmentalist-uniformitarian mentality—a type of mind that sought to show how through successive, cumulative, gradual advances of knowledge men may reach the millennium without turmoil—and that other, explosive, no less Puritan type of mind that sees the millennium as a product of progressive advancement, if we will, but an end requiring for its complete success violence, war, and even terror. There is no better representation of this latter, catastrophic type of Puritan mind than the Fifth Monarchy Men who sought desperately to turn Cromwell's war and revolution to their own apocalyptic ends. According to Fifth Monarchy belief there had already existed four great stages or "monarchies" in world history (described in Daniel when the Book is read properly, it was argued): the Babylonian-Assyrian, the Mede-Persian, the Greek, and the Roman. All had been evil, but all were necessary as steps toward the fifth which, inaugurated by the Puritans' own revolution, would result in earth and mankind being governed by Christ himself, who, however, would return only after the world had been cleansed utterly of the wicked and thus made good again. Such a cleansing was bound to be a drastic step, one inseparable from sword and torch. Fifth Monarchy Men could remember, even as had the millenarian Jews in the first century, struggling to protect Jerusalem from the Romans, that According to the Book of Daniel, triumph and fulfillment would only come as the result of "a time of trouble, such as never has been since there was a nation." They were prepared to act accordingly. What Guenter Lewy has written on the Fifth Monarchy movement is clarifying:

The first collective effort to establish the Fifth Monarchy and the emergence of the millenarians as an organized group or party took the form of a petition from Norfolk, presented to the leaders of the army in February, 1649. The authors of *Certain Queries Humbly Presented in Way of Petition by many Christian People Dispersed Abroad throughout the County of Norfolk* declared that they expected "new heavens and a new earth" and they warned against patching up the "old worldly government" of the ungodly. Instead a visible Kingdom of Christ and the saints was to be erected though it would come into being not "by human power and authority" but by mandate of God and Christ.

Let us not fail to see the reference in the petition to "a new earth" and the warning against patching things up instead of totally reconstructing. The revolutionary spirit of progress was very much in the breasts of these folk. And we might observe too that despite the belief that this total reconstruction on earth would be the work of God and Christ, not "human power and authority," it was precisely human power and authority that, before the

Puritan revolt was ended, reached heights in organized government only rarely seen before in European history.

By 1651, we read, there were regular meetings of the Fifth Monarchy sect in London where it grew rapidly, attracting both men and women in large numbers, chiefly from the urban lower classes. Then too there were the recruits from the New Model Army: officers with ranks as high as colonel as well as lower grade officers and, in substantial number, the unlettered but passionately committed enlisted soldiers.

The degree to which the Fifth Monarchy movement was bred in genuine social consciousness, that is, conscious and active desire to improve the lot of the poor and oppressed, is, I admit, debatable. The target was not the identifiable miseries of the masses; it was an absolute, a total transformation of the earth and all that lived on it through the power of Christ and his message. But we are obliged nevertheless to see—in the outright hatred of pomp, rank, and power among the mighty, especially in the established churches, but also in government and economy where opposition could be detected—that the Fifth Monarchy preachers and pamphleteers widely broadcast more than a few implications of purely social character. Granted: the touchstone for the devout was a spiritual one, a belief in the existence of a society of true saints on earth into whose hands all power on earth would eventually fall; the fact remains that a century and a half later, it was *virtue,* civic morality, that above anything else inspired the makers of the French Revolution, an event plainly enough endowed with social, economic, and political effects.

The ease with which Christ could be supplemented with purely earthly rulers and reformers as a means of instituting the fifth and golden age on earth is illustrated by the early liaison effected between Fifth Monarchy representatives and Oliver Cromwell himself. There was great joy in the hearts of most of the movement when they learned of Cromwell's interest, and he was even regarded as the Moses who would lead the way. Although there were some proto-populists who thought the government of saints should be chosen by ballot, there were many others, including the powerful and vocal John Rogers, preacher at St. Thomas Apostle, who argued for a Sanhedrin of seventy impeccable earthly saints to be chosen by Cromwell, "the great Deliverer of his people (through God's grace) out of the house of Egypt."

Nor, in the beginning, was Cromwell deaf to Fifth Monarchy preachings. In 1653, speaking before the Nominated or Little Parliament, a highly millenarian body of men, Cromwell with due reference to the Fifth Monarch gospel hailed the members of the newly formed body as true Saints, declaring (according to Professor Lewy):

. . . I confess I never looked to see such a Day as this . . . when Jesus Christ should be so owned as He is, this day, in this work . . . And why should we be afraid to say or think, That *this* may be the door to usher-in the Things that God has promised . . . Indeed I do think somewhat is at the door; we are at the threshhold . . .

At the threshold! Precisely the same spirit, albeit somewhat more secularized, would animate the leaders of the French and then the Russian Revolutions.

Of course the amity between Cromwell and the millenarian Fifth Monarchy did not last. Though sympathetic to their visions and cravings, he was one of the world's great political realists when the crunches came. It was inevitable that the day would come when he would be condemned by the progress-intoxicated millenarians, those who demanded not reforms in government and law but absolute destruction of all existing government and law and replacement of them with the laws found in the Bible. Cromwell's dissolving of the Little Parliament alienated them completely. From then on, conflict between the Lord Protector and a highly disillusioned Fifth Monarchy sect became ever more bitter. Cromwell castigated them and all other millenarians at a meeting of the next parliament; he referred with scorn to their pretensions that *they,* rather than Jesus Christ alone, could rule the earth well and wisely. We have a record of the strange, almost bizarre meeting between Cromwell and John Rogers that led up to this parliamentary denunciation.

But the Fifth Monarchy did not give up lightly. Merely consider the following title of a sermon delivered by Thomas Goodwin during September of the same year in which Cromwell had lastingly broken with, and denounced, the Saints: "A Sermon of the Fifth Monarchy, Proving by Invincible Arguments That the Saints shall have a Kingdom here on Earth, Which is yet to come, after the Fourth Monarchy is destroy'd by the Sword of the Saints, the followers of the Lamb." John Rogers was so convinced of the imminence of the Fifth Monarchy that in a pamphlet written in 1653 titled *Sagrir, Doomesday drawing nigh* he predicted that the Monarchy would be established in England well before 1660 and would have reached even Rome by that year, then to become "visible in all the earth" by 1666.

Although the coming of the Fifth Monarchy was rendered inevitable by divinely laid historical progression through time, and in the minds of Fifth Monarchy zealots could not possibly be altered, much less prevented, there was nevertheless much attention given to the practical aspects of the matter. In *A Standard Set Up,* published in 1657, various prescriptions, plans, and promises were set down. There would be complete equality before the law, and no one would be imprisoned save for just and recognized cause. All excise taxes, customs charges, and tithes would be abolished. So would unjust tenure of lands be terminated, as would rents of any kind. (Although the Levellers were no longer a genuinely active force, having been severely weakened by Cromwell in 1649, many of their egalitarian ideas were assimilated by the Fifth Monarchy Men.) Finally, in the same manifesto it is declared that the Saints through their Sanhedrin would make changes in the peoples' rights and liberties only when "the good of the people" demanded them. Given such promises as these, it is not difficult to understand the fact that the Fifth Monarchy would appeal to a great many of the lower classes. For them any golden future on earth would be best envisaged in terms of cessation of taxes and rents. The manifesto written in 1660, *A Door of Hope,* stressed the desire "to take off all yoaks and oppressions both of civil and spiritual nature from the necks of the poor people."

This is not the place to deal with the decline and fall of the Fifth Monarchy movement. Suffice it to say that Cromwell's influence proved too great. More and more of the members changed faiths, many of them becoming Quakers. Before the century had ended there were only fading memories of the glorious visions of the Fifth Monarch. Indeed by the end of the century, just about all Puritan millenarianism as such had been spent.

But let us not overlook either the intensity of Fifth Monarchy belief at the time or its capacity for becoming a precedent for later beliefs. As to the importance of the Fifth Monarchy at the time, Melvin Lasky in his *Utopia and Revolution* cites the result of one modern historian's investigation of the seventeenth-century pamphlet collection of the London bookseller George Thomason. During the period 1640–43, according to the study, 70 percent of the hundreds of works published can be properly regarded as millenarian. In such works is to be found belief in an impending golden age, a kingdom of glory and righteousness, and belief also in the absolute necessity of war and other forms of violence to make this kingdom possible.

In some ways the most remarkable aspect of the entire cause was the conviction in the minds of men as able and influential as John Rogers that what was already under way in England would quickly win success there and then pass to the rest of the world. According to Lasky, Rogers's calculations led to the prediction that by 1660 the transformation would reach Rome and by 1666 "be visible in all the earth."

As to the historic effects of the Fifth Monarchy mentality, it will suffice to quote Lasky's arresting summation:

"Thunder and lightning . . . overturning days . . . teetering and tumbling affairs . . . blood will have blood . . . domes-day drawing nigh . . . the rule of the just . . . a true reformation . . . . A flood tide of change . . . audacious men and dark prophecies . . . words are actions . . . the minds of men . . . purge the nation . . . overthrow

rotten structures . . . the holy destruction of the evil of oppression and injustice . . . the golden age is at hand . . . the fire and the sword.

Lasky continues:

For three centuries these basic accents, with a few historic variations, would remain the basic elements in the world of the radical temper. They are the constant links of the great chain of human hope. A modern cycle of revolution would begin with its saints and end with its scientists.

There are historians of modern Europe who are prone to distinguish sharply the explosive, catastrophic, and apocalyptic prophecies and manifestos of the Puritans (and indeed other groups answering to this description—the utopians of the nineteenth century, for example) from the mentality represented by the idea of progress. Progress, it is declared, always means slow, gradual, and cumulative change in time. Millennialists and utopians are interested only in the sudden, drastic, power-laden accession to the perfect society, with instruments of coercion, torture, and terror always at hand.

But this is too restricted and artificial a conception of the idea of progress. What the idea means, as we have seen, is first and foremost that humanity is advancing toward some goal continuously, inexorably, and necessarily. Such an idea is as valuable—indeed, it is indispensable—to the chiliastic mind bent upon sudden transformation through whatever means, as it is to a Turgot, Mill, or Spencer. Those who risk their own lives, who are not allowed to shrink from the most wanton acts of violence and terror against others, must have a faith unless they are mere masochists or sadists. From the post-medieval disciples of Joachim, eager to hasten through sword and torch the onset and completion of the time of terror that must precede the arrival of the millennium, through the zealots of the Puritan Revolution, through the Jacobins in the French Revolution, down to the Lenins, Stalins, Hitlers, and Maos of the twentieth century, the most awful of persecutions, tortures, massacres, and sieges of terror have had for their justification a sense of historical development, of *necessary* development, every bit as galvanizing as any Crusader's sense of God needing to be avenged against the infidel.

L'Envoi

Thomas Henry Buckle at the end of his famous chapter on the "influence exerted by religion, literature and government" on the progress of the intellect tells us that in the last part of the sixteenth century a child was born in Silesia with one tooth of gold. There was, Buckle informs us, great excitement all over Europe. A Dr. Horst came up with the most popular and widely believed answer for the phenomenon. The golden tooth, Dr. Horst explained, after making use of astrological and other arcane investigations, "was the precursor of the golden age, in which the Emperor would drive the Turks from Christendom, and lay the foundations of an empire that would last for thousands of years." And this, Dr. Horst added, in the spirit of the decades which would follow, is clearly foretold in Daniel, where, in the second chapter, the prophet speaks of a statue with a golden head.

Buckle, of course, in keeping with the theme of his great *History of Civilization* . . ., uses the incident as a means of piling on additional evidence of the intellectual backwardness and superstitiousness of Europe in the sixteenth and seventeenth centuries. But there is another way of interpreting the incident: as one small element of the growing, spreading, deepening faith in western Europe at the time in the imminent millennium, the most golden of ages in the world since that of the prelapsarian Adam.

Bossuet's Universal History

It is a long step from the passion of Puritan millenarianism to the serene erudition in France of the Bishop Bossuet, adviser to Louis XIV, tutor to the Dauphin, and one of the Catholic Church's wisest and most judicious of leaders during the seventeenth century. Had he never written his *Discourse on Universal History,* published in 1681, he would have gained an important place in intellectual history by virtue of such other impressive works as his profoundly analytical and prophetic *Histoire des Variations des Eglises Protestantes.* No one else foresaw as clearly and explicitly as Bossuet the course of accelerating fractionation that Protestantism would take and hold to this day. He was the most famous preacher of his day in France, and his orations rank among the best of literary works in that age of consummate style.

Our concern will be solely with his *Discourse on Universal History.* It is, and was almost instantly recognized by other scholars in Europe as, a masterly synthesis of world history. A century and a half later, Auguste Comte in his *Positive Philosophy* paid it high tribute, its Catholic, Providential orientation notwithstanding. Comte wrote:

Bossuet was unquestionably the first who proposed to survey, from a lofty point of view, the whole past of society. We cannot adopt his explanations, easily derived from theological resources; but the spirit of universality, so thoroughly appreciated, and, under the circumstances, so wonderfully sustained, will always preserve this admirable composition as a model, suggesting the true result of historical analysis; the rational coordination of the great series of human events, according to a single design . . ."

That Comte chose, as we shall see, a different design, in no way diminishes the respect he paid Bossuet. Such respect was forthcoming almost from day of publication, from Protestant, Catholic, and, later, secular scholars and philosophers. Among the last were Turgot and Condorcet in the eighteenth century.

Even today one is struck by the essentially modern cast of Bossuet's work, although its lineal descent from the early efforts at universal history by Eusebius and St. Augustine is evident. As we have just seen, there was an abundance of works in Bossuet's century, mostly Protestant, seeking with the aid of the prophetic books of the Bible to give unity to past and present and illumination to the future. But these were almost without exception sacred histories in which little attempt was made to fuse the sacred with the burgeoning secular—manifest in works of science, philosophy and art, and notable political events. What the historian Leonard Krieger has written of Bossuet is instructive:

. . . Bossuet's fusion of the Christian framework he inherited from Augustine and Eusebius with the humanist motifs of classical rhetoric and civic morals . . . gave a modern cast to his providential structure of history and equipped it for its transfer into the secularized rational schema that would loom so large in the universal history of the next two centuries. The coherence which the designs of a transcendent divinity lent to human history would pass over into the world histories from which the interventions of the divinity themselves had been excluded, and, once there, this universal connectedness would become an essential feature whose tension with the ideal of covering the whole extent of the multicultural human past has constituted the basic problem of world history ever since.

Indeed it has. I have noted on several occasions in this book that apart from the use of an omnipresent, omnipotent Providence conceived as author and executor of a design within which all human cultures however widely separated in space and time fit smoothly, there is no possibility whatever of dealing with "world history" in narrative, unilinear fashion. Such an impossibility would not, of course, prevent such secular minds as Condorcet, and Marx from essaying the feat, but in each instance the obvious and indispensable *modus operandi* is some metaphysical substitute for Providence.

For Bossuet, however, there is no problem posed at all by his world history. For he is frank in stating that the kind of universal history he is setting forth in his *Discourse* is meaningless apart from the comprehension and initiating presence of God. He is well aware of the problem posed by the existence of seemingly separated peoples in past and present. To the royal pupil to whom the *Discourse* is directed, Bossuet writes in the opening chapter titled "General Plan of this Work":

He who has not learned from history *to distinguish different ages* will represent men under the law of Nature or under written law as they are under the law of the Gospel; He will speak of the vanquished Persians under Alexander as he speaks of the victorious Persians under Cyrus; he will make the Greeks as free at the time of Philip as at the time of Themistocles or Miltiades, the Roman People as proud under Diocletian as under Constantine, and France during the upheavals of the civil wars under Charles IX and Henry III as powerful as at the time of Louis XIV, when, united under that great king, France alone triumphs over all of Europe. (Italics added)

In sum, Bossuet is saying to his pupil and to all readers, we shall become lost in the particularities of history, ignorant of the meanings of the great events and, above all, of their place in the larger design that is universal history. What is required is a panorama of the whole, "in condensed form, the entire course of the centuries." Bossuet continues:

This kind of universal history is to the history of every country and of every people what a world map is to particular maps. In a particular map you see all the details of a kingdom or a province as such. But a general map teaches you to place these parts of the world in their context; you see what Paris or the Ile-de-France is in the kingdom, what the kingdom is in Europe, and what Europe is in the world.

In the same manner, particular histories show the sequence of events that have occurred in a nation in all their detail. But in order to understand everything, we must know what connection that history might have with others; and that can be done by a condensation in which we can perceive, as in one glance, the entire sequence of time.

Such a condensation . . . will afford you a grand view. You will see all preceding centuries developing, as it were, before your very eyes in a few hours; you will see how empires succeeded one another and how religion, in its different states, maintains its stability from the beginning of the world to our own time . . .

It is the progression of these two things, I mean religion and empires, that you must impress upon your memory. And since religion and political government are the two points around which human affairs revolve, to see what is said about them in a condensation and thus to discover their order and sequence is to understand in one's mind all that is great in mankind and, as it were, to hold a guiding line to all the affairs in the world. (Italics added)

How often during following decades and centuries almost identical words would be written! To place the minutiae of times, places, events, and personages into a grand design that will give meaning to each and to all:

this, from Bossuet on, has been the justification of numerous universal or world histories. No one has improved upon Bossuet's statement of the matter; hence I have quoted him at length.

Bossuet realized and it cannot be overemphasized, that Providence alone can be made the true author of any condensation of history's multiplicities into a single, compressed, unilinear narration. And Bossuet is unsparing in his insistence upon the significance of Providence.

Bossuet introduces the concept of *epochs*. Just as we must have land-marks or certain principal towns in mind around which to place others according to their distance, so

> . . . we must have certain times marked by some great event to which we can relate the rest.
> That is what we call an *epoch,* from a Greek word meaning to *stop,* because we stop there in order to consider, as from a resting place, all that has happened before or after, thus avoiding anachronisms, that is, the kind of error that confuses ages.

There are for Bossuet twelve great epochs to be discerned in the past. I will not set down the specific identity of each here, for what is vital in any event is not the nature of each epoch but, rather, the idea of organizing world history into epochs irrespective of content. It is *this* that communi-cated itself so powerfully to such later secular minds as Turgot, Condorcet, Comte, and others. Suffice it to say that the first great epoch for the de-voutly Christian Bossuet is the Creation itself and all that went with it. We pass through other such epochs as the Flood, the contributions of Moses, the fall of Troy, the building of Rome, the coming of Christ, down to Charlemagne and the Holy Roman Empire. Each of the epochs is given precise meaning in its relation to the sequence of the rest by Bossuet. He apologizes for concluding this section of his book with Charlemagne, and tells us that in a later work (which, alas, Bossuet seems never to have gotten to or completed) he will bring the sequence of epochs down to his own illustrious time, the Age of Louis XIV. There is simply no question but that for Bossuet *progress* characterizes the whole of universal history.

Part Two of the *Discourse* is titled "Continuity of Religion," and there is no mistaking here either the sense of progress in Bossuet's treatment of Christianity and especially the Catholic Church. He leaves no doubt in our minds that the very heart of the progress of mankind through the ages has been religious in character and that Jesus Christ and the founding of Chris-tianity have all the majesty in the Age of Louis XIV that they had earlier.

The final part of the book is in some ways the most interesting to any modern reader. Titled simply "The Empires," it is a series of astute reflec-tions on the rise, fall, and other historical changes of the great empires of the past. He brings in review for us the Scythians, Ethiopians, Egyptians, Persians, Greeks, and the Romans. The second chapter of this section is titled: "Changes in Empires have Particular Causes Which it Behooves Princes to Study." The following passages will suggest the flavor of the chapter:

> But this spectacle will be more useful and interesting if you reflect not only upon the rise and fall of empires but also upon the causes of their progress and decadence.
> For the God who caused the universe to be linked together and who, though all-powerful in himself, willed, for the sake of order, that the parts of the great whole be dependent on one another—the same God also willed that the course of human affairs should have its own continuity and proportions. By this I mean to say that men and nations have had qualities proportioned to the heights they were destined to reach and that, with the exception of certain great reversals by which God wished to demonstrate the power of his hand, no change has occurred without causes originating in preceding centuries.
> And since there is something in every event to prepare it, to motivate its beginning, and to determine its success, the true science of history consists in uncovering for each age the hidden tendencies which have prepared the way for great changes and the important combinations of circumstances which have brought them about.
> It is, indeed, not enough to look only what is before our eyes, that is, to consider the great events which suddenly decide the fate of empires. If we truly wish to understand human affairs, we must begin further back; we must also observe the inclinations and ways or, to put it more succinctly, the character of the dominating nations in general, and of princes in particular, as well as that of the outstanding men, who, because of the important role they were given to perform in the world, have contributed for good or evil to the change in empires and the fate of nations.

The striking aspect of this third and final section of the *Discourse* is its remarkably secular character. We are never in any doubt, of course, that the first and final cause of everything is Providence; but, this accepted, we are presented with a sequence of social, economic, cultural, and political insights into the rise and fall of empires. The two chapters on Rome, its greatness and then decline, are as free of references to God and his intervention as most of the numerous eighteenth-century treatments of Rome's rise and fall are. It is not that Bossuet is denying Providence; only that he is concerned with demonstrating and illustrating the secular ways in which Providence works in history.

Millenarian Puritanism of the mid-seventeenth century did much to broadcast to unlettered and lettered alike the chiliastic excitement of a view of history founded upon a vision of progress, past, present, and future; so too, I would argue, did the Bishop Bossuet's learned and elegantly constructed *Discourse on Universal History* give the idea of progress so much of its power over the minds of scholars and philosophers, those for whom the Puritan bursts of religious enthusiasm were repugnant or alien. It is fair to say of the *Discourse*—and no higher compliment can be given it—that it did for the seventeenth *and eighteenth* centuries what *The City of God* had done for the post-Roman and indeed the whole medieval period.

The Assimilation of Voyage and Discovery

John Edwards, in a work earlier referred to in this chapter, wrote in 1699: "Diligent Researches at home, and Travels into remote Countries have produced new Observations and Remarks, unheard-of Discoveries and Inventions. Thus we surpass all the times that have been before us; and it is highly probable that those that succeed, will far surpass these . . ."

Edwards's words give us insight into the uses which could be and were made of the abundant materials on the great voyages and explorations available to all literate Europeans in the seventeenth century. The fascination with earthly paradises which we found in the High Middle Ages— leading to popular interest in whatever might be reported from time to time or made the subject of legend—underwent striking renewal in the late sixteenth century, a seizure of the public mind that would last well into the eighteenth century. The publication of Hakluyt's *The Principal Navigations* at the very end of the sixteenth century, followed by Samuel Purchas's *Purchas His Pilgrimage* in 1613 and then his longer work, based on unpublished Hakluyt papers and East India Company records, *Hakluytus Posthumus, or Purchas His Pilgrims* in 1625, guaranteed some exciting reading to the large, waiting lay audience in western Europe. It also provided data for those scholars eager to put western European civilization in proper geographical and also *temporal* perspective. For, as the opening citation suggests, Europeans found it very easy to connect the cultures which navigators and explorers discovered and reported on, with earlier stages of their own cherished and, in their eyes, advanced, civilization in the West.

Christianity made it easy for Westerners to find a certain kinship or affinity between their own culture and the exotic societies which had been uncovered in other parts of the world. After all, St. Augustine had given virtual canonic status to the unity of mankind. And from the very beginning of Christian missionary work, going back at least to Gregory the Great and his instructions to the other Augustine, the Christianizer of Britain, there had been a remarkable sympathy with and tolerance of the customs of the non-Western, non-Christian peoples. Hence the almost continuous willingness of the Christian explorers to accept large parts of the belief and custom they came upon, seeking only to infuse these with as much Christian significance as possible. Perhaps the greatest example of this is Joseph-Francois Lafitau's *Customs of Primitive Americans Compared with Customs of Early Times* published in 1724. The book is a remarkable instance of the tolerance, understanding, and high respect that could come from an educated French Catholic missionary who spent years among the American Indians. Even more striking, however, are the temporal overtones of the work. The Christian theory of human progress made it easy for Lafitau to find parallels between American Indian beliefs and customs and those of an earlier western European age. He could deduce from this the fact that Western civilization was more advanced and had once known such beliefs and customs, but had gone beyond them over a long period of historical time.

But the kind of thinking to be found in Lafitau's early eighteenth-century work is vivid in the seventeenth century and even earlier, as J. H. Elliott has stressed in his valuable *The Old World and the New: 1492–1650.* Without question, it was America that excited the greatest interest among Europeans after Columbus had duly filed his reports on his great voyages. Elliott writes:

To watch the process by which sixteenth-century Europe came to grips with the realities of America is to see something of the character of sixteenth-century European civilization itself, its strength and its weakness. Certain elements in Europe's cultural inheritance made it difficult to assimilate new facts and new impressions, but others may have given it certain advantages in confronting a challenge of this magnitude.

Here, of course, the idea of progress, the ecumenical idea of progress, proved to be of upmost help. How to resolve the huge problem of locating—that is, morally, economically, and socially—the peoples of the Americas and other parts of the world where human beings lived lives so utterly different, in many instances so "barbarically" different, from Europeans? For sixteenth-century Europeans, as for the ancient Greeks and Romans, there were at least two explanations available: one, that all these peoples represented corruptions or degenerations of once civilized races; the other, that these peoples were different, generally more primitive, savage, or barbaric, because they had not yet developed to the level of Europe. It was this explanation that proved to be the more popular. As Elliott notes:

In changing and refining Europe's conception of barbarism and civility, therefore, as in so many other areas of thought, the discovery of America was important,

146

less because it gave birth to totally new ideas, than because it forced Europeans to come face to face with ideas and problems which were already to be found within their own cultural traditions.

It was simply impossible for the reflective and Christianity-driven mind in Europe to overlook the classificatory problem posed by these peoples in their relationship to Christians in the West. They were different. Did that mean inferior? Were they to be conceived of as genuine members of the same human race to which Europeans belonged? Were the peoples of America different because they were made of different physical and spiritual stuff? These were some of the questions raised in a great many centers of thought in Europe as explorers returned to write their books about the exotic peoples they had encountered, often lived with for significant periods of time. Again it is useful to quote J. H. Elliott:

> By the end of the sixteenth century, then, the experience of America had provided Europe with at least the faint outlines of a theory of social development. But this theory was set into a general framework of historical thought which was European in its points of reference, and Christian and providentialist in its interpretations of the historical process. The criterion for assessing the development of non-European peoples remained firmly Eurocentric . . . .
>
> If the discovery of the New World, therefore strengthened the Christian providentialist interpretation of history as a progressive movement which would culminate in the evangelization of all mankind, it equally strengthened the more purely secular interpretation of history as a progressive movement which would culminate in the civilization of all mankind. Recent events had shown the superiority of modern Europeans, at least in some respects, to the men of classical times. But they had also shown their superiority to the barbarous peoples of a sizeable portion of the globe.

What Elliott does not tell us, however, is that the method of assimilating the non-Europeans into a progressive interpretation of history—with the newly-discovered barbarians deemed to be living examples of what Europeans once were in their habits and customs, and with the whole panorama cast in Eurocentric terms—is exactly the method we have seen the ancient Greeks and Romans employ in their own encounters with bizarre and barbaric peoples. As we noted, Thucydides begins his *History of the Peloponnesian Wars* with reflections upon how the Greeks, the most civilized of all peoples, had once themselves been like those now living on the fringes. Moreover, the method Elliott describes would remain for the next three centuries the principal method of relating Westerners to other peoples.

If these peoples of the Americas and other barbarians were in fact then but lower, inferior, stages of development through which Europeans had long since passed, then the interesting question was posed: What should

Europe's treatment of them be? They could be taken to be made of the same flesh and blood, however different their color, and thus members of the one human race St. Augustine had posited; but their rude, even savage cultures rendered them fair game for enslavement, exploitation, and colonization by Western nations—for profit, yes, but in the long run also with the intent to tutor and Christianize these peoples as a means of hastening their development.

Much that became highly visible in the political and military history of the eighteenth and nineteenth centuries had its clear intellectual roots in the various ways in which those peoples of Africa, Asia, Oceania, and the Western Hemisphere had been regarded, had been fitted, as it were, to the Western idea of progress that was asserting itself so strongly in the sixteenth and seventeenth centuries. True, Montaigne in his famous essay "Of Cannibals" could write tolerantly and indulgently, even admiringly, of the so-called savage peoples who killed one another for food. Montaigne contrasted them with his own Western Europeans who, as he tells us with dry relish, kill, torture, devastate, and slaughter for no reason at all save religious or political dogma. So too in the eighteenth century there would come into existence among certain intellectuals the "cult of the noble savage," the faith in exoticism. But these idealizations of the non-European world are rare by the side of those declarations which saw the non-Western world as composed largely of savages and barbarians. The Western idea of progress has been, as we have seen, Eurocentric from the beginning. Just as Homer and, then much later, Thucydides could look at the primitive peoples around them—Homer's Cyclopes, Thucydides' "pirates"—as examples of how the Greeks themselves once had been, so could the philosophers of the seventeenth and eighteenth centuries.

Nowhere did this use of the literature of exploration find broader and more diverse expression than in political theory. If we would know what kind of state is possible or necessary, it was argued, we must also know what kind of being man is by nature. We are accustomed to interpretations which say in effect that the Hobbeses and Lockes and Rousseaus first decided what kind of state they wanted built and then looked to whatever primitive people might best serve their purpose. But, as John Linton Myres pointed out a half-century ago, in his *The Influence of Anthropology on the Course of Political Science* it makes as much sense to assume—given the wide reading habits in the literature on primitive peoples around the world —that the ways in which a given political philosopher chose to describe the state of nature in which European man had aboriginally lived depended a great deal on just what books and reports concerning savage peoples he was most familiar with or had decided to accept as most authoritative.

How was it that Hobbes could deal so shudderingly with the state of nature, declaring it a place without property, security, any of the practical arts; a scene of violence and fear, where the life of man was "solitary, poor, nasty, brutish and short"? How was it that Locke a half-century later, by contrast, found the state of nature a rather different place, one in which property existed and was held secure, with natural property in agricultural land the rule? How did Montesquieu a half-century after Locke reach the conclusion that presocial man was chronically timid? How did Rousseau still later reach his celebrated views on the first, the natural, state of mankind?

I do not mean to imply that the direct impact of practical, contemporaneous conditions and events—the English Civil War, the Revolution of 1688, the decadent condition of so much of the ancien régime—did not shape significantly the kinds of states Hobbes, Locke, Montesquieu, and Rousseau hold up to us in their texts. Of course they did. But what is too little and too seldom noted is the fact that these men, Locke especially, were steeped in the anthropological literature of their times and were without question deeply influenced by what they read. Hobbes, as the famous paragraph in *Leviathan* makes evident, was sensitive to what he had read and heard about the warlike tribes of northeastern America. There are many more references to primitive peoples in Locke's works. In fact, as Myres shows us, we can come very close to tracing Locke's development as a political philosopher using the records we have of his readings in travel and ethnography. We can see his reading interests move, for example, from the same warlike North American Indians Hobbes had been struck by all the way down to the much more peaceful, landholding Indians of the Southeast. Montesquieu, while by no means ignorant of the writings on savages, was much more influenced by what he had read on the Persians, Russians, Japanese, Turks, and other peoples farther up the progressive scale than the American Indians. Rousseau's political attention went to the Indians of Central America, but he was not unaware of other preliterate peoples.

The important point here, however, is not the relation between ethnography and political theory or the influence the former exerted upon the latter. The point, rather, is the degree to which the faith in human progress became a means of assimilating all the non-Western peoples into a single progressive series reaching its apogee in Western civilization. Belief in progress and in its premise of the unity of mankind, drawn from Christianity, made it possible to convert perceived heterogeneity into a conceptualized homogeneity: the homogeneity of a single, temporally ordered progression of all peoples in the world from the simplest to the most advanced—which, of course, to the people of Western Europe meant themselves.

Granted that in the eighteenth century there were minds such as Montesquieu and Voltaire ready to deal with the Persians and Chinese as superior in civilization to Westerners. But this was at bottom ideological; a means of holding the glass up to Westerners just as Tacitus had done with the Germans in the first century. On the matter of human progress these thinkers did not really doubt the supremacy of the West and its vanguard position.

It is interesting to note too that as Western thinkers became exposed to masses of data accumulated by missionaries, explorers, and others concerning the rest of the world, their concept of the centrality of the West assumed increased importance. Arthur Lovejoy has nicely described the paradox inherent in this fact:

It was *after* the earth had lost its monopoly that its inhabitants began to find their greatest interest in the movement of terrestrial events, and presently came to talk of their own actual and potential racial achievements . . . as if the general destiny of the universe wholly depended upon them or should reach its consummation in them. It was not in the thirteenth century but the nineteenth that *homo sapiens* bustled about most self-importantly and self-complacently in his infinitesimal corner of the cosmic stage.

But that bustling about was well along by the seventeenth century. It merely reached a higher intensity in the nineteenth, the result of two centuries of gathering Eurocentrism based upon the idea of progress.

It is all quite amusing. Our stereotypes in Western history teach us to think of the consciousness of medieval man as more parochial than the consciousness of modern man. Perhaps in some ways this is true. But in more important ways it is not. With the diminution of the hold of Christian concepts upon the Western mind—concepts such as the unity of the human race, the chain of being in the universe, and the relative insignificance of both this world and this life in the total scheme of things—Western man became steadily more preoccupied not simply by the things of this world, but, more importantly, with the tiny portion contained in Western Europe. It is, I think, a fair statement that the reports Marco Polo made to his fellow Westerners in the thirteenth century did more to interrupt Western man's fascination with himself than did the torrential literature on the peoples and cultures of the world in the seventeenth and eighteenth centuries. For by then the spell of the idea of progress—and with it the Eurocentric view of the entire world—had grown to such proportions that little if anything in the world could be considered in its own right. Everything had to be seen through the West and its values.

The Quarrel of the Ancients and Moderns

However absurd this controversy may seem today, it had great importance in the minds of its participants in the seventeenth century, who included writers of the stature of Boileau, Swift, Bentley, and Perrault. Moreover, this is the literary battle from which the modern idea of progress emerged—in the judgments at least of Auguste Comte in the nineteenth century and J. B. Bury (in his *Idea of Progress*) in the twentieth. Bury gives the Quarrel two whole chapters and accords one of its combatants, Fontenelle in France, the honor of being "the first to formulate the idea of the progress of knowledge as a complete doctrine." We know better than that today, but all the same the event has its full share of importance in the history of the idea of progress.

The battle or quarrel was waged around this question: which are superior, the literary, philosophical, and scientific works of classical Greece and Rome, or, instead, the works of the modern world; that is, the sixteenth and seventeenth centuries? The battle was begun in Italy at the very beginning of the seventeenth century when the brilliant Tassoni, in his *Miscellaneous Thoughts* (1620) attacked Homer for all the faults of plot, characterization, and language he could find. No writer in his day, Tassoni declaimed, could survive for a moment if he made use of the ridiculous images and the unlikely occurrences which figure in *The Iliad* and *The Odyssey*. Tassoni went even farther. Modern writers are superior on the whole to all of those who composed their "classics" in the ancient world.

Tassoni may have started the battle, but the real ground proved to be France and England. It was in these two countries that the defenders of the ancients such as Boileau and Temple and in considerable degree Swift did fiercest battle with the Perraults, Fontenelles, and others who insisted that nothing done in ancient times could possibly be as fine in quality as that of the modern age.

In England Sir William Temple in his *Essay Upon the Ancient and Modern Learning* declared on behalf of the ancients, and with lamentable want of appreciation of modern science: "There is nothing new in astronomy to vie with the ancients, unless it be the Copernican system; nor in physic, unless Harvey's circulation of the blood." To which we can only reply: "Unless," indeed! Temple's volume was followed by William Wotton's *Reflections Upon Ancient and Modern Learning,* which is superior to Temple's if only because of Wotton's proper insistence upon the need to differentiate the sciences from literature and the arts. Science is cumulative in character, Wotton argues, and the works of a Newton are bound to be superior to those of, say, Archimedes. However, the works of art and literature are very different. It is quite possible that here the genius of an Aeschylus or a Praxiteles has not yet been surpassed if even equaled.

But the cream of the English battle over the question was Jonathan Swift's *Battle of the Books* published in 1704, the same year that saw issue of his other brilliant satire, *A Tale of a Tub*. Swift had been Temple's secretary, and was only too familiar with—in his contemptuous, biting words—the pedants, polymaths, upstarts, and ignoramuses he could find on both sides of the Quarrel. Swift follows the style of Homer in his delightful *Battle of the Books*. To this day the assertions and counter-assertions of representative books (at night, in an otherwise quiet library) in Swift's classic make enjoyable, and in our own day of modernist "upstarts" and "ignoramuses," highly pertinent reading. Swift may have thought the whole controversy inane and insipid, but he takes care to espouse the ancients and to lacerate painfully indeed those of his contemporaries who thought the classics outmoded.

But, from the point of view of the history of the idea of progress, it is the French rather than the English manifestation of the Quarrel that is the more important, even if no single work (except Boileau's in support of the ancients) quite matches the genius of, say, Wotton and Swift. Moreover, the French were somewhat earlier in publication of chief works than the English.

The French Academy, founded in 1635, later to become the arbiter in all literary matters, was for a time without either leadership or policy. A good deal of the fervor that went into the battle between defenders of the ancients and advocates of the moderns had struggle for control of the Academy as its base. The greatest of the minds in the Academy was Boileau, but his unalterable preference for the Greeks and Romans cost him dearly so far as influence in Academy affairs was concerned. For the majority of members consisted of those who could quite seriously regard such mediocrities and hacks as Maynard, Gombauld, Godeau, Racan, Sarrazin and Voiture (names all but meaningless after their brief burst of renown in their own age) as possessed of the same kind of genius that existed during the greatest ages of ancient Greece and Rome. Boileau saw quickly through the hollowness of such claims by the supporters of the moderns, and reacted with appropriate scorn as well as learning and critical judgment. But his cause was lost before it began. The soldiers of modernity held every crucial polemical position. They were determined to prove that modern artists— poets, dramatists, essayists, and so forth—as well as modern scientists were the superiors of the ancient Greeks and Romans.

No one has ever treated the French modernist strategy during the Quarrel with greater perspicacity and contempt than Georges Sorel in his *The Illusions of Progress,* published more than two centuries later in France. He went immediately to the heart of the matter, showing how the moderns in perfect circularity of reasoning "proved" that they were superior to the ancients because of the operation of the law of intellectual progress, and at the same time "proved" the validity of the asserted law of progress by the evident superiority of modern poets and dramatists over ancient. For Sorel, who was always on the attack, the whole episode was a part of the hypocrisy of seventeenth-century French intellectuals abasing themselves to contemporaneous bourgeois wealth and power which wanted nothing so much as evidence of its own importance drawn from spheres it knew nothing about—a desire, Sorel emphasizes, that intellectuals of the time were only to happy to satisfy, given the promise of patronage.

Two of the defenders of the moderns stand out, at least in effectiveness of polemic: Charles Perrault and Bernard de Fontenelle. The former was the more creative of the two. His anticipation of the future was not, however, a rosy one. He tells us in his *Comparison of the Ancients and Moderns* that his own age had "arrived . . . at the highest perfection." He doubted that we have very many things "for which to envy those who will come after us." Perrault is chiefly interesting, at least so far as the idea of progress is concerned (his largest niche in history comes, surely, from his authorship of "Cinderella," "Sleeping Beauty," and other children's tales) for the ingenious way he deals with that bugaboo of the Italian humanists: the Middle Ages. How can we speak of lineal, continuous progress from past to present when a thousand-year period of ignorance, tyranny, and corruption such as the Middle Ages may be shown to exist? So asked the humanists. Perrault has an ingenious answer. We may compare the progress of the arts and sciences, he suggests, with "rivers which are suddenly swallowed up, but which, after having flowed underground for a space, come finally upon an outlet . . . whence they are seen to reissue with the same abundance with which they vanished from sight." In sum, during the hateful Middle Ages, knowledge continued to advance, but in subterreanean fashion—in isolated monasteries, for example. Progress of knowledge has been slowed down from time to time, but thus far never halted altogether.

Fontenelle, however, was willing to carry all the way through to the future his panorama of progress. In his *Digression on the Ancients and Moderns* he tells us that the real question of human progress comes down to whether nature remains the same over centuries and millennia. Fontenelle, a devout Cartesian, thought that nature did remain the same:

Once clearly understood, the whole question of the preeminence between the ancients and the moderns reduces itself to whether the trees of yesterday were greater than those of today. If they were, Homer, Plato and Demosthenes cannot now be equalled; but if our trees are as great as those of former times, then we can equal Homer, Plato, and Demosthenes.

In short, if trees are just as tall, lions and tigers just as fierce today, then surely we are justified in assuming that the human mind is every bit as acute and susceptible to genius today as it was in the age of Aeschylus and Socrates:

Nature possesses a kind of paste which is always the same, which she ceaselessly moulds and remoulds in a thousand different ways, and of which she forms men, animals and plants; and certainly she did not form Plato, Demosthenes, or Homer of a finer or better-kneaded clay than our philosophers, our orators, and our poets today.

So much for the invariability of potential human genius in history. What about differing physical topographies and climates? These too can be ruled out, Fontenelle declares, because their merits and demerits in providing abundant food supply and tolerable living conditions for human beings are pretty much the same the world over, with the exceptions of "the Torrid Zone and the Two Polar Regions."

But are not the ancients to be lauded, given first place, for having been the first to invent, create, or otherwise achieve? By no means, argues Fontenelle. With all deference to those who were first in time, there are two points to add: first, had we, the moderns, been present in the beginning, everything points to the fact that we would have done precisely what the ancients did; second, and more important, it is often more difficult to *add* to what was first done than to be responsible for a first achievement. Fontenelle, it has to be said, does not pursue this dubious position beyond its simple statement. He is, however, much more eloquent in his argument for the moderns when he emphasizes the fact that we have what the ancients, not even the greatest of their creators and inventers, did *not* have: that is, their own works to build on, to be inspired by. "We have benefited intellectually by those same discoveries which we see before us; we have inspirations borrowed from others in addition to those which we have of ourselves; and if we outdo the first inventor, it is he himself who has helped us to outdo him. . . ."

However, it can well be asked why all ages since the times of the Greeks and Romans are not great ages; greater than those of Aeschylus and Plato, of Cicero and Livy? After all, nature turns out the same tall trees, the same abundance of human brains. Why, then, Fontenelle asks rhetorically, "the dark ages which followed the century of Augustus and preceded our own"?

What explains the pall of ignorance and superstition which hung over Europe for close to fifteen hundred years? As we have seen from the time of the earliest phase of the Renaissance, it was taken for granted by humanists and intellectuals generally that the whole period, roughly A.D. 300–1400, was one of unrelieved barbarism. Fontenelle is not lacking in his own devotion to this assumption. But, he argues, it is as though a single human being were to be seized by some disease from which all his knowledge and memory are temporarily destroyed, reduced to impotence. In time, such a man would ordinarily recover from his disease and his memory would be restored to him. Moreover, Fontenelle continues, disease notwithstanding, our hypothetical individual would have been growing and developing his natural powers and perhaps even, subconsciously, his knowledge, all the while he lay ill. So is it with nations and civilizations. Periodically they suffer setbacks from wars, religions, tyrannies; knowledge seems to languish, even to disappear. But in time such civilizations recover, and once again the process of intellectual growth resumes. The following quotation is amply illustrative of Fontenelle's central position in defending progress and also the superiority of the moderns:

The comparison we have just drawn between the men of all ages and a single man is applicable to our whole problem of the ancients and the moderns. A good cultivated mind contains, so to speak, all the minds of the preceding centuries; it is but a single identical mind which has been developing and improving itself all the time. Thus this man, who has lived since the beginning of the world up to the present had his infancy, when he occupied himself with the most pressing needs of existence; his youth, when he was fairly successful in imaginative pursuits, such as poetry and eloquence, and when he even began to reason a little, though with less soundness than fire. He is now in his prime, when he reasons more forcefully and has greater intelligence than ever before . . .

It is annoying not to be able to prosecute to the end a comparison which is in such a fair way; but I am obliged to confess that the man in question will have no old age . . .; that is to say, to abandon the allegory, men will never degenerate, and there will be no end to the growth and development of human wisdom.

So much for the Quarrel of the ancients and moderns to which Bury and other historians have accorded such seminal status in the history of the idea of progress. It was not of course the beginning of the idea's career. For that we have gone back to the classical and early Christian philosopher. Nor was the argument for progress, for the superiority of the present over the past and of the future over the present, stated with anything like the solid reason and the erudition we have found in others in the century who were not connected with the Quarrel. The French advocates of modernity and progress were, as Sorel was to stress with such fury, merely intellectuals engaged in verbal trickery; in no degree the equal of those who defended the ancients. Nevertheless, history was to decide in favor of the moderns; it is they, not the Boileaus, who make their way to the exponents of progress in the eighteenth and nineteenth centuries. It is they, and not their learned betters, who gave voice, however mild, to the idea that was to dominate the consciousness of the next two and a half centuries.

One final comment, though, is irresistible. There is something delicious in the spectacle of Fontenelle—Secretary of the French Academy, popularizer of the wonders of science, an intellectual as religiously emancipated as any of the time could possibly have been—using for purposes of clinching demonstration of the reality of human progress an analogy which had been made popular by St. Augustine and transmitted to the seventeenth century through impeccably Christian channels. And the spectacle is made the more amusing by the solemnity and obvious belief in his own originality that accompanied Fontenelle's use of the analogy.

Leibniz

One of the principal happenings of the eighteenth century, Lovejoy writes in his *The Great Chain of Being,* "was the temporalizing of the Chain of Being. The *plenum formarum* came to be conceived . . . as the program of nature, which is being carried out gradually and exceedingly slowly in cosmic history. While all the possibles demanded realization, they are not accorded it all at once." Actually, as we noted, there had been intimations of this temporalization in medieval thought, and more than intimations in some of the Puritan writings. But Lovejoy's statement can stand as apposite commentary on the eighteenth century. And no one had more to do with this temporalizing than the great Leibniz.

From his mind alone, no doubt, there could have come enough substance to guarantee the idea of progress the intellectual ascendancy it has had during the past three centuries. Only rarely since Aristotle has there been an individual as broadly, deeply, and diversely endowed in philosophical and scientific matters as Leibniz. His invention of the infinitesimal calculus was in advance of Newton's. He seems to have been abreast of every major discovery, invention, and formulation of theory in the sciences in his day. He is credited with being the founder of symbolic logic. He was a doctor of law. Despite the sheer richness and quantity of his philosophical and scientific works, after his student days he never found time to accept an academic position that would have afforded him full time to give these works. He was much too engaged in diplomatic and political labors.

But our concern with Leibniz relates more closely to what he *renewed* in European thought than to what he invented or discovered. His life falls in the very middle of what I have termed The Great Renewal, and in his renewal of the ancient and medieval ideas of plenitude and continuity, Leibniz contributed as much to the idea of progress as those who renewed interest in the millennium, in the practical arts and sciences as harbingers of the millennium, and in "earthly paradises" found by navigators and fitted into a linear philosophy of history.

Leibniz had been influenced by Spinoza and his confidence in the Great Design. Everything that ever will happen lies in the present. Spinoza, like the scholastics, deduced plenitude from the axiomatic truth that whatever an omnipotent, omniscient God would create would inevitably contain everything that was conceivable. So too would there be in this divine, cosmic order a hierarchy of being perfectly continuous in ascent from lowest to highest.

As Arthur Lovejoy has written:

But Spinoza (unlike Bruno) had not made a great deal of the aspect of the principle of plenitude which was to be most fruitful of consequences in the eighteenth century; what most interested him in his own doctrine was not the consideration that everything that logically can be must and will be, but the consideration that everything that is must, by the eternal logical nature of things, have been, and have been precisely as it is.

No such limitation (or chosen alternative) is to be found in Leibniz. Wrestling with Spinoza's (among others') doctrines, Leibniz succeeded in laying down a metaphysics so broad and flexible, and so attuned to the ideas of growth, development, and evolution, that he would be not only a powerful influence in the eighteenth but the nineteenth century in formulations of progress. Comte, Marx, and even Darwin found themselves quoting from Leibniz in important contexts.

What is chiefly important to us here is, first, Leibniz's insistence upon the absolute *necessity* of each thing to be found in the universe and world (even crocodiles, as he expounds at some illustrative length!): it could not be other than it is, it can only be the result of unalterable necessity, given the nature of God and His design; second, Leibniz's doctrine of infinite potentiality; and third, and perhaps most important of all, his theory of continuity.

It is from his doctrine of necessity that Leibniz derived his famous conclusion that this is the best of all possible worlds—a conclusion that Voltaire was to make sport of later. The emphasis, however, should be placed on the word "possible." Leibniz did not for a moment believe that everything in the world was "good" and that evil was absent, as *Candide* would have us believe. Not by any means! He was well aware of evil, but his argument is simply that when all "possibles" are reckoned with (as only an almighty God could so reckon) it must be concluded that the best *possible* world was in fact created and then developed into maturity. But however one chooses to interpret Leibniz, it cannot be doubted that his cogitations upon fulfillment and necessity in the world order were bound to give a great deal of impetus to the idea of progress.

In some ways, though, more important for the idea of progress was the Leibnizian monad, or, rather, the conception of dynamic potentiality embedded in the monad. In his *On the Ultimate Origination of Things*, Leibniz wrote:

. . . To realize in its completeness the universal beauty and perfection of the works of God, we must recognize a certain perpetual and very free progress of the whole universe, such that it is always going forward to greater improvement. So even now a great part of our earth has received cultivation [culture] and will receive it more and more . . . . And to the possible objection that, if this were so, the world ought long ago to have become a paradise, there is a ready answer. Although many substances have already attained a great perfection, yet on account of the infinite divisibility of the continuous, there always remain in the abyss of things slumbering parts which have yet to be awakened, to grow in size and worth, and in a word, to advance to a more perfect state. *And hence no end of progress is ever reached.* (Italics added)

Few statements in the whole of Western philosophy were to echo more loudly or to reach more diverse contexts of philosophical and scientific work during the next two centuries than that Leibnizian pronouncement. Greek to the very core, Aristotelian in distinctive nature, it yet has a unique power and contemporaneity.

Consider the following, from *New Essays on the Human Understanding:*

Nothing happens all at once, and it is one of my great maxims, and among the most completely verified, that *nature never makes leaps:* which I call the *Law of Continuity* . . .

Everything goes by degrees in nature, and nothing by leaps, and this rule as regards changes is part of my law of continuity.

That these pronouncements extend well below the level of abstract generality, down into the very particulars of nature, is well attested by the following passage, also from *New Essays:*

Letter, 1707. I think, then, that I have good reasons for believing that all the different classes of beings, the totality of which forms the universe, are, in the ideas of God, who knows distinctly their essential gradations, merely like so many ordinates of one and the same curve, the relations of which do not allow of others being put between any two of them, because that would indicate disorder and imperfection. Accordingly men are linked with animals, these with plants, and these again with fossils, which in their turn are connected with those bodies which sense and imagination represent to us as completely dead and inorganic . . . Therefore all the orders of natural beings must necessarily form only one chain, in which the different classes, like so many links, are so closely connected with one another that it is impossible for sense or imagination to determine exactly the point where any one of them begins or ends; all the species which border upon or which occupy, so to speak, disputable territory being necessarily ambiguous and endowed with characteristics which may equally be ascribed to neighboring species.

Such is the continuity in Western thought of the central elements of Leibniz's *Letter* that we may easily imagine Lucretius comprehending and admiring it in his own day and no doubt Heraclitus long before him. What is equally telling, however, is the fact that a century and a half later these same central elements would be found in such a work as Darwin's *The Origin of the Species.* No one appreciated more than Darwin, given his advocacy of natural selection as the key process in biological evolution, Leibniz's *Natura non facit saltum,* which Darwin cites in appropriate context. The same appreciation would have gone (perhaps did go) toward the final clauses of the *Letter,* for one of Darwin's acknowledged objectives was to rid biology of rigid *species thinking* and to replace it with the kind of understanding of nature that is to be found in his theory of natural selection —and, less specifically, in Leibniz's passage.

Still another line of continuity is to be seen in the following:

Whence it is easy to conclude that the totality of all spirits must compose the City of God, that is to say, the most perfect state that is possible, under the most perfect of monarchs.

This City of God, this truly universal monarchy, is a moral world in the natural city, and is the most exalted and most divine among the works of God; and it is in it that the glory of God really consists, for he would have no glory were not his greatness and his goodness known and admired by spirits. It is also in relation to this divine city that God specially has goodness, while his wisdom and his power are manifested everywhere.

This from the inventer of calculus, the founder of the Prussian academy of sciences, and the brilliant political adviser to the King of Prussia! St. Augustine would have approved. So would, and perhaps did, Isaac Newton.

Vico

In his *Autobiography* Vico refers to his masterpiece *The New Science* in the following words:

> By this work, to the glory of the Catholic religion, the principles of all gentile wisdom human and divine have been discovered in this our age and in the bosom of the true Church, and Vico has thereby procured for our Italy the advantage of not envying Protestant Holland, England or Germany their three princes [Grotius, Selden, and Pufendorf] of this science.

Herewith one of the reasons why Vico, whose life spanned the last part of the seventeenth and first part of the eighteenth centuries, was so little read by his contemporaries and so devoid of influence in his own day: for all the originality and creativity of his historical, sociological, philological, and economic works, he chose to cast them in the rigorous perspective of not merely Providence but faith in a church whose intellectual fortunes were fast waning in Vico's time. A second major reason for the neglect with which he was treated throughout the eighteenth century was his staunch and at times bitter opposition to Cartesianism. Descartes had enjoined upon truth-seekers the strict eschewal of empirical and especially bibliographical and archival data, and had enjoined upon them also the use of pure, deductive reason—the kind that underlies geometry—as the only possible way of distinguishing what is true and real in man from what is mere appearance. For Vico, however, all hope of a science of man depended upon precisely the opposite point of view. Apart from data to be drawn from direct observation and from records of the past, there can be no such science.

Although Vico was largely ignored in his own day, especially as a philosopher of history, his reward came a century later, well after his death, when the French historian Jules Michelet, on a trip to Italy in the early 1820s, came upon Vico's *New Science*. His admiration seems to have been instantaneous. Michelet brought about an immediate translation into the French, and in his monumental *History of France* declared Vico to have been a genius of the magnitude of Newton.

There is some irony in the fact that Vico's vindication came chiefly from Michelet, for the latter was an impassioned enemy of the Roman Catholic Church and of Christianity generally. Vico gives all indication of having been a faithful Catholic (although several commentators have observed that Vico nowhere makes reference to Jesus in his *New Science*) and an admirer of the Middle Ages, a period that Michelet regarded with profoundest contempt—a contempt that led him to introduce the concept of the Renaissance in European historiography, a concept that Burckhardt was to use with classic effect later.

Providence was as real a being for Vico as for any seventeenth-century Puritan. Nothing happened, ever had or ever would happen, except as caused by Providence whether directly or by original design. Leon Pompa, one of the most perceptive students of Vico today, argues that one can excise Providence from Vico's *New Science* without significantly altering his fundamental principles of history. Perhaps so, but then one could excise the General Scholium from Newton's *Principia* without altering the laws of motion. What is crucial, however, is the fact that neither Vico nor Newton imagined for a moment that a universe, a world, a mankind was even possible apart from a creative, guiding Providence.

Providence, Vico writes, has seen to it that no two nations follow exactly the same course of development—even though tracing parallels in the development of nations is part of Vico's major objective. And Providence, he writes, sees to it that although the history of every people is one of recurrent cycles of genesis and decay, each new cycle begins at a higher level culturally than its predecessor. The dissolution of Roman civilization, and thus the end of a cycle or *corso,* did not mean that the start of a new cycle in the early Middle Ages had to be at the same level at which the Roman cycle had begun. In the final pages of his *New Science* there are reflections (somewhat confusing reflections, to be sure) on the possibility that Christianity will make it impossible for barbarism to affect ever again the course of Western civilization. (Edward Gibbon later in the century would reach the same conclusion about barbarism, but for reasons in no way related to Christianity.)

The following passage cited by Leon Pompa in his valuable study of Vico is evidence enough of Vico's dependence upon God. Our purpose, he writes, must be:

> demonstration of what Providence has wrought in history, for it must be a history of institutions by which, without human discernment or counsel, and often against the designs of men, Providence has ordered this great city of the human race. For though the world has been created in time and particular, the institutions established therein by Providence are universal and eternal.

For Vico, Providence has some of the flavor, obviously, that the "invisible hand" had for Adam Smith's economics later in the century. And as Croce (strongly influenced by both Vico and Hegel) observed: "Vico, no less than Hegel, had the concept of the *cunning of reason,* and he called it Divine Providence." In Element 7 of the *New Science* there is an interesting reference to Providence as the means alone by which the naturally violent and avaricious passions of men are resolved through institutions into a stability for society. Vico writes:

This axiom proves that there is divine providence and further that it is a divine legislative mind. For out of the passions of men each bent on his private advantage, for the sake of which they would live like wild beasts in the wilderness, it [Providence] has made the civil institutions by which they may live in human society.

There is little wonder in the fact that Vico was so thoroughly ignored by his contemporaries, despite his almost frantic, often despair-ridden efforts to project himself and his *New Science* upon the mind of his age. For what Vico was insistent upon referring to as the work of Providence—the resolving of men's disharmonious, even belligerent natural impulses into some kind of social equilibrium—others whose works were read in the eighteenth century translated Providence into an assortment of secular concepts. As a concept, altruism served Francis Hutcheson, Adam Smith's teacher, as a sufficient moral force in the world. For Bernard Mandeville on the other hand (whom Hutcheson detested) the secret of equilibrium lay simply in human egos competing with one another. [*Private Vices, Public Benefits* is the subtitle of his famous *Fable of the Bees.*] Adam Smith who seems to have made his way to this book despite his teacher's loathing for it, made effective use of both Hutcheson's and Mandeville's ideas. If there is more Mandeville than Hutcheson in *The Wealth of Nations,* there is more Hutcheson in Smith's earlier *Theory of Moral Sentiments.* But all of these are at bottom but secularizations of Vico's idea of an "immanent Providence."

I have previously referred to Vico's hostility to Cartesianism, and it is interesting therefore to learn from the *Autobiography* that in his early years Vico had been an admirer of Descartes's royal road to knowledge of any kind, in whatever sphere, natural, human, historical, or social. He is quite frank about this as the following statement shows:

All my life I had delighted in the use of reason more than memory and the more I knew in philology the more ignorant I saw myself to be. Descartes and Malebranche were not far wrong, it seemed, when they said it was alien to the philosopher to work long and hard at philology.

But however taken Vico was in the beginning by the Cartesian approach, he changed his mind completely the longer he pursued his research into history. He gradually came to realize that Cartesianism is applicable as a method solely to mathematics or logic, not to any understanding of the external world, physical or social. There are, Vico learned, and repeatedly emphasized, two types of knowledge: *Verum* and *Certum.* The first is a priori truth, dependent upon axioms or principles which man himself constructs, and requiring only strict adherence to deduction for steadily more complex conclusions to emerge. *Verum* is absolute knowledge and, of course, the only kind that Descartes had been interested in, a kind marvelously exemplified by geometry. The second kind of knowledge or truth, *Certum,* is proximate, not absolute, and is dependent not upon intuitively arrived at axioms and rigorous deduction from "clear and simple ideas," but rather on the patient observation of things—past and present. Once Vico made his break with Cartesianism on the ground of its utter inapplicability to the study of human society, he abandoned *Verum* altogether. A passage in the *New Science* is revealing:

> Now, as geometry, when it constructs the world of quantity out of its elements, or contemplates that world, is creating it for itself, just so does our Science [create for itself the world of nations] but with a reality greater by just so much as the institutions having to do with human affairs are more real than points, lines, surfaces and figures are.

Not until the nineteenth century, when the study of history generally, and more especially social and institutional history had become so popular, when eighteenth century ideas of *natural* rights and *natural* law had become supplanted in the social sciences by *actual* rights, duties, customs, and codes of men, did Vico reap the rewards of his institutionalism. The eighteenth century was largely unprepared.

Vico had great admiration for Bodin's *Commonwealth,* and refers to Bodin as an "equally most erudite jurisconsult and political thinker." He even dedicated a chapter to Bodin in the *New Science,* praising in detail the major principles of Bodin's system of political theory. Vico does not, however, refer to Bodin's work on history and historical method. It is of course possible that he somehow failed to read this key work of a philosopher he so greatly admired, but it seems highly unlikely. There are too many parallels, too many instances of almost identical thinking on given matters, to support anything but belief that Vico was entirely familiar with the *Methodus* and built upon it. As Girolamo Cotroneo has pointed out in an important study, there is almost perfect similarity in the theories of the origin of human society we find in the pertinent writings of Bodin and Vico. The same is true of the systematic refutation of not only the Golden Age—so common, as we have observed, in Renaissance thought—but also of the prophecy of Daniel concerning the Four Monarchies, which as we have seen had so great an effect upon the minds of Puritans and others in the seventeenth century. Although Vico's refutation of this prophecy is virtually

Bodin's word for word, there is no mention of Chapter 7 of the *Methodus*. I am not—nor is Cotroneo—seeking to detract from the originality of Vico's work. I am much more interested in bringing out the fact that Vico is far more closely allied in his thinking with a century earlier scholar, Bodin, than with any of his contemporaries. Just as Bodin had to struggle against not only the influence of Machiavelli but currents of thought emerging from the Italian Renaissance well before Machiavelli's time, so later, did Vico, find himself deluged by the waters of Cartesianism.

I have referred to Vico's desire to put history in the realm of true science rather than leave it where it has been for so many centuries, in the sphere of narrative art. He understood brilliantly the necessity of *comparative* history if there is to be historical science. His *New Science* begins, in fact, with what he calls a "Chronological Table" and with this in parallel columns are the leading events and personages of some seven different histories: Hebrew, Chaldean, Scythian, Phoenician, Egyptian, Greek, and Roman. His declared intent is to extract, through detailed, empirical, and comparative examination of these histories, principles which would be genuinely scientific in character. Vico had all the admiration for Francis Bacon that so many religionaries in England in the seventeenth century had, Catholic, Anglican, and Protestant alike. For Vico, any dependence upon allegedly self-evident principles in the study of human society had to be futile. All genuine principles must be the outcome of patient, comparative study of the records of actual peoples. Is it strange, then, that this remarkable mind should have been consigned to oblivion by the eighteenth century, a century in which the very essence of a true knowledge of mankind was held to lie in axioms which would illuminate the development of humanity—when proper, rigorous deductions were made—as they illuminated geometrical propositions? When in his second discourse Rousseau wrote in a famous and too often maligned line "Let us begin then by laying the facts aside, as they do not affect the question," he was following the approved Cartesian route. What could dusty records of the actual histories of peoples supply that would be apposite to a true and rational understanding of mankind? It was precisely this mentality that Vico sought, and failed, to dislodge. Over and over he tells us that the method of pure reason, so applicable to mathematics, can never in the study of mankind take the place of hard, empirical investigation of the actual experiences of nations.

Even when we turn to Vico's famous principle of an "ideal eternal history," we are dealing with a construct (Providence-generated, to be sure) that, although somewhat more deductive in fact than Vico imagined, is nevertheless drawn from and given application in the concrete, recorded, histories of peoples and nations; not to some such abstraction as Mankind or Humanity.

The course of the institutions of the nations had to be, must now be and will have to be such as our science demonstrates, even if infinite worlds were born from time to time through eternity, which is certainly not the case. Our science therefore comes to describe an ideal history traversed in time by the history of every nation in its rise, development, maturity, decline and fall. Indeed, we make bold to affirm that he who meditates this science narrates to himself this ideal eternal history so far as he himself makes it for himself by that proof "it had, has, and will have to be."

Given the nature of man as it always has been and always will be, Vico is saying, there is necessarily a *corso,* a pattern or cycle of change through which each and every people must pass.

This "ideal eternal history" has much in common with what Max Weber would refer to at the beginning of the twentieth century as an "ideal type." Particular societies, in Vico's judgment, do not in their respective histories follow any absolutely fixed pattern; but there is enough similarity in the development through three major stages of all nations—or at least what Vico refers to as "gentile" nations—to make his generalization, his model or ideal type, possible. The reason for the ideal pattern or the overriding similarity of courses of history among peoples is, as Sir Isaiah Berlin points out in explicating Vico's text, "the structure of 'the mind' [which] is the same for all men and all societies . . . for it alone is what makes them human." Long before Hegel and Marx, as Berlin emphasizes, Vico described human nature and the mind as activities or processes inseparable from the social contexts in which they operate.

A brief account of the actual, mental, cultural, and social content of his law of historical development reveals that there is no "state of nature" in Vico resembling the sense of it that we find in Hobbes, Locke, and Rousseau. Human society began, Vico argues, when human beings frightened by one aspect or other of environment took refuge in first the family, then in religious and local groups. The earliest age of human history in any people we study is an "age of gods," one in which every act or thought is governed by the dictates of gods as these are to be found in myths and symbols. Blood ties are sanctified by the gods, as is the patriarchal character of society and each of its families and groups.

Vico sees the breakup of this first great age as the result of the incapacity of a society founded upon the blood tie to assimilate smoothly those—the *socii*—who come as strangers from afar, who seek protection, and who find themselves forced to be in, but not of, their new societies. Tensions develop, followed by bloody conflicts, and then there ensues, Vico tells us, the second great age, "the age of heroes." Change in social and political organization is followed by changes in governing symbols. Religion gradually is replaced by poetry. This is truly the epoch of human feeling, emotion, and of passionate urge to be loyal in human affairs. If the first age is an age of gods and kinglike priests, the second comes closer to what we ordinarily think of as feudalism.

The third age flows, as does the second, from imperfections gradually developing in its predecessor; imperfections which ripen into fresh conflicts that begin to involve more and more people. It is in the third age that the people of a state assume wider and wider power, aided in the beginning by powerful monarchs whose support of the people leads them into deadly conflict with the "heroes" of the aristocracy. As religion was the characteristic pattern of symbols men lived by in the first age, as poetry with its epic heroes was the pattern of the second age, so does the third age take on its cultural-philological character which is, in a word, prose. Poetry now becomes so formalized, so classical in nature, so devoid of heroic emotions as to be prose in actual substance.

But in due time this age will come to an end also. Its reliance upon rationalism, technique, ever-wider bodies of subjects or citizens, extensive commerce, and symbols from which human feeling is increasingly withdrawn has decline and collapse as its necessary consequence. A new cycle of history, a renewal of the *corso* will—though by no means in exactly the same fashion; Vico's determinism is not iron in nature—commence.

There is much here to remind us of the Greek and Roman doctrine of cycles. It can be properly assumed given Vico's substantial command of classical writing that his conception of *ricorsi*, recurrences, in history—like his Renaissance predecessors'—is rooted in the classical doctrine. But there is this major difference: Vico's constantly stated faith in Providence leads him to see each of the *corsi* followed by nations as individual in its relation to God (thus anticipating in some degree Ranke's view of history and God) and thus different in vital particulars from all other *corsi*. And, as already noted, the same faith in Providence allows Vico to see successive *corsi* in ever-higher levels of civilization, just as had the equally religious Bodin.

Before concluding with Vico, it is important to stress yet another notable element of this thought, one that divides itself into several closely related parts. For Vico there is a distinct and irreducible *pattern* that, in Sir Isaiah Berlin's summarizing words, "characterizes all the activities of any given society; a common style reflected in the thought, the arts, the social institutions, the language, the ways of life and action, of an entire society." Thus, still following Sir Isaiah, we are able to see in the succession of such patterns in time the dynamic, changing, alterable character of man; we are also able to comprehend the fact that, as Vico insisted, those who actually construct or create something can understand its true reality better than those who merely gaze upon it at a distance—temporal or spatial. Finally, the creations of man are for Vico not artificial entities capable of being altered and transformed at will, but, in Sir Isaiah's words, "natural forms of self-expression, of communication with other human beings or with God." Many in Vico's day tended to see—and would continue to see long after his day—fables, legends, and myths as so many absurd, meaningless "survivals". Vico long before Herder and then Hegel and his followers saw myths as perfectly intelligible, rational ways by which primitive man gave order and coherence to the world around him. It is this quality that makes Vico the sociologist of knowledge. Irrespective of whether we are considering a myth or superstition, a work of art that survives through the ages, or a philosophical theory of universe and mankind, it is important that we see each not set against some abstract and timeless principle but as a part of the culture within which it comes into being. Is it any wonder, then, that Vico, once brought by Michelet to the attention of the nineteenth century, would have been so widely respected by those—Comte and Marx, for example—who, although maintaining independent origins of their own thinking along this line, nevertheless rendered him praise? It is fitting to close with a tribute given Vico by Croce:

> In his view of the historical development of mankind he shed new light on primitive language, consisting in imagination, rhythm, and song; on the primitive thinking characterized by myths; on the primitive and genuine poetry of Homer in antiquity and of Dante in Christian times as distinct from the intellectualistic poetry of unpoetic eras and of the eighteenth century . . . Despite the pessimism which isolated him in an age of great revolutionary impetus, the substance and the particular characteristics of his thought presented an ensemble of doctrines and of historical interpretations which were destined to integrate, correct, and transform the rationalism of the eighteenth century.

All of this is correct and important. But if there were but one element of his whole, complex, and tortuous system of thought to seize upon as the means of establishing Vico's importance to the history of the idea of progress, it would have to be, I think, the idea contained in the very title of his greatest work, *The New Science*. For, what best characterizes the post-Christian, the *modern* idea of progress is its containment in systems of thought believed by their authors to be as scientific as anything to be found in the physical or biological sciences. Vico accepted and emphasized the governing role of Providence. But within this belief lay a belief in science that would become ever more autonomous and self-sufficing in the generations which followed.

Part II

The Triumph of the Idea
of Progress

Introduction

DURING the period 1750–1900 the idea of progress reached its zenith in the Western mind in popular as well as scholarly circles. From being *one* of the important ideas in the West it became the dominant idea, even when one takes into account the rising importance of other ideas such as equality, social justice, and popular sovereignty—each of which was without question a beacon light in this period.

However, the concept of progress is distinct and pivotal in that it becomes the developmental *context* for these other ideas. Freedom, equality, popular sovereignty—each of these became more than something to be cherished, worked for, and hoped for; set in the context of the idea of progress, each could seem not merely desirable but historically necessary, inevitable of eventual achievement. It was possible to show—as did Turgot, Condorcet, Saint-Simon, Comte, Hegel, Marx, and Spencer, among many others—that all history could be seen as a slow, gradual, but continuous and necessary ascent to some given end. Clearly, any value that can be made to seem an integral part of historical necessity has a strategic superiority in the area of political and social action. The relatively small things which can be achieved in one generation toward the fulfillment of the idea or value are greatly heightened in importance when they are perceived as steps in the inexorable march of mankind. Marx was probably more aware of this than any other mind in the nineteenth century, but he was very far from being alone.

What we also find in the period we are now concerned with is the beginning and development of secularization of the idea of progress—detaching it from its long-held relationship with God, making it a historical process activated and maintained by purely natural causes. From Turgot's notable lectures and discourses in 1750–51 through Condorcet, Comte, Marx, Mill, Spencer, and others, there is a manifest desire to liberate progress from any crucial relationship with an active, guiding, ruling Providence. Throughout this period we find that system after system in philosophy and the social sciences was concerned primarily with demonstration of the *scientific* reality of human progress and of the laws and principles which make progress necessary. The philosophers of progress considered their productions in exactly the same light that they considered the productions of Darwin and Wallace, or of Faraday and Maxwell. For Condorcet or Marx it was preposterous to hypothesize God as a means of explaining what could far more plausibly and simply be explained by natural and purely human forces. This process of secularization of the idea of progress which began significantly in the eighteenth century, steadily gained momentum during the next two centuries, and has without doubt reached its height in the second half of the twentieth century (which I shall discuss further in chapter 9).

However, having pointed to secularization as a major force in the modern and contemporary formulations of belief in progress, it is immediately necessary to warn the reader that secularization is a long way from being the whole story of the idea in this period. Even in the Enlightenment when the process of secularization had its start, there were highly respected and influential minds still insistent upon the crucial place occupied by Providence in the progress of mankind. Few if any minds were more honored by the philosophers of the Enlightenment in Western Europe than Lessing and Herder in Germany and Joseph Priestley in England. All three were profound believers in progress; and all three made their faith in God and Christianity repeatedly evident. Nor did Christian devotion disappear in the nineteenth-century history of the idea. Scientists of the stature of Louis Agassiz in America and philosophers of the eminence of Hegel combined their faith in the scientific demonstrability of progress with devout and expressed faith in the Christian god.

Yet it is much more than Christianity that we are really talking about here: it is the religious (irrespective of creed), the sacred, the mythological, and, not to be overlooked in the nineteenth century, one or other entelechy that from today's point of view has to be seen as a substitute for religion. In all truth the nineteenth century must be accounted as one of the two or three most fertile periods in the history of religion in the West. It is a century rich in theological writing, the spread of evangelicism through all classes of society, the rise of the Social Gospel (in Protestantism and Catholicism alike), and, perhaps most important, in the mushrooming of new faiths: Christian Science, Mormonism, Adventism, the religion of Positivism, and others.

Such efflorescence could hardly fail to touch the idea of progress, thus limiting or qualifying its secularization. Even Saint-Simon, often credited with the founding of modern socialism and also the then new science of sociology, recanted his earlier atheism and came increasingly to see his imagined utopia under the label of "the New Christianity." Comte, very probably the most famous and influential philosopher of progress of the nineteenth century, the founder of *systematic* sociology, indeed coiner of the word and arch-exponent of science, had become an ardent believer in what he called the Religion of Humanity by the time he wrote his *Positive Polity* at midpoint in the century—a work devoted to the highly detailed character his Positivist utopia would have. All true Positivists, he enjoined, unite science and religion, will worship the *Grand Être*, and there will even be appropriate litanies and rituals.

But there are other, equally potent, instances in the nineteenth and twentieth centuries of what I am referring to. We need only think of the use made —chiefly in Germany and by virtue of export from Germany in other countries as well—of such concepts as Spirit, *Zeitgeist*, the Dialectic, and First Cause. Marxists will of course take issue with respect to the Dialectic, insisting, as they have from the beginning, that there is not a hint of either religion or metaphysics in the idea, only scientific substance. But to those whose minds are not befuddled by Marxist script, the supra-rational, neo-religious character of the word is evident—in the writings of Hegel from whom Marx acquired it and in the works of Marx himself. Marx may have, as he insisted, turned the dialectic right side up, putting it on its feet, but the quasi-religious character of the concept remained. Similarly, Herbert Spencer, without doubt the most influential social philosopher and social scientist of his day, wrote in his *First Principles:* [T]he Atheistic theory is . . . absolutely unthinkable." For Spencer the necessary substitute for an out-and-out God was what he called the First Cause. He wrote: ". . . we have no alternative but to regard this First Cause as Infinite and Absolute"— attributes, obviously, of the Augustinian God.

Nevertheless, having recognized all of this persisting religiosity in the nineteenth century, we cannot properly ignore the powerful spell that was cast by the word "science." Both "science" and "scientist" in their contemporary senses are coinages of the early part of the century, and as the century progressed each became a more and more sacred symbol in Western vocabularies, both scholarly and popular. The awe that has until very recently attended science and the scientist is a product of the nineteenth century. So overriding was the desire in all parts of the population to participate in or at least exalt science that even religions began to cite "scientific" evidences of their reality. Mary Baker Eddy's Christian Science, as a phrase, epitomized a great many sects and churches founded in both the nineteenth and twentieth centuries. In sum, while we are obliged to recognize the infusions of religion in science, especially social science, we are equally obliged to recognize the extraordinary luster and appeal of science in its own right.

Another point must be made in general introduction to the chapters which follow. Today we tend to differentiate, with good reason, between the words "progress" and "evolution" or "development." But as Kenneth E. Bock has pointed out in detail, no such differentiation was made in the eighteenth and nineteenth centuries. Just as the eighteenth century made "natural history," "conjectural history," and "hypothetical history" synonyms of "progress," so the nineteenth century used "progress" and "evolution" interchangeably. This is nowhere better illustrated than in Darwin's *The Origin of the Species* published in 1859. Repeatedly "progress" is used to describe a process or phenomenon that would today be put under the label of "evolution" or "development" in biology. And what was true of Darwin in biology was just as true of Lyell in geology, Tylor in anthropology, and Spencer in sociology—indeed of any writer in the nineteenth century concerned in any way with processes of cumulative and processual change.

Closely related to this point about terminology in the nineteenth century is another: the relation of "social evolution" to "biological evolution." Even today we encounter references to the derivation of the concepts of social evolution and social progress from Darwin's "revolutionary" announcement in 1859 of the origin and descent of the species. Seemingly, scholarship will never rid the world of this gross misconception. What is alone original in Darwin's great work is his theory of *natural selection,* at its best a statistical-populationist theory in which neither progress nor cumulative development plays any vital role. *This* theory had no counterpart, nor has it today, in any of the social sciences. (Let readers remember at this point, though, the anticipation of Darwin's conception of natural selection by Lucretius, and also, it should be added now, by Darwin's own grandfather, Erasmus.)

But, as Kenneth E. Bock has made clear, "social evolution" as a theory not only must be sharply distinguished from what Darwin's central point about evolution was but, more to the point, it long preceded Darwin's biological writings. The social evolutionary theories we find in the post-Darwinian world have their easily identifiable roots in the works of such pre-Darwinian philosophers as Condorcet, Comte, Hegel, and many others of the late eighteenth and early nineteenth centuries. I have said that Darwin used the words "progress," "evolution," and "development" interchangeably, which is true and easily demonstrable. And without doubt such usage contributed substantially to the extraordinary popularity after Darwin of ideas of social evolution. But this in no way alters the validity of what I have just stressed: theories of *social* evolution in the nineteenth and twentieth centuries (right up to the contemporaneous works of Talcott Parsons and the late Leslie White and their followers) have their origin in what Comte referred to in the 1830s as his "law of progress"; emphatically *not* in the works of Darwin, Wallace, and Mendel.

Now to a different point. I have chosen to exhibit the idea of progress in the period 1750–1900 in two chapters on freedom and power respectively. But such selectivity should not distract any reader from the universality of the idea in the scholarly, scientific, literary, and other spheres of thought and imagination in this period. Philosophy was literally saturated in the temper of progressivism—and I refer to the core areas of metaphysics, ontology, ethics, and esthetics as well as to the philosophy of history. All of the social sciences without exception—political economy, sociology, anthropology, social psychology, cultural geography, and others—were almost literally founded upon the rock of faith in human progress from Turgot and Adam Smith on through Comte, Marx, Tylor, Spencer, and a host of others. If it is difficult to perceive the idea of an unfolding civilization in the strict classical economists let us not forget the immense part played by the idea in John Stuart Mill's *Principles of Political Economy,* and most spectacularly in the works of the (chiefly German) historical school of economics.

I have mentioned Darwin in a different context. But, in order to suggest the importance of the idea of progress in the biological sciences in the nineteenth century, the following passage from Darwin's *The Origin of the Species* is helpful:

> . . . we may feel certain that the ordinary succession by generation has never once been broken, and that no cataclysm has desolated the world. Hence we may look with some confidence to a secure future of great length. And as natural selection works solely by and *for the good of each being,* all corporeal and mental endowments will tend to progress toward *perfection.* (Italics added)

Or this: "Although we have no good evidence of the existence in organic beings of an innate tendency towards progressive development, yet this necessarily follows, as I have attempted to show in the fourth chapter, through the continued action of natural selection." And to show that even Darwin could combine at least the rudiments of what had once been an all-out faith in Christianity with progressivism, there are the final words of the book:

> There is grandeur in this view of life, with its several powers, *having originally been breathed by the Creator* into a few forms or into one; and that, whilst this planet has gone cycling on according to the fixed law of gravity, from so simple a beginning endless forms most beautiful and wonderful have been, and are being evolved. [Italics added.]

Is it any wonder that innumerable professed Christians, lay and scientific and scholarly, could find so much in Darwin's historic work to agree with and to find compatible with views already arrived at? True, Darwin had his critics. But their number and intensity have been grossly exaggerated; and from fellow naturalists at least, such criticisms were more likely to be aimed not at any impiety in Darwin, but at lapses of logic and evidence which in later editions Darwin himself came to acknowledge, however reluctantly. (Not until Mendel's remarkable discoveries became well-known for the first time in the early twentieth century was it possible to give true scientific support to Darwin's theory of evolution.)

Darwin's contemporary and co-discoverer of the principle of natural selection, Alfred Wallace, was even more progressivist in his thinking than Darwin. He did not doubt that the evolutionary process must someday reach fulfillment in "a single homogeneous race, no individual of which will be inferior to the noblest specimens of existing humanity." Subjection to baser instincts and passions will be replaced, Wallace declared, by free participation in a world of reason and humanity once the members of the race "develop the capacities of their higher nature, in order to convert this earth which had so long been the theatre of their unbridled passions, and the scene of unimaginable misery into as bright a paradise as ever haunted the dreams of seer or poet."

In historiography the idea of progress became with rarest exceptions the very foundation of the field. On both sides of the Atlantic there were literally hundreds of historians to echo in one way or other the faith in progress that is constitutive in a Macaulay or a George Bancroft. Nor was Christian theology unaffected. One classic will suffice here: John Henry Newman's *Development of Christian Doctrine* (1845), written to demonstrate to certain critics of Christianity that the complex character of its theology in the nineteenth century—by comparison with apostolic Christianity—was the result not of deviation from or corruption of the original, but of the *progress* of Christian doctrine.

Literature, although not without some striking dissenters, was, too, a repository of the religion of progress. Alexander Pope, before our present period of interest even began, wrote: "All full or not coherent be, / And all that rises, rise in due degree." Edward Young in the eighteenth century could say: "Nature delights in progress; in advance / From worse to better." In the nineteenth century Browning, in virtually the same words Herbert Spencer would use, declared: "Progress is a law of life." And Tennyson (who would in his final years change his mind drastically) wrote: "For I dipt into the future, as far as human eye could see / Saw the vision of the world, and all the wonder that would be." Coleridge concluded that while a cursory reading of history might dispose one toward cynicism, history properly studied "as the great drama of unfolding Providence, has a very different effect. It infuses hope and reverential thoughts of man and his destination." And countless must be those who have read and cherished Arthur Clough's "Say Not the Struggle Naught Availeth." These few examples must suffice. Jerome H. Buckley, in his *The Triumph of Time,* has shown in rich detail the impact the idea of progress had on Victorian literature.

One other general observation about the role of the idea of progress in the late eighteenth and the nineteenth centuries must be made. There was very close affinity between faith in progress and faith in what today we call economic growth. This affinity was particularly strong in the Age of the Enlightenment. Voltaire believed, and repeatedly wrote, that commerce, liberty, and progress were inseparable. We shall see in chapter 6 attitudes of this kind in the writings of Turgot, Adam Smith, and Malthus. It is worth mentioning here that even that prodigious experimenter in the sciences, Joseph Priestley—honored throughout the Western world for his works on science and on Christianity—was heart and soul behind economic growth and affluence. In his *The Perfectibility of Man,* John Passmore has stressed the difference between the twentieth century intellectual's characteristic repugnance for things economic, particularly if they are capitalist in setting, and the attitudes of enlighteners and philosophical radicals at the end of the eighteenth and early part of the nineteenth century. Passmore quotes Priestley on commerce and how "it tends greatly to expand the mind and to cure us of many hurtful prejudices. . . . Men of wealth and influence who act upon the principles of virtue and religion, and conscientiously make their power subservient to the good of their country, are the men who are the greatest honor to human nature, and the greatest blessing to human societies."

Condorcet, inspired egalitarian, fanatical believer in the French Revolution (even while he was being hunted down by Robespierre's Jacobin police), was hardly less rapturous about economic production and commerce.

These pursuits may not have yet rendered their full potential for good in the world, he declared, but they would once the Church and political despotism had been abolished.

There were indeed pessimists and antagonists in the nineteenth century in so far as industry and trade were concerned. Even John Stuart Mill lamented some of the most visible ills of the economic system and wrote a famous chapter in his *Principles of Political Economy* on the virtues of what he called "the stationary state," the state that has renounced the objective of economic advancement. And well before mid-century, poets, novelists, and artists were recording their distaste for what Blake referred to early on as the "dark Satanic mills" which the industrial revolution had brought into being. But if writings of the major philosophers of progress of the century are examined—Saint-Simon, Comte, Marx, Spencer, among them—there is nothing but laudation to be found in comments on industry. Marx, as we know, yearned and worked for socialism, but he and Engels were adamant in their belief that the technological and even organizational substructure of socialist and communist society must remain largely what capitalism had created. As every reader of the *Manifesto* knows, capitalism for Marx and Engels was one of the wonders of world history, consigning to oblivion the so-called seven wonders of the ancient world.

But whether the claimed foundation was some physical, biological, economic, technological, religious, or metaphysical principle, faith in the progress of mankind was almost universal among the light and leading in the period stretching from 1750 to the middle of the twentieth century. There were, as I shall indicate in some detail later, skeptics and outright antagonists to this faith, but they were in the small minority. For the vast majority of Westerners progress was, in Herbert Spencer's famous phrase "not an accident but a necessity."

It is impossible to do full justice in a single volume—or a dozen volumes, for that matter—to this faith in progress. I have felt obliged therefore to be thematic and selective in chapters 6 and 7, devoted to eighteenth- and nineteenth-century theories of progress. Inasmuch as no two values were more important to the intellectuals of these centuries than freedom on the one hand and the legitimacy of power on the other, I have chosen these two values as contexts for illustrations of how faith in progress could manifest itself.

Chapter 6

Progress as Freedom

T HE eighteenth and nineteenth centuries were not lacking in historians, scientists, philosophers, and, in general, intellectuals who considered *freedom* and *liberty* sacred. It was thus inevitable that for a great many minds the very purpose, the ultimate objective, of progress would be the steady and evermore encompassing advance of individual freedom in the world. The reality of progress was attested to by the manifest gains in human knowledge and in man's command of the natural world, but such gains were possible only when all possible limits were removed from the individual's freedom to think, work, and create. The test of progress was thus the degree of freedom a people or nation possessed.

Turgot

No one in the eighteenth century united progress and freedom more closely than did this remarkable individual. He is known to history in two quite different roles: first, as philosopher of progress (the *founding* philosopher of progress, Condorcet and others would declare); second, as theoretical and practical economist whose writings and achievements in government administration on fiscal matters were of such distinction as to lead to his eventual appointment by Louis XVI as Controller-General of France. He brought about important, long-needed, and acclaimed reforms, but his very success led to his early undoing, his fall into political disgrace resulting from having antagonized very powerful nobles who were in no mood for reform of any kind. What the two Turgots—youthful philosopher of progress and mature finance minister—have in common is devotion to individual freedom.

He was just twenty-three years old when in December 1750 he delivered an address to the public at the Sorbonne titled "A Philosophical Review of the Successive Advances of the Human Mind." His reputation among the philosophes and other intellectuals in Paris was established immediately. By general assent among historians, Turgot's address is the first systematic, secular, and naturalistic (apart from a couple of rhetorical flourishes at Providence) statement of the "modern" idea of progress. Here he described in rich colors "the general course of advancement of the human mind," an advancement determined "by a chain of causes and effects which unite the existing state of the world with all that has gone before." As we look out on the world today, Turgot declared, the world that European navigators and explorers have made known to us, we can see "every shade of barbarism and refinement . . . every step taken by the human mind, the likeness of every stage through which it has passed, the history of all ages." Nor need we depend for our understanding of progress upon anything but science. "The natural philosopher forms hypotheses, observes their consequences. . . . Time, research, chance, amass observations, and unveil the hidden connections which unite phenomena." And what are the mechanisms responsible for the progress of mankind? It could be Mandeville speaking: "Self-interest, ambition, vainglory" are the prime movers, "and in the midst of their ravages manners are softened, the human mind enlightened, isolated nations brought together; commercial and political ties finally unite all parts of the globe; and the total mass of human kind, through alternations of calm and upheaval, good fortune and bad, advances ever, though slowly, towards greater perfection." Turgot's conclusion was in perfect keeping with the ethnocentric character of reflections on progress we have seen since the Renaissance. "Century of Louis the Great, may your light grace the precious reign of his successor! May it endure forever, may it extend over all the earth! May men continue to advance along the pathway of truth! Rather still, may they become ever better and happier!" But the preceding words refer to the French image of betterment and happiness, we cannot help but note wryly.

What gives distinction to Turgot's address at the Sorbonne is his weaving of truths and errors, advances and retardations, periods of rise and periods of decline, and glories and debasements into one single, unified advance of all mankind. Bury is quite correct in his characterization of Turgot: "He regards all the race's actual experiences as the indispensable mechanism of Progress, and does not regret its mistakes and calamities."

Turgot's accomplishment is truly remarkable. But for the sake of full and illuminating context, there are certain points which must be made. First, it is interesting to know that Turgot was enrolled at the time of his address on progress in the Maison de Sorbonne, a part of the theological faculty of the University. Second, his career objective when he entered the University was ecclesiastical—to serve the Catholic Church in one capacity or other (to be sure, this objective changed by the time he left the Sorbonne). Third, only six months prior to his giving the address I have just described, Turgot delivered another, also publicly, with the title: "The Advantages which the Establishment of Christianity has Procured for the Human Race." This address given in July 1750 was not only about Christianity and its boons but was, in structure, the familiar Christian philosophy of history that began with Eusebius and St. Augustine. Progress extolled, yes, but in the form we have come to know well: Providence-as-progress. Fourth, Turgot by his own admission had been deeply influenced by the Bishop Bossuet's *Discourse on Universal History;* it became indeed, albeit in secularized contemplation, the very model of the "Plan for Two Discourses on Universal History" that Turgot drafted in 1751, just before his entry into government service which I shall come to shortly.

The first conclusion to be drawn from all this is clear: sometime between July 1750, when he delivered his public address on Christianity's gifts to world history and in the process hailed the Christian Providence, and December 1750, when he delivered his more secular and rationalist (though with due references to Providence) "Philosophical Review" to an appreciative Paris audience, Turgot seems to have lost at least some of his faith in God, or if nothing quite so drastic, his desire to serve God and the Catholic Church. For, as noted, it was in the following year that he forsook ecclesiastical ambitions and went into government service and a career that both in administrative accomplishment and theoretical works in economics won him the admiration of France's greatest minds. I am concerned here, however, with the single fact that, with respect to the idea of progress, Turgot, without abandoning the structure or framework of his first address at the Sorbonne, secularized it. He was not the first, nor would he be the last, to put rationalist-naturalist content into a framework born of Christian dogma.

But the second point I want to make is the more important. Turgot's experience within a single year can be seen as the very epitome of the processes of intellectual development we have been concerned with: processes which take us, as it were, from Providence-as-progress to progress-as-Providence. Bodin, the Puritan historians and prophets, Bossuet, Leibniz, and Vico—all were, as we have seen, deeply committed to the progress of humanity in material as well as spiritual respects. But though all of them paid increasing attention to natural and social factors, Providence was the ultimate and continuing cause of progress and the Providential order the grand, unfolding context—just as it was for Isaac Newton, as set forth in the General Scholium.

Turgot certainly did not, in the six months which elapsed between his July 1750 address on Christianity and the December address that so impressed his generally secular audience, abandon Providence utterly. There is indeed in the later discourse a passage beginning: "Holy religion! Could I forget the perfection of morals . . . the enlightenment of mankind on the subject of Divinity!" But the evidence is clear enough that during that six months, from whatever motivation or cause, Turgot's attention turned more and more emphatically to subjects secular rather than sacred.

His greatest work on progress is the "Universal History," which he wrote in outline apparently in 1751, and which he acknowledged had been inspired by reading Bishop Bossuet's *Discourse*. But such recognition should not diminish appreciation of the originality and comprehensiveness of Turgot's draft for a universal history. He begins with reference to "a supreme being" and "the imprint of the hand of God," but what follows is the outline of a strikingly modern treatise on social evolution. Bossuet's epochs of advancement had been, as we observed, religiously designated; Turgot's epochs are presented in the terms of mankind's primitive beginnings of culture, ascent to the stage of hunting, pastoralism followed by the stage of agriculture, and then navigation and commerce. He deals with the rise of the first governments, uniformly despotic and monarchical, and the beginnings of human liberation from political despotism. "Despotism perpetuates ignorance and ignorance perpetuates despotism. . . . Despotism is like an enormous weight which, resting on wooden pillars, weakens their resistance and crushes or submerges them from day to day." Over and over Turgot affirms the necessity of freedom for human creativity of any kind, and declares the achievement of freedom—by women, by slaves, by subjects of all orders—the greatest goal of human progress. He deals with migrations, invasions, even wars in the light of their effects in breaking down cultural fixity and inertia, the consequence of geographic and cultural isolation.

His stress on freedom becomes even greater in his draft of the second discourse on universal history. Here his overriding concern is the development of the arts and sciences through all time. He dismisses Montesquieu's emphasis on climate and terrain for the understanding of despotism and freedom, finding cultural and social factors entirely sufficient. We are treated to the probable naturalistic origins of speech and of written language; of the physical sciences and the practical arts; of the disciplines of history, mathematics, logic, ethics, and politics. One of the most brilliant elements of Turgot's outline of the progress of human knowledge is the succession of insights into the failure of given nations to progress beyond a certain point and into the reasons why, for individual peoples, decadence so quickly follows the heights of achievement, although for mankind as a whole overall progress is constant and certain. Turgot is sensible of the immense effect a people's language and its mode of development can have on creativity.

> If a language which has acquired too early a fixity can retard the progress of the people who speak it, a nation which has too rapidly assumed permanent form can be . . . arrested in its scientific progress. The Chinese became fixed too early; they have become like those trees which have been pruned at the stem and which put forth branches near the ground. They never advance beyond mediocrity.

There were many in the eighteenth century who sought natural causes (as did, for instance, Montesquieu) and natural laws for the explanation of the different types of culture and polity to be seen in the world. Turgot, however, was the first to place all of the differences in progressive terms; that is, to describe them as differences in degree of advancement. He was fascinated by geography, but unlike Montesquieu's interest in this subject, Turgot's interest (which he expressed in a draft manuscript titled "Plan for a Work in Political Geography," written apparently at about the same time as his "Universal History") was set forth in developmental and historical terms. Thus he gives us tantalizingly brief accounts of what would be "political world-maps"—the first of which would deal with the locations and movements of the races of mankind, the second with the establishment of nations, considered in aggregate, and still other sequentially, developmentally arranged "political maps" reflecting the rise to power of each of the great nations which make up Western history. It is really historical geography that Turgot gives us in outline. He emphasizes repeatedly the danger of ascribing causal effectiveness to geographic data alone, without reference to their place in human history and in stages of development of humanity.

Over and over Turgot employs the three-stage typology that we have already seen as a cardinal part of the history of the idea of progress from its beginning. But for Turgot the stages are invariably rooted in the substance of whatever he happens to be describing. Mankind as a whole may be seen to have progressed through three stages—hunting-pastoral, agricultural, commercial-urban—but each of its major institutions may also be observed as passing through three stages: language, mathematics, painting, and so forth, each with its own distinctive pattern of advancement drawn from the nature of the entity.

Had Turgot never written anything or done anything besides the discourses on progress I have briefly described, he would without question loom up as one of the signal eminences of the eighteenth century. It was admiration almost wholly for Turgot's writings on progress that led his contemporary, Condorcet, to write a biography of him. When one reads the often fragmentary, telegraphic type of sentences and phrases which make up his "Universal History," and reflects on what these could and doubtless would have been developed into had Turgot remained at the Sorbonne for the rest of his life, one has intimations of a monumental work on progress that very probably has not been nor ever will be done by anyone else.

But, as we know, Turgot left the Sorbonne, abandoned his objective of becoming a scholar within the Church, and went into the career for which he is probably most widely known, that of government administrator, reaching ever-higher levels of achievement and distinction before his eventual fall from political grace. And within this career, oriented almost entirely toward financial and taxation matters, Turgot found the time to write some essays on economics which at their best were not surpassed in quality, if even equalled, by Adam Smith himself. The late Joseph Schumpeter, in his *History of Economic Analysis*, wrote of Turgot: "It is not too much to say that analytical economics took a century to get where it could have got in twenty years after the publication of Turgot's treatise had its content been properly understood and absorbed by an alert profession." Not, Schumpeter also asserts, until the late nineteenth century would work as good in the realm of wages, prices, and capital be done by European economists.

Turgot's masterpiece in economics is the long essay "Reflections on the Formation and Distribution of Wealth." Written in 1766, published in 1769, several years before Adam Smith's *Wealth of Nations* appeared, Turgot's work anticipates Smith's in a number of important respects. Its thesis, like Smith's, is vital necessity of an economic system based upon individual freedom, upon autonomy from government decree and caprice, upon, above all else, free, private enterprise.

From our point of view the greatest importance of Turgot's *Reflections* is to be seen in the relation of the work to Turgot's papers on progress. In his "Universal History," chiefly in the first part, he had outlined the normal progress of economic enterprise from "hunting" to "pastoral" to "agriculture," with the next natural stage of progress that of, or to become that of, free commercial enterprise. For Turgot, each of the stages is a progressive emergent from its predecessor in time, and this holds no less for the manufacturing-commercial system Turgot could see forming in his own time than for any of the preceding stages of economic progress. As the English economist Ronald Meek in his edition of Turgot's basic writings observes:

> Turgot's main aim in the *Reflections* was to investigate the way in which the economic "machine" operated in a society where there were three main classes or "orders" of economic agents—landowners, wage-earners, *and capitalist entrepreneurs*. . . . But even more remarkable was the way in which he appreciated . . . that one could arrive at an understanding in depth of such a society by beginning with an analysis of the working of the "machine" *in the the type of society which historically preceded it,* and then asking oneself what alterations in its working were brought about when a new class of capitalist entrepreneurs entered upon the historic scene.

In short, almost a full century before Karl Marx dealt with capitalism as the historical-developmental emergent of the stage of economy which had preceded it, we find Turgot dealing with the new economic system in exactly the same terms: the terms of progress and advancement in time.

For Turgot, the essence of a successful system of manufactures was freedom: the freedom of the individual from the thicket of customs, privileges, ranks, and laws that everywhere in Europe seemed to be threatening to stop the progress of the new system even before it was well started. In his first address at the Sorbonne, in July 1750, Turgot had lauded Christianity above all else for its role in giving freedom to slaves and others, including women, who had been in pagan bondage. In his next and more famous address of December 1750, Turgot made the natural progress of the arts and sciences through all history his major subject, and, as I have observed, he frequently comments on the indispensability of individual freedom and autonomy for upsurges in the arts and sciences. In his drafted "Plan for Two Discourses on Universal History" Turgot seeks to demonstrate how the progress of social institutions and political laws has been toward an ever-higher degree of freedom. From this to his *Reflections,* written fifteen years after his "Universal History," it was but a short step. For that work may properly be seen as a detailed presentation of the very form of economic liberty that was for Turgot the essence of human progress. We may well consider Turgot as the very first of philosophers and advocates of economic growth in the modern world. Both in the "Universal History" and in the *Reflections* he emphasizes strongly the dependence of all forms of progress in the arts, sciences, and elsewhere upon economic growth and "economic surplus." As a young man of twenty-three Turgot had designated the arts and sciences as true measures of progress. By the time of his *Reflections* he had come to realize fully the relation of intellectual to economic progress, and the dependence of each upon individual liberty.

Such indeed was Turgot's devotion to individual freedom of enterprise that he criticized in a letter to Richard Price (this after Turgot's forced retirement from his finance ministry) the bicameral system of legislature and independent executive in the American states. Such multiplication of authorities, Turgot argued, would constrict individual freedom of thought and action to a degree far greater than would a government composed simply of a single-house legislature and a very rigorously limited executive. After Turgot's death in 1781 Price published the letter from Turgot, which eventually reached John Adams, causing him in strong disagreement with Turgot's position to write his notable three-volume work, *Defense of the Constitutions of Government of the United States.* I shall come back to that book when we deal with philosophies of progress among the Founding Fathers in America.

Edward Gibbon

About halfway through *The Decline and Fall of the Roman Empire* Gibbon, reflecting on the power of the Germanic barbarians to destroy an entire civilization, muses over the question of whether a like destruction of his own Western civilization could ever take place. The result of his musing is wholly optimistic. There will be ups and downs among states, but they will not "injure . . . the system of arts and laws and manners which so advantageously distinguish, above the rest of mankind, the Europeans and their colonies."

But, he continues, may not those parts of the earth still inhabited by "savage nations" spew forth invaders just as Asia and Eastern Europe did at Rome's expense? Gibbon is serenely confident, to say the least. In the first place the progress of the military arts in the West renders it invulnerable to savage peoples necessarily devoid of these arts. More important, though, is the fact that these very savage nations will themselves undergo progress in the arts and sciences, and such progress will be under the tutelage of the West. Europe, Gibbon assures us,

. . . is secure from any future irruption of Barbarians; since, before they can conquer, they must cease to be barbarous. Their gradual advances in the science of war would always be accompanied, as we may learn from the example of Russia, with a proportionable improvement in the arts of peace and civil policy; and they themselves must deserve a place among the polished nations whom they subdue.

The dread possibility that new and more terrible forms of barbarism might arise from *within*, under their Stalins and Hitlers, progress in the arts and sciences notwithstanding, seems not to have disturbed Gibbon in the slightest. We cannot be certain, he writes,

to what height the human species may aspire in their advances toward perfection; but it may safely be assumed that no people, unless the face of nature is changed, will relapse into their original barbarism. . . . We may therefore acquiesce in the pleasing conclusion that every age of the world has increased, and still increases, the real wealth, the happiness, the knowledge, and perhaps the virtue of the human race.

Not for Gibbon any parallel between Rome and Western civilization!

Adam Smith

The same year, 1776, that yielded the first volume of Gibbon's historic work on the Roman Empire yielded also Adam Smith's *Wealth of Nations*. Without very much question, it is Adam Smith above all his contemporaries, including Turgot and the Physiocrats, who most vividly represents individual economic freedom—the system of "natural liberty," to use Smith's words. The influence of the book was almost immediate, and this influence expanded steadily during the half-century following its publication, reaching the highest levels of government on both sides of the Atlantic.

An Inquiry into the Nature and Causes of the Wealth of Nations was not Smith's first book. Seventeen years before, while still strongly (though not completely) under the influence of his great Glasgow teacher Francis Hutcheson, Smith wrote *The Theory of Moral Sentiments*. Hutcheson, himself a devout follower of Shaftesbury, had put his entire emphasis on the "passions" toward altruism and cooperation which, he argued, are the major sources of society and of the capacity of human beings to live together amicably and constructively. A great deal of Smith's *Theory of Moral Sentiments* is best understood in light of Hutcheson's teachings, although the careful reader will detect here and there the interest in individual self-interest that would become overriding in the *Wealth of Nations*. I do not know how carefully Smith had read Mandeville's *The Fable of the Bees*, published first in 1714 and then in enlarged editions in 1723 and 1728. Clearly, he knew the book and its argument so well expressed in the subtitle *Private Vices, Public Benefits* if only because his teacher Hutcheson had made incessant attacks upon Mandeville's thesis: it is through complex interplay of individuals' egoisms and self-interests that both the stability and the prosperity of society emerge. Such attacks were bound to send Smith to the book and to its easily comprehended and memorable argument.

In some slight degree the Mandevillian thesis can be found in Smith's *Theory of Moral Sentiments*, but in much larger part this book is a reflection of Hutcheson's stress on altruism and cooperation as the building blocks of social order. It is to the *Wealth of Nations* that we must turn for evidence of the influence of the Mandevillian theme of self-interest as the only reliable mainspring of human behavior and society at large. This influence is vivid in what is perhaps the most famous single passage in the *Wealth of Nations*:

> It is not from the benevolence of the butcher, the brewer, or the baker that we expect our dinner, but from their regard to their own interest. We address ourselves, not to their humanity but to their self-love, and never talk to them of our own necessities but of their advantages.

In sum: "private vices, public benefits." And yet, as a succession of students of Adam Smith's classic work have concluded (starting, in my own experience at least, with Eli Ginsberg's profoundly interpretative *The House of Adam Smith*, published nearly a half-century ago), the entry of Mandeville into Smith's mind by no means drove out all of Hutcheson. We look harder, of course, to find consciousness of altruism and cooperation in the *Wealth of Nations* than in the earlier book, and nowhere does Smith make a principle of these two traits in order to explain the economy and its best mode of operation. But it is well within reason to declare that Smith advanced the individualistic arguments of the later book in light of or within the premises of the earlier one. We are justified in saying that it is *because* the social order has been cemented securely by all the values and institutions which spring from altruism and cooperation that an economic system driven by enlightened self-interest is possible within that order. And as far as Smith's notable precept of "natural liberty" or *laissez-faire* is concerned —that is, avoidance by political government of direct management of individual lives—one can as easily argue this on the basis of prepolitical social bonds as on the basis of an "invisible hand" in the marketplace.

It is inevitable that we classify the *Wealth of Nations* as economic in theme, indeed as the principal source of what would come in time to be called economics or political economy. But it is also a text in the history of the idea of progress. I would argue indeed that the major purpose of the book is that of not only describing human progress, especially economic progress, but also of seeking to demonstrate the pattern of this progress, and above all the root causes of economic progress. The book abounds in such phrases as "progress of institutions" and "progress of opulence"; a count of the uses of the simple word "progress" inevitably would be high. Smith was fascinated by the kind of history that in his age was variously referred to as "hypothetical," "natural," "conjectural," or "speculative"; that is, the kind of history that aims not at event-by-event, person-by-person recital of the actual, concrete experience of a given people or state, but, rather, the kind of history that through a combination of historical, ethnographic, and psychological means tries to set forth the *real* history of man through the ages. It was the kind of history that involved looking to the universal forces at work and the stages of social and cultural development through which mankind has actually passed, or would have passed had there not been interruptions of the progress that for Smith as for so many of his contemporaries is natural to man. Much of Smith's book falls under what today we term "economic growth," and needless to say Smith was wholeheartedly for it.

A variety of works by Smith attests to his keen interest in progressive development: those on the origin of language, the history of astronomy, and the development of jurisprudence; but there are others. Ronald Meek has recently stressed the point that Adam Smith utilizes in his lectures on jurisprudence modes of subsistence in mankind's progress—just as Turgot had in his "Universal History"—to supply the stages of progress, pointing to four major stages which humanity has passed through. And Andrew Skinner has provided us with a sufficient amount of textual evidence that Smith can very properly be seen as working within pretty much the same progressive-developmentalist perspective of types of economy as Marx and many others in the next century.

But for clinching testimony of Adam Smith's dedication to the idea of progress in economic and other spheres, we have the eloquent words of his contemporary, friend, and admirer Dugald Stewart, also a professor of political economy. He wrote in his *The Life and Writings of Adam Smith*:

In Mr. Smith's writings, whatever be the nature of his subject, he seldom misses an opportunity of indulging his curiosity in tracing from the principles of human nature or from the circumstances of society, the origin of the opinions and the institutions which he describes. . . .

. . . the great and leading object of his speculations is to illustrate the provisions made by nature in the principles of the human mind, and in the circumstances of man's external situation, for a gradual and progressive augmentation in the means of national wealth; and to demonstrate that the most effectual plan for advancing a people to greatness, is to maintain that order of things which nature has pointed out; by allowing every man, *as long as he observes the rule of justice,* to pursue his own interest in his own way, and to bring both his industry and his capital into freest competition with those of his fellow-citizens. (Italics added)

Too often when references by friends or foes are made to Smith's devotion to competition and free enterprise, there is omission of the crucial statement: "as long as he observes the rule of justice." To return to my earlier observation on "the Adam Smith problem" as it used to be known, there is really little to search for in establishing the continuity of the *Wealth of Nations* and the earlier *Theory of Moral Sentiments.* As noted, we may see the early work as Smith's sociology, concerned with the forces which hold a social order together, thus making possible specializations and other expressions of individual enterprise coupled with competition which without the preeconomic social bonds would lead to sheer anarchy. Competition, yes; but only within "the rule of justice."

Despite continuing belief to the contrary in our time, Adam Smith was deeply sensitive to the needs of the poor and the working class. One of the strongest points he makes about economic competition is that workers, "the laboring poor," will be benefited. Smith writes:

It deserves to be remarked, perhaps, that it is in the progressive state, while the society is advancing to the further acquisition, rather than when it has acquired its full complement of riches, that the condition of the laboring poor, of the great body of people, seems to be the happiest and the most comfortable. It is hard in the stationary, and miserable in the declining state. The progressive state is in reality the cheerful and the hearty state to all different orders of society. The stationary is full; the declining melancholy.

Nothing seemed more inimical to either economic effectiveness in a country or to the liberty, in all spheres, of its citizens than endeavours by government to manage or direct economic processes. Over and over Smith presents us with instances of the harm done—not only to the business class or to the wealthy, but *especially to* the poor—by political interventions, however well intended, which destroy the equilibrium of the economic machine. Government, when so oriented, "retards, instead of accelerating, the progress of the society towards real wealth and greatness; and diminishes, instead of increasing, the real value of the annual produce of its land and labor." Hence Adam Smith's incessant adjurations to governments in the West to remove altogether, or at least reduce, existing limitations on individual freedom. He states:

> All systems either of preference or restraint, therefore, being thus completely taken away, the obvious and simple system of natural liberty establishes itself of its own accord. Every man, as long as he does not violate the laws of justice, is left perfectly free to pursue his own interest his own way, and to bring both his industry and capital into competition with those of any other man, or order of men.

In a system of genuine, "natural" liberty, there is no room in Smith's view for government to intervene in matters where it "must always be exposed to innumerable delusions, and for the proper performance of which no human wisdom or knowledge could ever be sufficient; the duty of superintending the industry of private people, and of directing it towards the employments most suitable to the interest of society."

For Adam Smith there are but three legitimate functions of a political government: defense of country from foreign attack; administration of justice; and maintenance of a few vital public works.

Now, the crux of all this, at least from our point of view, is that Adam Smith is setting forth his "system of natural liberty" *not* primarily on the ground of personal preference or even individual reason, though both were surely involved in Smith's thinking. The essential and for him unchallengeable ground is that of the nature of progress, or the normal, necessary "progress of opulence." Thus his famous chapter titled "The Natural Progress of Opulence," and thus his insistence therein that whereas "according to the natural course of things . . . the greater part of the capital of every growing society is, first, directed to agriculture, afterwards to manufactures, and last of all to foreign commerce," what has in fact happened in all the modern states of Europe is that this natural course of progress has been in many respects "entirely inverted." He continues: "The manners and customs which the nature of their original government introduced, and which remained after that government was greatly altered, necessarily forced them into this unnatural and retrograde order."

The mainspring of human progress for Adam Smith—nowhere expressed more powerfully than in the economic sphere—is "the natural effort of every individual to better his own condition." When this natural effort is allowed "to exert itself with freedom and security," it is capable "alone, and without any assistance" of "carrying on the society to wealth and prosperity," even of "surmounting a hundred impertinent obstructions with which the folly of human laws too often incumbers its operations; though the effect of these obstructions is always more or less either to encroach upon its freedom, or to diminish its security."

So devoted to *individual* liberty and the free play of *individual* self-interest is Adam Smith that he even warns against those more or less voluntary associations or combinations of men which by their existence are bound to put a check upon individual inclination and movement. Smith shrewdly recognizes and condemns the powerful tendency of people in the same trade to fix or raise prices with the public the victim. "People of the same trade seldom meet together, even for merriment and diversion, but the conversation ends in a conspiracy against the public, or in some contrivance to raise prices." He is no less hostile to corporations, declaring that the "pretence that corporations are necessary for the better government of the trade is without any foundation." All necessary discipline will be furnished in a genuinely free economic system by either fear of losing a job or customers.

It is interesting to note that Smith sees a strong and pervasive equality of talents among human beings. "The difference of natural talents in different men is, in reality, much less than we are aware of." It is "habit, custom, and education" which account for the major differences. What does bring about the more useful and creative differences among men—or, putting it differently, social differentiation—is "the disposition to truck, barter and exchange. . . . As it is this disposition which forms that difference of talents, so remarkable among men of different professions, so it is this same disposition which renders that difference useful."

Precisely this same disposition lies behind the rise and progress of that most vital aspect of prosperous societies: division of labor. It is division of labor and, with it, the rise of individual talents which would not otherwise emerge that marks the accomplishments of the most progressive nations.

This division of labor, from which so many advantages are derived, is not originally the effect of any human wisdom, which foresees and intends that general opulence to which it gives occasion. It is the necessary, though very slow and gradual consequence of a certain propensity in human nature which has in view no such extensive utility: the propensity to truck, barter, and exchange one thing for another.

Others—for example, the Physiocrats in France from whom Adam Smith learned so much during the years immediately following publication of his *Theory of Moral Sentiments*—had proposed on the grounds of their lack of consonance with the laws of nature the abolition of guilds, syndicates, and other artificial interferences with individual liberty. Still others after Smith would do the same, under whatever auspices. But no one, I believe, either before or after Smith, has so ingeniously allied the doctrine of individual freedom to what he had no hesitation in calling "the natural progress of opulence." His celebrated reference to "an invisible hand" which, he argues, leads individuals pursuing their own private interest to achieve a maximum of public good, must be seen in the context of Smith's larger philosophy of human progress.

By pursuing his own interest he frequently promotes that of the society more effectually than when he really intends to promote it. I have never known much good done by those who affected to trade for the public good. It is an affectation, indeed, not very common among merchants, and a very few words need be employed in dissuading them from it.

Adam Smith was an ironist, obviously, as well as a libertarian and a prophet of economic progress.

The Founding Fathers

If 1776 has been made notable by Adam Smith's and Edward Gibbon's classics (to which should be added Jeremy Bentham's seminal *Fragment on Government,* it has been made world historic by the *Declaration of Independence* which issued forth in that year from the American colonies to make its way quite literally to every part of the earth. The *Declaration* is not a primary text in the history of the idea of progress, strictly interpreted, but it is the product of minds, beginning with its drafter's, Jefferson's, which were steeped in faith in human progress.

In 1748, it is interesting to note, Turgot predicted the colonies' liberation from British rule just before his admission as a student to the Sorbonne. The prediction is contained in his "Researches into the Causes of the Progress and Decline of the Sciences and Arts . . . "—a somewhat disjointed, fragmentary, if brilliant set of notes on rise and fall in history and without doubt the immediate source of the two better composed, more mature addresses at the Sorbonne which we have already examined. In the "Researches" Turgot muses at one point on colonies in history; they are "like fruits which cling to the tree till they have received from it sufficient nurture; then they detach themselves, germinate and produce new trees." Turgot writes: "Carthage did what Thebes had done and what America will do some day." We know that Turgot throughout his life had genuine admiration for the American accomplishments in the New World. Even in his final years, after he had been forced from political office and was virtually sequestered in his home, his interest in and respect for America continued. In the letter to Richard Price I have already referred to, Turgot went so far as to declare that "America is the hope of the human race."

Turgot was not alone in his sentiment. True, there had been earlier in the century those, the great Buffon among them, to declare the American continent an impossible base for a true civilization. It was, they declared, lacking in sufficient natural resources; and all forms of animal and human life native to the continent were inferior by their nature. So went the argument of Buffon and others against the possibility of real progress. But Americans were quick to reply. Franklin, Jefferson, John Adams, and Benjamin Rush were at the forefront of the counterattack. With an immense wealth of every relevant kind of evidence—geological, botanical, zoological, physiological, and so forth—the Americans quickly demonstrated that America was in every respect youthful and strong, capable of furnishing far more resources necessary to the progress of civilization than any European country. Franklin in his *Observations Concerning the Increase of Mankind* in 1755 used America's fast-developing population as a principal argument in behalf of his prediction that America would become a great and powerful civilization. As late as 1785 Jefferson was still replying—in his *Notes on the State of Virginia*—to Buffon's insistence that nature in America was inferior to nature in other parts of the world. He declared that Americans, including the native Indians, were at least equal and probably superior to European physical types. He did not hesitate to utilize America's victory over the English and other European troops in the Revolutionary War as evidence for the fact that not only were Americans physically superior but that such defeat of the English argued their own degeneration of body and mind.

By the latter part of the eighteenth century in Europe there was a good deal less of the kind of assessment Buffon had made. The achievements of the Americans in so many spheres were all too obvious for any indictment on grounds of regress to survive. Much more common were the kinds of comments which came from Turgot in 1748 and were echoed by such minds as Voltaire and Condorcet. In his *Philosophical Letters* Voltaire declared America the improvement of all that was excellent in England. The Quakers in Pennsylvania, Voltaire asserted, had already created "that golden age of which men talk." The Abbé de Raynal (earlier on Buffon's side) came to hail America with such words as "a new Olympus, a new Arcady, a new Athens, a new Greece." And Condorcet in his prediction of what the next stage of human progress would contain used America to represent all that he believed to be best and most advanced in his own, a very model of what the entire world must become in time if it is to progress to the very highest levels of civilization.

Needless to say, there were abundant assessments of this kind in America. The greatest of the Founding Fathers were emphatic in their conviction of past progress over vast lengths of time for humanity, and of progress, with America in the vanguard, through a long future. Such individuals, steeped as most were in the classics of the ancient world, may have expressed neo-cyclical views now and then about a single given nation, or about human nature and its persisting fallibilities. But these are of slight importance when set against the stately affirmations of the progress of civilization which we shall see in Jefferson, John Adams, Franklin, Paine, and others of the time.

There is much the same relationship between Puritanism in America and the burgeoning of a philosophy of secular progress as we found in Europe. There is not space to enter here into a full account of the relevant Puritan beliefs of the seventeenth and eighteenth centuries. But something must be said, all the same. The historian David Levin in his recent study of the young Cotton Mather greatly illuminates our subject. Levin notes that in 1669, Cotton's father, Increase Mather, expressed publicly and repeatedly his confident assertion that the millennium was on the way, and his personal belief that New England—by then separated from British rule— would become the New Jerusalem. And, as Levin also makes clear, Cotton Mather himself even as a young man combined in his thinking the same strands of millennialist fervor and interest in the practical arts and sciences which we found so richly evident in Puritan England. Cotton Mather thought that the three greatest events of the modern age were the discovery of America, the revival of the arts and sciences, and the Reformation. As Levin writes, Cotton "would praise Francis Bacon, revere Robert Boyle, admire Isaac Newton, and he would write about devils, angels, and witches as phenomena no less real than men and the force of gravity." In his early years Cotton Mather declared his conviction, based upon assiduous study of Biblical prophecies and on observation of what was going on in his own age, that the millennium would come in 1679. It is interesting to note that long before Benjamin Franklin, Mather used the rate of population growth in America compared to what it was in Europe to bolster argument for New England's eventual ascendancy in the millennium.

There is a steady, continuous development of Puritan thought on progress—overwhelmingly spiritual and millennium-oriented throughout the seventeenth century in New England, but less and less so as the eighteenth century advances—to the affirmations we shall see coming from the Founding Fathers. Perry Miller argues this in impressive detail in his study of Jonathan Edwards, who would remain for a long time in American history the only mind of philosophical stature that could properly be compared with European thinkers. Edwards, without ceasing to be deeply religious and passionately Puritan (he is, after all, the primary figure in America's "Great Awakening" of 1730–60), was able nevertheless to give to his theological writing evidences of keen interest in issues of a psychological, sociological, economic, and political character. I recognize that Perry Miller's interpretation of Edwards, his "modernization" of this towering religious mind is controversial among students of Puritanism, but it is hard for any interested outsider to conclude other than that there are without question strong intimations of modernity in Edwards, intimations which were bound to be appreciated and built upon during the years following his writing. And this holds emphatically for the ideas of millennium and of progress. What Sacvan Bercovitch in his *The American Jeremiad* has to say is highly appropriate here; Bercovitch is referring to the direction of Edwards's thought: "It indicates, first of all, that Edwards drew out the protonationalistic tendencies of the New England Way. He inherited the concept of a new chosen people, and enlarged its constituency from saintly New England theocrats to newborn American saints."

Bercovitch sees in Edwards an "emphasis on process." While I cannot agree with his view that such emphasis was largely lacking among the English-based Puritans (more interested, Bercovitch writes, in the final millenarian event than in the fulfilling process by which it comes about), there is no question whatever of the American emphasis on process that Berkovitch is stressing. "Edwards," he writes, "by changing the scenario for this last act of the errand, welded the whole progression into an organic human-divine (and natural-divine) whole." Precisely. Edwards's roots are indeed Puritan; the origins of his own "human-divine" philosophy of history with its inevitable millenarian outcome cannot be separated from the seventeenth-century Puritan Americans who saw progress as essentially divine. But the kind of view of human progress contained in the *Virginia Gazette* letter of 1737 that I have already cited, and the kind of outlook that we find ever more luminously revealed in the pre- and post-Revolutionary writings of the Founding Fathers and their contemporaries are hardly intelligible apart from neo-secular, human, and material emphases in the writings of the greatest American theologian of his age. As in Europe, the imprimatur of the sacred was required for the legitimation of the political and social.

None of the foregoing will, I trust, suggest any lack of appreciation of the forces emanating directly from the Enlightenment in Western Europe. Americans, religious leaders included, were reading with close attention the writings of Locke, Hume, Montesquieu, Priestley, Price, many of the Encyclopedists, and a great many other European luminaries. And, we should not forget, America had its own Enlightenment in the latter part of the eighteenth century, one that has much in common with that of Europe. But, as Henry May has brought out strongly in his *The American Enlightenment*, it is virtually impossible to separate religious and secular strands of the American efflorescence, or to understand it except in its still hardy Protestant shell. There were more than a few Enlighteners in Europe who were able to maintain—as did Lessing, Herder, Kant, and Priestley—faith in Christian principle side-by-side with faith in science. But there were also in the European (and especially the French) Enlightenment, to a degree hardly known in America at the time, those who would mount a powerful onslaught against Christianity.

Ernest Tuveson, in his *Redeemer Nation: The Idea of America's Millennial Role,* has brought together illuminatingly the religious-apocalyptic and the rational-political forces in American thought. As I indicated earlier, one of the casualties of the Great Renewal was the Augustinian dogma of a single, indivisible mankind as the true and sole body of progressive fulfillment. Such a dogma couldn't survive the explosive nationalisms which went with the Protestant Reformation, and, as we have seen, a sense of the political-national was very strong indeed in the Luthers and Calvins of the sixteenth century. So, gradually, was the sense of the nation as a kind of redeemer in the process of historical development. Religionaries vied with political nationalists in creating this last sense. As Tuveson demonstrates, however, nowhere was the sense of a single nation as redeemer of mankind as strong and lasting as in America. He writes:

> . . . when Protestant millennialist theory was formed, logically there came with it a need to find a new chosen nation, or nations. If history is theodicy, if redemption is historical as well as individual, if evil is to be finally and decisively found through great conflicts, God must operate through cohesive bodies of men; there must be children of light and children of darkness geographically, and the city of God and the City of the World should be susceptible of being designated on maps.

The affirmations of progress we find in America in the eighteenth and nineteenth centuries are rarely if ever separable from the profound conviction that America was not only a destined nation, but a redeeming nation for that huge part of mankind that lay still bound (in Europe as well as other, more distant parts of the world) to obsolete and unfree ideas. The success of the Revolutionary War only heightened the sense of a millennium achieved or a millennium near. As Bercovitch has written, the terms "political millennium" and, the more frequently used, "American millennium" were common in the speeches and writings which flourished in the final decades of the eighteenth century—and would go on flourishing well into the nineteenth century. Bercovitch writes:

> American millennialism pervaded the entire spectrum of social thought. Educators planned for a "spiritual revolution" that would bring humanity to perfection. Political and moral reformers advertised their programs as the "revolutionary consummation of God's plan." Prominent thinkers urged that technology would "revolutionize the land" into being a "human-divine paradise," where "mechanical

power [would] be matched by a new access of vitality . . . imaginative, utopian, transcendent; and the acquisitive spirit would "typify" the "infinite" reaches of the soul. Labor leaders found in the Revolution a "post-millennial justification for trade-unionism."

Just as the Puritan-bequeathed sense of millennium became transposed into the politics of millennium, with American government the vessel, so did the Puritan-bequeathed sense of the *advance* of mankind toward a future millennium become transposed in America into an ever more secular view of the nature of this advance. It was a view nevertheless in which the religiously inspired attributes of inexorability and necessity were maintained. Just as many Americans could think of the new nation as a kind of earthly redemption, with the idea of the expanding political community high in their thoughts, so could they see the whole human past as a long preparation for exactly those elements of material and spiritual culture which were prominent in American life. The Revolution had been the midwife for the birth of the new, hallowed republic, but nothing more. Far more important to grasp was the *place* of the newly-formed United States of America—which occupied but a tiny part of a vast continent—in the march of mankind to advanced stages of knowledge and welfare. And this place, in the minds of substantial numbers of Americans, was at the vanguard of humanity's march. In one of the most fascinating passages to be found anywhere in the literature of progress, Jefferson, at age eighty-one, just two years before his death, surveyed the advancements he had seen during his life. And what gives special piquancy to his survey is his use of the entire American continent as a kind of tableau which, properly envisaged, could serve as illustration of the progress of the whole human species.

> Let the philosophical observer commence a journey from the savages of the Rocky Mountains eastwardly towards our seacoast. These he would observe in the earliest stage of association, living under no law but that of nature. . . . He would next find those on our frontiers in the pastoral state, raising domestic animals to supply the defects of hunting . . . and so in his progress he would meet the gradual shades of improving man until he would reach his, as yet, most improved state in our seaport towns. This, in fact, is equivalent to a survey, in time, of the progress of man from the infancy of creation to the present day. And where this progress will stop no one can say. Barbarism has, in the meantime, been receding before the steady step of amelioration, and will in time, I trust, disappear from the earth.

Not Turgot, not Condorcet, not any European philosopher of progress could have improved upon that combination of the anthropological method and conviction of the inevitable amelioration of man's lot on earth.

Even the often dour, occasionally pessimistic John Adams was capable of most eloquent appreciation of human progress. Thus Adams commences the Preface in his notable *Defense of the Constitutions of Government of the United States* with the words:

> The arts and sciences, in general, during the three or four last centuries, have had a regular course of progressive improvement. The inventions in mechanic arts, the discoveries in natural philosophy, navigation, and commerce, and the advancement of civilization and humanity, have occasioned changes in the condition of the world, and the human character, which would have astonished the most refined nations of antiquity. A continuation of similar exertions is everyday rendering Europe more and more like one community, or single family. Even in the theory and practice of government, in all the simple monarchies, considerable improvements have been made.

But the overriding theme of the book is to assert the still greater improvements which have been made in America as the result of state and national constitutions. What these amount to, for John Adams, is the vital separation of powers: executive, legislative, and judicial. This is not the proper place to describe Adams's ingenious and learned defense of the principle of separation of powers. I am only concerned with emphasizing the relation of his defense to his faith in progress, past, present, and future. His confidence in the future can be seen in the following—and also his sense of the forward movement of time:

> The institutions now made in America will not wholly wear out for thousands of years. It is of the last importance, then, that they should begin right. If they set out wrong, they will never be able to return, unless it be by accident, to the right path. After having known the history of Europe, and of England in particular, it would be the height of folly to go back to the institutions of Woden and Thor, as the Americans are advised to do. . . .

The last is a somewhat acerbic reference to the criticism Turgot had made of American constitutions. It is interesting to note, as a measure of how seriously John Adams held to those sentiments of progressiveness, that years later in one of the many letters he exchanged with Jefferson, Adams made reference to, indeed quoted from, the Preface. One gathers that he had been stung by what he felt were unjust charges from certain quarters of "recommending to Youth 'to look backward instead of forward' for instruction and improvement." He therefore cites the passage from the Preface beginning "The Arts and Sciences . . . have had a regular course of *progressive* improvement," this time adding italics.

In a variety of places Benjamin Franklin gave vent to his own sentiments regarding the progress of mankind. A letter written in 1788 to the Reverend John Lathrop serves sufficiently as illustration of both thought and intensity of feeling:

... I have been long impressed with the same sentiments you so well express, of the growing felicity of mankind, from the improvements in philosophy, morals, politics, and even the conveniences of common living, by the invention and acquisition of new and useful utensils and instruments, that I have sometimes almost wished that it had been my destiny to be born two or three centuries hence. For invention and improvement are prolific and beget more of their kind. The present progress is rapid.

Franklin concludes his letter with the reflection that if the "art of physic" improves in proportion to the improvements which may be seen in other areas of learning, "we may then be able to avoid diseases, and live as long as the patriarchs in Genesis." And in a letter of 1780 to Joseph Priestley Franklin writes: "It is impossible to imagine the Height to which may be carried, in a thousand years, the Power of Man over Matter." (The "thousand years" came natually, we may assume, to anyone as acquainted with Puritan millenarianism as someone of Franklin's roots had to have been.)

It is not inappropriate to cite here the very Priestley to whom Franklin wrote; for this great scientist, although born in England, with his most famous work done there in the experimental sciences, came to America for refuge after he had been subjected by a Birmingham mob to personal torment and the burning of house, library, and laboratory as the result of his sympathy for the French revolutionists and his criticisms of Burke. Needless to say, he was welcomed—indeed had been invited—by eminent Americans. He was met at New York Harbor by Governor Clinton himself, was offered a professorship of chemistry at the University of Pennsylvania, and was invited by Jefferson to assist him in the planning and development of the University of Virginia. But Priestley chose instead to live on the Pennsylvania frontier, ever in hope that European friends and students would join him there in the building of a libertarian utopia.

Priestley is one more of those prominent in the Enlightenment who found it both possible and necessary to combine experimental work in science with deep and continuing faith in religion. He could write with deadly aim on Gibbon and Hume for their delinquencies in Christian faith. And he remained a devout Unitarian to the end of his life. His faith in the progress of mankind continued to be strong as the following, cited by Commager, suggests:

I view the rapture of the glorious face of nature, and I admire its wonderful constitution, the laws of which are daily unfolding themselves to our view. . . . Civil society is but in its infancy, the world itself is but very imperfectly known to the civilized inhabitants of it and we are but little acquainted with the real value of those few of its productions of which we have some knowledge and which we are only beginning to name and to arrange. How must a citizen of the world wish to know the future progress of it?

In America, Priestley, living close by, could enjoy the intellectual stimulation that went with membership in The American Philosophical Society in Philadelphia, founded by Benjamin Franklin many years earlier as a means of bringing together at regular meetings individuals in all the colonies who were interested in the development of science and the practical arts. Of the millenarian nature of Priestley's faith in science and progress, there can be no doubt, as the following rapturous lines make clear:

[Men] will make their situation in this world abundantly more easy and comfortable; they will probably prolong their existence in it, and will daily grow more happy, each in himself and more able (and, I believe, more disposed) to communicate happiness to others. Thus, whatever was the beginning of this world, the end will be glorious and paradisiacal, beyond what our imaginations can now conceive.

Only William Godwin in England, whom we come to shortly in this chapter, outdid in rhetoric that confident hope in the future.

Jefferson was one of those in America who while believing in the certainty of progress did not hesitate to suggest the social conditions under which progress would occur most easily. His inclination toward the agrarian life is well-known, and the following is as much evidence of this as it is of his interest in progress; the passage comes from his Query 19 in his *Notes:*

The natural progress and consequence of the arts, has sometimes perhaps been retarded by accidental circumstances: but, generally speaking, the proportion which the aggregate of the other classes of citizens bears in any state to that of its husbandmen, is the proportion of its unsound to its healthy parts, and is a good enough barometer whereby to measure its degree of corruption.

It is interesting to discover that François Jean Chastellux, author of *Travels in North America, 1780, 1781, and 1782,* based upon his experiences as a French general in the Revolutionary War, had a somewhat mixed view of Jefferson's prescription. Chastellux years before had written a widely read, if controversial, book on the progress of human happiness—linking its highest developmental achievement to the instituting of complete freedom. Asked by the President of William and Mary College, where he had been welcomed and accepted as virtually a member of the faculty, to write out his views of the propects for the arts and sciences in America, Chastellux declared just before his return to France his complete confidence that knowledge in America will progress steadily, as will, he thought, the fine arts. But Chastellux urged, let Americans pay more attention to the development of their (five) cities; for, he argued, it is only in an urban atmosphere that the arts and sciences can develop. The countryside is important, but its inhabitants should be close to cities.

Tom Paine, born in England but every inch the American patriot, and whose best-known work, *The Rights of Man*, was written to refute in detail Burke's pessimistic and highly antagonistic view of the French Revolution, was also rapturous about the future of American society.

From the rapid progress which America makes in every species of improvement, it is rational to conclude that if the governments of Asia, Africa, and Europe had begun on a principle similar to that of America, or had not been early corrupted therefrom, that those countries must, by this time, have been in a far superior condition to what they are.

Nor was the new nation devoid of poetic expressions of confidence in America's unique greatness and in its inevitable improvement throughout the future. The American poets had, to be sure, some distinguished European precedent: in what may be Bishop Berkeley's most famous lines, he wrote in 1726:

> Westward the course of empire takes its way;
> The four first Acts already past,
> A fifth shall close the Drama with the Day;
> Time's noblest offspring is the last.

Timothy Dwight, one of the "Connecticut Wits," added to Berkeley in 1794 the following lines of West-oriented poetry:

> All Hail, thou western world; by heaven designed
> Th'example bright, to renovate mankind.
> Soon shall thy sons across the mainland roam;
> And claim, on far Pacific shores, their home;
> Their rule, religion, manners, arts, convey
> And spread their freedom to the Asian sea.

Philip Freneau, the best known of American poet-celebrants of the Revolution and its mission in the world, wrote:

> And men will rise from what they are;
> Sublimer and superior, far,
> Than Solon guessed, or Plato saw;
> All will be just, all will be good—
> That harmony, "not understood,"
> Will reign the general law.

We will close on a contribution by Joel Barlow in *The Columbiad*. America, Barlow preaches, was appointed by Providence for the mission of demonstrating by example and precept the nature of true progress to all the world:

> For here great nature with a bolder hand,
> Roll'd the broad stream and heaved the lifted hand;
> And here, from finisht earth, triumphant trod,
> The last ascending steps of her creating God.

There is no better way of epitomizing the respect in which the arts and sciences were held in the age of the Founding Fathers and the close relationship which was perceived between knowledge and progress than to call the reader's attention to Article I, Section 8 of the Constitution. It reads:

The Congress shall have Power . . .
To promote the Progress of Science and useful Arts, by securing for limited Times to Authors and Inventors the exclusive Right to their respective Writings and Discoveries.

The Constitutional scholar, Dr. Robert Goldwin—to whom I am indebted for directing me to the aforementioned—adds that this passage is the only one in the entire Constitution (amendments excepted, of course) in which there is any explicit reference to individual "right" or "rights." Clearly, in the judgment of the makers of the Constitution, nothing was more important by way of generating and advancing American prosperity and well-being than security given to the creative mind.

What began so lushly in the eighteenth century with respect to the progress of knowledge and America continued grandly in the nineteenth. Whether it it was a George Bancroft devoting a half-century of historical research and writing to the publication of his ten-volume work on American history, its theme nothing less than the inexorable unfolding of the "epic of liberty," or a John W. Draper speaking to large audiences in New York City, propounding his thesis that American history embodies a "social advancement . . . as completely under the control of natural law as is the bodily growth of an individual," or any one of the innumerable Fourth of July orators whose number once seemed infinite, faith in progress was widespread and deep. Even Emerson, so often critical of American values, asked in his "Progress of Culture": "Who would live in the stone age or the bronze or the iron or the lacustrine? Who does not prefer the age of steel, of gold, of coal, petroleum, cotton, steam, electricity, and the spectroscope?" From the East Coast to the West, throughout the century and well into our own century for that matter, newspaper editors vied with one another in singing the praises of progress, with the emphasis almost invariably upon industry and technology, and upon their power to effect political, social, and moral advancement of Americans. "You can't stop progress" was a national colloquialism (how rarely we hear it at the present time!), on a par with any aphorism out of Poor Richard's Almanack. Nothing gave more dramatic evidence of American fascination with progress than the celebrated Chicago Fair in 1893. More than 27,000,000 people were drawn to that immense (600-acre) exhibit of scientific, mechanical, architectural, and industrial progress. The Chicago Fair did for both America and Europe (large numbers of its visitors came from Europe and other parts of the world) in 1893 what the almost equally famous, earlier Crystal Exhibition Palace in London had done to confirm faith in progress. The aim of that exhibition, one visitor declared was "to seize the living scroll of human progress, inscribed with every successive conquest of man's intellect."

By the second half of the nineteenth century, the concept of progress had become almost as sacred to Americans of all classes as any formal religious precept. What tended to be stately philosophical wisdom limited largely to the educated in, for example, France or England was grass-roots evangelism in America from one coast to the other. I can testify on the basis of personal exploration of volumes of newspapers in the cities of Pittsburgh, Chicago, and San Francisco that not only editorials but innumerable letters from readers in the last part of the nineteenth century echoed with this litany of progress—all human progress, but American most particularly. If the great majority of such expressions in America had their due recognition of God and His wisdom, the emphasis and the enthusiasm were on progress itself.

One final note on the nineteenth century in America is important. No discussion of the American belief in progress in that century could be complete without reference to the brilliant Henry George and his *Progress and Poverty*. Never mind the inapplicability of the book's central thesis today or even the questions which attended his proposal at the time his book appeared. It was published first by George himself in 1879 and then accepted by D. Appleton & Co. for national and international publication the following year. It was almost immediately recognized in England—by *The Times* and also *The Edinburgh Review*, as well as other newspapers and journals—as the work of a genius. Tolstoy thought its central argument unassailable, and praised Henry George as an authentically creative mind and potential deliverer of the impoverished masses. Within a very few years the book had been translated into several languages and, with the aid of cheap editions which George encouraged from the start, sold millions of copies around the world.

The great question Henry George addressed himself to was: Why, amid all the incontestable evidences of the progress of mankind, does the misery of the poor increase almost in direct proportion to progress in technology, science, government, the arts, and so many spheres of the social order? What must be done to bring the poor into general human progress? As is well known among social scientists and historians, George found the answer solely and exclusively in the system of ownership of land that prevailed everywhere in the world, the United States included.

> The ownership of land is the great fundamental fact which ultimately determines the social, the political, and consequently the intellectual and the moral condition of a people. . . . On the land we are born, from it we live, to it we return again— children of the soil as truly as is the blade of grass or the flower in the field

This is not the place to enter into the intricacies of his argument—his analysis of the whole problem of land ownership and rent, his celebrated single tax—for our concern is with his theory of and faith in social progress. It must do to say that George found the basic and abiding cause of poverty amid riches and progress to lie in individual, rather than common, ownership of land. Once this fact was recognized by the people and their governments, all taxes could be abolished save only that on the economic rent of land and on the immense increases in the value of land, especially unimproved land, which came not from any individual enterprise or ingenuity but from the sheer pressure of an expanding population.

The interesting point for us, however, is the fusion George effected between his theory of poverty, land rent, and the single tax on the one hand, and "the laws of progress" on the other. There was not the slightest question in his mind that all major energies in man and society were harmoniously directed toward progress, or, rather, would be once the problem of land ownership were taken care of.

The general tendency, he writes, in the section on "The Law of Progress," throughout all human history has been toward the reduction or removal of the grosser inequalities: slavery, hereditary privileges, the substitution of parliamentary for absolute government, the instigation of private judgment in religion for ecclesiastical despotism, equal justice before the law instead of differential justice, and so forth. "The history of modern civilization is the history of advances in this direction—of the struggles and triumphs of personal, political and religious freedom." There remains but one signal and ultimately fatal (for any human society) inequality: ownership of land and unjust accrual of profits and other income from the land. Progress will have become fixed forever on its onward and upward course when we the people and our governments remedy through legislation this last vestige of barbarism.

It is a mark of Henry George's faith in America that he believed it the likeliest country to set in motion for the world the reform, the vital reform, that was alone necessary to abolish the dismal, direct ratio between progress and poverty. He speaks eloquently on the liberties we already enjoy in America:

> . . . where political and legal rights are absolutely equal, and, owing to the system of rotation in office, *even the growth of a bureaucracy is prevented;* where every religious belief or non-belief stands on the same footing; where every boy may hope to be President, every man has equal voice in public affairs, *and every official is mediately or immediately dependent* for the short lease of his place *upon a popular vote.* [Italics added. Henry George, thou shouldst be living . . .]

With but one single and indispensable change in our treatment of land and its accruals of value there would be, George declaimed, no end to the heights which civilization would reach.

> Words fail the thought! It is the Golden Age of which poets have sung and the high-raised seers have told in metaphor. It is the glorious vision which has always haunted man with gleams of fitful splendor. It is what he saw whose eyes at Patmos were closed in a trance. It is the culmination of Christianity—the City of God on earth, with its walls of jasper and its gates of pearl! It is the reign of the Prince of Peace.

Thus Henry George ends his book. Joachim de Fiore, the Fifth Monarchy Men, Condorcet, William Godwin—all would have understood George's words and rejoiced.

Condorcet

This remarkable figure, at once scion of nobility and fierce supporter of revolutions, the American and French alike, mathematician and permanent secretary of the Academy of Sciences but also eager contributor to both the literature and the action of politics, was only seven years old when Turgot delivered his December 1750 address on progress. But not many years could have passed before Condorcet became acquainted with Turgot's creative achievements in the theory of progress and the theory of economics. It was Condorcet who wrote the first biography—more nearly eulogy—of Turgot, hailing him as the real discoverer of the "law of progress," an appreciation that both Saint-Simon and Comte would echo later.

Such was the ardor of Condorcet's own passion for this "law" that he wrote his celebrated *Sketch for an Historical Picture of the Progress of the Human Mind* (to be published in 1795, one year after his death) while in hiding for a number of weeks from Robespierre's Jacobin police. Condorcet, although nearly ecstatic about the greatness in history of the ongoing French Revolution, was associated with the Girondist party, and several of his blunt observations on Jacobin leadership led to Robespierre's hostility and orders to put Condorcet in confinement. He was eventually caught, or rather, in effect, gave himself up, and would no doubt have been guillotined as an enemy of the people had he not died (apparently through self-administered poison) the first day of his imprisonment.

He had, however, succeeded in composing a work that would exert a great deal of influence upon not only liberalism, but the rise of the social sciences, especially sociology, in the early nineteenth century. Both Saint-Simon and Comte declared that Condorcet, proceeding from the works of Turgot and Priestley, had first established progress as one of the vital laws of the study of mankind. This, of course, in his *Picture of the Progress of the Human Mind.*

We are given in that little work ten stages of humanity's progress from primitive savagery, the tenth stage reserved for the future that as Condorcet believed the French Revolution was to make possible. He was himself living, he thought, in the ninth stage of mankind's progress, one made notable by the works of the great scientists of his own and the preceding century. They, he declares, are the ones who at long last made it possible for man to liberate himself from superstition, to become intellectually free and thus able to move forward toward eventual perfection. At the beginning of the book we are told:

Nature has set no term to the perfection of our human faculties, that the perfectibility of man is truly indefinite; and that the progress of this perfectibility, from now onwards independent of any power that might wish to halt it, has no other limit than the duration of the globe upon which nature has cast us. This progress . . . will never be reversed as long as the earth occupies its present place in the vast system of the whole universe, and as long as the general laws of this system produce, neither a general cataclysm nor such changes as will deprive the human race of its present faculties and its present resources.

What follows is a series of chapters, each reflective of a vital and necessary stage in human progress, commencing with the very first which is "that of a small society whose members live by hunting and fishing, and know only how to make rather crude weapons and household utensils and to build or dig for themselves a place in which to live. . . ." Condorcet deals with the social organization of primitive man; his clans and kindreds; the ways through which language, abstract thought, and moral ideas made their appearance; and the circumstances surrounding the rise of arts and letters, of cities, commerce, and ever expanding knowledge of world and man himself. We are treated to the rise of rational philosophy in the ancient world—the solid foundation upon which all science rests—and the development of this rational philosophy and of the sciences through the ages leading up to the ninth stage. This stage he has beginning in Descartes's seminal philosophy and culminating in the "foundation of the French Republic." Condorcet writes in the opening of his chapter on the ninth stage:

We have already seen reason lift her chains, shake herself free from some of them, and, all the time regaining strength [from the effects of the Christian Dark Ages], prepare for and advance the moment of her liberation. It remains for us to study the stage in which she finally succeeds in breaking these chains, and when, still compelled to drag their vestiges behind her, she frees herself from them one by one; when at last she can go forward unhindered, and the only obstacles in her path are those that are inevitably renewed at every fresh advance because they are the necessary consequence of the very constitution of our understanding—of the connection, that is, between our means of discovering the truth and the resistance that it offers to our efforts.

What we are then given, in some forty pages, is a capsule account of the progressive changes which had taken place in the seventeenth and eighteenth centuries and which were continuing to take place in philosophy, science, the arts, and in the understanding of the proper foundations of government, economy, and society. Condorcet is lavish in his praise of the individual accomplishments of such minds as Descartes, Locke, Leibniz, Bayle, Fontenelle, Montesquieu, and others, with whose writings Condorcet was not only acquainted but could virtually quote from in his enforced isolation. He discusses the American revolution and, although he has the highest respect for its achievements, contrasts it nevertheless unfavorably with the French. The American revolution, he argues, did not ever go to the real roots of despotism and inequality.

The French, on the contrary, attacked at once the despotism of kings, the political inequality of any constitution only partly free, the pride of the nobility, the domination, intolerance, and the wealth of the priesthood, and the abuses of the feudal system, all of which are still rampant in most of Europe, so that the European powers inevitably united on the side of tyranny.

But for all his pride in the political acts which formed the substance of the French Revolution, Condorcet is far more concerned with setting forth the great contributions of the sciences during the ninth stage. Science, for Condorcet, is the golden avenue to the future and to the final perfection and egalitarian spirit of the future. Until superstitions, especially those of all religions, are erased everywhere, the attainment of future happiness must be delayed.

All errors in politics and morals are based on philosophical errors and these in turn are connected with scientific errors. There is not a religious system nor a supernatural extravagance that is not founded on ignorance of the laws of nature. The inventors, the defenders of these absurdities could not foresee the successive perfections of the human mind. Convinced that men in their day knew everything they could ever know and would always believe what they then believed, they confidently supported their idle dreams on the current opinions of their country and their age.

Condorcet's inexhaustible faith in science and its laws of movement and structure led him to the view that prediction of the course that political, social, and economic history would take during the centuries ahead was a relatively simple matter. He was by no means the first "futurologist," but no one has ever exceeded Condorcet's confidence in the matter of prediction. "If man can, with almost complete assurance, predict phenomena when he knows their laws . . . why, then, should it be regarded as a fantastic undertaking to sketch, with some pretense to truth, the future destiny of man on the basis of his history?"

With relish, therefore, Condorcet turned from the ninth epoch in which he lived to the tenth, still ahead in time, though not distantly. What is the picture Condorcet offers us? There are scholars—Frank Manuel is one— who have argued with a good deal of logic, based upon Condorcet's specific forecasts, that for Condorcet this tenth and probably final stage of mankind's progress would be a kind of despotism governed by scientists, not radically different from the society Francis Bacon had presented in his *New Atlantis*. If reason was to dominate the age, if science was to take command of society as well as of the natural world, then scientists as a class would have to enjoy ascendancy, would have to form a ruling class comparable to that formed by scientists and engineers in Saint-Simon's and Comte's later utopias. In sum, if we follow the interpretation of Condorcet that Frank Manuel presses upon us with much evidence, treatment of Condorcet in this book should not be in a chapter devoted to progress-as-freedom but, rather, in the next chapter where we shall be concerned with the different forms of absolute power (utopian included) which were held by large numbers of minds to represent fulfillment of progress.

But, with all respect to Manuel, I am obliged to conclude that Condorcet was on the whole the devotee of freedom rather than power. There are three thematic questions Condorcet asks at the beginning of his chapter on the shape of the future: first, are there peoples who will never "enjoy liberty"; second, will present large inequalities in all countries be reduced to "such an inequality as is useful to the interest of all?''; third, is humanity destined to improve either "by reason of new discoveries in the sciences and arts" or "through progress in the principles of conduct and in moral practice" or through "the real improvement of the intellectual, moral and physical faculties"?

Condorcet's answers to all three questions are affirmative. "There will come a time . . . when the sun will behold henceforth on earth free men only, recognizing no master but their own reason. . . ." True, Condorcet is firm as to the hallowed place that science and scientists must play, and we can guess that irrespective of Condorcet's own confidence in the compatibility of liberty and a government of scientists the results might in fact be more nearly a scientific bureaucracy than a genuine society of free men. But we must still take Condorcet at his word. And in his long and fevered appreciation of education Condorcet stresses the importance of educating every possible individual in the laws and techniques of science in order to spread scientific knowledge and discovery as widely in the world's population as is possible. He proposes the same for the arts. Everyman-his-own-scientist, or artist, is not an inaccurate rendering of Condorcet's dream of future betterment. I find the future that Condorcet puts on scientific pillars a decidedly different and more liberal form of society than that which Bacon had sketched in the *New Atlantis*.

Second, in addition to a preview in which freedom plays or is marked to play a large role, Condorcet supplies us with a forecast of the development of equality. Several years before he wrote his *Sketch* he had prepared an article "On the Admission of Women to the Rights of Citizenship." He argues that the rights of men,

> . . . result simply from the fact that they are sentient beings, capable of acquiring moral ideas and of reasoning concerning these ideas. Women, having these same qualities, must necessarily possess equal rights. Either no individual of the human species has any true rights or all have the same. And he who votes against the rights of another of whatever religion, color or sex, has abjured his own.

There is nothing in the *Sketch* that runs counter to that statement of equality. It is not absolute, total equality that Condorcet seeks and predicts for the future; not a levelling of human beings for its own sake. As we have already seen, Condorcet, for all his animosity toward the kinds of inequality that abounded in the ancient régime, for all his hope of a liberating equality, took note of the importance of preserving the possibility of those inequalities which will be "useful to the interest of all." And as we have observed also, Condorcet's admiration was nearly infinite for Turgot's ideas, which do not want for emphasis upon individual freedom—intellectual, moral, and economic. A few phrases notwithstanding, Condorcet's treatment of equality is in the main not different from what Turgot might have written and what John Stuart Mill would write in the next century. In our own day, even Hayek or Milton Friedman is not oblivious to the necessity of an equality—chiefly legal—that is the prerequisite for genuine freedom.

In considering the histories of past civilizations Condorcet writes, "there often exists quite a difference between the rights which the law recognizes in the citizens and the rights which they actually enjoy, between the equality established by political institutions and that which actually exists between individuals. . . . " So might Jefferson have written, and so might Jefferson have endorsed Condorcet's explanation for these discrepancies: "inequality of wealth," "inequality of condition," and "inequality of instruction." The following passage by Condorcet is reassuring on the relation between equality and freedom:

It will behoove us, then, to show that these three sorts of real inequality are bound to diminish continually, without, however, disappearing altogether; for they have natural and necessary causes which it would be absurd and dangerous to wish to destroy; nor could we even attempt to destroy their effects entirely without opening up more fruitful sources of inequality, without giving to human rights a more direct and fatal blow.

Whether with respect to individuals within a nation or among nations, it is an equality of opportunity, an equality that merits individuals and nations alike to seek and to realize their highest potentialities that Condorcet—like the Founding Fathers—cherishes, and predicts for the future.

There is, finally, the theme of ultimate perfectibility of human beings, their attainment of an estate on earth that will be highlighted by "individual well-being and general prosperity" and a "real improvement of the intellectual, moral and physical faculties." This too will come about as the result of the laws which have brought mankind to its present advanced condition in the civilized parts of the world and, not to be missed, of a constantly intensified education available to all. Education, properly directed

. . . corrects the natural inequality of the faculties . . . just as good laws remedy the natural inequality of the means of subsistence; just as in those societies whose institutions shall have effected this equality, liberty, though subjected to regular laws, will be more extensive and more complete than in the independence of savage life.

The advantages which result from progress "can have no limit other than the absolute perfection of the human race."

Condorcet then considers the possibility of overpopulation. If mankind becomes ever more perfect in condition, ever more prosperous, as the result of advancement of the arts, must there not come a time "when the increase in the number of men [surpasses] that of their means," with the result manifest in "decrease in prosperity and in population" and with "at least a sort of oscillation between the good and the bad . . . a constant source of almost periodical calamities"? This, of course, is precisely the question Malthus (whom we shall come to momentarily) would ask and answer in two very different ways through successive editions of his famous *Essay on Population*. Condorcet very evidently recognizes the seriousness of the problem, and admits that, all else equal, the perfection of man's estate would lead to an unmanageable, intolerable surplus of people with respect to food supply. But, just as Malthus would reach the point in his thinking where the continued growth of knowledge and reason might be accepted as a "moral check" upon procreation, so does Condorcet. Well before the time of a calamitous and destructive overpopulation on earth, there would surely be, Condorcet argues, a change in men's contemplation of those ancient "superstitions" which enjoin unlimited fertility:

> . . . if we suppose that prior to this time the progress of reason shall have advanced on a par with that of the arts and sciences . . . men will know then that, if they have obligations towards beings who are yet to come into the world, they do not consist in giving them existence only, but happiness; they have for their object the general welfare of the human race, of the society in which they live, or of the family to which they are attached, and not the puerile idea of encumbering the earth with useless and unhappy beings. There could, then, be a limit to the possible means of subsistence and, in consequence, to the greatest possible population, without there resulting that premature destruction, so contrary to nature, and to social prosperity, of a portion of the beings who have received life.

As I say, Malthus himself would eventually come to a conclusion not radically different from this, but before we treat Malthus, we should recognize the philosopher who along with Condorcet stimulated Malthus into writing the *Essay on Population* in its first form.

William Godwin

Philosophical anarchist, radical libertarian, utopian perfectibilitarian— these are a few of the labels which have been put on Godwin. Not even the fanatical Condorcet outdid him in the intensity of his devotion to individual freedom: freedom from state and church primarily, but from any form of social interdependence, including the family, that restricted individual freedom of thought and action.

His *Enquiry Concerning Political Justice and its Influence on Morals and Happiness* was published in 1793 when he was thirty-seven years old. He had been born in a deeply Calvinist family, and the imprint of Calvin's doctrine of individual grace and salvation would lie permanently on Godwin's mind even though from age thirty-two on he declared himself completely emancipated from all religion. Emancipated he may have been, but the kind of millennialist perfection and happiness which the Puritans had held forth to mankind as the inevitable outcome of the unfolding of God's design was at the heart of Godwin's philosophy of progress, God's design, of course, set aside. Godwin had utter faith in mankind's inherent capacity for advancement in knowledge, morals, and above all in respect for the individual.

"Individuality is of the very essence of intellectual existence." This statement is the *leitmotif* of Godwin's *Political Justice*, as indeed it is of most of his other writings as well. All that restricts individuality in its natural development is to be condemned. This included cooperation, which for the majority of anarchists of the nineteenth century was the cornerstone of their faith. Godwin writes (referring to his principles of individual development of freedom and virtue):

From these principles it appears that everything that is usually understood by the term cooperation is in some degree an evil. A man in solitude is obliged to sacrifice or postpone the execution of his best thoughts in compliance with his necessities or his frailties. How many admirable designs have perished in this conception by means of this circumstance . . . . Hence it follows that all supererogatory cooperation is carefully to be avoided, common labor and common meals.

How relentless Godwin was in his pursuit of individuality and liberation from all restraints whatever may be sensed from his prescription of avoidance even of orchestras and other "cooperative" representations of individual excellence, for true musical ability can best be developed and then expressed by the solitary musician. Nor as I have already intimated is the family or what Godwin calls "cohabitation" spared. "The evils attendant on this practice are obvious . . . . [I]t is absurd to expect the inclinations and wishes of two human beings to coincide through any long period of time. To oblige them to act and to live together is to subject them to some inevitable portion of thwarting, bickering and unhappiness."

The idea of progress is the very warp of Godwin's reflections on the future attainment of perfect, unfettered individuality. That there has been from the beginning a powerful tendency toward improvement, Godwin did not doubt. There is,

> . . . a degree of improvement real and visible in the world. This is particularly manifest in the history of the civilized part of mankind, during the last three centuries . . . . It [mankind's improvement] has struck its roots deep, and there is no probability that it will ever be subverted. It was once the practice of moralists to extol past times and declaim without bound on the degeneracy of mankind. But this fashion is nearly exploded . . . . And, as improvements have long continued to be incessant, so there is no chance but that they will go on. The most penetrating philosophy cannot prescribe limits to them, nor the most ardent imagination adequately fill up the prospect.

Godwin is being too modest in that last sentence. For one of the charms of his often tedious book is the limitless reach of his own imagination when it comes to describing the future men might look forward to if they but put behind them once and for all restraints upon individual freedom. Consider the following contemplation of man's future state; we should have to go back to Joachim de Fiore or to one of the more inspired Puritan apocalyptics of the English seventeenth century for its equal: "The sum of arguments which have been here offered amounts to a species of presumption that the term of human life may be prolonged and that by the immediate operation of intellect, beyond any limits which we are able to assign." Godwin will not permit himself to predict individual immortality on earth in the future; that is, the eradication of death. But he comes very close indeed to such prediction. He does not believe that death is necessarily inherent in the human cycle.

Like those Christians beginning with Joachim who foresaw a long stage in which human spirit succeeded human body on earth, with absolute happiness—true, spiritual happiness—the result, William Godwin foresees the decline of present human pleasure in gratification of the bodily senses, especially the sexual. As individual freedom and virtue take command, the sway of the merely sensual will diminish.

> The men therefore whom we are supposing to exist when the earth shall refuse itself to a more extended population will probably cease to propagate. The whole will be a people of men, and not of children. Generation will not succeed generation, nor truth have, in a certain degree, to recommence her career every thirty years. Other improvements may be expected to keep pace with those of health and longevity. There will be no war, no crimes, no administration of justice, as it is called, and no government. Beside this, there will be neither disease, anguish, melancholy, nor resentment. Every man will seek, with ineffable ardor, the good of all. Mind will be active and eager, yet never disappointed. Men will see the progressive advancement of virtue and good, and feel that if things occasionally happen contrary to their hopes, the miscarriage itself was a necessary part of that progress.

Godwin is sufficiently restrained to conclude the chapter in which those words appear with the admonition to the reader that his idea is based upon conjecture, is a statement of probability only. But his admonition, we may reasonably assume, was not taken very seriously either by him or by the numberless readers whose vision of a perfect state ahead in time has been excited by their reading of Godwin's "probable conjecture." The following passage suggests the depth of his vision within the larger concept of necessity in history:

. . . [T]he doctrine of necessity teaches us that all things in the universe are connected together. Nothing could have happened otherwise than it has happened. Do we congratulate ourselves upon the rising genius of freedom? Do we view with pride the improvements of mankind, and contrast with wonder man in the state in which he once was, naked, ignorant and brutal, with man as we now sometimes behold him, enriched with boundless stores of science, and penetrated with sentiments of the purest philanthropy? These things could not have existed in their present form without having been prepared by preceding events.

And once again we are given the analogy of the single individual mind and the history of all mankind:

The human mind is a principle of the simplest nature, a mere faculty of sensation or perception. It must have begun from absolute ignorance; it must obtain its improvement by slow degrees; it must pass through various stages of folly and mistake. Such is, and could not but be, the history of mankind.

And yet Godwin, for all his at times nearly blind faith in historical necessity, does not let us forget that the condition as well as ultimate purpose of progress is the greatest possible degree of freedom of the individual.

Can we arrest the progress of the enquiring mind? If we can, it must be by the most unmitigated despotism. Intellect has a perpetual tendency to proceed. It cannot be held back but by a power that counteracts its genuine tendency, through every moment of its existence. Tyrannical and sanguinary must be the measures employed for this purpose.

Therefore it must be the unvarying policy of government henceforth to encourage every possible form of thought and discussion. Beyond this, there must be an ending to the kind of bitter factionalism, the organized movements for immediate salvation of human beings, and the like which, Godwin declares, exist at the present time.

The genuine progress of political improvement is kind and attentive to the sentiments of all. It changes the opinions of men by insensible degrees; produces nothing by shock and abruptness; is far from requiring the calamity of any. Confiscation and the proscription of bodies of men form no branch of its story.

It is a far cry from the humane, gentle, and pacific sentiments of Godwin the utopian, devoted as he is to individual freedom and to an equality that will never be allowed to level minds, to the kinds of utopias we shall have occasion to consider later in this book: those which are inseparable from the limitless uses of power. In an early draft of *Political Justice* there is a section titled "Three Principal Causes of Moral Improvement Considered." He describes them as the study of literature; unremitting, universal education; and political justice—the last meaning freedom of the individual. "These are the three principal causes of which the human mind is advanced toward a state of perfection . . . " Any thought of the uses of the kind of absolute power over human beings that, for instance, Comte would symbolize with his *Grand Être* and Marx with his "dictatorship of the proletariat" would have been utterly repugnant to Godwin. His was a mind seized by almost total innocence, if we like, but one dedicated nevertheless to the principle that the movement of humanity has been toward ever-greater liberation of the individual with final, complete liberation the objective toward which history has been working from the beginning and will continue to work until perfect freedom has been established over the entire earth.

Thomas Malthus

It may perhaps seem strange to many readers to place Malthus in the context of this chapter; that is, in the context of optimism and human progress. Is not Malthus the figure who, through his famous *Esssay on Population* with its iron law of geometric growth of population and arithmetic increase in food supply declared, in effect, the hopelessness of even a good, much less perfect, society? The answer to this question is very different from the one usually associated with this remarkable mind. Through the scholarship of Gertrude Himmelfarb and William Petersen and a few others in recent years we have been allowed an understanding of Malthus and his *Essay* that was seemingly absent during all the years when Malthus was thought of only in the context of "the dismal science."

An Essay on the Principle of Population made its first appearance in 1798. It was written by Malthus in direct response to the kind of perfectibi-litarianism we have seen in Condorcet and Godwin. Malthus himself describes the *Essay* as "remarks on the speculations of Mr. Godwin, M. Condorcet, and other writers." As we have seen, Godwin had dealt expressly with the possibility of overpopulation, but insisted that the progress of reason would reduce human desire for fertility, adding, "myriads of centuries of still increasing population may pass away, and the earth be yet found sufficient for the support of its inhabitants."

It was this Godwinian supposition that Malthus found utterly unacceptable, at least while he was composing the first edition of the *Essay*. Malthus is entirely respectful in his observations on Godwin's and Condorcet's desire for reform of the human condition and their belief that the laws of progress would insure this reform, leading to an eventual perfection and happiness without limit. But his respect for the motives of the two men did not prevent him from addressing clearly and sharply what he believed to be the fatal flaw in their conception of progress and the future.

This is not the place for a detailed account of Malthus's powerful thesis in the *Essay*. It must suffice to recall simply that in his attack upon doctrines of future perfection for mankind Malthus pointed out that population will always increase in a geometrical ration (2, 4, 8, 16, and so forth) by virtue of constant indulgence in procreative activities; however, Malthus argues, the food available to generations so multiplying must be seen as increasing at but an arithmetical rate, one that spells inevitable famine and wretchedness of human condition instead of the perfection foreseen by Godwin and Condorcet through man's constantly increasing knowledge and his use of reason. So long as sexual desire remains imperious, therefore, any thought of a perfect or even an improved social order must be futile.

Malthus's thesis was a powerful one, and was immediately recognized as such by his readers among whom, naturally, was Godwin himself. In a letter, Godwin congratulated Malthus on the brilliant thesis of the *Essay*. But in this letter Godwin reiterated his faith in the power of human reason to supply a moral check upon processes of fertility. Malthus, Godwin wrote, failed to give proper due to "another check upon increasing population which operates very powerfully and extensively in the country we inhabit . . . " This positive check Godwin identified as "that sentiment, whether virtue, prudence, or pride, which continually restrains the universality and frequent repetition of the marriage contract . . . . The more men are raised above poverty and a life of expedients, the more decency will prevail in their conduct and sobriety in their sentiments."

Whether it was Godwin alone we cannot be sure, but the record shows powerful effect upon Malthus of these Godwinian views. For, in the second and all subsequent editions of the *Essay* Malthus gives full recognition to the efficacy of "positive checks," those induced by reason directing "moral restraint." The fact, as professors Gertrude Himmelfarb and William Petersen have emphasized and documented, is that Malthus moved over a period of years from pessimism rooted in biology to an optimism that sprang from conversion to a sociological-progressive perspective. We find Malthus the pessimist succeeded by Malthus the social democrat and believer in the forthcoming improvement in the human condition. Even in his *Principles of Political Economy* he indicated his belief that with the advance of economic prosperity and the increase in and spread of wages, the working class will become the middle class with altered tastes and, for the first time, capacity for the use of moral or prudential restraint upon procreation.

And now we come to Malthus the believer in individual liberty. He writes in the *Principles*:

> Of all the causes which tend to generate prudential habits among the lower classes of society, the most essential is civil liberty. No people can be much accustomed to form plans for the future who do not feel assured that their industrious exertions . . . will be allowed free scope . . . . [Moreover] civil liberty cannot be permanently secured without political liberty . . .

And in the later editions of the *Essay on Population* we find these words:

> In most countries, among the lower classes of people, there appears to be something like a standard of wretchedness, a point below which they will not continue to marry and propagate their species . . . . The principal circumstances which contribute to raise [this standard] are liberty, security of property, the diffusion of knowledge, and a taste for the comforts of life. Those which contribute principally to lower it are despotism and ignorance.

Adam Smith or William Godwin could have, and in their respective ways did, write that Malthusian diagnosis of society. Let us look at one more Malthusian affirmation that has to come as a shock to those whose knowledge about Malthus is confined to the inexorable ratio of population and food supply in the first edition. This statement also appears in the second edition, and all succeeding editions of the *Essay*:

> On the whole, though our future prospects affecting the mitigation of the evils arising from the principle of population may not be so bright as we can wish, yet they are far from being entirely disheartening, *and by no means preclude that gradual and progressive improvement in human society* which before the last wild speculations on the subject was the object of rational expectations . . . (Italics added)
> And although we cannot expect that the virtue and happiness of mankind will keep pace with the brilliant career of physical discovery, yet if we are not wanting in ourselves we may confidently indulge the hope that, to no unimportant extent, they will be influenced by its progress and will partake in its success.

Why, given such expressions of faith in the capacity of mankind to advance in knowledge, reason, morality, and comfort on earth, does the myth of Malthus persist and so largely prevail: the myth that Malthus spent his life seeking to demonstrate that progress was impossible and that the condition of the poor would always remain squalid, at the near-starvation level, and devoid of all hope?

The answer, as William Petersen has brought out and emphasized in his recent study of Malthus, is that until recently the only Malthus the overwhelming majority of us ever made our way to was the Malthus of the first edition of the *Essay*. And, Petersen observes trenchantly, *this* Malthus attained immediate popularity with the radical critics and antagonists of capitalism. The Malthus of the first edition could be used effectively to demonstrate that *under capitalism* the grim ratio between population and food would inevitably prevail, leaving the working class in a permanent straitjacket of poverty and unemployment, the result of its unalterable procreative activities. Thus, as Petersen points out, Malthus (of the first edition of the *Essay*) becomes for Marx an exceedingly useful stick with which to beat the bourgeoisie and all other supporters of capitalist free, private enterprise. If Marx was aware of later editions of the *Essay* and the striking changes of content, he does not so indicate. He confines himself entirely to the original edition, and even with it he takes liberties of exposition which make a virtual caricature of Malthus's work.

In summary, Malthus has to be seen among those of his century who did in fact believe in progress. Even in the first edition of the *Essay* we are given what is in substance a natural history of mankind from its primitive beginnings through discovery of domestication of animals, agriculture, commerce, and through the successive advances of the arts and sciences—making for a civilization, Malthus thought, far higher, its infirmities recognized, than any that had existed before. There are many likenesses between Malthus's treatment of the historical progress of mankind from past to present and Condorcet's. There was a great deal even in the first edition on which Malthus, Godwin, and Condorcet could have reached easy agreement. The differences, to be sure, are striking. The plagues, catastrophes, and other natural checks upon population increase, which *all three* recognized in the past and present, were for Malthus in the beginning checks which will always be with us and which must be with us if the earth is to be saved from a stupendous mass of population that could lead only to disasters and setbacks worse than any ever known in the past. It was this early Malthusian belief and this alone that formed the principal barrier to agreement between Malthus and Godwin—although even the later, mature Malthus doubtless would have and did reject the more extreme expressions of Godwin's confidence in a blissful future.

And yet, as Gertrude Himmelfarb and William Petersen have made us see, the real Malthus came to hold very positive views indeed on the possibility of progress—social and economic progress for the whole population—in the future. And Malthus is one with Adam Smith, Godwin, and Condorcet in emphasis upon the indispensable role that must be played by education: education through schools made available by political government for the entirety of the people. Petersen quotes Malthus to this effect: "No government can approach to perfection that does not provide for the instruction of the poeple, . . . and as it is in the power of governments to confer these benefits, it is undoubtedly their duty to do it." Neither Condorcet nor Jefferson could have put the matter better.

Malthus has suffered in reader understanding and esteem precisely as Adam Smith so long did—still does, it must be added, although the outcome for Smith is far better than the outcome for Malthus has been or, unhappily, is likely to be, given the sheer succinctness and memorability of the Malthusian "law of population increase." There are not many intellectual historians today who fail to understand that Adam Smith's *Wealth of Nations* has to be read with his *Theory of Moral Sentiments* in mind, and that Smith's stress in the one book on self-interest as the mainspring of economic abundance has to be seen within the context of the altruism and sympathy Smith had made fundamental to the social order within which any economic system must exist. But there are all too many historians who are seemingly unconquerable when it comes to their image of Malthus as the writer who sought to demonstrate the impossibility or inutility of all social, economic, and cultural improvement.

But the hard fact remains: Malthus clearly believed in the progress mankind had undergone in the past, from savagery to civilization as it was known in the West; and on the basis of the second and following editions of the *Essay* and also his *Principles* he believed in not merely the possibility but the high probability of continued progress in the future as the result of continued advances in knowledge and man's predictable desire to avail himself of the benefits of these advances.

Immanuel Kant

Not very many German names of the period we are dealing with spring to mind when we think of *individual* freedom—at least in the sense that is so widely present in England, France, and the United States, the sense in which we have been using the phrase in this chapter. The characteristic and dominant referent of German theories of progress during the period is some supraindividual entity—nation, people, working class, race, and so forth. But Kant is among the exceptions within the tiny group that also includes Wilhelm von Humboldt for whom the individual is the overriding object of attention and moral regard.

Anyone who knows anything at all about Kant knows the large role played in his moral philosophy by the individual—the individual as the autonomous rational being who lives or should live in accord with the categorical imperative. Without individual autonomy, or freedom, there can be no morality in the true sense of the word, Kant argues in his *Critique of Practical Reason*. What is less well known in Kant's thought is his interest in progress. His *Idea of a Universal History from a Cosmopolitical Point of View* published in 1784 is probably our best single source of Kant's views on the nature of progress and its relation to individual freedom. One point should be stressed immediately: we will look in vain, in this or any other Kantian work, for as forthright, confident, and perspicuous a view of human progress as we find in others dealt with in this chapter. There are too many antagonistic elements in Kant's thought, too great an aversion, I should add, to any idea that human happiness or moral perfection is the necessary outcome of the history of humanity for there to be found a theory of the order of, say, Condorcet's or even Turgot's. All the same, Kant was as renowned as anyone else of his time for his interest in and exploration of man's progress.

The first sentence of the *Universal History* reads: "Whatever metaphysical theory may be formed regarding the freedom of the will, it holds equally true that the manifestations of the will in human actions, are determined like all other external events, by universal natural laws." He then goes on to observe that "when the play of the freedom of the human will is examined on the great scale of universal history, a regular march will be discovered in its movements." What at first sight appears to be a tangled undergrowth of human beings and actions at cross-purposes, without design or ordered progression, turns out to be when carefully examined a collectivity "continually advancing, though slow, development of its original capacities and endowments." He is referring, of course, to the human species. God plays a definite role in the progress Kant finds, and there is clear Augustinianism in his theory. Once again we are reminded that wherever we turn in the eighteenth century, the religious origins of the "secular" idea of progress are to be discerned.

For Kant, all capacities and powers in an individual or his species which are implanted by nature are destined, as he tells us, "to unfold themselves, completely and conformably to their end, in the course of time." In man, the only entity or being on earth possessed of reason, the direction progress takes over the whole history of mankind is toward the perfection and ever freer use of this individual reason.

Nature, according to this view, does nothing that is superfluous, and is not prodigal in the use of means for her ends. As she gave man reason and freedom of will, on the basis of reason, this was at once a clear indication of her purpose in respect of his endowments. With such equipment, he was not to be guided by instinct, nor furnished and instructed by innate knowledge; much rather must he produce everything out of himself.

Precisely as Augustine utilized conflict as the efficient cause of the march of mankind to ever-higher levels that had been designed in the first instance by God, so does Kant utilize what he calls "mutual antagonism." Man possesses an "unsocial sociability," he argues, and although his nature inclines him inexorably to the social life, to life with other human beings, this same nature endows in man a resistance to sociality, a protection of self and will from others that leads to mutual antagonism, to unsocial sociability. Without this conflict the human race would lie passive, would never have accomplished what it has, would never reach higher levels of achievement in the future. "Without those qualities of an unsocial kind, out of which this antagonism arises . . . men might have led an Arcadian shepherd life in complete harmony, contentment and mutual love, but in that case all their talents would have forever remained hidden in their germ."

As we have seen, the object, the driving purpose, of the advancement of mankind has been, will continue to be, the attainment of ever more perfect conditions for the exercise of individual freedom. These conditions, for Kant, are political. "The history of the human race, viewed as a whole, may be regarded as the realization of a hidden plan of nature to bring about a political constitution . . . as the only state in which all the capacities implanted by her in mankind can be fully developed." Thus Kant falls among those in his century and nation who helped give the idea of the political state its appeal to modern intellectuals in the West. And there would be others, working basically from Kant's views (Fichte among them), who would endow Kant's liberal state with an increasingly collectivist, power-oriented character that we find in so much German, especially idealist, philosophy in the nineteenth and twentieth centuries. But having conceded this, we cannot doubt the highly liberal nature of Kant's own view of the state. There is really little difference between the kind of state that Kant describes as just and the kind we have seen to exist in the thinking of Turgot and Adam Smith. Any serious limitation of what Kant calls the individual's "civil liberty" would carry with it, he tells us in concrete terms, malignant implications to economic prosperity. There must be on every count—moral and political as well as economic—a maximum of autonomy granted the individual in all areas of his life.

> . . . if the citizen is hindered in seeking his prosperity in any way suitable to himself that is consistent with the liberty of others, the activity of business is checked generally; and thereby the powers of the whole state, again, are weakened. Hence the restrictions on personal liberty of action are always more and more removed, and universal liberty even in religion comes to be conceded.

Kant had the utmost respect for Rousseau and drew gratefully from Rousseau's formulation of a social contract that must underlie the just social order. But where Rousseau tended to draw conclusions chiefly oriented toward the nature and absoluteness of the General Will and, of course, equality, Kant draws conclusions pertaining to individual autonomy and freedom. Nor does Kant see the national state in any of its existing forms as the ideal or the progenitor of the ideal form of polity. For Kant the ascent that began with primitive savagery, animated only by "unsocial sociability," that has gone through such mighty civilizations as those of Greece and Rome and that now has modern Western civilization as its highest point, will continue until there is brought into being a "Federation of Nations." This vision becomes the basis of Kant's equally famous *Perpetual Peace*, a project or proposal for the uniting of all nations into one great and supreme body that will make national wars impossible.

How deeply Kant could be moved by the perspective of progress, despite occasional doubts or ambiguities, may be inferred from the following words, almost French in character:

> I will . . . venture to assume that as the human race is continually advancing in civilization and culture as its natural purpose, so it is continually making progress for the better in relation to the moral end of its existence, and that this progress, although it may be sometimes interrupted, will never be entirely broken off or stopped.

There is, it seems to me, a certain humor in the fact that those words are found in a short piece Kant wrote with the title: "On the Saying: That a Thing may be Right in Theory, but may not Hold in Practice."

Triumph of the Idea of Progress

Heinrich Heine

Cosmopolitan though events in Germany forced him to become, thoroughly saturated by the culture of Paris in which he took residence in 1831 and helped invigorate intellectually, Heine remains nevertheless German—one of the greatest of German lyric poets. While in Paris, he participated for a time in the Saint-Simonian movement, and there is no evidence that despite bitterness and a sense of betrayal by contemporary events and by individual intellectuals, Heine ever lost the sense of buoyancy and belief in mankind's progress that the French Revolution's heritage helped so largely to stimulate. The following brief extract epitomizes Heine's belief in progress:

When mankind regains its complete health, when peace is restored between body and soul, and they blend again in their original harmony, we will scarcely be able to comprehend the unnatural discord that Christianity has sown between the two. The happier and finer generations, who, begotten in an embrace of free choice, come to flower in a religion of joy, will smile sadly at their ancestors who gloomily refrained from all the pleasures of this earth . . . . Yes, I say it with conviction—our descendants will be finer and happier than we. For I believe in progress, I believe mankind is destined to happiness, and I therefore cherish a grander conception of the Divinity than those pious people who fancy that man was only born to suffer. Even here on earth I would like to establish, through the blessings of free political and industrial institutions, that bliss which, in the opinion of the pious, is to be granted only on the Day of Judgment, in Heaven.

We need not doubt that the kind of "pious people" Heine castigates did indeed exist, and still do. Nevertheless, it is a pity that he could not have known some equally pious Lessing, Schelling, or Priestley who could combine devout religious—Christian—piety with an anticipation of future worldly happiness on earth that was a match for Heine's.

John Stuart Mill

Mill is best known today for his *On Liberty*, published in 1859, and within this work for what he called "one very simple principle" of human freedom. Mill writes:

That principle is that, the sole end for which mankind are warranted, individually or collectively, in interfering with the liberty of action of any of their number is self-protection. That the only purpose for which power can be rightfully exercised over any member of a civilized community, against his will, is to prevent harm to others.

The theme of the paragraph in which the words just quoted are found contrasts strikingly, as Gertrude Himmelfarb has pointed out in a fascinating study of Mill's personal evolution of mind, with what he had written in 1831 in his "The Spirit of the Age." There, although committed to liberty, Mill had stressed the necessity of limits to liberty, the kind constituted by morality and the judgments of the recognizedly wise and learned in a social order.

Such limits are scarcely to be found in the later *On Liberty*, although if we read on beyond the paragraph with its "one very simple principle" as prescription, we find that Mill does not extend this principle of liberty to the feeble minded, to those not yet in their majorities (which for Mill would have excluded all university students, among others), or, most interesting, to peoples who have not yet progressed to a level of civilization exemplified by Western Europe. Moreover, when we come to Chapter 3 of the work, we find further limits set upon the "one very simple principle." For instance:

> No one pretends *that actions should be as free as opinions* . . . . On the contrary, even opinions *lose their immunity* when the circumstances in which they are expressed are such as to constitute their expression a positive instigation to *some mischievous act* . . . . The liberty of the individual must be thus far limited; *he must not make himself a nuisance* to other people. But if he refrains from molesting others *in what concerns them* and merely acts according to his own inclination and judgment *in things which concern himself* . . . he should be allowed, without molestation, to carry his opinions into practice at his own cost. (Italics added)

Such expressions, it is clear enough, denote a good deal more restraint upon individual liberty than anyone is likely to conclude from a mere reading of the paragraph that sets forth the famous principle. From our point of view the single most interesting of all Mill's qualifications upon the freedom he prescribes in *On Liberty* is that which pertains to peoples in "backward states of society." He is forthright and blunt:

> Liberty, as a principle, has no application to any state of things anterior to the time when mankind have become capable of being improved by free and equal discussion . . . . Until then there is nothing for them but implicit obedience to an Akbar or a Charlemagne, if they are so fortunate as to find one. But as soon as mankind have attained the capacity of being guided to their own improvement by conviction or persuasion . . . compulsion, either in direct form or in that of pains and penalties for non-compliance, is no longer admissible as a means to their own good, and justifiable only for the security of others.

From the point of view dominant in our own day, that is, in the final part of the twentieth century, we might have been prepared for Mill's exclusion of the infirm and the feeble minded; possibly, though not so certainly, youth below the age of legal majority. But "races" in a "backward state"? Outright despotism for them? We are not prepared for these limits Mill puts upon his famous principle of freedom (which could easily be seen as contradictory to his almost impasssioned laudation of cultural diversity) unless we know how profound an influence the idea of progress was on Mill's mind.

The fact is, the principle of progress underlies or is implicit in almost everything Mill wrote, even though he perhaps makes less use of the word than do many of his contemporaries. In his *Logic*, in the famous sixth book in which he is concerned with the method appropriate to the moral or social sciences, he leaves us in no doubt whatever of his commitment to progress. He writes:

> It is my belief that the general tendency is, and will continue to be, saving occasional and temporary exceptions, one of improvement—a tendency towards a better and happier state . . . For our purposes it is sufficient that there is a progressive change, both in the character of the human race and in their outward circumstances so far as moulded by themselves; that in each successive age the principal phenomena of society are different from what they were in the age preceding, and still more different from any previous age.

And, a little farther on: "The progressiveness of the human race is the foundation on which a method of philosophising in the social science has been of late years erected, far superior to either of the two modes which had previously been prevalent, the chemical or experimental and the geometrical modes."

How close Mill's certainty regarding human progress was to his liberalism, his insistence upon near-absolute freedom of thought and action, can be inferred from the following assertion in his *Logic*: "From this accumulated evidence, we are justified in concluding that the order of human progression in all respects will mainly depend on the order of progress in the intellectual convictions of mankind, that is, on the law of successive transformations of human opinions."

But there is much more in Mill's devotion to the principle of progressive development:

> By its aid we may hereafter succeed not only in looking far forward into the future history of the human race, but in determining what artificial means may be used, and to what extent, to accelerate the natural progress insofar as it is beneficial; . . . Such practical instruction, founded on the highest branch of speculative sociology, will form the noblest and most beneficial portion of the political art.

Mill was lavish in his praise of Comte's *Positive Philosophy* which was published in France shortly after Mill wrote his "The Spirit of the Age." He accepted utterly Comte's Law of Three Stages and its implications, and he agreed with Comte that only by acceptance of the reality of social science can the "anarchy" which both men found in the intellectual life of the West in the early nineteenth century be terminated.

So devoted was Mill to *general* laws of historical progress, the kind that Comte had outlined in detail, that he declared geniuses must be considered secondary to nonindividual, social, or collective processes operating toward the progress of society. While recognizing the immense contribution of Newton, Mill yet asserts there would have been had Newton never lived another Newton in due time; or, equally important, Newton's contribution would have been made slowly, gradually, and continuously by a succession of minds, each inferior to Newton in mentality, but in continuous incremental succession bound to equal his own achievement.

We do not often think of John Stuart Mill—son of James Mill and young disciple of Bentham, both of whom ignored historical development altogether, both of whom relied solely upon those causes and processes which could be deduced directly from the individual, his reason, and instincts—as being a philosopher of progress. We are more inclined to think of the didactic passages of his more famous essays, such as "On Representative Government," "On Liberty," and "Utilitarianism" than we are that long section in *Logic* in which Mill reveals himself as much a social evolutionist, as much a prophet of human progress over the ages, as anyone else in the century. As I have noted, Mill was deeply indebted to Comte in this respect, just as he was indebted to another Frenchman, Alexis de Tocqueville, for his rising interest in voluntary association as an offset to too rigorous an individualism and for his stress upon social and cultural diversity, localism, and decentralization as the means of preventing political centralization and the rise of the homogeneous masses and regimentation of mind.

As we learn from his *Autobiography*, Mill found himself becoming more and more interested in socialism during his later years, and there have been those readers of Mill willing to declare that the end of progress ceased for Mill to be the maximum of individual liberty and became instead socialism. But when one looks at the content of Mill's "socialism" and, equally important, the limits he places upon socialist interference with freedom of any kind—property, income, enterprise, as well as philosophical and political thought—it is evident that a broad gulf separates Mill from the real socialists of the time. Even in the final edition of his *Political Economy* he distinguishes rigorously between the principles and processes which must underlie production on the one hand and distribution on the other. Only in the latter area, he tells us, may interventions take place in the interest of the poor; emphatically *not* in the sphere of production. But even with respect to distribution, although government may use its powers to establish channels, or institutions, it "cannot arbitrarily determine how these institutions shall work." It is hard to take very seriously any socialism within which no graduated income tax may exist, no restraints are placed upon production, and no interference with private property of whatever kind or quantity exists, not even through the uses of an inheritance tax! Mill is on record as hoping, as did his wife, Harriet Taylor, that the gross inequalities among individuals and also nations would through the continuation of progress eventually disappear, leaving only those inequalities which are natural and creative. But he would have found direct and immediate action by the government toward the achievement of this lessening of inequality wholly repugnant. There are assuredly differences of treatment of socialism in the first edition of the *Principles of Political Economy* published in 1848 and in the third edition of 1852. He is much more open to the possibility of commonly held property, in contrast to individual ownership, and, with this, of continued urge to work constructively, in the third edition. He is willing to state indeed that *if* the choice were between communism and the current economic condition with labor continuing to be dealt with harshly in many instances and with too many people living without working at all, he would take communism.

But the all-important "if" must be noted and remembered. Not for a moment did Mill, given his immense confidence in the continuity and necessity of progress and his absolute belief in individual liberty as the vital mechanism of progress, think that the abhorrent conditions in 1852 would last very long. His humane reaction to the sordid and squalid and insecure lives lived by so many in his time drove him to speculate on the advantages of socialism. But such was his conviction of the utter necessity of individual liberty and his fear of the kind of homogeneous, regimented, levelled population that government-instigated and government-directed socialism would bring about that he could never really bring himself to much more than experiment with small, voluntary communities in which property might be held in common.

There is one other element of Mill's economic thought that must be mentioned here, one that also, at first sight, would appear to contradict his devotion both to progress and individual liberty. This is his treatment in Chapter 6 of Book 4 of the *Principles* of "the stationary state." Bear in mind that it comes immediately after a long treatment of the "Influence of Progress of Society on Production and Distribution" in which Mill convincingly argues the harmony of complete liberty of individuals and progressive advancement of society. Nevertheless, Mill finds it possible to consider wistfully if not enthusiastically the advantages which men might come to see some day in a society that is not constantly advancing in accord with the criteria of population expansion, increase of economic goods, and the like.

There is room in the world no doubt, and even in old countries, for an immense increase of population, supposing the arts of life to go on improving, and capital to increase. But, although it may be innocuous, I confess I see little reason for desiring it . . . . A population may become too crowded, though all be amply supplied with food and raiment. It is not good for man to be kept perforce at all times in the presence of his species. A world from which solitude is extirpated is a very poor ideal. Solitude, in the sense of being alone, is essential to any depth of meditation or of character; and solitude, in the presence of natural beauty and grandeur, is the cradle of thoughts and aspirations which are not only good for the individual, but which society could ill do without . . . . If the earth must lose that great portion of its pleasantness which it owes to things that the unlimited increase of wealth and population would extirpate from it, for the mere purpose of enabling it to support a larger but not a better or a happier population, I sincerely hope for the sake of posterity, that they will be content to be stationary, long before necessity compels them to it.

That passage shocked many in Mill's time and it continues to shock those of us who believe that, on the evidence of human history, nothing so generates processes of political, social, and moral decay as the cessation of economic growth. It would be idle to attempt to reconcile Mill on the stationary state and Mill on economic progress, but this must be said. Even in his fond reflections on the cessation of material progress, on the appearance of the stationary state, the independence, autonomy, and intellectual freedom of the individual remains his highest justification for such a state.

Herbert Spencer

Without question, Herbert Spencer is the supreme embodiment in the late nineteenth century of both liberal individualism and the idea of progress. No one before or since so effectively united the two philosophies of freedom and of progress, or so completely anchored the former in the latter. The whole of organic evolution for Spencer must be seen as a long process of change in which "homogeneity" is replaced everywhere by "heterogeneity." Lifted from the merely organic to the social realm this translates into evolution or progress from the monolithic, static, and repressive type of social organization to the diversified, plural, and individualistic type of social organization. All forms of authoritarianism—religious, caste, racial, moral, and political—are destined to decline and eventually become extinct just as surely as the homogeneous is destined in the physical and biological spheres to be succeeded by the heterogeneous. That, in a nutshell, is the philosophy of progress and freedom Spencer presented to the world during the second half of the nineteenth century; not merely the Western world but the entire world, including the Far East where his ideas were among the most powerful in shaking ancient doctrines and practices.

His commitment to individual freedom, born of the religious Nonconformism of his family, probably preceded his interest in and devotion to the principle of cosmic progress. We know that as early as 1842, when twenty-two years of age Spencer published a series of articles in the newspaper *The Nonconformist*, each in the form of a letter, to which he gave the general title "Letters on the Proper Sphere of Government." There we learn that the state, irrespective of form of government—monarchical, republican, democratic, and so forth—has for its overriding function that of "preventing one man from infringing upon the rights of another." At this point in his life Spencer would not even allow the political state a right to supervise in any degree education, manufacture, religion, public health, and sanitation, even the waging of war. There is little to distinguish his philosophy of government from that of the earlier William Godwin.

From these early articles proceed all of Spencer's mature views on the subject of liberty. He tells us in his *Autobiography* that all of the reflections which were to appear in the *Social Statics* (1850) and *The Man versus The State* (1884) and which made Spencer's name a byword throughout the literate world for liberal individualism grew out of what he had written for *The Nonconformist* in 1842. "My aim" he wrote, "is the liberty of each, limited alone by the like liberty of all." And futher: "Every man has freedom to do all that he wills, provided he infringes not on the equal freedom of any other man." Those words were written nine years before Mill published his *On Liberty*. But whereas Mill tempered his advocacy of individual freedom by acceptance of a voluntary type of socialism in certain areas, and lost faith to some degree in economic growth and the development of society, Spencer never to his dying moment retreated an inch. Everywhere we turn in those works by Spencer concerned with human behavior the emphasis is upon freedom, individual freedom, with all forms of authority accordingly deprecated. We see this in his *The Principles of Morality*, in *Education, The Study of Sociology, The Data of Ethics*, and most famously in *Social Statics* and *The Man versus The State*. The mere recital of a few chapter titles from the latter two works is sufficient to convey their common theme: "Derivation of a First Principle" (freedom!), "The Rights of Life and Personal Liberty," "The Right to Use the Earth," "The Right of Property," "The Right of Exchange," "The Right of Free Speech," "The Rights of Women," "The Rights of Children," "The Right to Ignore the State." Those chapters are found in *Social Statics,* and they precede the long section in which Spencer effectively limits the uses of state power almost entirely to protection of the rights just listed. Similarly, in *The Man versus The State,* the following are the chapter titles for the book: "The New Toryism" ("liberal" and "socialist"acceptance of the state as the chief force for the instituting of "social justice"), "The Coming Slavery" (political, in the name of democracy and freedom), "The Sins of Legislators," and "The Great Political Superstition." In the last Spencer shows how mankind's earlier universal *religious* superstition had become replaced in modern times with equal infatuation with the political state as the cause and context of social progress.

If one wishes to acquire from a single article an accurate and full appreciation of Spencer's liberalism, there is no better place to go than to his remarkable and altogether prescient essay "Over Legislation," first written for *The Westminster Review* in July 1853 and later included among his published essays and articles. This article is at once a powerful affirmation of individual freedom as the only freedom worth considering and a demonstration of the intrinsic incapacity of the political state to deal effectively or justly with any social or moral problem. It is the second that he makes the chief subject of the essay, and much of it reads as though it were directed to problems of bureaucracy in our own day. He adamantly believes government or government agencies unable to plan for the population at large.

> . . .[W]hen I remember how many of my private schemes have miscarried, how speculations have failed . . . how the things I desperately strove against as a misfortune did me immense good—how while the objects I ardently pursued brought me little happiness when gained . . . I am struck with the incompetence of my intellect to prescribe for society.
>
> There is a great want of this practical humility in our political conduct . . . . Though we have ceased to assume the infallibility of our theological beliefs and so ceased to enact them, we have not ceased to enact hosts of other beliefs of an equally doubtful kind. Though we no longer coerce men for their *spiritual good,* we still think ourselves called upon to coerce them for their *material good*: not seeing that the one is as useless and as unwarrantable as the other.

What follows in more than fifty pages is a detailed, logical, step-by-step analysis of each and every function the modern state had assumed in institutional life, ranging from war making, through the administration of justice, to welfare of any kind whatever. And the conclusion, soberly stated and abundantly illustrated, is that in every instance there has been not only failure to achieve objectives but, worse, the perpetration of new and worse evils than those which political legislation was initially designed to correct.

It is the vice of this empirical school of politicians that they never look beyond proximate causes and immediate effects . . . . They do not bear in mind that each phenomenon is a link in an infinite series—is the result of myriads of preceding phenomena, and will have a share in producing myriads of succeeding ones. Hence they overlook the fact that, in disturbing any natural chain of sequences, they are not only modifying the result next in succession, but all the future results into which this will enter as a part cause. The serial genesis of phenomena, and the interaction of each series upon every other series, produces a complexity utterly beyond human grasp.

Spencer's dissection of governmental administration, what would in time be known widely as bureaucracy, is merciless but, by any rational standard, including that of Max Weber, perceptive and fair. "Officialism," he tells us, is slow; it is also stupid:

Under the natural course of things each citizen tends toward his fittest function . . . . But it is quite otherwise in State-organizations. Here, as everyone knows, birth, age, backstairs intrigue, and sycophancy, determine the selections rather than merit. The "fool of the family" readily finds a place in the Church, if "the family" have good connexions. A youth too ill-educated for any profession does well for an officer in the Army. Grey hair, or a title, is a far better guarantee of naval promotion than genius is . . . .

Officialism is also by its unalterable nature financially "extravagant," "unadaptive," and "corrupt." The last follows inexorably, Spencer argues, from all the other ills inherent in state officialdom. Finally, as Spencer notes, the state, by entering into a multitude of areas where it cannot possibly succeed, forecloses its capacity to do honestly and efficiently the two things it is alone fitted and valuable for: the protection of individuals from potential assailants and the administering of justice.

Despite common belief that the upshot of Spencer's passion for freedom was merely giving license to the rich and powerful (he is responsible for the phrase, used in his earliest works on evolution, "survival of the fittest," a phrase that Darwin in *The Origin of the Species* praises and adopts), there is a strong and persisting vein of humanitarianism in his works. No one was more aware than Spencer of the evils of his age, the profiteering and plundering, the grinding down of large numbers of able, hard-working people into a class of the poor, the appalling wastefulness of the new rich, and their all too typical disdain for the condition of others. Spencer's essay

"The Morals of Trade," first published in 1859, is an admirable reflection of his views on these matters. Nor can his devotion to individual liberty be declared neglectful of the social bond. In "From Freedom to Bondage" (1891), he tells us that the great objective to be sought is "voluntary cooperation" and that the only really important distinction between societies is between "that in which the individual is left to do the best he can by his spontaneous efforts and get success or failure according to his own efficiency, and that in which he has his appointed place, works under coercive rule, and has his apportioned share of food, clothing, and shelter." He concludes his book *The Inductions of Ethics* with the observation that for those who look back upon the changes which have taken place during thousands of years past, and forward to those which will take place during the thousands of years ahead, "it will be a satisfaction to contemplate a humanity so adapted to harmonious social life that all needs are spontaneously and pleasurably fulfilled by each without injury to others."

The real key to Spencer's view of the valid source of social improvement is found in a phrase he uses in the essay referred to previously, "Over Legislation": *social vitality.* By this he means the kinds of energy which spring spontaneously from human beings, either alone or in voluntary, cooperative association.

It is not simply that social vitality may be trusted . . . to fulfill each much-exaggerated requirement in some quiet spontaneous way, it is not simply that when thus naturally fulfilled it will be fulfilled efficiently, instead of being botched when attempted artificially; but it is that until thus naturally fulfilled, *it ought not to be fulfilled at all.*

This brings us properly to the second great principle in Herbert Spencer's works: that of adaptive evolution and progress. His faith in individual freedom and responsibility and his repudiation of all artificial forms of constraint and coercion commencing with the political state itself, which he believed to be no more than a survival or persistence of primitive-savage use of force, could not have taken the solid, prophetic form it did had it not been linked with, actually set in, a faith in natural progress. It is a matter of record (and attested to in his *Autobiography*) that Spencer's discovery of what he called "the development hypothesis" well before Darwin's great book was published took place at about the same time he had become aware of the indispensability of individual freedom and of the perniciousness of the political state.

There is hardly a volume, even chapter, in Spencer's vast expanse of writing that does not in some way make use of what he came to call the "law of progress," a law that for him as for others in the century was identical with the "law of evolution." Let us, though, draw simply and solely from the essay "Progress: Its Law and Cause," published in 1857. Spencer himself declared it the earliest full and systematic statement on the subject and the source of all that he was later to write in so many different areas of thought. A paragraph early in the essay demonstrates sufficiently the scope and aim of the work:

Now, we propose in the first place to show that this law of organic progress [which he has just described, drawing heavily from the works of the Germans Wolff and von Baer in biology] is the law of all progress. Whether it be in the development of the Earth, in the development of Life upon its surface, in the development of Society, of Government, of Manufactures, of Commerce, of Language, Literature, Science, Art, this same evolution of the simple into the complex, through successive differentiations, holds throughout. From the earliest traceable cosmical changes down to the latest results of civilization, we shall find that the transformation of the homogeneous into the heterogeneous is that in which progress essentially consists.

In a fifty-four page essay Spencer offers us what amounts to an epitome of his entire life's work—in geology and biology as well as in psychology and sociology. Wherever we look, he argues, we observe development or progress defined as change from the homogeneous to the heterogeneous. We see it in the individual organism itself, and we see this change in the whole panoply of organic life on the planet. The oldest and simplest forms of life are the most homogeneous; the latest and most advanced reveal a high degree of specialization and variegation. "The change from the homogeneous to the heterogeneous is displayed in the progress of civilization as a whole, as well as in the progress of every nation; and is still going on with increasing rapidity." We see this change in each institution or social form, but we also see it in the totality of institutions and forms which have existed in the past and continue to exist in all stages of evolutionary development on the earth. The law of progressive heterogeneity or differentiation "clearly exemplified in the evolution of the social organism, is exemplified with equal clearness in the evolution of all products of thought and action; whether concrete or abstract, real or ideal."

It serves no point to detail here each and every illustration Spencer adduces in support of his principle of evolution or progress. It is enough to know that for Spencer this principle is cosmic and penetrates every recess of planet, life, humanity, and society. He concludes his essay with the following words:

It will be seen that as in each event of today, so from the beginning, the decomposition of every expended force into several forces has been perpetually producing a higher complication; that the increase of heterogeneity so brought about is still going on and must continue to go on; and that thus progress is *not an accident, not a thing within human control, but a beneficent necessity.* [Italics added.]

No one, not St. Augustine, not Joachim de Fiore, not any of the millenarians of the Puritan Revolution, had invoked the idea of necessity, of necessary movement toward a given goal, with greater, more dogmatic certainty than does the rationalist-secularist Spencer in the concluding words of the passage just quoted. Nor is his declaration of the necessity of progress confined to that essay alone. It had been uttered in almost the identical words in *Social Statics* a few years earlier: "Progress, therefore, is not an accident, but a necessity." And so far as the thought itself is concerned, it would be utilized in almost countless variations of wording and style to the end of his days.

In *Social Statics* the phrase follows a discussion of what Spencer refers to as "the evanescence of evil." All that we define as evil, he writes, springs from "imperfection," that is, "unfitness to the conditions of existence." But such is the power of the inherent strain in all forms of life and culture toward "fitness" or adaptation to necessary conditions of life that ultimately "all deficiency must disappear; that is, all unfitness must disappear; that is, all imperfection must disappear." Spencer continues with the following fervent and unambiguous testament to progress and freedom:

The ultimate development of the ideal man is logically certain—as certain as any conclusion in which we place the most implicit faith. . . . As the experiences of all people in all times . . . go to prove that organs, faculties, powers, capacities, or whatever else we call them, grow by use and diminish from disuse, it is inferred that they will continue to do so. And if this inference is unquestionable, then so is the one deduced from it—that humanity must in the end become completely adapted to its conditions—unquestionable also.

It is impossible to think of any single name more deeply respected, more widely read among social philosophers and scientists, and more influential, in a score of spheres, than was that of Herbert Spencer. His influence in the social sciences was immense, not least in American colleges and universities during the last quarter of the nineteenth century. Even though the kind of liberalism Spencer espoused—based solely upon the increase and enhancement of individual freedom and "social vitality"—was, as we shall note in chapter 8, to be effectively altered, in the name of a greater use of state power to effect economic and social reform, by such men as L. T. Hobhouse and J. L. Hobson in England, and Lester Ward and Thorstein Veblen in America, it is a matter of record that one and all of the exponents of the New Liberalism proceeded from, and with expressed admiration for, Herbert Spencer.

Today, we are more likely to think of Spencer as some form of "conservative," given his unrestrained preference for governmental nonintervention and for *laissez-faire* in all spheres possible, economic included. But up until his death in 1903 Spencer's reputation around the world was anything but that of a conservative or traditionalist. His fame and writings penetrated Eastern Europe (including Czarist Russia) and these writings became intellectual pillars of the liberalism in those countries—brief-lived and insufficient though it was to be. Well before the writings of Karl Marx made entry into Hungary, to use but one example, the way for interest in his doctrines had been opened up (paradoxical though it must seem) by the writings of Spencer. In parts of the Middle East, in India, in China, and other non-Western countries, Spencer's was the most honored of all Western names in those circles of intellectuals which were striving to reform educational, religious, and governmental systems in the name of enlargement of individual freedom and also of rationalism. Not in the minds of Japanese and Chinese educators—or, rather, those seeking to modernize ancient curricula—was Spencer thought to be a "conservative." His relentless rationalism, his unquenchable faith in the individual and in voluntary cooperation, and his conviction of the necessity in the entire world of human progress toward ever higher levels of freedom, gave him an influence in social and economic areas that has been exceeded only by Karl Marx.

What began with Turgot and Adam Smith, the American Founding Fathers, Godwin, and Mill reached its grand culmination and fulfillment in Spencer. No one since has added an iota to what is set forth so eloquently in Spencer's writings: the belief that freedom is necessary to progress, and that the goal of progress, from most distant past to the remote future, is ever-ascending realization of freedom.

Chapter 7

Progress As Power

DURING the same age in which individual freedom was being hailed as the criterion and ultimate objective of progress, we find a very different value also being celebrated as the necessary means toward and purpose of progress: *power*. Not often, if ever, power in its own right; not coercion for the sake of coercion; and never laudation of despotism as such; but, power nevertheless.

I have in mind the development during the period 1750–1900 of new doctrines of nationalism and statism, along with utopianism and racism. In each of these we find power linked with the perspective of progress—always of course in the name of some kind of liberation, some kind of redemption or salvation on earth. It is power of a type rarely if ever before seen in history; power less concerned with the limitation or constraint of human action than with the bending and shaping of human consciousness. Rousseau, Fichte, Hegel, Saint-Simon, Comte, Marx, and Gobineau are among the major names in this tradition.

It should not be thought that these minds were insensitive or hostile to freedom—at least as they variously defined it. Rousseau made freedom central in his *Social Contract*. Hegel could write: "The history of the world is none other than the progress of the consciousness of freedom." Marx, from beginning to end, voiced man's need for restoration of freedom, liberation from private property, competition, bureaucracy, alienation, and so forth. Saint-Simon, Comte, and Fourier, among others, all paid their respective devotions to human freedom in the utopias they wrote. Even in

Gobineau's powerful *Essay on the Inequality of the Races* there is high respect for freedom of mind and action—linked, however, as we shall see, with a single master race.

But there is a very wide chasm separating the concept of freedom we have just dealt with from Turgot to Herbert Spencer, and that which we find diversely in the writers we shall be concerned with in this chapter. For Turgot or Spencer, freedom always and unwaveringly meant freedom *from* any kind of oppression, political, religious, and so forth, and freedom *to* develop individual faculties, powers, and talents with the least possible constraint or even guidance.

The idea of freedom that we shall see embodied in the theories dealt with in the following pages differs vastly. Freedom here is inseparable from some proffered community—political, social, racial, or other—and from the uses of coercion and strict discipline, when needed. Only through closer and more devoted awareness of himself as an organic part of the absolute state would the individual achieve, in Hegel's perspective, true freedom—a "higher freedom" than that posited by an Adam Smith. Marx made what he called "the revolutionary dictatorship of the proletariat" crucial to the commencement of socialism and, then, the reshaping of man. Absolutism is the essence of Saint-Simon's New Christianity and of Comte's four-volume description of Positivist Society—the absolute power of scientists and industrial technologists over human beings, the power of "intellectuals" over "emotionals," in one of Comte's more candid phrasings. Gobineau and his many followers thought freedom of thought to be inextricably linked with one great race on earth, the Germanic. Only as this race became purified and protected from genetic corruption and only as it governed the world absolutely would it be possible for the kind of civilization we associate with individual creativity to flourish once again, and at increasingly higher levels.

For those we considered in the preceding chapter freedom is always connected with individuals *as they actually are*; in the line of thinkers we shall now consider, freedom is inseparable from membership in some collectivity or community—state, proletariat, race, and so forth—and from the creation through absolute power if necessary of *a new type of human being*. This view of power is far from unique in the modern world. Its seeds lie in Plato's *Republic*. And as Dostoevski's allegory on the Grand Inquisitor reminds us, it is a form of power, a conception of freedom-through-power, that is not absent from some of the world's religions. No one has described this kind of power more eloquently than Tocqueville in his famous chapter on the type of despotism democracies have to fear, in his *Democracy in America*.

The Utopians

"Utopia," Leszek Kolakowski has written, "is a desperate desire to attain absolute perfection; this desire is a degraded remnant of the religious legacy in nonreligious minds." Kolakowski also writes:

> [The] unconsciously platonic belief that the essence of humanity can be defined theoretically so that the existential aspirations and desires of people are irrelevant to its definition, explains the hidden readiness of the utopian mentality to accept despotic means on the way to the promised land, even though many, indeed most, of the utopian writers expected their visions to be fulfilled without violence or coercion. In fact only the most penetrating minds among them did not shrink from admitting the necessity of violence in driving mankind to paradise.

Kolakowski's description of the utopian mentality, especially as we encounter it in the nineteenth and twentieth centuries, is excellent. It is a pity, therefore, that he does not see the connection that can exist, that demonstrably does exist, between utopian consecration and faith in an unfolding, linear progress through the long past. He sees the utopian mind as bereft of any sense of the past, save as something evil and oppressive, devoid of any comprehension of stage-by-stage advancement from past to present. For this mentality, Kolakowski writes, "History is portrayed as catastrophic . . . . There is a radical discontinuity between the world as it is and as it will be; a violent leap is needed to do away with the past; a new time will start."

But Joachim and the Joachimites, the Fifth Monarchy Men, and *revolutionistes* such as Saint-Just and then Babeuf at the end of the eighteenth century were all able to combine belief in the necessity of a period of catastrophic violence to usher in the golden age on earth with a philosophy of cumulative, stage-by-stage progress from the past to the future. Precisely the same is true of the utopians of the nineteenth century. Saint-Simon, Comte, Marx, and other utopians were apocalyptic and millenarian indeed. They came to burn with a passionate zeal for the earliest possible inception of their respective golden ages; each was willing to employ any degree of power necessary to achievement of the ideal society they dreamed of. But nowhere in the nineteenth century are there to be found more devoted and influential expositors of theories of progress, of the stage-by-stage, inexorable, and necessary advancement of mankind from past to future. Indeed their apocalyptic visions were declared—by Saint-Simon and Comte as well as Marx—*scientific* in contrast to the idle utopias that others, such as Robert Owen, were concerned with. Utopianism at its most influential is, then, an expression of both power and faith in progress.

Rousseau

Although we may not ordinarily think of Rousseau as a utopian, he is. *The Social Contract* is, at its core, the work of a law-giver. It is in such powerful and evocative chapters as those on the social compact, the sovereign, the infallibility of the General Will, the Legislator, voting, censorship, and, perhaps above all, the civil religion that we see what is really central to the book and to the mind of its author. And that is *prescription*, not different in the slightest, save in volume, from what we encounter in a Saint-Simon or Comte. The kind of interest Rousseau manifests in political power in both *The Social Contract* and the earlier *Discourse on Political Economy* is the kind of interest which has been at the core of political utopias since Plato (whom Rousseau lauds as the greatest of all influences on his mind).

Rousseau came early to his utopianism. In the *Confessions* he tells us that it was in 1743 while serving as an attaché in the French embassy in Venice that he reached the momentous conclusion "that everything is radically connected with politics and that however one proceeded, no people would be other than the nature of its government made it." There is no evidence that Rousseau ever changed his mind, ever lost his fascination with the social and moral uses of power. He literally was obsessed by power. We see this in *La Nouvelle Héloïse*; everything of significance that takes place in the family is the result of the behind the scenes, sinister figure of Wolmar, truly a *deus ex machina*. We see this adoration of power in *Emile*, represented by the tutor and his covert but absolute domination of *Emile*. The following words of the tutor (Rousseau) are expressive of the kind of power Rousseau most loved. "You can't guess how docile Emile, at age 20, is . . . . I leave him, admittedly, the consciousness of independence, but never has he been more completely subjected to me, for he is subject because he wishes to be."

It is not power that Rousseau fears and hates, but *inequality*. He is the consummate egalitarian in the history of political thought. The urge to extirpate inequality and to establish equality can be seen in the three discourses and in *The Social Contract*. In the first of the discourses, on the arts and sciences and their corruption and corrupting influence, he declares inequality the root evil. In the second discourse, which I shall come to in some detail shortly, we are given an evolutionary treatise the purpose of which is to show how inequality rose in the first place. In the third discourse, on political economy (written for the *Encyclopedia* at Diderot's request), the substance through and through is the kind of political order that would be required to stamp out inequality in all its forms. In that discourse occurs the pregnant sentence: "If it is good to know how to deal with men as they are, it is much better to make them what there is need that they should be. The most absolute authority is that which penetrates into a man's inmost being, and concerns itself *no less with his will than his actions.*" (Italics added) And also in this same discourse: "If you would have the general will accomplished, bring all the particular wills into conformity with it; in other words, as virtue is nothing more than this conformity of particular wills with the general will, *establish the reign of virtue!*" (Italics added)

Is there really further need to establish either the fact of the utopian cast of Rousseau's mind or his obsession with power? I shall content myself with but three more brief illustrations, all from *The Social Contract.* First, it must be noted that the title phrase has nothing whatever to do with the kind of social contract that Hobbes, Pufendorf, Locke, and others had written of, which was a real or hypothetical compact made among men and between men and a ruler in the distant past. For Rousseau the social contract is that covenant that men must make if they are to enter into his redemptive political state. There is no nonsense about rights or liberty. There must be "the total alienation of each associate, together with all his rights, to the whole community." Following this comes what Rousseau terms the "essence" of the social contract (the entire passage is set by Rousseau in italics): "Each of us puts his person and all his power in common under the supreme direction of the general will, and, in our corporate capacity, we receive each member as an indivisible part of the whole." Clearly rights and liberty of individuals have no place in Rousseau's utopia! Not that he is oblivious to freedom. Shortly after the above passage comes his Lycurgus-like injunction "that whoever refuses to obey the general will shall be compelled to do so by the whole body. This means nothing more than that *he will be forced to be free.*" (Italics added) Others had justified absolute power in the name of order, and protection from eruption of a Hobbesian state of nature. Rousseau is the first, though not the last, to actually *define* absolute power as freedom.

How radically utopian Rousseau was can be suggested by one more citation, taken from the famous chapter on "The Legislator." No ordinary legislator is Rousseau's subject.

He who dares to undertake the making of a people's institutions ought to feel himself capable, so to speak, of changing human nature, of transforming each individual, who is by himself a complete and solitary whole, into part of a greater whole . . . . He must in a word take from man his own resources and give him instead new ones alien to him, and incapable of being made use of without the help of other men.

With equal fervor, the Committee on Public Safety in the forthcoming Revolution would so enjoin; so would Saint-Simon and Comte and Marx, and, not least, those who in 1917 set about making the new Soviet Man.

We must turn now to Rousseau the theorist of progress. What, it properly may be asked, does his dedication to absolute and transforming power have to do with the idea of progress? Although there are minor evidences of his progressive-evolutionism in other works, including *The Social Contract*, it is the famous second discourse "What is the Origin of Inequality among Men, and is it Authorized by Natural Law?" that reveals Rousseau the theorist of progress in brightest light. The discourse is in every sense of the word a conjectural history or, as Rousseau preferred to label it, a "hypothetical history," precisely the same in structure as any of the conjectural or natural histories written by Adam Smith, Adam Ferguson, and, before them, Turgot. In content, the discourse is at once anthropology, ethnology, sociology, economics, and politics—all set, of course, in the unfolding, developmental terms of the established idea of progress.

Before describing this remarkable work, two points must be impressed upon the reader, given the widespread misunderstanding of each. First, Rousseau did *not* recommend man's retreat from civilization on any ground, including that set forth in the first discourse on the decadence and corruption of the arts and sciences and of the culture he lived in. Second, he did *not* ever recommend return to the state of nature. What he recommended in the third discourse, in *The Social Contract*, and in other works was the total reconstitution of political society as the means of reconstituting all culture, all human nature.

The underlying aim of Rousseau's hypothetical history is that of showing, first, how human society has reached its present level of degeneration and corruption, and, second, why only the most radical kind of political reconstruction can be counted upon to restore virtue, to restore, above all, equality. Just as Adam Smith felt obliged to demonstrate the *natural* path of progress in economic matters and how society had strayed from this natural path, as the means of underscoring his recommendations for a proper economy based upon natural liberty, so Rousseau does the same, but with equality rather than liberty the object and ideal. What follows is a necessarily brief condensation of the content of Rousseau's second discourse.

We begin with the state of nature before any institutions whatever had come into being. Natural man free of all interdependences, marriage included, roams the landscape drawing food from the bushes and trees and soil, forming liaisons of the sexes for procreation, protecting himself by wile from the fiercer animals, sheltering himself in caves or other natural retreats, and maintaining health in large degree as the very result of ignorance or necessary independence of the luxuries and also the medicines of contemporary life. In sum, writes Rousseau, we behold in man in his orginal state

> . . . an animal weaker than some, and less agile than others; but, taking him all around, the most advantageously-organized of any. I see him slaking his thirst at the first brook, finding his bed at the foot of the tree which afforded him a repast; and, with that, all his wants supplied.

Tempting, almost irresistible and worthy of return, this Rousseauian state of nature? Without doubt. And there were many in Rousseau's day as in our own to recommend such return. But Rousseau, as I have indicated, was not one of them. Even though he professes to validate his lush and exciting state of nature through ethnographic reference to the Caribs of Venezuela in his own day, Rousseau is resistant to any such idea of return.

It was, Rousseau argues, impossible for mankind to stay in the state of nature, happy though existence was when it is compared with our own time. The reason for this is an instinct deep in the nature of man: that of self-improvement. It is "the faculty of self-improvement which, by the help of circumstances, gradually develops all the rest of our faculties, and is inherent in the species as in the individual. . . . " Turgot at the very beginning of his address on progress at the Sorbonne five years earlier had contrasted man, equipped with this instinct and enabled to conserve in his culture each fresh advancement of mind, with the subhuman organic creatures, each generation of which is obliged to start at exactly the same mark occupied by each of all preceding generations. So does Rousseau make this contrast.

Once again the limits of space prevent our going into the details of one of the most remarkable ethnological essays of the eighteenth century. Let it be emphasized, though, that Rousseau takes us step by step, stage by stage, through mankind's acquisition of moral sentiments, spoken and written language, social attachments, including family and village and even "nation," and numerous other elements of the culture that lifts man above all others in the biological world. All of this, Rousseau acknowledges, required very long ages of development, with trial and error inevitable, with occasional setbacks unavoidable. But the progress of mankind continued nevertheless. As men grew enlightened they grew, in proportion, industrious. They invented utensils and weapons, and built huts to live in. "This was the epoch of the first revolution, which established and distinguished families, and introduced a kind of property. . . . " Everything began to change. "Men who have up to now been roving the woods, by taking a more settled manner of life, come gradually together, form separate bodies, and at length in every country arises a distinct nation, united in character and manners." And now the key passage: "The more we reflect on it, the more we shall find that this state was the least subject to revolutions, and *altogether the very best man could experience*; so that he can have departed from it only through some fatal accident, which, for the public good, should never have happened." (Italics added)

What was the fatal accident that deflected the course of progress which had been going on for "countless ages"? In a word, the rise of inequality. But what led to the rise of inequality? First, the proliferation of what Rousseau calls "combinations fatal to innocence and happiness." For a time men remained content with "rustic huts," "clothes made of the skins of animals," and the like:

. . . [and] so long as they undertook only what a single person could accomplish, and confined themselves to such arts as did not require the joint labor of several hands, they lived free, healthy, honest and happy lives . . . . But from the moment one man began to stand in need of the help of another . . . equality disappeared, property was introduced, work became indispensable, and vast forests became smiling fields which man had to water with the sweat of his brow, and where slavery and misery were seen to germinate and grow up with the crops.

Agriculture and metallurgy along with private property, Rousseau tells us, mark the obvious beginnings of the servitude of man, his loss of the equality and happiness which had survived the progress of mankind through the development of morality, language, thought, knowledge, and all the necessary material conveniences. But much more important than either agriculture or metallurgy as such in the debasement of the human condition is *the context of private property united with social interdependences from which man could not liberate himself.* We are permitted by Rousseau to infer that had agriculture and metallurgy evolved within those relationships which characterized the best and happiest stage of mankind's progress, the outcome would have been different.

Eventually, given the conflicts of class, nation, and territory, the institution of the political state was made necessary.

The rich man, thus urged by necessity, conceived at length the profoundest plan that ever entered the mind of man: this was to employ in his favor the forces of those who attacked him . . . to give them other institutions as favorable to himself as the law of nature was unfavorable . . . . All ran headlong to their chains, in hopes of securing their liberty. . . .

Such was, may well have been, the origin of society and law, which bound new fetters on the poor, and gave new powers to the rich; which irretrievably destroyed natural liberty, eternally fixed the law of property and inequality, converted clever usurpation into unalterable right, and, for the advantage of a few ambitious individuals, subjected all mankind to perpetual labor, slavery, and wretchedness.

Such is Rousseau's theory of human progress coupled with his account of how humanity became diverted from its progress. Such is his developmental explanation of all the avarice, cupidity, and exploitation he had indicted in the first of his three discourses. And such is the background he provides for his depiction of the mighty work necessary to liberate man from the torments and tyrannies caused by the deflection of progress: the depiction we have already at the beginning of this chapter had opportunity to examine, that is, construction of a form of government based upon the General Will which will give man the advantages of the civilization that had developed prior to the "fatal accident" of the rise of inequality but at the same time emancipate him from the bonds of servitude which private property and inequality had created.

"The problem," Rosseau writes early in *The Social Contract*, "is to find a form of association which will defend and protect with the whole common force the person and goods of each associate, and in which each, while uniting himself with all, may still obey himself alone, and remain as free as before.

Rousseau's answer to the problem is among the boldest and most imaginative in the history of political thought: a political order free of all ties or relationships save those which proceed directly from the state, itself based upon the sovereign General Will, and empty of all rights and liberties of individuals—whose renunciation or "alienation" of these is the condition of entry into the redemptive state. This political monolith is given sacredness through a "civil religion" whose "dogmas" are binding; "if anyone, after publicly recognizing these dogmas, behaves as if he does not believe them [he must be] punished by death: he has committed the worst of all crimes, that of lying before the law."

Neither the extreme partisans of the left nor those of the right in the next century had to search far, obviously, for justification of their monuments to absolute power over individual lives. It is no wonder that the more inflamed of the Jacobins and the *sans-culottes* (Babeuf chief among the latter) read their Rousseau during the high point of the French Revolution. From the Declaration of the Rights of Man all the way to the de-Christianization decrees, not excluding the Terror, there could be found rationalization eloquently written in Rousseau's Herculean effort to put mankind back on the track of progress through political force and legerdemain.

Saint-Simon

Interestingly, for all the ambitions and perspectives held in common by Rousseau and Saint-Simon, there was no love, only hatred, for Rousseau by the latter and—Condorcet and Turgot excepted—for the other principals of the French Enlightenment. From Saint-Simon's (and also Comte's) point of view it was the battery of Enlightenment ideas— "false and iniquitous ideas"—coupled with the drastic legislation of the Revolution which had put Western Europe into what both Saint-Simon and Comte regarded as a profound malaise, a sickness of the spirit, which, as they perceived it, formed the immediate points of their respective departures into the philosophy of progress and then utopianism.

"The future belongs to us," Saint-Simon declared on his death bed, attended by disciples. Activist in the extreme, he yet thought in terms of historical inevitability. "Our intention is to promote and explain the inevitable," he once wrote. Born into a devout Catholic family, apparently deeply committed during his youth, then a convert for a number of years to ideas imbibed from the philosophes and also some of the more moderate of the Revolutionists, a return to religion in whatever form seems to have been foreordained given Saint-Simon's temperament. His return was to what he called the *New Christianity*, a religion complete with ritual, dogma, and ceremony, but its substance a combination of technology and sociology that occupied his efforts—very passionate, messianic, efforts—during the last years of his life.

There is nothing of the Enlightenment in Saint-Simon's mind save dedication to reason, albeit with different import. He detested ideas of individual liberty, equality, and popular sovereignty on the ground that not one was compatible with a scientific reordering of society. Furthermore, each was a product, he argued, of a period—the whole Age of Reason—in which critical dissection, even destruction, of the social order was intellectually dominant rather than the more positive ideas of building a new society.

There can be no question whatever of the power of Saint-Simon's mind and the range of his learning. He attracted such luminaries as Augustin Thierry and Auguste Comte early in his post-Revolutionary career, and there is no doubt at all that some (many would say most) of Comte's key ideas were derived from Saint-Simon; Saint-Simon was probably correct in calling Comte a faithless, disloyal ingrate when the two men broke, utterly and bitterly, while Comte was still a young man. And after Thierry and Comte left Saint-Simon, he attracted an even larger number of young men (scarcely one over age thirty-five), most of whom had been well trained in the physical sciences, including engineering, and mathematics. Among them were Enfantin, son of a banker, graduate of the Ecole Polytechnique, and destined to lead the Saint-Simonians after the master's death in 1825 but who, after the gradual waning of Saint-Simonian faith, became a major industrialist in France. Others who joined Saint-Simon were Rodrigues, a mathematician; Buchez, a physician and medical researcher; and D'Eichthal and the Pereires, bankers and financiers. Not all were scientists or businessmen. There were newspaper reporters, artists, and coffeehouse intellectuals. What they all had in common was, first, profound faith in Saint-Simon as a charismatic temperament and mind, and, second, complete agreement with Saint-Simon that a glorious future lay ahead for mankind, one that would be composed of the achievements of science, technology, and industrialism.

As Lewis Coser has noted, there was a manifest need among intellectuals of this time in France to bring to a rational end the sense of disorder, alienation, and malaise they felt existed everywhere in Europe. Unable to accept traditional religions or a return to the medieval past (as some of that time were urging), they took refuge in what they saw as the highest achievements of human progress: science and the new industrial-technological age being built by science. Coser writes:

They envisaged a new and stable order to replace the anarchy around them, but this order would have to embody science and progress, the deities they had worshipped at the Ecole Polytechnique and other scientific schools. To them, science was holy, as was industry, but the most consecrated task was to bring to France a new integration, a drawing together of all its citizens.

The power inherent in the contemplated new society, itself a product of not only Saint-Simonian enthusiasm and teaching but, much more important, the laws of historical progress, was to be absolute. It was to be humanitarian, yes—devoted to the welfare of all the people, the poor and humble as well as the wealthy and successful, and, above all inspired by scientific knowledge—but absolute all the same. Precisely as there is no room for "freedom of thought" when one is concerned with the laws of mathematics or physical science, neither is there room for such obsolete libertarianism in a society governed by scientists, industrialists, and others working from true knowledge.

What Saint-Simon's New Christianity called for practically was a supreme power vested in an utterly new type of parliament: one composed of three distinct houses. The first would be a "house of invention" composed of scientists, inventors, and also poets, painters, architects, novelists, and sculptors. This house alone would propose laws, inaugurate projects in the people's welfare, and, in general, supply necessary initiative. The second house would be one of "examination." Physicists and mathematicians and also generalists equipped with substantial powers of critical examination would inhabit this house of parliament. The third house would be related to execution of laws and projects initiated in the first house and examined and approved in the second, and would be composed largely of businessmen, bankers, and industrialists.

After Napoleon's fall, Saint-Simon intensified his efforts to attract a significant following. He established a series of periodicals—L'*Industrie,* L'*Organisateur,* and *Du Système industriel;* the titles make sufficiently evident the mission and contents of the journals—which proved moderately successful. In article after article, some by Saint-Simon and others by disciples, the message was preached that the new society should be national in scope (rather than composed of small entities), and should be as completely open class as possible. Not that Saint-Simon believed for a moment in equality; like Plato he wished only to make it possible for the best, irrespective of origin, to rise as quickly as possible to leadership and participation in absolute power over the nation; absolute power based, of course, upon the laws of science. Saint-Simon foresaw, given the eventual achievement of his New Christianity, the abolition for once and all of hunger, squalor, disease, and war. Through a new science—one that he conceived as emerging directly from the existing physical and biological sciences—to be called "social physiology," it would be possible to find the basic laws of social equilibrium or organicism and, through their application, bring the social order itself to the highest possible level.

Nor was Saint-Simon insensitive to the working class. He told his disciples when on his death bed that the golden age lying ahead for mankind would be the result of the laws of social development in the first instance, but also of the united efforts of the working class once it had been enlightened as to its own interest. The point is, whereas Marx would disdain any thought of classes other than the proletariat so far as accomplishment of the revolution was concerned, Saint-Simon wanted the working class in close harmony with the other, scientific and business classes. There is one other signal difference between Saint-Simon and Marx. Saint-Simon's fear and hatred of the violence he had witnessed in the French Revolution led to his categorical eschewal of all violence, even for purposes of bringing his adored New Christianity into being.

For all Saint-Simon's passion for change and worship of the secular future, there is a strong measure of conservatism in his writing, a measure that he himself recognized both in source and content. He is the first of the new breed of sociological utopians after the Revolution to pay explicit tribute (Comte would echo it later) to the Conservatives in Europe whose own ideas had been generated in strong reaction to the Enlightenment and the Revolution. Saint-Simon pays high respect to Bonald, de Maistre, and Chateaubriand, among others, for their "profound understanding" of the need for and the nature of social order. True, they were Catholic, monarchist, and in favor of a hereditary aristocracy. Saint-Simon was not. But no one reading his *New Christianity* can fail to recognize the similarity of the *structure* of his imagined utopia and that of the Catholic Christianity that the Conservatives venerated. It is in content, not form, that the differences between Saint-Simon and the Conservatives are most visible; a point he was well aware of.

Although Marx and his followers were to treat Saint-Simon with some scorn because of the "utopian" character of his "socialism," and because of what Marx felt was Saint-Simon's unhistorical, undevelopmental, and therefore unscientific procedure, the truth is entirely to the contrary. His proclaimed new science of "social physiology (which Comte was to change to, first "social physics" and then "sociology") deals not only with matters of structure and organization—that is, statics—but also matters of dynamics, that is, development and progress of society. It is Saint-Simon and not Comte who is initially responsible for the panoramic vision of the history and progress of the sciences, with each new science taking its departure from a preceding one and capable of becoming a science in the full sense only when its predecessor had become a definite and exact science. The *social* physiology that Saint-Simon prized was made possible, he argued, only in his own day; this by reason of the fact that *human* physiology had just attained full scientific stature. I shall say more about this view of the progress of knowledge in the section below on Comte who, although the beneficiary of Saint-Simon's earlier insights and dependent upon them despite his own claims to the contrary, nevertheless sets them down in more systematic and logical fashion than Saint-Simon had.

For Saint-Simon the entire past could be seen in the terms of an orderly progression of civilizations, each reflecting a different degree of advancement. Within the larger picture of the progress of mankind Saint-Simon could see alternating periods which he termed "organic" and "critical." The importance of the first is positive; that is, the truly great achievements of man have been products of epochs characterized by an organic articulation of ideas, values, and institutions. In the development of Western civilization, Saint-Simon argues, there have been two great organic periods. The first is that of ancient Greece and Rome, founded upon a polytheistic system of religion, with all other advancements in knowledge rooted in this religion. Saint-Simon is strong in his appreciation of the intellectual debt that is owing the ancient, classical world. But it is the second great organic epoch, that of the medieval world, highlighted in the thirteenth century, that Saint-Simon regards as superior; and this by reason of its having been anchored in a monotheism that made possible a more rational theology and therefore a more rational structure of knowledge and society generally. The first organic age had contained, for all its manifest virtues, slavery and a type of despotism that imperial Rome best exemplified. The second organic age, that of the Christian Middle Ages, was, on the other hand, free from slavery, separated the temporal and the ecclesiastical realms, and brought into existence a much more humane form of society than the first had known.

In between organic ages are, as I have noted, what Saint-Simon called "critical" periods. These are characterized not by order but disorder, disintegration, and a general absence of intellectual and moral roots. They are in no sense ages to take as models of the good society, from Saint-Simon's point of view, but they have been vital, he argues, to the continuing ascent of mankind. Only through the negative, critical ideas of late Greece and Rome was it possible for the structure of the first great organic period to become weakened and the way opened for the emergence of the second and higher organic epoch, that of the high Middle Ages. Saint-Simon tells us that what has existed since the late Middle Ages is still another critical age, that of the age of Reason and the Enlightenment. The basic ideas of the Enlightenment are false in themselves, but they had the merit simply by reason of their negative, even nihilistic quality of bringing medieval organicism to ultimate decay and thus making possible the beginning of the third great organic age, that of the New Christianity, resting not upon religion in the traditional sense, but, as we have seen, science, technology, and industrialism.

It is this elaborate and detailed theory of human development that gives the lie to Marxists and others who accused Saint-Simon of being merely utopian and fanciful and of constructing his ideal society simply out of the resources of his imagination. On the contrary, Saint-Simon's ideal society of the future, like Marx's, is inconceivable for him except as the final stage of a progression that began millennia earlier. Moreover, not even Marx outdid Saint-Simon in demonstrating how each of the preceding epochs was a distinct pattern, a pattern based upon some one major theme—polytheism, monotheism—but having all other aspects of thought and life take their form and content from this major theme. Law, economy, education, political rule, and family each bore the mark of polytheism in the ancient world, just as each bore the mark of monotheism in the Middle Ages. The same holds true for Saint-Simon in the "critical" epochs. For all their negative, disintegrative effects upon prior organic periods, they too each have a distinctive, unitary quality with the parts in interrelationship.

It was thus as the social evolutionist or theorist of necessary progress from past to present that Saint-Simon was able to utter the statement quoted at the beginning of this section: "Our intention is merely to promote and explain the inevitable." Neither Marx nor any prophet of progress put the matter more succinctly. Zealot, fanatic, millenarian, utopian, and apocalyptic Saint-Simon may have been—to use adjectives so often applied to him by biographers and historians. But we cannot even begin to understand the real nature of Saint-Simonian utopian optimism until we realize that beneath it lay in its larger outlines exactly the same vision of an inexorably advancing mankind that we find in Marx and others of the century who had boundless admiration for their own "scientific" work in contrast to that of the mere "utopians."

The essential point is that the absolute power which in Saint-Simon's imagination would someday be wielded benevolently over the citizenry by scientists and savants and by engineers and industrialists, thus forming at long last the golden age, would come about as Saint-Simon saw it all through the inexorable working of the same laws of historical progress, those he identified in his "Social Physiology," which had brought man up to his present point.

The imagination of poets has placed the golden age in the cradle of the human race. It was the age of iron they should have banished there. The golden age is not behind us but in front of us. It is the perfection of social order. Our fathers have not seen it; our children will arrive there one day, and it is for us to clear the way.

To clear the way. A great deal and in fact most of the social reform and also the revolutionary strategies of the nineteenth century had precisely that objective. The "way" did not have to be constructed. The laws of progress had taken care of that in iron fashion. All that was required was to clear it of artificial impediments.

Auguste Comte

All of this was, certainly, Comte's view of the matter. In Comte we also have a complex fusion of elements. His *Positive Philosophy* published between 1830 and 1842 established him almost immediately as one of Europe's greater minds. So discerning a critic as John Stuart Mill, as we have already noted, virtually adopted Comte's prescriptions for the method of social science, making them the substance of the book in his *Logic* that deals with the moral or social sciences. Whatever Saint-Simon's role in the formation of modern, systematic sociology may be, it was Comte—who actually coined the word—who from the beginning has been regarded as the father of this discipline. For Comte sociology was the only social science, in the large. Political economy, social psychology, and the other social sciences would all take their ancillary roles in the one great science of man, sociology. It would be hard to find a more scientifically *inspired* book than the *Positive Philosophy,* with its careful, ordered review of the history of all the sciences, its placing of them in hierarchical and logical relation to one another, and its long finale, the outline of what Comte first called social physics and then sociology, which would do for the social or human sphere exactly what astronomy, physics, chemistry, and biology had done for their respective spheres. It is an imposing book, and was widely regarded as such shortly after its publication. By virtue of lectures which Comte had given in Paris announcing in advance many of the seminal perspectives of the *Positive Philosophy*—lectures which had attracted some of the best minds in not only Paris but other parts of the Continent as well—Comte was already well known when his volumes began to come off the press. He enjoyed, in sum, substantial respect as a scientist or at least a scientifically oriented philosopher.

That is one Comte. There is, however, another powerful being contained in the same body: that of a prophet, messiah, redeemer of mankind from the "anarchy" which Comte saw all over the social landscape of Europe, indeed of the world. Frank Manuel has found in *Positive Polity*—the huge work Comte would publish twenty years after his first work, devoted to the detailed character which true positivist society would have after Comte's principles had been sufficiently accepted by savants and citizens—a revealing reference to Joachim de Fiore. With evident pride, Comte names Joachim as among his messianic forerunners. Elsewhere Manuel cites the fact that Comte makes specific reference in the third volume of the *Polity* to the intellectual breakdown, the insanity, he had suffered in 1826, before publication of the science-oriented *Positive Philosophy.* During this year of madness, Comte tells us, he had acquired more than an intellectual knowledge of the validity of his fundamental scientific principles, chiefly the principle of the three stages in human development; he had come to understand the suprascientific truth of his principles, and gone so far, Manuel remarks, as to describe the regression he had undergone during the year, a regression that took his mind from the positive back through the metaphysical, to the religious, even the fetishistic. The regression was followed,

Comte writes, by a curative return of his mind through the three states, from the religious back to the positive or scientific. Clearly, Comte's statement here is far more in line with what we find all through the world literature of messianism than it is with the world of science or rationalist philosophy. Careful reading of Comte's *Positive Philosophy* and also of the essays he had published during the 1820s which lead up to this work makes only too clear that the soul of an eschatological, a messianic, thinker was already formed—a soul that would only enlarge, stimulated by diverse influences including his short-lived but profoundly shaping association with Clothilde de Vaux, whose death in 1846 seems to have been all that was necessary to transform Comte completely into the religious-prophetic figure he had become by the time of his death in 1857.

What provides common ground for the two Comtes is faith in progress, past, present, and future. From adolescence on, Comte was obsessed by belief that the West was in crisis, that misery and spiritual anguish were to be found in Europe, that Christianity had ceased to be the kind of spiritual and intellectual authority it had once been, and that paramount among all needs was a new system of thought that would do for the contemporary world what Christianity had done for the medieval and late Roman periods. In the essays of the 1820s there are frequent references in one form or another to what Comte called "spiritual anarchy." Such anarchy had been caused by the succession of mighty buffets the West had received from the Reformation, the Enlightenment, and finally, the Revolution. The makers of the Revolution and the philosophes had believed, Comte argues in these essays, that only a political reconstruction was required, whereas in fact what was absolutely necessary was *spiritual* reconstruction. The mistake that many of the readers of the *Positive Philosophy* made in the nineteenth century, John Stuart Mill included, was to see this book as an exclusively intellectual-rationalist-scientific enterprise. Comte intended it to be that; but he intended it to be also a body of principles, however rational and abstract, which would be *moral* and *spiritual* in their impact upon people.

The *Positive Philosophy* is in structure a masterful (if nevertheless flawed) historical synthesis of the physical and biological sciences in Western Europe from earliest times on. Comte's objective is to demonstrate historically that the human mind has progressed through three stages: the theological, the metaphysical, and finally, the positive or scientific. In the first all explanations are made in terms of deities; in the second by recourse to abstract spirits or entities without empirical foundation; and in the third stage explanations become genuinely scientific, rooted in the study of nature and the discovery of her laws.

Each of the major sciences has passed through these three stages, with

253

the single exception of the study of society. Most of the book—the first four volumes—illustrates how each of the sciences: astronomy, physics, chemistry, and biology, in that order (Comte does not accept the reality of psychology as a discipline or science) has passed through the three stages. He futher seeks to show that only when in the whole process a given discipline has passed into its third and scientific stage does it become possible for the next science in the hierarchy to gradually evolve into *its* positive stage. Thus, for Comte, there is not only a hierarchy of the sciences to be seen, but also a historical filiation. Physics could not become scientific until astronomy had; only when physics became a real science was it possible for chemistry to develop into its third, or scientific, stage. The same applies for biology.

This idea of the progressive filiation of the sciences is crucial to Comte's strategy. Through it he is able to declare that since biology, chronologically the latest of the sciences, has just become in Comte's own lifetime a genuine science, or has just reached its third stage, is it is now possible—inevitable —that the study of society may become a true science: that is, pass from the "metaphysical," or second, stage to the positive, or scientific, stage.

What will the nature of the new social science (the *only* social science) be? It is in the final two volumes of his work that Comte outlines with extraordinary ingenuity and insight that science which is at once the capstone and the necessary historical emergent of the history of the sciences in the West. Sociology will be divided into the two broad areas of statics and dynamics just as are all of the other sciences. In the first it is the nature of order, stability, and equilibrium in society that will be the object of sociological concern. The second, dynamics, which Comte is plainly more interested in, will consist in the study of progress: its laws, stages, causes, and manifestations.

As we have seen to be the case with so many minds involved in the history of the idea of progress, Comte believes that he alone is the discoverer of "the law of progress." Others, particularly in the Enlightenment, had helped show the way. As I mentioned previously, Comte is the author of the common belief that absolutely no idea of progress existed in the classical and medieval worlds: that its beginnings are to be found in the Quarrel of the Ancients and Moderns and its first tentative assertion, regarding society as a whole, in the writings of Turgot and Condorcet. Comte lauds these two and a few other philosophers of the Enlightenment for their "pioneering" work in what he calls social dynamics. So does he laud, as Saint-Simon also had, the Catholic conservatives of his day—Bonald, de Maistre, and Chateaubriand—for positing what the Enlightenment and the Revolution never had, the principles of order. What Comte defines as his momentous contribution to the world of knowledge is the uniting of the principles of order and progress into one master law.

No real order can be established, and still less can it last, if it is not fully compatible with progress; and no great progress can be accomplished if it does not tend to the consolidation of order . . . . Therefore, in positive social science, the chief feature must be the union of these two conditions, which will be two aspects, constant and inseparable, of the same principle . . . . [I]deas of order and progress are, in social physics, as rigorously inseparable as the ideas of organization and life in biology.

The conception of progress as an invariable scientific law belongs exclusively to Comte's new discipline, sociology—so he insists repeatedly. As I have noted, he is generous in his citation of those from the early modern era on who have been instrumental in setting down useful intimations of progress. Pascal, Bossuet, Leibniz come in for praise, along with those I have already mentioned. What they all had in common, Comte tells us, is realization that human history has been linear, that it has progressed in stages or epochs, and that it resembles nothing so much as the intellectual development of a single individual. This analogy which, as we observed, began among the Romans and then was seized upon and made the key to *world history* by St. Augustine, is just as vital an element in Comte's thought as in the work of any predecessor.

I will, Comte writes, "consider the continuous succession of human development, regarded in the whole race, as if humanity were one." St. Augustine did not say it better!

The true general spirit of social dynamics then consists in conceiving of each of these consecutive social states as the necessary result of the preceding, and the indispensable mover of the following, according to the axiom of Leibniz—*the present is big with the future.* In this view, the object of science is to discover the laws which govern this continuity, and the aggregate of which determines the course of human development. In short, social dynamics studies the laws of succession, while social statics inquires into those of coexistence; so that the use of the first is to furnish the true theory of progress to political practice, while the second performs the same service in regard to order; and this suitability to the needs of modern society is a strong confirmation of the philosophical character of such a combination.

There is not the slightest doubt in Comte's mind that progress and development or evolution are exactly the same. Amelioration is inevitable because it springs from the development process.

To me it appears that the amelioration is as unquestionable as the development from which it proceeds . . . . Taking the human race as a whole, and not any one people, it appears that human development brings after it, in two ways, an ever-growing amelioration, first in the radical condition of man which no one disputes; and next, in his corresponding faculties, which is a view much less attended to.

Comte has precisely the same view of plenitude and organic continuity that we have found from the Greeks on in European thinking about progress, and not least in the Middle Ages, though Comte has no awareness of that fact. What he writes in this respect could have been written by Aristotle or Thomas Aquinas, as well as by Leibniz, from whom Comte probably got it directly. "Adhering to our relative, in opposition to the absolute view, we must conclude the social state, regarded as a whole, to have been as perfect, in each period, as the coexisting condition of humanity and its environment would allow. Without this view, history would be incomprehensible. . . ."

So much for Comte the theorist of the laws of progress, the positive *philosopher*. We must turn now to the second, though intimately related, side of Comte; the Comte of utopianism, of construction of the *Positive Polity*. It is this work to which Comte gives the subtitle "Treatise on Sociology," and in many ways it is precisely that. Here he provides, especially in the second volume (it was published in four volumes, 1851–54) a substantial number of insights into the "Positive" theory of society and of each of its components. Many of these, in almost unchanged fashion, have made their way into contemporary social science. But the real aim of this book, written when Comte was in a virtual frenzy of belief in Positivism and also in the imminent realization of a society grounded in and based upon Positivism, is depiction of life as it would—or rather *will*—be in that society. Rarely has any utopia ever been written in the detail that Comte's was. Everything from the rites and ceremonies of the Religion of Humanity (which is Positivism in its religious rather than scientific form for Comte) to the actual dress of scientists and laymen is dealt with.

No detail is spared. We are introduced to the Positivist calendar, a reformed calendar with thirteen shortened months, each bearing the name of a great philosopher or scientist of the past rather than those names "derived from pagan superstition," and with Positivist holidays and festivals duly noted. The precise structure and workings of the Positivist family are described, and it should be noted that for Comte this "utopian" family must be patriarchal in nature. Women are not, however, neglected. Positivist society will mark the final emancipation of women and their incorporation into the community of love, fellowship, and intellect for the first time. Positivist education commencing in the family and extending to school and university or institute is described extensively. It is hard to think of a single aspect of human life that Comte does not touch, in each instance limning with fanatic intensity the nature of the structure or process as it will be in Positivist society.

Above all, though, it is the nature of the hierarchy and ruling class that interests him. Comte has no use whatever for the individualistic, liberal ideals of the Enlightenment. He is contemptuous of what he calls the "metaphysical dogmas" of liberty, equality, and popular sovereignty. As I have noted above, he had been strongly influenced by the conservatives of his day, Bonald and the others. It is order and stability and above all "spiritual authority" that is needed. In a striking phrase, Comte calls individualism "the disease of the Western world." He at one point divides society into "intellectuals" and "emotionals." The great mass of the people must be cared for, treated humanely, given every opportunity to rise in the social and economic scale; but it is folly, Comte argues, to expect true sovereignty to lie in the people as a whole. The real rule of Positivist society must lie in the hands of those who will be at the top of the the the Positivist religion—that is, the *sociologists*, whose position will be exactly like that held by the Sacred College of Cardinals during the Middle Ages. Comte makes no effort to conceal or disguise his admiration for the Middle Ages and the medieval Church. He had been born into a deeply Catholic, monarchist, traditionalist family, and although he had broken with this in his youth and indeed never returned to Catholicism or support of a monarch, it is impossible to miss the hold that early faith in the church had on Comte's mind. Positivism, he tells us at one point, is Christianity denatured of its superstitions and converted into worship of the Grand Being, which is society or humanity. Not without reason did a wit describe Comte's utopia as medieval Catholicism minus Christianity.

Like his early master Saint-Simon, Comte accepts industrialism utterly. Industrialists will come only below the priest-scientists in the Positivist hierarchy. All crucial decisions will be made by these two classes, though final authority, absolute and irrevocable in character, will reside with the scientists, the true leaders of Positive society. The religious, not to say medieval, cast of Comte's mind is revealed in his insistence upon *two* powers in this society: the political and the spiritual. And they must be kept separate, just as they were or were intended to be in the Middle Ages. "The peculiar goal of the 'spiritual power' is . . . the direction of public opinion; that is, the establishment and maintenance of principles which must preside among diverse social relationships. . . . No social entity may lack the influence of this 'spiritual power.' Its main task is, however, the supreme direction of education." Like all religious prophets and self-proclaimed messiahs, Comte obviously had proper respect for the crucial role of education. Rousseau (whom Comte detested) had laid down in his third discourse the vital importance of education, which for Rousseau carried with it the implication of centralization and monopoly to the point where he even recommended abolition of the family. Comte doesn't abolish the family in his utopia; far from it! It must be made patriarchal and absolute in its own sphere. But once children reach a certain age, family-controlled education ends and that supervised by the scientists-priests replaces it.

Albert Salomon in his *Tyranny of Progress* stresses the combination of the spiritual, the absolute, and the redemptive in Comte's vision of the future. When Comte spoke of progress (in the *Polity*, that is), "he hoped to recreate a catholic universe of meaning. By reconstructing the patterns of superiority and submission, he wished to provide a new systematic spiritual home for the individual that would take the place of religious sanctity."

There is not the slightest reason for believing that had Comte lived longer, had found it possible to take his disciples with him to a new continent and to found there a microcosm of Positivist society, he would have shrunk from use of any form of coercion and discipline in order to give fulfillment to the basic principles set forth in the *Positive Polity*. In him as in most self-declared messiahs, there were no real limits to desire to transform an eschatology into the work of practical social and human reconstruction.

Karl Marx

There are few if any intellectual oddities in our time more pronounced than that among Western Marxist scholars who seek to disengage Marx from the evolutionary-progressivist tradition in the nineteenth century. It is impossible to think of any major figure of that century in which the perspective of inexorable, irreversible, stage by stage progress toward a golden age on earth is more vividly evident than in Marx's key works. For those who today believe that the "real" Marx is the Marx of the so-called Paris essays and fragments written in the early and middle 1840s, and that the "real" Marx remained primarily interested in the individual self's emancipation from the alienation that had sprung from the rise of private property, it is useful to cite here some highly illuminating words of Lewis Feuer. Feuer has shown conclusively, I believe, that while Marx did *not* ever write Darwin to ask permission to dedicate any of the volumes of *Capital* to him, Marx without any question was impressed profoundly by Darwin's *Origin of the Species*, declaring that that book provided him (Marx) with "a basis in natural science for class struggle in history." Moreover, as Feuer has pointed out, Marx in his Preface to *Capital* in 1867 stated plainly that his standpoint was one from which the evolution of society is "viewed as a process in natural history." As Feuer concludes: "Class struggle founded on biological drives is about as far as one can get from a view of history that would regard its mainspring as man's quest to realize his essence."

From Marx's point of view the similarities between his own *Capital* and Darwin's notable work must have seemed obvious. Just as the primary objective of the *Origin of the Species* is to demonstrate the essential *process* —that is, natural selection involving incessant conflict within the species for survival—so from Marx's point of view the chief contribution of his *Captial* was to synthesize and make scientifically irrefutable all that he had written earlier on class conflict. He had previously given the world his broad outline of the course of social progress, and had offered many references to history as the story of class struggles. In *Capital*, which Marx regarded as his masterwork, he brought all of this to a focus, one in which class struggle could be seen as a *necessary* process in the "species" capitalism: made necessary, from his point of view, by the dynamic, dialectical relation of the elements of the capitalist system. He had declared repeatedly and more or less *ex cathedra* the inevitability of the breakdown of capitalism through internal forces of destruction, with socialism and then communism equally inevitable stages of development in the future. The prime, overriding purpose of *Capital* was to show in minute detail how the necessary processes leading to destruction of capitalism actually operated.

Lenin is said to have declared that *Capital* cannot be understood fully until one has mastered Hegel's *Logic*; Lenin came very close to echoing what Marx himself wrote in the Preface to the second edition of *Capital* when he expressed strongly and eloquently what Hegelian principles of development had meant to him. His own use of the dialectical method, Marx writes, is the "direct opposite" of Hegel's, which, Marx tells us, is "mystifying" by virtue of its centering upon the world of thought, that is, "the Idea" conceived as the "demiurgos of the real world." And, Marx continues, "the mystifying side of Hegelian dialectic I criticized nearly thirty years ago when it was still the fashion." But in the intervening period the Hegelian dialectic had gone out of fashion, had become subject to attacks by "the peevish, arrogant, mediocre epigoni" who failed to understand Hegel and sought to defame him.

I therefore openly avowed myself the pupil of that mighty thinker, and even here and there, in the chapter on the theory of value, coquetted with the modes of expression peculiar to him. The mystification which dialectic suffers in Hegel's hands by no means prevents him from being the first to present its general form of working in a comprehensive and conscious manner. With him it is standing on its head. It must be turned right side up again if you would discover the rational kernel within the mystical shell.

In its mystical form, Marx observes, the dialectic was capable of being used to support or to justify the permanent existence of bourgeois society, but when the Hegelian dialectic is applied in its rational form it makes us aware not only of the existing state of things, but

. . . at the same time also, the . . . negation of that state, its inevitable breaking up; because it regards every historically developed social form as in fluid movement, and therefore takes into account its transient nature not less than its momentary existence; because it lets nothing impose upon it, and is in its essence critical and revolutionary.

How committed Marx was to a unilinear perspective of historical advancement or progress may be be seen vividly in the Preface he wrote to the first edition of *Capital*. There he explains that although because of the advanced state of English capitalism he gives it primary attention in his study, the message is nevertheless universal.

If . . . the German reader shrugs his shoulders at the condition of the English industrial and agricultural laborers, or in optimist fashion comforts himself with the thought that in Germany things are not nearly so bad, I must plainly tell him: *De te fabula narratur* [It is a tale told for you].

Intrinsically it is not a question of higher or lower degree of development of social antagonisms that result from the laws of capitalist production. It is a question of these laws themselves, or these tendencies working with *iron necessity towards inevitable results*. The country that is more developed industrially only shows, to the less developed, the image of its own future. (Italics added)

Marx puts the point even more strongly a page or two later:

One nation can and should learn from others. And even when a society has got on the right track for the discovery of the natural laws of its movement—and it is *the ultimate aim of this work to lay bare the economic law of motion of modern society* —it can neither clear by bold leaps nor remove by legal enactments the obstacles offered by the successive phases of its normal development. But it can shorten and lessen the birth pangs. (Italics added)

In 1859, the very year in which Darwin's *Origin of the Species* appeared, Marx published his *Critique of Political Economy*. Here as in his later works he is cautioning against actions, however well intended, which are out of harmony with the historical stage of development in which a society finds itself. It is a gross error, Marx tells us, to seek solutions out of hand to problems which can only be met when history itself has furnished the vital materials of the solutions.

[We will] always find that the problem itself arises only when the material conditions necessary for its solution already exist or are at least in the process of formation. In broad outlines we can designate the Asiatic, the ancient, the feudal, and the modern bourgeois methods of production as so many epochs in the progress of the economic formation of society. The bourgeois relations of production are the last antagonistic form of the social process of production . . .; at the same time the productive forces developing in the womb of bourgeois society create the material conditions for the solution of that antagonism. This social formation constitutes therefore the closing chapter of the prehistoric stage of human society.

It would be impossible to discover in eighteenth- or nineteenth-century thought any statement of the principle of necessary progress more positive in character than that. In form and thrust it varies not the slightest from stated laws of progress we have found in such minds as Kant and Condorcet and will in the next section find in Fichte, Hegel, and many others. That "alienation" Marx had in his earliest years of writing found to be the inevitable condition of the human spirit so long as private property existed, would have its eventual relief (though after about 1846 Marx never referred to alienation as such again) through the necessary, "iron" laws of historical development which carry mankind through its several stages to eventual arrival in the advanced state of communism we shall shortly see described in Marx's criticisms of the Gotha Program.

The felicitous state the future would bring human beings is described charmingly by Marx in *The German Ideology* (written with Engels), published in 1845–46. Marx and Engels describe the necessarily subjugating effects of division of labor upon human beings in capitalist society, effects which require each human being to perform some small, highly specialized role in the productive process and thus prevent him from enjoying all his faculties and from having a spontaneous, diversified, and therefore stimulating life. Communist society, "where nobody has one exclusive sphere of activity but each can become accomplished in any branch he wishes," will be very different. With all society regulating the general production under communism, it is thus "possible for me to do one thing today and another tomorrow, to hunt in the morning, fish in the afternoon, rear cattle in the evening, criticize after dinner, just as I have a mind, without ever becoming hunter, fisherman, shepherd, or critic."

Such idyllic thought is not characteristic of Marx, but it is there all the same and can take its place with other utopian dreams in the nineteenth century. Much more characteristic of both Marx and Engels is the discussion which shortly follows the passage just cited. I refer to his discussion of the vital, controlling reality of the struggle among *classes* in history, of the merely illusory nature of those struggles of political character—"between democracy, aristocracy, and monarchy, the struggle for the franchise, etc." —and the necessary emergence of, and then domination by, the proletariat, just as historically earlier classes had their emergence, dominance, and disappearance. How universal, how nearly cosmic in nature, the progress toward the communist ideal is and must be, is manifest in the following lines:

> Empirically communism is possible only as the act of the dominant peoples "all at once" or simultaneously, which presupposes the universal development of productive forces and the world intercourse bound up with them . . . . The proletariat can thus exist only *world-historically*, just as communism, its movement, can only have a "world-historical" existence. World-historical existence of individuals, i.e., existence of individuals which is directly linked up with world history. . . .

St. Augustine's spirit and the spirits of more than a few other Christian eschatologists, live in Marx's words! The struggle between the "two cities," of man and of God, was for St. Augustine the vital means for mankind's eventual, worldwide ascent to salvation. For Marx it is the struggle among classes, a struggle that will last until the proletariat has destroyed all other classes and then eventually, with the development of communism, will lose its own class existence. It will be lost to that egalitarian whole of society in which, to quote the words from his *Critique of the Gotha Program*,

> the enslaving subjugation of individuals to the division of labor, and thereby the antithesis between intellectual and physical labor have disappeared . . . when the all-round development of individuals has also increased their productive powers and all the springs of cooperative wealth flow more abundantly. . . .

For the first time in all history it will be possible for men to live by the ideal, "From each according to his abilities, to each according to his needs."

How seriously Marx took his own stated "law of motion" for society, his statement of the necessity of each society following with only minor variations a "normal," single track of progress, may be gathered from a piece he wrote on the English in India. He is referring to the depredations of the English upon the ancient traditions of the Indians, and describes how all conquerors of that country with the exception of the English had failed to penetrate below the political surface of Indian society, and had left intact the family, village community, and caste. The English were managing "through the brutal interference of the British tax-gatherer and the British soldier" and also through economic and political erosion of Indian authori-

ties and communities to effect a virtual transformation of Indian civilization. Marx's view is two-sided. He can refer to the uprooting of Indian
traditions and communities as "sickening . . . to human feeling" and to the
"myriads of industrious patriarchal and inoffensive social organizations
disorganized and dissolved into their units, thrown into a sea of woes . . . ."
But, given his devout belief in the philosophy of human progress, necessary
and unilinear progress, Marx can also see the English doing a great favor to
India in the long run. He writes:

> England, it is true, in causing a social revolution in Hindustan, was actuated
> only by the vilest interests, and was stupid in her manner of enforcing them. But
> that is not the question. The question is, can mankind fulfill its destiny without a
> fundamental revolution in the social state of Asia? If not, whatever may have been
> the crimes of England she was the unconscious tool of history in bringing about that
> revolution.

In the *Manifesto of the Communist Party* and in a good many other
writings Marx stressed the progressive character of human history—from
primitive savagery through barbarism, slavery, and feudalism to capitalism. When Lewis Henry Morgan's *Ancient Society* was published in 1877
with its summarizing principle that all states of culture, past and present,
"are connected with each other in a natural as well as necessary sequence of
progress," both Marx and Engels fell upon it, regarding this product of a
conservative New York lawyer's anthropological imagination as absolute
confirmation of the view of progress which both Marx and Engels had long
believed in. (Morgan's book coupled with the works of Edward B. Tylor in
England at about the same time can be seen as the real foundation of the
systematic discipline of anthropology. Tylor was just as convinced as Morgan that the panorama of the human past illustrated absolute, continuous,
and irreversible progress.)

There is still another expression of Marx's progressivism that should be
cited for its intrinsic interest. This is to be found in Marx's *Grundrisse*,
written in 1857–58. It has to do with poetry, which Marx loved throughout
his life. But, like Vico, Marx saw the really great poetry of the ages as
reflective of a mentality that was born of "the childhood of humanity," a
mentality that has long since been outgrown through the progress of mankind to ever-higher states of consciousness. But is this any reason, Marx
asks, for disdaining poetry? Not by any means. Social development is like
an individual's development from childhood to maturity. It is not possible
for the man to become the child again. "But can he not find joy in the child's
innocence, and can he not seek to reproduce its truth at a later age? . . .
Why should not the historic childhood of humanity . . . a stage never to

come back, exercise a timeless charm? . . . The charm of [Greek] art is not in opposition to the undeveloped stage of society's growth in which it appeared." On the contrary, it was the very fact of the relatively primitive condition of Greece, when compared to the modern world, that made possible the art that can no longer rise naturally from our own developed stage of history. Progress, in short, need not deny us the opportunity to enjoy and respect works of the imagination which belong to (earlier) stages of growth.

But let us turn now from Marx's progressivism to the goal he foresaw for man's future: socialism and then, following continued social and intellectual development, true communism. Nowhere does Marx present us with a picture of his ideal society that even begins to compare with what Comte and a host of other utopians of the century set forth. Marx was publicly scornful of all forms of "utopian" socialism, whether in the form of blueprint or actual settlement, as with the American products of Cabet's and Fourier's dreams and calculations. But this does not for a moment belie Marx's fundamental interest in the future golden age. From early youth, the transformation of world society and human nature was foremost in his mind. He prided himself to his life's end on being the scientist of society, the first *true* scientist, and this was a self-evaluation that Engels took respectful note of in his graveside eulogy of Marx. But the biographical facts are irrefutable: long before Marx thought in terms of the science of society, he was consecrated to the transformation of society, one to begin with the abolition of private property, competition, and profit. "Science" Marx's *Capital* may be, at least in the eyes of his followers, but what that book seeks to demonstrate and validate is a set of utopian aspirations Marx had acquired while still a very young man. In every proper sense of the word, in short, Marxism is—despite Marx's own rhetoric of disdain for it— utopianism: of course supplemented, as were Saint-Simon's and Comte's, with the philosophy of history that lifted it from the kind of utopianism we find in More or Bacon.

Marx was fully aware, at least in his older age, of the uses of absolute power which achievement of socialism would require. There are still a few who deny altogether that Marx was absolutist in his contemplation of power, but the overwhelming reason why the anarchists and also many non-Marxian socialists of his time refused to accept his system was the collectivist, centralized use of political power that lay in Marx's doctrines. Perhaps the best insight into Marx's dedication to power lies in his famous *Critique of the Gotha Program*:

> The question then arises: What transformation will the state undergo in a communist society? In other words, *what social functions will remain that are analogous to present functions of the state?* . . . [Italics added]

Between capitalist and communist society lies a period of revolutionary transformation from one to the other. There is a corresponding period of transition in the political sphere and in this period the state can only take the form of a *revolutionary dictatorship of the proletariat*.

Those words were written late in Marx's life when he seemed to have become increasingly obsessed by the hope of a revolution coming into being sooner than might be inferred from a reading of *Capital*. Hence his keen interest in the Russian revolutionary underground, despite the fact that Russia didn't even come close to the kind of capitalist society Marx had so often in his major and minor writings alike declared historically necessary to the proletarian revolution. Sufficient uses of an aroused revolutionary power based in the lower class, as expressed by revolutionary leaders, would appear to have become more and more attractive to Marx.

Marx was far from oblivious to power in his earlier years. Well before the philosophical and then the "scientific" Marx became realities, Marx had indicated in poetry, pamphlet, and letter his passionate belief in revolutionary transformation and his acceptance of the kinds of power and violence which would be involved. And in the final pages of the *Manifesto* in which he and Engels outline the steps which would be necessary after the proletariat had won its revolution against the capitalists, the dominant notes are centralization of power on the one hand and nationalization on the other—the latter referring to the "vast association of the whole nation" within which all production would henceforth exist. True, Marx declares that after class distinctions disappear and after production has been firmly "concentrated" in the nation, "the public power will lose its political character." Such a statement is obviously nonsense, but that is not to take away its mesmerizing influence on generations of Marxists. Precisely as Rousseau could declare the state's coercion of the individual a means of forcing him to be free—an equally nonsensical but hypnotic declaration—Marx can concentrate all the major forms of economic production in the nation, that is, the government, and yet conclude that government, "the public power," will have lost its political character.

Viewed in retrospect, how logical, even necessary, was the development from Marx's "revolutionary dictatorship of the proletariat" to Lenin's proposal of the dictatorship of the party and of democratic centralism, a proposal that Trotsky came to accept thoroughly and to hold onto even after exile when his life was in constant danger from Stalin's agents. Indeed, Trotsky added to Lenin's doctrine the idea of dictatorship of the "center," meaning the most central core of government and party, and from this it was but a short and natural step to Stalin's total monopolization of power. Only in the light of religion, religious consciousness, and the mentality of

265

true believers is it possible to understand the appeal of Marxism. Such a view is regarded as heresy or nonsense by many, even today. But from the time Marx took over Hegel's dialectic and the belief in necessary, inexorable development toward a single, inevitable, golden end, Marxism, despite its pretensions to and rhetoric of science, was fundamentally a religion. As I stressed at the beginning of this section, only rarely did a full and genuine secularization of thought take place in the nineteenth century. Rousseau's civil religion, Saint-Simon's New Christianity, Comte's religion of Humanity, and Marx's faith in the dialectic—all of this is as religious in essence as anything we could possibly find in any of the declared religions or sects in history.

One final note is worth stressing: Marx's view of equality. His announced goal almost from his earliest social and political writings is the extermination of social classes and the private property which underlies them. From the extermination of classes would come equality for the first time in history. But Marx had no illusions about the ease or quickness with which human beings actually could become equal. He had nothing but contempt for those sections of the Gotha Program which implied that equality must become the law of the land the moment the revolution was successfully over. Marx had the same contempt for social reformers of his day who agitated for political and civil and economic equality within the capitalist system.

So far as the Gotha Program's easy optimism was concerned, Marx had this to say:

> We are dealing here with a communist society, not as it has *developed* on its own foundations, but on the contrary, just as it *emerges* from capitalist society. In every respect, economically, morally, intellectually, it is thus still stamped with the birthmarks of the old society from whose womb it has emerged. . . .
>
> Hence *equal right* is here still—in principle—a *bourgeois right*, although principle and practice are no longer at loggerheads, while the exchange of equivalents in commodity exchange only exists *on the average* and not in the individual case.

Like Rousseau, Marx realized that the achievement of equality would take a long time, would require a great deal of evolutionary development even after the beginnings of socialism had been fixed, would necessitate an unlimited amount of guiding power, and finally, would demand a total remaking of personality, a sloughing off of all attributes of the personality formed in prehistory—that is, the history anterior to the eventual emergence of socialism. In Marx's characteristically blunt words, to give priority immediately to redistribution of goods after the revolution in the interest of "dogmas . . . which may have made some sense at a particular time but which are now only a load of verbal rubbish" is to fail utterly to see the nature of the problem.

Marx also writes:

> Vulgar socialists (and from them, in turn, a section of democrats) have followed the bourgeois economists in their treatment of distribution as something independent of the mode of production and hence in the presentation of socialism as primarily revolving around the question of distribution.

Marx, like other founders of universal or world religions, was well aware of the discipline and self-discipline, the sacrifices, and above all the "rebirth" that would be required before mankind could shake off all evolutionary vestiges of the exploitativeness, the covetousness, and the spirit of self-aggrandizement which had entered the nature of all human beings during the eons leading up to the revolution. Power—constant, unremitting—alone would make it possible for this eventual rebirth of man to take place.

This is of course the abiding theme of all the utopias of the nineteenth century: power! Fourier advertised widely for some political ruler, however despotic, who would be willing to establish through his absolute power Fourier's minutely detailed, cooperative, regimented system of phalansteries, each with an identical number of people, chosen with meticulous regard for the harmonizing of the "passions" which Fourier identified, classified, and made the molecular bases of his entire complicated utopia. Saint-Simon and Comte were not less eager to find a despotic ruler to bring their respective utopias into quick existence. Comte actually sent a copy of his *Polity* to Emperor Nicholas I of Russia, accompanied by a respectful hope that the Czar would see fit to establish in Russia Comte's ideal system of human governance.

But let us not forget that behind all of the utopian, religious, and power-obsessed minds of the utopians we have dealt with here, there lies a faith in history-as-progress, as progressive unfolding of potentiality, just as devout as any belief in the millennium and its progressive achievement that we found in the minds of Fifth Monarchy Men and other Puritans of the seventeenth century.

Statism

To German philosophers and ideologues above any others in the nineteenth century must go credit (if that be the proper word) for uniting the perspective of human progress with the power of the national state. I am not suggesting that other countries—France, England, and the United States, among others—were without partisans of the sovereign state and a full-blown nationalism. And we have just reviewed the degree to which French as well as German utopians could join the theory of progress to a construction of some future society that would be every bit as repressive of individual liberties as any historically formed national state of the nineteenth and twentieth centuries. But the fact remains that there is no other country apart from Germany, chiefly Prussia, in which there is to be found a succession of thinkers dedicated to progress and the absolute state alike in any degree comparable to Fichte, Hegel, and their intellectual progeny in the nineteenth and twentieth centuries. For them the political state was more than a structure of law and polity; it was an exalted form of moral perfection or of a special kind of freedom, spiritual grace, or idealistic purity that was held to be man's supreme loyalty in the world, his consecrated duty of service, and his highest mode of true freedom.

To be sure, the idea of the state, of the state's absolute power in service to the achievement of social and individual moral perfection really began in France during the Enlightenment. We have seen what political power—the power arising from the General Will—meant to Rousseau in the transformation of society and human nature. And although few in the Enlightenment in France came close to Rousseau in his apotheosis of power and in his denial of any individual rights whatever in the state that would rest upon his prescribed social contract, power was nonetheless an attractive, tempting, even irresistible thing for a great many of the philosophes. Despairing of gaining what they desired in their individual ways through reliance upon ordinary social and political processes, a substantial majority of the philosophes turned to the possibilities of fulfilling their reformist or revolutionary aims through use of absolute, centralized, and *enlightened* power. Hence the fascination held for so many of the philosophes by such rulers as Frederick the Great in Prussia and Catherine the Great in Russia. Even the Physiocrats, apostles of the natural, free, economic order, were not loath to think of such centralized political power as the best means of cleaning away all the detritus of the *ancien régime* which made their cherished system impossible.

If the philosophes were the first to hold up a theoretical vision of the moral and psychological values inherent in proper use of absolute power, it was the Jacobins and then Napoleon who gave the world its first sight of the conversion of theory into practice along these lines. Through decrees, manifestos, declarations, and actual laws, beginning about 1791 and reaching the heights in 1794, the Revolutionary government made plain the burning desire of such men as Robespierre and Saint-Just to effect a total transformation of French society and of human nature, a purification of the human spirit that would make true virtue possible for the first time in history, through the legislative and executive powers of the new state, one and indivisible. Very little that was prized by Jacobin zealots ever actually came into effect, although they were not without their successes when it came to demolishing or profoundly altering ancient institutions and laws. It was Napoleon who, in his own words, took power to fulfill, not destroy, the goals of the Revolution and who did the most to glorify and dramatize absolute political power. His impact on the German intellectuals was fully as great as, if not greater than, his impact upon French ideologists. Not since Cromwell or perhaps Frederick II in the thirteenth century had there been a political figure in Europe with the combination of personal charisma, redemptive essence, and almost total political and military power that was to be seen in Napoleon. His unification of the German states and principalities was temporary, but it was bound to give immense stimulus or encouragement to all in Germany who dreamed of permanent unification. His power at home and abroad was all the greater for his insistence that it was rooted in the people, the masses. To speak and to rule, as he claimed to, directly for the people conceived as an indivisible unity rather than for special areas, classes, or interest groups; to put power at work, again as he claimed to, for the moral and intellectual as well as the social and economic and political welfare of man; and above all to convince the educated classes and particularly the intellectuals that power as Napoleon wielded it, or professed to wield it, was at once liberating and ethically elevating—this was what made Napoleon the figure he was for Hegel who, on sighting Napoleon riding through Jena in 1806, wrote that he had just seen the World Spirit pass by.

But with all regard to the French contribution to magnification of the national state in the late eighteenth and early nineteenth centuries, it is still to Germany and its philosophical idealists that we must look for understanding of how the political state became what it did in the nineteenth century. And at the heart of the German philosophers' achievement was, as I have noted, the linking or organic fusing of national political power to a conception of the progress of humanity, a conception that remains saturated with idealism from beginning to end. Who, we are obliged to ask, but a German idealist—Hegel—would declare: "The state is the Divine Idea as it exists on earth." Well into the twentieth century through Weimar and the Third Reich would the essense of this affirmation remain a beacon light.

Johann Gottfried von Herder

I do not have to be told that the author of *Ideas Towards A Philosophy of History of Mankind*, published in 1784-91, presents a real difficulty in present context. It is not possible to make of Herder the worshipper of the unified, organic, collective state that both Fichte and Hegel were. Herder had been deeply influenced by Lessing's *The Education of the Human Race*, which was anything but a statement of national-political power. He was devoted to the idea of Germany as a plurality of autonomous, self-developing, free, and small nations or national communities. He detested the centralized, militarized Prussia. There is a good deal in common between Herder and Wilhelm von Humboldt, whose early individualistic conception of freedom so akin to that of William Godwin gradually evolved into a philosophy of freedom that recognized the vital importance of free communities and associations as contexts of individual liberty. All of this is true.

But, as Sir Isaiah Berlin has written, Herder's works "bristle with contradictions." And, again quoting Berlin, it is indeed possible to see Herder as "in some sense a premonitory symptom, the albatross before the coming storm." While it must be granted that he believed in kinship, social solidarity, and a high degree of dispersion of political authority, it cannot be denied that he was devoted to *Volkstum*, to nationhood, and to progress seen as a realization of these. He died in 1803, and therefore could not know how powerfully his name and ideas affected a widening number of philosophers and intellectuals who would retain the concept of *nation*, who would see all history as working toward this end, but who for the most part gave little fealty to those other ideas Herder cherished: localism, decentralization, and multiplicity of loyalties. It is therefore useful and I believe proper to say something about Herder's philosophy of progress before turning to Fichte and Hegel, the two greatest exponents of the state-as-progress.

There is a religious intensity about Herder's contemplation of mankind's progress from the most primitive of beginnings, through stage after stage, to the present and thence to a glorious future. He accepts fully the idea of plenitude which we have seen to be so vital to the idea of progress from the start.

> When the door of creation was shut, the forms of organization already chosen remained as appointed ways and gates by which inferior powers might in the future raise and improve themselves . . . . New forms arise no more: but our powers are continually varying in their progress through those that exist, and what is termed organization is properly nothing more than their conductor to a higher state. . . .

He is equally devoted to the idea of a chain of being and to the idea of continuity. Everything, we are told, is connected in nature and time. Since man is the "last and highest link, closing the chain of terrestrial organization, he must begin the chain of a higher order of creatures as its lowest link"; thus it was possible for Herder to see a truly magnificent unfolding, a mighty advancement, into the long, even endless, future. He likens, as had

Augustine, the education of a single individual, his development of mind and learning from infancy on, to mankind as a whole. "In this lies the principle of the history of mankind, without which no such history could exist . . . . There is an education, therefore, of the human species; since every one becomes a man only by means of education, and the whole species lives solely in this chain of individuals." Indeed, there have been errors, failures, and wrecks in history; great nations have weakened, fallen, and disappeared. But there is a higher order of reality than this. "The chain of improvement alone forms a whole of these ruins, in which human figures indeed vanish, but the spirit of mankind lives and acts immortally . . . ."

Without question, humanity is the protagonist of Herder's great work on progress, and as I have emphasized, Herder is the enemy of all that constricts man's individual faculties, all that prevents the individual or the people from realizing its highest potential. He repeatedly condemns the despotic state as one of the most powerful of checks upon human development. But, for all that, there is an unmistakable vein of devotion to the nation, the *Volkstum*; this he sees, we must not forget, in linguistic, literary, traditional, and cultural more than in political terms. Hence Herder's expressed fear of foreign languages, fear of what they might do to the purity of the language that is and must be the deepest source of unity of a true nation. "I am able to stammer with immense effort in the words of a foreign language; its spirit will evade me." He castigates all efforts by a people, a true people—that is, a nation—to take on a character that is alien to its constitutive nature. To seek to go back, to use a people of the past, however great, as a model, to draw from even the best of contemporary peoples—this for Herder is unconscionable.

What we must do, Herder declares, is "be characteristic of our nation, language, and scene." As Berlin points out, it is in this context that Herder, for all his acceptance of world diversity and cosmopolitanism, strikes his deepest nationalist chord. "I cry," Herder writes, "to my German brothers . . . the remnants of all genuine folk songs are rolling into the abyss of oblivion . . . the night of so-called culture is devouring all about us like a cancer. . . . We speak the words of strangers and they wean us away from our own thought." As Berlin immediately comments, following his citation of Herder's words, "Herder appeals to Germans to know themselves, to understand their place and respect their role in the cosmos, in time and in space."

Once again, then, acknowledging the lack in Herder of any of the glorifications of national power we find in German thought from Fichte on, the important fact remains: Herder united the idea of nationalism and the idea of progress in so compelling a way as to set the intellectual scene for the

German political idealists of the nineteenth century. The strength of his belief in human progress is boundless, and even those who did not share Herder's views about the Germanic nation found his litanies to progress almost mesmerizing.

> Every return to ancient times is a fiction, is, from the ideas of the World and Time, an impossibility. We float onward: and the stream that has once flowed, returns no more to its source.
> All the doubts and complaints of men respecting the uncertainty and little-observable progress of good in history arise from this, that the melancholy wanderer sees too little on his way. If he extended his view, and impartially compared with each other the times that we most accurately know from history; if he dived into the nature of man and weighed what truth and reason are, he would as little doubt of their progress as of the most indisputable truths of the physical sciences.

Herder's ideals of political diversity, localism, and decentralization were to become almost lost in Germany during the next century and a half, but there is probably no single work that did as much to fix the idea of progress in the German intellectual mind, and, with it, the idea of the nation, as Herder's *Ideas Towards a Philosophy of History of Mankind*; nor, it is only fair to add, in the intellectual minds of other countries as well.

Johann Gottlieb Fichte

It has been said of Fichte that he did more than any other single philosopher to effect the transition from a German philosophical scene largely dominated by Kant to one dominated by Hegel. There is a wide gulf between Kantian individualistic liberalism and Hegel's idealistic political absolutism, but not so wide that Fichte could not bridge it through such works as *The Closed Commercial State* and *Addresses to the German Nation*. He is the first to provide systematic philosophy to the extension of the national state from a largely legal-political entity to one in which all needs of human beings—moral and spiritual as well as social and economic—were to be met. He is the true author of national socialism, a phrase I use here generically.

Fichte began as a Kantian. At age thirty he produced a book, *A Critique of all Revelation*, that for a time was believed by many to have been written by Kant, so close was the correspondence of views. It was a book that the great Kant publicly praised. Four years later, in 1796, Fichte published his

Foundations of Natural Law According to the Principles of Science, and although the astute reader today, with the advantage of hindsight, may detect premonitory signs of Fichte's gradual alienation from Kantianism, it would still be difficult on the basis of this work to predict a Fichte who could, less than a decade later, write the *Addresses to the German Nation*. Here all Kantian limits are taken from political powers and responsibilities.

In *The Closed Commercial State* Fichte describes the state as the only agency capable of providing for individuals the conditions necessary to their work, which he declared to be "the highest and general purpose of all free activity" in individual life. The state alone gives man his property, and only the state is qualified to protect man and property "by licensing all economic activity and subjecting it and the social groupings formed around it to a strict control with the view to the equal distribution of all available means of subsistence among the individual citizens." For Fichte the state is the individual's greatest hope, in both material and nonmaterial respects. As the title of the book suggests, Fichte was keenly interested in the kind of security and care the state could provide in economic matters but he is hardly less interested in the state's potential for becoming the dominant *teaching* influence in the individual's life; and it is moral education that Fichte has chiefly in mind.

In Fichte we observe starting with *The Closed Commercial State* the clear beginning of one of the most powerful contrasts in nineteenth-century idealistic thought: the contrast between a *social* order, rooted in economy, that is governed largely by man's base desires—ambition, avarice, covetousness, conflict, and the like—and a political order in which man's highest qualities alone may take root and grow. No other strain of thought in the nineteenth century did as much to advance the cause of the state and its absolute power as did the strain that begins with Fichte and achieves such majesty in Hegel. One would have to go back to Plato's *Republic* to find equal adoration of the state; but there it was set in the abstract world of perfect ideas. In nineteenth-century Germany it is set in the process of evolution and of progress; that it was never doubted made necessary the eventual achievement of the perfect state on earth—and with the Prussian or German state without question the model.

By the time Fichte delivered his hugely popular *Addresses to the German Nation* (1807–8), the philosophy of total nationalism was almost complete. Hegel would add metaphysical and ethical layers to this philosophy, and also embed it in a dialectical process operating throughout history that so many students in German universities would find enchanting; he would also develop the idea of alienation and the state's role in moderating this psychic state, still another exceedingly attractive conception in the nine-teenth century. But Hegel did not and could not improve upon the essence, the substance, of the perspective of national power that Fichte gave to large crowds who heard him and to a much larger public who read him. No wonder that a grateful government gave him a rectorship at one of the greatest of German universities.

Individual, nation, and state become mystically fused in Fichte's thought. As Leonard Krieger clearly points out:

> The nation, as *the* earthly embodiment of the eternal, is the form of human society which comprehends and establishes the order of both. The individual is integrated into the nation by the dependence of his own seed of eternal moral being upon the national totality of eternal moral being, and the state is encompassed by the nation by receiving the fundamental sanction and direction of its power therefrom.

It is an interesting development of thought, though by no means a unique one in Fichte's country and century. Begin with the individual and his moral nature, as Fichte did in his younger years, bring in the social order in its plurality and its capacity for nurturing the individual's moral nature, and then, finally introduce not only the nation—Herder's nation—but also the state that could alone give identity and protection to the nation and, thus, also to the social order and the individual. Before Fichte died, he had juxtaposed the individual with the power of the state so closely that literally nothing else could serve as an intermediate agency.

We must not forget that this cultivation of absolute power for the nation-state by Fichte is set as is so much German thought of the century in the context of *cosmic* evolution. Just as with liberty and equality, it wasn't enough in the nineteenth century merely to propose or to plead for the absolute power of the national state. It must be shown to be as much an inexorable outcome of a long evolutionary process as anything to be found in the world of nature. No historians and philosophers in the nineteenth century could equal the Germans in demonstrating the cosmic necessity of the national state.

In the *Addresses to the German Nation*, where Fichte's exaltation of national power reaches its height in his writing, he specifically condemns any cyclical theory of history, arguing the unassailable rationality of the long, unilinear view of mankind's progress. We must look elsewhere, though, to find Fichte's most inspired declaration of unilinear rather than cyclical pattern in history: "The universe is to me no longer that ever-recurring circle, that eternally repeated play . . . it has become transfigured before me, and now bears the one stamp of spiritual life—a constant progress towards higher perfection in a line that runs into the Infinite." That statement appears in his earlier *The Vocation of Man* (1800), the book in which the nearly complete transition from Kantian individualism to nationalist collectivism can be seen easily. This is the work in which Fichte's ingrained progressivism is most evident. The following is indicative:

All those outbreaks of unregulated power before which human strength vanishes into nothing . . . can be nothing less than the last struggles of the rude mass against the law of regular, progressive, living, and systematic activity to which it is compelled to submit in opposition to its own undirected impulses;—nothing but the last shivering strokes by which the perfect formation of our globe has yet to be accomplished . . . . This dominion of man over Nature shall gradually be extended until at length no further expenditure of mechanical labor shall be necessary than what the human body requires for its development, cultivation and health; and this labor shall cease to be a burden;—for a reasonable being is not destined to be a bearer of burdens.

William Godwin could scarcely have put the matter in more hopeful and elegiac terms in his *Political Justice*, published seven years before Fichte's *Vocation of Man*. Fichte is still enough of the Kantian internationalist to foresee the progress of all races, including those at present most savage, toward the same civilized terminus now represented by Western civilization.

Savage races may become civilized, for this has already occurred—the most cultivated nations of modern times are the descendants of savages . . . . They must no doubt at first pass through the same dangers and corruptions of a merely sensual civilization, by which the civilized nations are still oppressed, but they will thereby be brought into union with the great whole of humanity, and be made capable of taking part in its further progress.
It is the vocation of our race to unite itself into one single body, all parts of which shall be thoroughly known to each other, and all possessed of a similar culture . . .

All of this, in 1800, has, as I say, a strongly Kantian quality to it. It is humanity as a whole that is the essential referent of the progress Fichte sees taking place from the creation of mankind to the distant but foreseeable future. What a profound, radical change in Fichte, then, during the few years which followed *The Vocation of Man*: a change from Kantian universalism to a pre-Hegelian adoration of the nation-state, from humanity as a whole to the omnipotent, omnicompetent German nation that has become for Fichte the crowning achievement of progress. The national state, touching each citizen in all his spheres of activity from birth to death, ever-watchful, ever-custodial, ever-providing, all-benign and, necessarily, all-powerful: this is for the Fichte of 1808 the culmination of progress. It is no wonder that Lasalle and a good many other proponents of national socialism would for a long time treat Fichte with reverence. It was Hegel who made progress-as-political power virtual gospel for the European mind, but Fichte's are the truly seminal works in this respect.

Georg Wilhelm Friedrich Hegel

Apart only from Plato, Aristotle, and St. Augustine, Hegel may well be the single most influential philosopher in Western history. He was without question the preeminent philosopher of the nineteenth century, and the renascence of Hegelianism during the last two decades, one that has actually led to a Hegelianizing of Marx, suggests that his influence may be with us for a long time. In no philosopher or scientist of the nineteenth century did the idea of progress or of unfolding advance through successive stages marked by great civilizations of the past have greater weight than in Hegel's thought. There is scarcely a work in Hegel's voluminous writings that is not in some fashion or degree built around the idea of becoming, of growth and progress. His posthumously published *Philosophy of History*, which we shall come to momentarily, is perhaps the prime example of his progressivism. But even in such works as his *Philosophy of Art* and the *Philosophy of Religion*, there is to be found essentially the same division of world history into great ascending stages, leading to the Germanic present, that we find in the *Philosophy of History*.

Hegel's all-important *Logic* has to be seen also in the light of his perspective of progressive development. It is here that the most systematic and thorough analysis of both structure and process is to be found. It seems doubtful that what we today call the "systems method," "functionalism," and "structuralism" in the social sciences would have ever come into their current estate had it not been for the omnipresent influence of Hegel during tha last century and a half, whether direct or through Marx or others who had been influenced deeply by Hegel and particularly this work. Here is where Hegel describes in detail the famous dialectic and its working from thesis to antithesis to synthesis; and here is where we are given the pregnant thesis that an understanding of the part-whole relationship, organic in character, is the key to understanding all nature and society. There is of course very close connection between the Hegelian dialectic and his theory of progress. Quite simply, the dialectic is the mechanism, the dynamic essence or cause of the pattern that progress has taken in the world. Everything must be seen in organic terms—that is, structurally but also dynamically; as process, as *becoming*. Hence from Hegel's point of view the falsity of categorical contrasts, of any insistence that a thing is or isn't. Unfolding, becoming, the continuous passage from state to state: each is different but is related functionally by the process of development as the man is related to the child and the plant to the seed—different but of the same essence. It is no wonder that Marx paid tribute to Hegel and the dialectic.

Progress is one sweeping force in Hegel's thought. We turn to the other now. It is the political state. Whatever may have been Hegel's idols during his very early years when he was in substantial measure carried away by the zeal of the French Revolution, he had but one real subject of worship during his mature and final years, and that was the national, specifically the Germanic, absolute state. So seized was Hegel by the national state in its Germanic form that he literally constructed his world histories, whether in politics, art, or religion, around the respective progress of each of these to a final, triumphant resting place in the political state. More successfully than any other philosopher in all Western history, Hegel united absolute faith in inexorable progress with equally absolute faith in the absolute political state. I say "successfully"; I mean this, of course, in the sense of the extraordinary appeal this union of faiths had for so many diversely located minds in the nineteenth century: in England, in France, in Eastern Europe, even in America.

The Nation State is Spirit in its substantive rationality and immediate actuality; it is therefore the absolute power on earth . . . The State is the Spirit of the People itself. The actual State is animated by this spirit in all its particular affairs, its Wars and its Institutions . . . . The self-consciousness of one particular Nation is the vehicle for the . . . development of the collective spirit; . . . in it, the Spirit of the Time invests its Will. Against this Will no other national minds have rights: *that* nation dominates the World.

These words are cited by Karl Popper from Hegel's *Philosophy of Law*. Popper errs, I believe, in his declaration that "Hegel introduced the *historical theory of the nation*." That work had been done in some part by Bodin and in still larger part by Herder. But the words which are extracted by Popper from Hegel's work on law are fully reflective of the political philosophy that governed his teaching and writing for many years at the University of Berlin. Granted that the Prussia of Hegel's adulation was, at least by twentieth-century standards of political repressiveness, relatively mild; it bore the effects of the reforms effected by Scharnhorst and others who had learned from French military successes how important to military strength a nation is that has some degree of popular participation in government and social and economic security for its citizens. Granted too that the society described in ideal terms by Hegel in the *Philosophy of Right* is a constitutional monarchy with representative institutions, a moderately autonomous religion with quasi-independent "corporations" (for Hegel, guildlike organizations), and the family principle well ensconced. And granted, finally, that there is no evident reason to believe that Hegel would have been other than shocked and horrified by the Third Reich.

We are still, however, left with ideas, perspectives, and unalterable utterances which give evidence to Hegel's sincere belief that the political state, the national state—with Prussia as paradigm—is the "march of God on earth," "the realization of the ethical Idea," "the basis and center of all the concrete elements in the life of a people: of Art, Law, Morals, Religion, and Science." The inescapable fact is that no matter how the "real Hegel" may come to light in the various guises given him by those who in our own time are engaged in his sanctification as political, economic, and social liberal or humanitarian, there is simply no way of separating him from ideas and expressions which were in themselves acts of obeisance to the national state and which, on the ineffaceable record, led others to ever-higher levels of intensity in the glorification of the state. It is not necessary to imply that Hegel was in some way a "servant" of the Prussian bureaucracy, that his professorship at Berlin was payment, or vantage ground, for celebration of the existing government. Allow him all the individual autonomy and self-direction we will: he still emerges as the preeminent philosophical influence in the glorification of human progress as attainment of national power.

His *Lectures on the Philosophy of World History,* not published in his lifetime but delivered by him at Berlin (1822–23), went beyond insistence upon the proposition that "reason governs the world" and that world history is "a rational process"—a proposition that St. Augustine could have endorsed fully. For Hegel, in this work, nations have been from the beginning the key actors in world history, with each nation expressing some particular idea or purpose. The history of the world "travels from east to west, for Europe is absolutely the end of history." The first phase is the Orient.

In the political life of the east we find a realized rational freedom developing itself without advancing to subjective freedom. It is the childhood of history . . . . The glory of oriental conception is the one individual as that substantial being to which all belongs, so that no other individual has a separate existence, or mirrors himself in his subjective freedom.

Thus the first great world stage of progress becomes one in which through the absolute dominance (freedom) of one individual—the ruler—all others are consequently led to feel the organic relatedness that will constantly grow in time. Through incessant conflict—between the Oriental state and invading barbarians—that expresses itself dialectically, thesis versus antithesis, a still higher form of political life is realized. The Oriental resting place of the Spirit is, Hegel tells us, "the boyhood of history, no longer manifesting the repose and trustingness of the child, but boisterous and turbulent," most notably in central Asia. But progress continues. "The Greek world may then be compared with the period of adolescence, for here we have individualities forming themselves. This is the second main principle in history."

Progress carries us next to Rome.

The third phase is the realm of abstract universality (in which the social aim absorbs all individual aims); it is the Roman state, the severe labors of the manhood of history. For true manhood acts neither in accordance with the caprice of a despot, nor in obedience to a graceful caprice of its own; but works for a general aim, one in which the individual perishes and realizes his own private object only in that general aim.

Dialectical change alone has made possible this emergence of the political spirit to manhood in the Roman Empire. "At the very outset we have the antithesis between the aim of the state as the abstract universal principle on the one hand, and the abstract personality of the individual on the other." Synthesis requires the harmonization of this opposition, one that is paralleled by the antithesis in the third stage between the secular state and the spiritual power represented by Christianity.

"The German world appears at this point of development—the fourth phase of world history. This would answer in the comparison with the periods of human life to its old age. The old age of nature is weakness; but that of spirit is perfect maturity and strength." Now the conflict between individuality and the state, between spirituality and the secular power, is at last and finally reconciled. This synthesis, Hegel declares triumphantly,

attained concrete reality only in the history of the German nations . . . . The antithesis of church and state vanishes. The spiritual becomes reconnected with the secular, and develops this latter as an independently organic existence . . . . Freedom has found the means of realizing its ideal—its true existence. This is the ultimate result which the process of history is intended to accomplish, and we have to traverse in detail the long track which has been thus cursorily traced.

As I have several times noted in this book, there has always been an ethnocentric quality to the Western idea of progress. From the Greeks and Romans, through the Christians, to the eighteenth- and nineteenth-century philosophers of progress, the West or some part of it always has been accepted as the kind of civilization toward which mankind's progress is proceeding. Hegel carries this ethnocentrism much farther. It is not Western civilization as a whole that is for him "the ultimate result" of human progress, but, as we have just seen, the Germanic people alone; more precisely, the Germanic state which Hegel saw most resplendently formed in the Prussia of his day. We shall meet Teutonism again, in the next section.

We should say something about the mechanism or process by which this grand progression from East to West, from Oriental despotism to Germanic political order, is made possible. This too we are given in the *Philosophy of History*. The "grades of progress," let us be reminded, "are the characteristic 'national spirits' of history . . . . To realize these grades is the boundless impulse of the world-spirit—the goal of its irresistible urging;. . ." What, then, is the activating force, the inherent cause?

The answer is not unfamiliar to those of us who have seen the persistence through Western history of the Augustinian fusion of development and conflict, and the Augustinian adaptation of the Aristotelian idea of potentiality becoming actuality. We begin with that impulse which for countless philosophers of progress has been crucial: in Hegel's own words, "an impulse of perfectibility." From Hesiod on, this is the impulse that best characterizes the difference between man and the lower orders of organic being. At bottom we are of course dealing with the Greek idea of development.

"The principle of development," Hegel writes, "involves also the existence of a latent germ of being—a capacity or potentiality striving to realize itself. This formal conception finds actual existence in spirit; which has the history of the world for its theatre, its possession, and the sphere of its realization." Leaving out only the "history" and "theatre of the world," we are in the presence in such a statement of Aristotle and, of course, Leibniz. Development, Hegel continues, is a property of nature as well as humanity. But the "development of natural organisms takes place in a direct, unopposed, unhindered manner"—a contention that would have astounded Darwin, I cannot resist noting. But it is the Spirit we are concerned with here. And with the Spirit, "it is quite otherwise."

[It] is at war with itself; it has to overcome itself as its most formidable obstacle. That development which in the sphere of nature is a peaceful growth, is in that of the spirit, a severe, a mighty conflict with itself. What spirit really strives for is the realization of its ideal being; but in doing so, it hides that goal from its own vision, and is proud and well satisfied in this alienation from it.

Its expansion, therefore, does not present the harmless tranquillity of mere growth, as does that of organic life, but a stern reluctant working against itself. It exhibits, moreover, not the mere formal conception of development, but the attainment of a definite result.

Of course the result is, as we have seen, the ascent to the fourth and final stage of the development of nations in the theatre of world history: the Germanic nation.

The history of the world is the discipline of the uncontrolled natural will, bringing it into obedience to a universal principle and conferring subjective freedom. The east knew and to the present day knows only that *one* is free; the Greek and Roman world that *some* are free; the German world knows that *all* are free.

What Hegel means by that last is nothing that Kant or Mill or Spencer would have recognized as "freedom." For Hegel freedom is not individual rights against the state but, rather, the conscious, accepting participation in the state. Rousseau would have understood. Hegel clothes the absolute state, just as Rousseau had, in the garments of freedom; but there cannot be the slightest doubt of Hegel's dedicated belief in the absolutism, the sanctity, even the divinity of the national state's power.

Thus in his *Phenomenology of Mind* he writes: "The state power is . . . the achievement of all, the absolutely accomplished fact, wherein individuals find their essential nature expressed, and where their particular existence is simply and solely a consciousness of their own universality. . . . it stands as the absolute basis of all their action."

He is no less positive of this nature of freedom in his *Philosophy of History*. There he declares the state to be "that form of reality in which the individual has and enjoys his freedom, *but on the condition of his recognizing, believing in, and willing that which is common to the Whole.*" (Italics added)

And in the *Philosophy of Right* occurs the famous, or notorious, statement: "The march of God in the world, that is what the state is. The basis of the state is the power of reason actualizing itself as will."

It is true that in his description of the kind of state that approximates most closely the ideal, Hegel draws heavily from the conservatives of his day, not all of whom by any means shared Hegel's reverence for the state. It was the conservatives from Edmund Burke on—reacting bitterly to the combined atomism and political centralization of the French Revolutionary state under the Jacobins—who were the first to reinstate family, local community, church, social class, guild, and other forms of intermediate association to a position of theoretical importance they had not enjoyed in the mainstream of European political thought since at least Jean Bodin at the end of the sixteenth century. Hegel disliked the English state which, he believed, rested upon aggregates of discrete individuals brought together in artificial unions solely for political purposes. In his *Philosophy of Right*, therefore, there is a strong articulation of these traditional groups into what he calls civil society. Hegel thus in pluralist fashion distinguishes sharply between state and society. The principle of intermediation of authority in the state is a vivid one in Hegel.

But, this noted, we cannot overlook the ascendant and powerful place that Hegel gives to state in distinct contrast with church, family, community, and all other component groups of civil society. What he calls "the German Principle" is the complete fusion of the spiritual and secular and the social and political into a single unity, presided over by an absolute monarch. As Leonard Krieger has written in his *The German Idea of Freedom*, there are three different aspects of human liberty to be found in Hegel's theory of the state: first, the right of citizens to manage all those affairs which are not necessary to the well-being of the state; second, the voluntary "cooperation" of the citizens with the agencies of government and with all the authorities which are vital to the health of the state; and third, "the guarantees of the freedom of the citizens by the concentration of supreme state-power in one center—the monarch." And, Krieger adds, "of these three elements . . . the third was for Hegel the most fundamental; it was, indeed, both the condition and the measure for the existence of the others."

It would be difficult to exaggerate the influence that Hegel's transmutation of freedom from a state that has individual autonomy and rights as its essence to one in which the true measure becomes not autonomy or independence for the individual but his *willing* participation in a centralized, absolute structure of power. If Rousseau is the initial architect of this transmutation, his influence, great as it is, does not equal Hegel's; for, from Hegel this conception of freedom as membership or participation in a collectivity moved directly to powerful movements in the nineteenth and twentieth centuries as diverse as military nationalism, Marxian and Leninist socialism, and the kind of racism that was extolled by Richard Wagner.

The historian Treitschke writing years after Hegel's death felt himself, and with all reason, in Hegel's spiritual company when he wrote: "War is not only a practical necessity, it is also a theoretical necessity, an exigency of logic. The concept of the State implies the concept of war, for the essence of the State is Power. The State is the 'People organized in Sovereign Power."

Compare Treitschke with the Hegel whom Karl Popper cites from *The Philosophy of Law*: "War has the deep meaning that by it the ethical health of a nation is preserved and their finite aims uprooted . . . . War protects the people from the corruption which an everlasting peace would bring upon it." There is really nothing surprising in Hegel's statement, given our observation that, in general, conflict is central to the progress of the human spirit through the ages. As Popper notes, Hegel had a surprisingly modern conception of the war that he justified on ethical and progressive grounds. He may or may not have been acquainted with Clausewitz and his ideas (Clausewitz died in the same year Hegel did, 1831, though his classic *On War* did not appear until after his death), but there is striking similarity between the ideas of the two men on the nature of modern war. The lessons Clausewitz drew from the Napoleonic wars were no doubt drawn independently by Hegel, and they consisted essentially in the realization that individual valor no longer has pertinence in the strategy of nations at war. Clausewitz could have concurred, *did* concur, with these Hegelian words: "In civilized nations true bravery consists in the readiness to give oneself wholly to the service of the State, so that the individual counts but as one among many. Not personal valor is significant; the important aspect lies in self-subordination to the universal." Popper further presents us with Hegel the sociologist, if not actual partisan of modern weaponry. It was, Hegel asserts, the conversion of war from a state in which the individual is decisive to one in which the mass counts that caused the invention of the gun: ". . . it is not a chance invention," Hegel declares. And of gunpowder's invention in the later Middle Ages Hegel tells us: "Humanity needed it, and it made its appearance forthwith."

There is no space here even to sketch the outlines of Hegel's influence upon political and social thought in the nineteenth and, as noted, in the twentieth century to this very moment. What is most remarkable perhaps is the multiple character of his influence as philosopher of progress and of power. From the time of his death there were "left" and "right" Hegelians, and to this day Hegel is as often cited by those of radical disposition as by conservatives. Marxism as we know it is deeply rooted in Hegelian philosophy, and so were other, non-Marxian varieties of radical thought in the late nineteenth century. But so is a great deal of conservative thought in law and politics of the same period rooted deeply in Hegel. In truth, there are elements of logic, metaphysics, epistemology, and philosophy of history in Hegel to serve just about all philosophical or ideological causes—most especially those in which the principle of necessary, unfolding, progressive change is integral.

Much of Hegel's philosophy of history is quickly recognizable as something of a secularization of Christian themes of conflict and synthesis going back at least to St. Augustine. Hegel had a deeply religious mind and a high respect for the place of religion in the good society. But the achievement of Hegel, for ill or good, was the fixing of inherently Christian perspectives of progress to a world in which the high point of advancement was symbolized by the national state. If for no other reason this gave timeliness and power to Hegelian thought. For, after all, the central institution in European society, and in many other parts of the world given the penetration of European political and economic values to these parts, was the national, increasingly popular state. It was during the nineteenth century that the national state rose to the zenith it enjoyed until the horrifying devastation of World War I made plain for once and all what the spirit of nationalism, when locked into the sovereign territorial state, could bring about.

Make all the allowances we will for the wars, strokes of diplomacy, dynastic unions, acts of political executives and legislatures and, of course, economic titans of that time, we still cannot explain the sheer power, the almost religious intensity of political nationalism, and the boundless patriotism of tens of millions of citizens to their respective states in the nineteenth century apart from intellectual currents ranging from outright, contrived propaganda in school and marketplace to systems of political idealism as exalted as that of Hegel—systems which became parts of even English intellectual life through the so-called English Hegelians such as T. H. Green and Bernard Bosanquet. Hegel's ideas extended even to America, land of rugged individualism and pragmatism, chiefly in the famous *Journal of Speculative Philosophy* published in St. Louis during the last third of the nineteenth century.

Space does not allow more extensive treatment here of Hegel's wide, deep, and diverse influence upon Western thought during the decades following his death. It was at its height, of course, in Germany, touching not only philosophers, scientists, and scholars, but also statesmen, bureaucrats, military leaders, and prominent members of the business class. Rarely if ever in history has a single man's philosophy exerted the appeal Hegel's did, especially up to World War I and its aftermath of defeat for German polity and *Kultur*.

But the lure of the Hegelian synthesis of political absolutism and inexorable progress did not by any means disappear amid the ashes of German political humiliation. Keith Bullivant in his recent and important *Culture and Society in the Weimar Republic* (which he edited and contributed to) has emphasized how strong the legacy of Hegel and the Hegelians remained during this period. One of the book's contributors, Godfrey Carr, quotes tellingly from the Weimar intellectual, Friedrich Sieburg, who wrote: "Only Germany can decide the future, for only Germany has produced formulas of universal validity." Among the formulas Sieburg listed are the categorical imperative, Hegelianism in politics, and, not least, militarism. Hugh Ridley observes in the same volume how easily the left and the right could mistake for Soviet ideas exported in the 1920s to Germany ideas which were actually German, rooted in the tradition of progress-as-national power going back to Fichte and Hegel.

In an especially illuminating essay Keith Bullivant demonstrates in detail how firmly anchored in precisely this Fichtean-Hegelian tradition were some of the ideas Thomas Mann gave voice to in essay, novel, and speeches. Mann, who moved to the United States in 1938, could at once thrill and disturb American audiences unaccustomed to the kind of authoritarianism that could exist even in a mind as antifascist as Mann's. Mann's intellectual roots may be, as he claimed, in Schopenhauer and Nietzsche, but no one could have come of age during Mann's early period without coming into full contact with Hegelianism.

I do not want to conclude this section without indicating once again the fact that though progress-as-power was triumphant and all-pervasive in Germany in the nineteenth and twentieth centuries, the idea existed in other nations also. France is a prime example, especially after her defeat by Prussia in 1870. It would be hard to find the idea of progress more firmly embedded in nationalism and sovereignty than in this country. That holds not only for the fiercer exponents of *revanche* and for French militarists and imperialists, but for minds as civilized as Taine, Renan, Durkheim, and Péguy. Nor was this conception of progress lacking in tradition-bound, "muddling through," empiricist England. I have mentioned the role of the English Hegelians; it was by no means insignificant despite the blows from other philosophers which almost immediately fell upon Bosanquet and Green. But there were many other forces at work as well to make possible that state of mind which led young English men to volunteer by the hundreds of thousands even after the appalling casualties of trench warfare were widely known. The British Empire had not yet become, save in a few minds, the repugnant entity for intellectuals that it became after the War.

Prior to 1914 there were large numbers of brilliant and educated thinkers in England who saw something akin to manifest destiny in the Empire. Progress burned brightly in English minds, and so did the fierce desire to extend the English heritage to all parts of the world.

Nor, as Ernest Lee Tuveson in his *Redeemer Nation: The Idea of America's Millennial Role* has shown us in vivid detail, was nineteenth- and early twentieth-century America devoid of this same passion for use of the nation-state as the instrument of progress, or, in commoner form, as the exemplar of human progress. A single citation will serve us here, one from Albert J. Beveridge, notable statesman and writer:

God has not been preparing the English-speaking and Teutonic peoples for thousands of years for nothing but vain and idle self-contemplation and self-admiration. No. He made us master organizers of the world to establish system where chaos reigned. He has given us the spirit of progress to overwhelm the forces of reaction throughout the earth. He has made us adept in government that we may administer government among savage and senile peoples. Were it not for such force as this the world would relapse into barbarism and night. And of all our race, he has marked the American people as His chosen nation to finally lead in the redemption of the world.

Truly, in the New World as in the Old, the compounding of the idea of progress and the idea of the nation-state could result in an intensity of millennialism and messianism the like of which had never been seen on earth.

Racism

One other, final manifestation of progress-as-power must be described: racism, the belief that human progress is inseparable from the existence of certain racial stocks in history—racial stocks which embody progress in their own histories and which are the indispensable generators of progress for mankind as a whole.

Consciousness of race and of racial superiority is of course very old. It is unlikely that any people of long history and accomplishment, however modest, has been free of such consciousness. Certainly we find it among the Chinese ("the Middle Kingdom"), the Jews, the Greeks, the Romans, and countless other ethnic strains. The Greeks distinguished between themselves and the "barbarians," a term that covered almost though not quite

the rest of mankind. Romans were no less convinced of their racial substance and destiny. True, classical ideas of race were more resilient than
those of modern Europe and America, for it was possible for a captured
barbarian to emerge from the status of slavery and become a full citizen
following due assimilation of the culture.

Ideas of race and racial basis of civilization persist through all intervening centuries to our own day, though as long as Augustinian Christianity
dominated Western Europe in its Catholic form—which is to say, the Middle Ages—the religious was more important than the racial or ethnic as a
decisive category. St. Augustine's absolute insistence upon the unity of
mankind and upon the single origin of mankind helped guarantee that.
During and after the Reformation, racist thought mushroomed. Far more
Old Testament-oriented than the medieval Roman Catholics, Protestants
became imbued with a consciousness of "good" and "bad" peoples, one
derived from the innumerable struggles involving the true people of God
and their enemies. The impact of European discoveries of exotic peoples in
other parts of the world upon European consciousness inevitably invited
comparison of peoples in terms of their visible cultures but also in terms of
putative biological differences of mental capacity. The spreading popularity
of polygenetic theories of the origin of mankind, in vivid contrast to Augus-
tinian-unitary thought, also gave impetus to increasingly invidious classifications of peoples in the period following the sixteenth century. During a
short period of the eighteenth century there was a waning of interest in race
as such. Turgot, Condorcet, and others devoted to progress thought in
terms of cultures and civilizations arranged in linear scale, rather than in
terms of races. Nevertheless it is in the late eighteenth century that racist
hypotheses became increasingly common as explanations of the vivid differences of cultures on the earth. Voltaire, who derided the Jews and denied
their historical importance in the history of civilization, thought Negroes
incapable of true civilization. Even David Hume, so generally respectful of
the power of custom and habit, thought civilization probably the exclusive
domain of the whites. Lord Kames, among the most highly respected of
Scottish moral philosophers, reached the reluctant but real opinion that the
inferiority of Negro cultures to those of the Caucasians and Orientals was
based in racial biology.

George L. Mosse in his recent, valuable *Toward the Final Solution: A
History of European Racism*, stresses the critical importance of the Enlightenment in the genesis of the kind of fascination with race that was to be one
of the major identifying characteristics of the nineteenth and twentieth
centuries. There was, he says, first the Enlightenment faith in science; all

things, however complex and ambiguous, would be in time reduced, it was thought, to scientific principles and classifications. Second, there was Enlightenment devotion to Greek and Roman art and thought—one way of escaping from and putting the cudgel on the hated Middle Ages and their contributions—and this in turn led to the seizing upon the shapes of Greek and Roman bodies, as evidenced by statuary, as criteria for the biological best in the modern world; biological and also mental and cultural best! The fusion of these two Enlightenment obsessions—science and belief in Greco-Roman superiority—helped popularize the use of "scientific" measurements and other tests for the determination of who among modern peoples were closest to the Greeks and Romans, and who were farthest and therefore the most primitive or backward. Mosse's discussion of all this is highly illuminating. For without late eighteenth- and early nineteenth-century establishment of a "scientific" basis for belief in discrete races and in their discrepant contributions to civilization, it is unlikely that there would have occurred that union of racism and the theory of progress that is the essential subject here.

But it did occur; and before the nineteenth century had ended there were tens of millions of Westerners on both sides of the Atlantic who believed implicitly in the racial basis of progress. The key figure in this uniting of race and progress was Joseph Arthur de Gobineau. Without question, his *Essay on the Inequality of the Human Races* (1853–55) is the source of racist conceptions of human progress which, during the late nineteenth century, spread throughout Western civilization. In the Dedication (to George V of Hanover) Gobineau writes: ". . . I convinced myself at last that everything great, noble, and fruitful in the works of man on this earth, in science, art, and civilization, derives from a single starting point; it belongs to one family alone, the different branches of which have reigned in all civilized countries of the universe."

To race alone Gobineau ascribed both the triumphs and the failures in the history of mankind's efforts to build civilizations. He was as much occupied by the decline and death of civilizations as by geneses and developments. In point of fact, had Gobineau not been chained to the superstition of race, had he devoted himself simply to the social, cultural, and intellectual processes involved, the problem he set for himself and the comparative methodology he employed would have given him a seminal place in modern comparative history. Gobineau was a learned man and, apart from his conception of the crucial importance of race, had a humane mind. Tocqueville disagreed strongly with Gobineau's racist theories, as is evidenced in their correspondence, but he respected Gobineau all the same as a mind and as a man of civilized sensibilities.

But, alas, race was Gobineau's obsession, and the sad truth is that above any other single figure in modern history he is responsible for the place that race has had in Western political and historical thinking. Any civilization, he declared in the *Essay,* "will certainly die on the day when the primordial race-unit is so broken up and swamped by the influx of foreign elements, that its effective qualities have no longer a sufficient freedom of action."

There are ambiguities and even inconsistencies in Gobineau's work. From the statement just quoted one could assume that "purity" of race was invariably the ideal so far as human progress is concerned. It is assuredly true that for Gobineau the "strong" races on earth are white, but he is fully appreciative of the role of contact and of intermixture of "bloods" in the liberation of a given people from fettering tradition. He tells us that very often in history it is the "secret repulsion from the crossing of blood" that condemns an inferior race to primitivism or barbarism. Again, it is worth stressing that Gobineau was utterly correct in his stress upon *historical contacts of peoples* and their intermixture—wrong only in centering his explanation of the results in biological rather than cultural terms. One must not expect consistency from Gobineau. He can stress the utter necessity of mixture of races and their "bloods" as the means of lifting the cultural level of a given race, but he can also write that "peoples degenerate only in consequence of the various admixtures of blood which they undergo." Moreover, "their degeneration corresponds exactly to the quantity and quality of the new blood."

Gobineau is primarily responsible for that most insidious and false of conceptions: *the Aryan race.* Long before Gobineau, philologists in Europe had come to the conclusion that far back in time there had been a culture and a language which could be seen as the parent cultural-linguistic source of all the Indo-European languages and cultures. Such, it was argued, are the strong similarities among these modern languages that the hypothesis of original common linguistic source was unavoidable. The philologists for the most part had not concerned themselves with race; only language and culture. But Gobineau was among those—the most eloquent and persuasive indeed—to argue that the original "Aryan" culture was more than that; it was *Aryan race,* and that this race was the parent stock of all the more recent races—Greeks, Romans, Germanic, and others—which have been alone responsible for all the major advances in civilization. Gobineau was not precise in his delineation of probable physical characteristics of the original Aryan "race" or of the descendants chiefly responsible for the development of high civilization. Sometimes he has them with round heads, sometimes with long; sometimes eye color is brown, other times black for the superior races. It was the German disciples and followers—and also

English and American—who gradually made the original Aryan people into the now familiar blond, blue-eyed, tall, and white complex that has exerted so much power and done so much evil in modern thought about culture and politics.

Gobineau sees the past and present as composed of ten major civilizations. There is no need for listing, much less describing them here. It is Gobineau's considered judgment on them that is alone important: "If there is any element of life in these ten civilizations that is not due to the impulse of the white races, any need of death that does not come from the inferior stocks that mingled with them, then the whole theory on which this book rests is false."

It is to the Germanic peoples that Gobineau looks with most ardent appreciation and hope. It was the German race, he declares, that rescued civilization from the decadence and weakness of late imperial Rome. Western civilization owes everything for its unrivaled cultural advancement to the German race. "Where the Germanic element has never penetrated, our kind of civilization does not exist." So obsessed was Gobineau by the genius inherent in the Germanic peoples that he credits this specific genius with the initial creative spark that raised even the Alleghenian, Mexican, and Peruvian cultures to a reasonably high level. His ranking of the races of the world may easily be guessed. At the bottom are the Negroes; next come the Chinese and related Asians, who are "clearly superior to the black" but dominated by impulses to conform and to avoid the bold or daring. Whites, as already noted, rank highest not only in mental capacity but physical beauty. "The peoples who are not of white blood approach beauty but do not attain it." Whites alone know "honor" and "reflective energy" of an intensity that leaves them with no peers on earth.

Gobineau had his critics, among them, as I have noted, his friend Tocqueville, who in a letter declared: "There is an entire world between our beliefs." But more to the point here, Gobineau had his followers—almost instantly, and nowhere in such abundance and with such willing resources as in the German areas. Germany, Gobineau once wrote to a friend, had become his second home. Richard Wagner, Germanist supreme, inevitably found Gobineau's views admirable. In 1894 a Gobineau Society was formed in Germany, with Wagner's widow the first inscribed member. The historian John Lukacs in the preface to his edition of the Tocqueville-Gobineau correspondence, writes: "Six thousand volumes on race, together with the Gobineau manuscripts were collected in the Gobineau Library of the University of Strassburg, which was opened on 14 July 1906, on the ninetieth anniversary of the race prophet's birth."

There is a certain amount of humor in the Germans' adoption and commemoration of Gobineau. For, although he was unstinting in his consecration to "Germanic genius" and its unique role in the progress of civilization, he made plain that he did not consider this genius a necessary part of the peoples, or all of them, living in the Germany of his day. In his own words: "Les Allemands ne sont pas d'essence germanique." Indeed there were qualities in nineteenth-century Germany which Gobineau regarded as portents of decay and degeneration. But none of this was seen by or in any event considered of importance by the thousands upon thousands of German intellectuals, politicians, scholars, scientists, and military officers for whom Gobineau's *Essay* was simply and primarily tribute to them and their fellow countrymen.

Let us pass to the second most influential prophet of progress-as-racism in nineteenth- and twentieth-century history: Houston Stewart Chamberlain. It is amusing to realize that neither of Germany's two greatest racist celebrators were born German. Gobineau of course was French. Chamberlain was the son of an English admiral, although he received nearly all of his education in France and Germany. Germany became the country of his preference and after marrying Richard Wagner's daughter he became a German citizen. His *Foundations of the Nineteenth Century* (1911) is without equal as a testament to first the absolute and exclusive role played in history by race, and second, to the Germanic people. Its distortions and fabrications of history are nearly limitless, but it would be difficult to exaggerate the influence Chamberlain's book had on racist thought on both sides of the Atlantic.

The "foundations" referred to in the title are a mixed bag. There is first the Greek contribution: art and philosophy. Second comes the Roman heritage: law and statecraft. Third, and darkly, the alien, corrupting, and potentially lethal (to civilization) presence of the Jews in Europe. Fourth, the incomparable role played by the German peoples from the end of the Roman Empire in the West, and the equally incomparable redemptive position they hold in the present. (There are other "foundations" but these four are most important.)

It would be impossible to find a more relentlessly racist philosophy of progress than Chamberlain's. "Race lifts a man above himself: it endows him with extraordinary—I might almost say supernatural—powers." The ambivalence on "pure" and "mixed" races we find in Gobineau is absent in Chamberlain. "A noble race does not fall from Heaven; it becomes noble gradually, and this gradual process can begin anew any moment." There must first be "excellent racial material." But strict inbreeding in the interests of purity condemns even the best of races to specialized and limited contributions. Thus "such races as the Greeks, the Romans . . . the Italians and the Spaniards in the period of their splendor . . . pass away before our eyes." To achieve true greatness there must be a mixing, a crossing, of races—*good* races, naturally—over a substantial period of time. Natural selection has made possible the rise of the great races including the German, but what is important in our time is "artificial selection." Any inferior qualities in a race must be eliminated, or if present in a neighboring race, avoided; through interbreeding, there must be calculated, systematic favoring of racially superior qualities.

Unlike Gobineau (of whom he is critical in a number of respects) Chamberlain gives little if any credence to the notion of an orginal Aryan race. "To speak of the Aryans of three thousand years ago is to express a gratuitous hypothesis; while to speak as if they existed today is simply to utter an absurdity." Such fastidiousness does not, however, keep Chamberlain from referring approvingly in one section to "moral Aryanism," itself the product of the "blood relationship" that exists among "all the Indo-Europeans from the Atlantic Ocean to India."

It is "Teuton" and "Teutonism" which play the largest role in Chamberlain's thought and hope. The terms cover the great majority of northern European peoples, although Slavs are included with some reluctance by Chamberlain. "That Celts, Slavs and Teutons are descended from a single pure stock may today be regarded as certain in the light of anthropology and ancient history." Most of what is great, noble and enduring in Western culture is the product of Teutonic genius. "It was Teutonic blood and Teutonic blood alone that formed the impelling force and the informing power" of Western civilization in the world. In science, art, music, literature, military strategy, and statesmanship the great minds are Teutonic. Chamberlain is not at all diffident in declaring Marco Polo, Giotto, and Galvani "Teutonic" minds.

Nor does he balk when it comes to Jesus and Christianity. There is no evidence, we are told, that Jesus's parents were Jewish. The Galileans "were bound to have had" a significant infusion of Aryan blood (another instance of defection from his position on Gobineau's Aryanism). The native Aryanism of Jesus is evident from his utterances in the New Testament. St. Paul receives the same treatment. It is inconceivable that a man of such consummate genius could have been "a pure Jew by birth." The very purest Teutonism the world has ever known was that which Tacitus wrote about in the first century. That Teutonism became crossed with Celtic and Slavic blood in due time. The Germans of the present do not have the purity of their ancient ancestors, but no existing people can come even close to them. They alone have the potential for regenerating and reinvigorating the whole world, for preserving culture, for saving it from the corruptions and debasements springing from the Jews. Chamberlain arrays the Teutons and the Jews of his day in much the fashion that St. Augustine had the City of God and the City of Man. The conflict Augustine posited between the two Cities is posited by Chamberlain between Teuton and Jew.

> No arguing about "humanity" can alter the fact of the struggle. Where the struggle is not waged with cannon-balls, it goes on silently in the heart of society by marriages, by the annihilation of distances which further intercourse . . . . But this struggle, silent though it be, is above all others, a struggle for life and death.

If Germany in the nineteenth and twentieth centuries has been the most hospitable of countries to racism as the clue to progress, it has been by no means alone in regard for race. In France, doctrines of Celticism and Gallicism flourished. G. Vacher de Lapouge at the end of the nineteenth century in two widely read books, *Les Selections sociales* and *L'Aryen, son Rôle Social?*, did much to further racism and to provide it with "scientific" attributes which helped a great deal to make the study of races almost standard curriculum in Western schools and universities by the early twentieth century. Lapouge discerned three major races in Europe, the first of which was the Aryan race—its physical characteristics tallness, blondness, and long face, and its psychological and social qualities the gaining rather than the preserving of wealth and that audacity of mind which leads to "incomparable successes." "Progress is [the] most intense need" of this race. Second come the Alpines—shorter, brown in color, broad of head, "frugal, laborious, remarkably prudent . . . . Mental vistas limited, and do not like progress." Third are the Mediterranean people—dark, squat, head somewhere between those of the other two races; impossible to assess mentally and temperamentally because of too many strains of blood in their composition, but decidedly incapable of generating progress.

It was Lapouge, probably above any other racist-minded investigator, who devised the techniques and criteria of measurement and assessment of the physical and mental characteristics of the "races." Underlying all such "scientific" works, however, and indeed giving inspiration to them, was his belief in the superiority of the Aryan, the Nordic, race or races over all others in every field of endeavor in which the progress of mankind is measured. For him, as for Chamberlain or Gobineau, geographic, social, economic, commercial, and military factors are minor if significant at all in comparison with race.

Nor was England of the nineteenth century without its eminent support-ers of the racist theory of progress. We shall content ourselves with but one, Charles Darwin, for his eminence assured respect for his beliefs. Toward the end of chapter 5 of his *Descent of Man*, he muses on the forces which have ensured the "remarkable success of the English as colonists, compared to other European nations" and reaches the preliminary conclusion that such success is owing to what Darwin calls the "daring and persistent energy" of the English, as compared, say, with the French. He continues:

> Looking to the distant future, I do not think that the Rev. Mr. Zincke takes an exaggerated view when he says: "All other series of events—as that which resulted in the culture of mind in Greece, and that which resulted in the empire of Rome—only appear to have purpose and value when viewed in connection with, or rather as subsidiary to . . . the great stream of Anglo-Saxon emigration to the west."

As Kenneth E. Bock has pointed out, the extraordinary part of Darwin's discussion of the "superiority" of Europeans to other peoples is the compla-cent *assumption* of that superiority. Given such an assumption, all that remained was discovery of the "causes." I know of no evidence that Darwin ever questioned the assumption itself. And as Bock also points out, Darwin in his *Expression of Emotions in Man and Animals* takes for granted the racial-biological basis of the facts that Englishmen do not shrug their shoul-ders as much as Italians, do not cry as much as Frenchmen (or English *women*)—with the clear implication that these English traits indicate, first, more highly advanced development, and, second, the operation of natural selection among the races. Sir Francis Galton, Darwin's cousin, in a tribute to the remarkable progress of the United States declares it to be the result only of the most daring, intrepid, energetic, and courageous of Europeans having gone to this new country.

Even so, in spite of the presence of Darwinian natural-selectionists spec-ulating on race and the eugenicists, commencing with Galton, seeking to improve the race, it cannot be said that racism as the key to progress ever experienced a vogue in England such as it enjoyed in Germany and other countries, including the United States. Just when the myth of "American Anglo-Saxonism" was planted, we do not know accurately. It is enough to note that well before the nineteenth century had run its course in America, the belief that the essence of America was its Anglo-Saxonism—traceable back to pre-Norman England—was prevalent. Certainly this continent-wide belief in the Anglo-Saxon racial character of Americans—that is, true Americans—had a great deal to do with setting the scene for the hostility which successive waves of Eastern Europeans, and also Asiatics, were greeted by in the late nineteenth and early twentieth centuries. Interestingly, Herbert Spencer, who seems not to have shared Darwin's views on Western European and Anglo-Saxon supremacy, wrote that the most beneficial event that could take place in the United States was the immediate mixture through marriage of native Americans and the immigrants pouring into America in the late nineteenth century. There were not many in this country, however, who agreed with Mr. Spencer.

Teutonism and Nordicism had their increasingly numerous followers in the United States. So great and seminal a scholar-teacher as John W. Burgess of Columbia University judged Teutonism, in his hugely influential *Political Science and Comparative Constitutional Law* (1890-91), vital to the progress of humanity. The "mission of conducting the political organization of the world," Burgess wrote, is so supremely that of the Teutons that "the Teutonic nations can never regard the exercise of political power as a right of man."

The great races for Burgess are "the Greek, the Latin, the Celt, the Teuton and the Slav." But, Burgess continues, true political genius lies in the Teuton alone. "The Celt, for instance, has shown almost none, the Greek but little, while the Teuton really dominates the world by his superior genius." The Germanic nations, Burgess concludes, "are the political nations *par excellence.*"

Burgess, his views on race and progress notwithstanding, was one of the most renowned scholars and academic leaders in America at the beginning of the twentieth century. A great deal of his writing is as valuable today as it was when published. He was known as an individual of generous and humane disposition. If a man of his virtues could hold to the racist views I have drawn from, it is not difficult to imagine the breadth and depth of racist thought in the United States in the early part of this century. Madison Grant's *The Passing of the Great Race or the Racial Basis of European History* (1916) was as extreme in many respects as Houston Stewart Chamberlain's *Foundations*, but the preface to it was written by one of America's most distinguished naturalists, Henry Fairfield Osborn. And the book came close to being a bestseller throughout America.

As a final note, it is evident from the contents of this chapter that, as is unhappily true of all moral values, the idea of progress is susceptible—has been and always will be—to corruption. The same fundamental purview that could lead Adam Smith, Jefferson, Mill, and Spencer to conclude that humanity is moving toward higher levels of material prosperity and moral accord as the result solely of increasing individual liberty, could lead Comte, Marx, Hegel, and Gobineau to doctrines in which—irrespective of the rhetoric of freedom in their works—power is triumphant: utopian, political and racial.

I would not go so far as to suggest that the totalitarianism implicit in the ideas we have examined in this chapter is crucial to an understanding of the rise in the twentieth century of the totalitarian society in Russia, Germany, Italy, China, and elsewhere. Ideas alone are never sufficient to explain such results. Military victories and defeats, collapsed governments, economic dislocations, and presence of revolutionary movements eager and ready to capture governments must all be recognized if we seek to explain the phenomenon of a Soviet Union or a Nazi Germany. But just as ideas do not exist in a social and economic vacuum, neither do military, political, and economic events. The full consequences of events flow from the perceptions of the events as much as from the events themselves, and our perceptions are in turn deeply influenced by the ideas we choose to accept or expunge. Given the sheer number of people in the nineteenth and early twentieth centuries who believed deeply in the kind of national power that Hegel and Fichte had given voice to early in the nineteenth century, who were passionately committed to utopianism in one or other of its several forms, Saint-Simonian, Marxian, or whatever, and who accepted the doctrine of Nordic, Germanic, or Anglo-Saxon superiority as the key to progress, it would be absurd to rule out altogether these beliefs and convictions in seeking to explain the precise form twentieth century totalitarianism has taken—absolute power compounded of absolute, idealistic faith in utopia, political state, and race.

Nevertheless, with full attention to the tragedies which have been perpetrated by corruptions of the idea of progress—and also, let us remember, of such other ideas as freedom, equality, and democracy—I see no more reason for abandoning an idea that was vital to the thinking of those we considered in chapter 6 than I do the ideas of freedom, equality before the law, and democracy. Its flaws and corruptions understood, the idea of progress has been overwhelmingly a noble idea in Western history, noble for what it has celebrated in countless philosophical, religious, scientific, and historical works and, most of all, for what it has meant to the motivations and aspirations of those who have made up the human substance of Western civilization.

Chapter 8

The Persistence of

Progress

THERE is no want in our age of declarations by historians and other intellectuals that the idea of progress "died with Herbert Spencer," "ended with the nineteenth century," and "was banished forever by World War I" —to draw at random from several dozen such statements in my files.

But the truth lies elsewhere. I am well aware that there is now and has been for most of the century an abundance of challenges to faith in progress: to be found in literature, philosophy, history, and the sciences. We shall come to these in the next chapter. They make an imposing assemblage of arguments, and it may well be that in this, the final quarter of the twentieth century, the dogma of progress is at death's door. Nevertheless, this much accepted, it would be negligent to suppose that belief in progress in the West and especially in the United States has been without powerful support among intellectuals and laity in the twentieth century; particularly in the first half. Consider the following passage, written by one Alexander Mackendrick in the pages of the prestigious *The Hibbert Journal* in 1927, nearly a decade after World War I:

The remarkable increase in the efficiency of industry through the achievements of science and the multiplication of tools and machinery seems to justify the belief that the age of plenty has dawned. Whatever may have been the case a century ago, it is now fairly certain that the power of production and the means of transport are such that the entire human race might be comfortably housed, clothed, and nurtured. . . . A consciousness of social solidarity has manifested itself that is a new fact in human history. . . . The daily press and fictional literature have done much to focus the minds of all classes on the subjects of common interest, and to promote that sense of mutuality, of membership one with another, which must form the basis of any just demand for the establishment of rights and recognition of duties. . . . Such considerations would seem to offer some support to the belief in a natural law of progress, and to strengthen that unquenchable hope that by the gradual evolution of sweeter manners and purer laws, the *Civitas Dei* will ultimately be reached, and the Apocalyptic visions of seers realized.

The author concedes that it is not yet clear which precise course progress will take, whether through "sweeter manners and all that this implies of a deeper spiritual culture" or "by the enactment of new laws which will delimit and define the area of each citizen's liberties and make man's inhumanity to man so largely unconscious and accidental as it now is, no longer possible." But Professor Mackendrick is not troubled. "A deeper insight and a broader look may . . . beget the thought that these two attitudes are not mutually exclusive, but complementary and interdependent."

Never mind that neither the author nor the journal was or is exactly a household name in the Western world. Never mind either what the author's eventual judgment may have proved to become. The important point is that the words I have cited epitomize perfectly what tens of millions of people in the West felt about progress when Mackendrick's article was written, well into the twentieth century. Current disillusionment and malaise in the West may make us forget the enthusiasm and conviction which attended belief in progress in earlier decades of our century. One need but go back and sample newspapers, popular magazines and books, social and physical science journals, political party platforms, and the varied manifestos and policy-statements of groups across the entire spectrum of ideology in the first half of our century, to appreciate the sturdiness of what then seemed an indestructible faith in progress in the West generally and, overwhelmingly, in the United States. Nor is the idea of progress without adherents here and abroad at the present moment. I find nothing extraordinary or bizarre in this fact. Quite apart from the devastations of war and tyranny which have occurred in this century, an idea as intrinsically redemptive and millennial in nature, that has been believed in for so many centuries, that has activated so many religious and secular movements of thought and action from early Christianity on, is not an idea that is likely to disappear lightly from the Western mind. Thus World War I, with all its unprecedented slaughter, devastation, and disintegrative effect upon the political and moral fabric of Europe, actually seems to have strengthened Western faith in the idea.

After all, it was in 1920 that J. B. Bury produced his historically designed celebration of the idea, dealing with it so proudly as a distinctively modern idea. Let us turn to a few of the major expressions or vehicles of devotion to progress in our century.

Consider liberalism. The beliefs of Adam Smith, Mill, Spencer, and others of classical-liberal mind in the nineteenth century assuredly made their entry into the twentieth. They can be seen in the philosophy of free private enterprise that for the first few decades of the century so largely dominated textbooks in economics on both sides of the Atlantic; that constituted the working faith of the vast majority of owners, managers, and workers in industry; that lay behind countless editorials in the major newspapers and magazines in the country; that was consecrated regularly and faithfully at every national festival.

The belief that progress lay through free private enterprise was only a part of a larger faith that individual freedom in all spheres—speech, assembly, press, religion, and so forth—was, as Mill and Spencer had argued, the key to progress. Even so, it was belief in economic progress and in the indispensability of this form of progress to all others that was perhaps the most spectacular manifestation of the philosophy of progress prior to the Great Depression of the 1930s.

Without doubt this depression presented liberalism of the classical kind with a severe challenge. And as I shall indicate shortly, it brought to the fore a different form of liberalism that had come into being in the early part of the century. But the buffets of the Depression notwithstanding, classical (or at least neoclassical) economic liberalism survived. And at the present moment there is a veritable renascence taking place, manifest in the works and influence of Hayek, Friedman, and the Chicago School. Hayek is a very strong voice among our continuing prophets of progress. In his monumental work *The Constitution of Liberty* published in 1960, Hayek opens the third chapter with these words:

> Writers nowadays who value their reputation among the more sophisticated hardly dare to mention progress without including the word in quotation marks. The implicit confidence in the beneficence of progress that during the last two centuries marked the advanced thinker has come to be regarded as the sign of a shallow mind. Though the great mass of the people in most parts of the world still rest their hopes on continued progress, it is common among intellectuals to question whether there is such a thing, or at least whether progress is desirable.

Hayek concedes that some meretricious, even false, defenses of "laws of progress" were mounted in the last century, and that the demolition of these defenses has been salutary. But he is even more solidly of the opinion that faith in progress is justified by history, and that the imperative of our time is that of support of the reality of progress in this century. "The preservation of the kind of civilization that we know depends on the operation of forces which, under favorable conditions, produce progress." For Hayek, civilization is progress, and progress is civilization. Granted that along with the good things which the progress of knowledge yields us, and which are absolutely indispensable in our day to civilization at whatever level, there are consequences which may make us sad, which offend our esthetic, moral, or religious perspectives. Hayek continues:

> The question whether, if we had to stop at our present stage of development, we would in any significant sense be better off or happier than if we had stopped a hundred thousand years ago is probably unanswerable.
> The answer, however, does not matter. What matters is the successful striving for what at each moment seems unattainable. It is not the fruits of past success but the living in and for the future in which human intelligence proves itself. Progress is movement for movement's sake, for it is in the process of learning, and in the effects of having learned something new, that man enjoys the gifts of his intelligence.

Obviously, for Professor Hayek the idea of progress has served in modern Western history as a spiritual motor force equal if not superior to the Protestant Ethic, so far as the political and industrial advancement of Western civilization is concerned. If that is indeed his conviction, he is correct. All evidence suggests that the surge of technological, industrial, and commercial development in the West commencing in the High Middle Ages and, with only occasional interruptions, becoming constantly larger and more encompassing in scope of faith of the people, especially the middle classes, and touching by the nineteenth century literally all aspects of life, economy, social order, culture, and government, was in large measure the result of near-religious faith in the ascent of mankind from past to future. To an astonishing degree this traditional faith in an intellectual and cultural progress buoyed up by economic growth and liberty holds firm in the minds of the American people, though not of most intellectuals it would appear. Remove the present governmental fetters upon economic enterprise, it is argued by libertarian progressivists, and economic growth will continue, carrying with it progress in all spheres of life.

But that is only one form of liberalism-cum-progress. There is another and much more popular form, especially among social scientists, that makes political intervention the very core of economic and social progress. I refer to the so-called New Liberalism that sees the direct use of the central government's planning, regulatory, and directive powers as the key to progress. Michael Freeden in his recent *The New Liberalism* has shown us how this form of liberalism grew up in England—the result primarily of those two devoted disciples of progress, J. A. Hobson and L. T. Hobhouse. In the United States at about the same time there were L. T. Ward, Thorstein Veblen, and John Dewey, though other names will surely come to the reader's mind.

The New Liberalism, without lessening or relaxing advocacy of individual liberty in the sense that Mill and Spencer gave it and that is at the core of the Bill of Rights in the American Constitution, came to see, however, a role for the state that one does not find in classical, nineteenth century liberalism. Hobson, for example, in England, was throughout his youth an ardent admirer of both Mill's *On Liberty* and Spencer's *Social Statics*. He remained throughout his life a defender of civil and political rights for individual citizens. But as Freeden points out, Hobson, largely through his fascination with the idea of an evolving, progressing society, came to believe that liberalism itself had begun and must be made to continue a progressive development, one in which the natural process of progress would be heightened and accelerated through enlightened political legislation. Hobson made great use of the concept of the social organism, which he admitted acquiring from Spencer's sociology, but for Hobson, unlike Spencer, the image of organism carried with it an articulation of functions in society, functions which could best be supervised and regulated by the state. The slower, if natural and inexorable, advancement of mankind's social condition could be stimulated and widened in impact by the intelligent application of the basic principles of the social sciences to economy and society. The use of planning and regulation did not for a moment signify to Hobson that either freedom or progress was in jeopardy; only that each could be magnified and hastened in its fulfillment through the enlightened state.

L. T. Hobhouse is an equally apt example of what the founding of the new liberalism meant. His studies in social evolution and in the progress of society became notable, and he never lost his faith in the "laws" of social development. But he too came to believe that what was required to offset the hardships created by industrialism was greater use of the power of the state —to shore up security and also freedom for individuals. His *Development and Purpose* was a milestone in his intellectual development. Published in 1913, it quickly became virtually the bible of the New Liberalism. What Hobhouse calls "conditional teleology" in this work is simply the fusing of biological, social, and moral progress—the progress that has been going on for countless millennia and that will continue to go on—with the kind of planning and governmental guidance that the accomplishments of the social sciences had made possible, in his judgment. Only today, Hobhouse argued, has it become for the first time in history possible for mankind to use knowledge and also the democratic state as the means of accelerating the fulfillment of what he called "social purpose." The line between the new liberalism of Hobson, Hobhouse, and their followers in England and the democratic socialism of the Fabians is not always a distinct one, but there is a substantial difference between the central propositions set forth by the new liberals, at least in the beginning, and the key tenets of the Fabianism of the Webbs and their associates. As Hobson emphasized in the memoirs he wrote toward the end of his life, the Spencerian principles of individual freedom he had absorbed in his youth remained shining lights for him even if he had come to choose an un-Spencerian means of giving them effect.

In America, the paleobotanist and sociologist Lester Ward reached analogous ideas somewhat earlier than had Hobson and Hobhouse. For Ward, as for Hobhouse, the progress of cosmos, civilization, and the human mind was as real and certain as any of the laws of physical science. He had also been impressed in the beginning by Spencer's works and never lost admiration for them. But to his listing of stages of human progress from past to present Ward adds a new stage, one that Western man was just entering, one in which "telic evolution" or progress was possible. "Social telesis" for Ward is, as for his English counterparts, the use of government and education to give more precise guidance and also acceleration to the natural processes of advancement. True liberalism for Ward meant, in sum, political and social planning, enlightened controls, and a conception of government as both liberating and protecting in its relation to citizens.

So did Thorstein Veblen seek to unite a constant criticism of capitalism with evolutionary-progressive rationale. Almost everyone knows of Veblen's harsh strictures on the leisure class, on the kinds of nonscientific mentalities which directed the economic system, and on what he regarded as irrational lags in necessary development of economy and society. Fewer realize how deeply set these strictures were in a coherent, consistent theory of human progress. He had very early become fascinated with the developmentalism that was associated with Hegel, Marx, and many of the English anthropologists. Throughout all of Veblen's writings, ranging from *The Theory of the Leisure Class* (1899), through *The Instinct of Workmanship and the State of the Industrial Arts* (1914) to *The Engineers and the Price System* (1919), there is a solid, ever-utilized substructure that is developmental in character; more, anthropological-developmental. It was Veblen's underlying theory of human progress replete with reference to a substantial number of stages, that led him to his conviction that certain crucial "lags" in progress were present in his time—the dominance of capitalist managers over scientists being one of them—and to his further conclusion that only by expanding the powers of government, by extending legislation into areas of human life hitherto free of such legislative guidance, and by letting reason rather than economic interest alone govern our lives could we simultaneously speed up the normal rate of evolutionary progress and ameliorate the social conditions of large numbers of people in capitalist society.

Veblen's *Instinct of Workmanship* presents most systematically his theory of human progress and its stages. The earliest is what he calls "the savage state," a stage that bears considerable resemblance to the "primitive communism" in Marxist thought, though it was undoubtedly from Lewis Morgan's *Ancient Society* that Veblen drew his view of mankind's earliest condition, one in which there was neither private property nor war. From this primal condition mankind develops, Veblen tells us, into "predatory society," the first phase of which is "barbarism," with the military and priestly classes dominant. This is followed by "pecuniary society," beginning in handicraft and evolving gradually to the machine age. The emergence of the machine age makes it possible for the first time in history for reason—largely represented by engineers and scientists—to guide humanely and rationally the processes of evolutionary progress.

The third of the major intellectual figures responsible in America for the transformation of classical liberalism is John Dewey. Although there is much less of a formal or systematic nature in Dewey's treatment of progress than there is in Ward's and Veblen's, the current of progressive-developmentalism runs nevertheless through almost all of his work. He began his intellectual career as pretty much a Hegelian. And although he eventually renounced Hegelianism, it would be difficult to comprehend Dewey's lifelong opposition to all forms of dualism, his conception of freedom as realization by the individual of innate potentialities, with the central purpose of education and other institutions that of aiding in this realization, and, perhaps most important, his conception of all norms, laws, and values as being in a dynamic process of becoming, without understanding Dewey's early Hegelianism.

Like Ward and Veblen and Hobson and Hobhouse, Dewey believed strongly in the uses of intellect for the purpose of rational, progressive reform. His defense of liberty was just as solid and lasting as that of any of the other makers of the new liberalism, but the whole point of what he and others called his "instrumentalism" was the utilization of thought and planning to supplement the natural processes of society and change. His *De-*

mocracy and Education (1916) is of course the classic work in the development of what came to be called "progressive education." Dewey cannot be held liable for the extravagances and fatuities which eventually became identifying marks of Deweyan progressivism in education, but the fact remains that confidence in natural progress underlies all of Dewey's manifestations of social reform, education, and morality.

In sum, whether in Europe or America, liberals old and new never doubted at least until recently that there was progress easily to be discerned in the long struggle by man toward release from the torments of poverty, insecurity, and deprivation and, to make this release possible, toward a strongly interventionist, humanitarian, and policy-setting political state. In America both Theodore Roosevelt and Woodrow Wilson made the Presidency what the former called a "bully pulpit" for the gospel of progress through political intervention. Rarely were liberals down through the 1950s loath to set their faith in government planning and control of the economy in the rhetoric of progress. They may not often have had the panoramic outlook on progress that their forerunners Hobhouse, Ward, and Veblen had, but there is high significance in the fact that "progressive" became in rising degree the preferred adjective to describe their works and their recommended policies, with "reactionary" and "regressive" always at hand for use against opponents.

The same faith in progress is to be seen in twentieth-century radicalism. Lincoln Steffens's celebrated remark "I have seen the future and it works," made on his return from a visit to Russia shortly after the Bolshevik Revolution, has its roots in a philosophy of economic progress that was memorialized if not begun by Marx and Engels. It was this revolution—vying in importance with the French Revolution at the end of the eighteenth century as far as stimulus to belief in progress is concerned—more than any other single event of the twentieth century that gave or seemed to give validation to socialist and communist belief in the necessity of capitalism's eventual decay and death and of socialism's progressive mastery of the earth. To read the literature of radicalism through most of the twentieth century is to read the literature of secular millennialism. There must be strategy employed, to be sure—the strategy of revolt, strike, and organization of the working class, all preparatory to the Revolution—but such strategy took on its persuasiveness to intellectuals and some workers by virtue of the philosophy of progress in which it was set. However we may choose to evaluate it morally, there is no stronger affirmation of mankind's progress anywhere in the twentieth century than that contained in the books, articles, manifestos, and speeches of the socialists and communists. Parenthetically, I suggest that the largest difference between the radicalism of the first half of the century and that which began to flower during the 1960s in campus settings, with vandalism and terror sanctified, is reducible to faith in inevitable progress toward socialism. Such faith was smaller in the New Radicalism. And it is smaller still, one would judge, in current radicalism.

For a great many radicals and new liberals the Great Depression had much of the significance that famines, plagues, and other disasters had upon the minds of Joachimites and other millenarians of the late Middle Ages. It, like those catastrophes, could seem to be in its very intensity and scope precisely that time of torment, deprivation, and conflict which both the Book of Revelation in the Bible and Karl Marx in *Capital* declared to be a necessary prelude to the onset of the millennium.

But let us not forget that on the record there were many millions of Americans during the Depression whose continuing faith in progress required no radical, millenarian underpinnings whatever; only sustained belief in basic American values and institutions. In 1933, at the very bottom of the Depression, the city of Chicago staged a world's fair to celebrate "A Century of Progress." When Robert and Helen Lynd first visited Muncie, Indiana in the 1920s for research on their classic *Middletown*, they found faith in progress religious in character. More surprising is the fact that when the Lynds revisited Muncie during the Depression, to prepare their *Middletown in Transition*, they found confidence in progress largely undiminished.

And let us not forget the Technocrats about whom William E. Akin has recently written a fascinating study. The Technocrats flourished in the 1930s and counted among their membership some of America's foremost engineers. For progress to continue there must be, argued the Technocrats, replacement of businessmen by engineers as masters of the economy. So attractive was this idea that even as eminent an engineer as Walter Rautenstrauch, head of the Department of Engineering at Columbia University, helped form with the tacit backing of the University a high-level Committee on Technocracy. It cannot be said that Technocracy as a movement had anything like the national influence that other, more directly social and economic movements (such as Dr. Townsend's, for example) had during the Depression, but it nevertheless left an impact that has not disappeared altogether even today. And behind the interest of those who filled the ranks of Technocracy was the prior interest in human progress and also faith that progress could be resumed and hastened by turning over the powers of government to engineers.

Somewhat comparable to the American technocratic prophets of progress during these two decades were the English, Marxist-oriented scientists who preached the gospel of progress-through-science, taking the last word in a sense that went greatly beyond the engineering-obsessed dream of the Technocrats. Among them as among the American group were some of the foremost biologists, chemists, and physicists of the day: J. D. Bernal, Joseph Needham, and others. All had absorbed the Marxian doctrine of progress, and what they added to faith in the coming of classless society devoid of private property and capitalists was the somewhat more Comtean than Marxian conviction that scientists would and should have a dominant role in that society. For them as for the Technocrats, as well as for the New Liberals, the problem was not that of *effecting* progress, but rather, of merely activating what was already latent in society, of accelerating what would be taking place naturally were there not certain artificial obstacles, chiefly economic and fiscal, the results of the blindness of capitalists and the managers of industry.

I have been writing about America and Western Europe. Consider the Draft Program of the Communist Party in the Marx-saturated Soviet Union in 1961: We learn from it that

> . . . the epoch-making turn of mankind from capitalism to socialism, initiated by the October Revolution, is a natural result of the development of society. . . . The high road to Socialism has been paved. . . . Many more peoples are already marching along, and it will be taken sooner or later by all peoples. . . . Harmonious relations will be established between individual and society. . . . Family relations will be based solely on mutual love and friendship.

We have no way of knowing how many living Russians who may be aware of that lofty statement of principle feel other than disillusioned and betrayed, as they look about them; but it would be extraordinary if the Soviet Union even today were entirely devoid of true believers.

And here is a similar statement from that other massive communist state in our time, China. It was written by Liu Shao-Chi, spokesman some two decades ago for the Communist Party in China. Describing the China of Mao's creation, Liu Shao-Chi declares that "this is the road that all humanity must inevitably take, in accordance with the laws of the development of history." Western European and American Marxists at the present time mostly ignore or are embarrassed by such emanations from Marx's clearly written endorsement of the inevitability of progress toward socialism, and take refuge in the humanizing of Marx currently going on in the West—the Marx of "praxis." It would appear to be different, however, in the communist areas of the world.

The emphasis in the two quotations on laws of development in history suggests still another abode of the historic idea of progress. I refer to faith in what is called "social evolution" or "social development," terms which for all their nineteenth-century origins have a very contemporary status in the social sciences. It was thought earlier in the century that this manifestation of the nineteenth-century idea of progress had been killed off—through the devastating criticisms of the methodology involved written by such imposing minds as the anthropologists Kroeber, Lowie, Radcliffe-Brown, and Malinowski, and such comparative history-oriented critics as Flinders Petrie, F. J. Teggart, Toynbee, Spengler, and many others.

But during the last few years we have seen a considerable revival of nineteenth-century social evolutionism in the writings of the sociologist Talcott Parsons and his followers and in the works of the anthropologist Leslie White and his students. Much is made in these works of the affinity they have with current evolutionary theory in biology, but apart from some phrases borrowed by the social scientists from evolutionary biology, there is no affinity whatever; any evolutionary biologist will assert this immediately, once he has looked at the representations of social evolution. The largest difference between the theory of evolutionary biology and the theory of social evolution is that the first rests squarely and immovably upon the Darwinian theory of natural selection coupled with the genetic principles originally established in the mid-nineteenth century by Mendel but vastly expanded and improved in the present century. Evolutionary biology is inseparable from population-statistical theory, whereas social evolution as we find it in the nineteenth century and in the current age is ineradicably typological in character: dealing not with arithmetic means and statistical averages of vast population aggregates, and with laboratory-induced speciation which invokes these means and averages, but instead with cultures, civilizations, institutions, and other structures or types. The social evolutionist is inherently and unavoidably the typologist. And, as the Harvard biologist Ernst Mayr writes, "Many of the basic concepts of synthetic theory [in evolutionary biology], such as that of natural selection and that of the population are meaningless for the typologist." There is simply no theoretical or substantive relation whatever between what the geneticist or molecular biologist does in his studies of evolution and speciation and what the sociologist or anthropologist does with his classifications and categorizations of whole civilizations or institutions spread out over the world and through history.

The real appeal of social evolution at this time, I would argue, and the prime reason for recent revival of systems which do not differ markedly from those of Comte, Marx, and Spencer, is *moral*. The panorama provided by constructions of so-called social evolution, is a stimulant to desire for unity, for the sense of community among all nations and all "stages" of past and present in the long saga of mankind. In secular terms, social evolutionary theories of the present serve precisely the same function that was served for St. Augustine in his doctrine of the unity of mankind and his theory of the six stages or epochs humanity had already gone through and of the two that yet lay ahead. In sum, the idea of progress has at this very moment a substantial following in the social sciences by those committed, by moral faith as well as intellectual interest, to one or other scheme of social evolution. Marxists and other radicals, liberals old and new, and even conservatives must be counted among the adherents to this current manifestation of the philosophy of progress.

Continuing belief in this philosophy may be seen, in significant degree, in Western (and especially American) contemplation of the rest of the world. More specifically the philosophy of progress is observable at the roots of our foreign policy and of our sense of mission in the world. Two different and opposed perspectives—both, however, resting solidly on the historic idea of progress—are to be seen at the moment. On the one hand, perpetuating an old if now rather decrepit view is the conviction that the essential values and political and economic structures in the West are not only superior to those of the rest of the world but are symbols of what the non-Western nations should and *will* know in due time—when these values have developed, or will have been developed by those educated and trained in the Western tradition. The abundance in the social sciences of foundations and government agencies dedicated to such concepts as "underdeveloped" "modernization" and "developed" is tribute to the persisting hold of the idea of progress in the West.

There is, however, a different, diametrically opposite perspective in the West that has grown up since World War II and that also is rooted in the philosophy of progress. In this perspective it is no longer the West that is perceived to be in the vanguard of progress. On the contrary, it is fundamental to this viewpoint to describe Western civilization in terms of decadence and decline. True progress, it is argued, is to be seen in the non-Western socialisms, so-called, especially in those of the Third World. These are the peoples, it is declared, who provide us with the spectacle of the true march of progress, a march that has China or the Soviet Union at the head of the column. Matters as practical as American foreign policy, as ideological as human rights in the world, are dealt with and resolved in light of a conviction that socialism, with all its current repressions of life and liberty, is the real road to the future.

One of the more interesting legacies of the idea of progress of old is the great vogue of what is called futurism or futurology. It too is inseparable from a foundation of imagined progress from past to present to future. Much is made of our computer technology, allowing us, it is solemnly said, to foresee scientifically what the Tocquevilles and Marxes of the past could only guess at. But in fact we are still operating just as the prophets Tocqueville and Marx were when their gaze was toward the future. Some apparent trend in history is identified: it may be egalitarianism, as with Tocqueville, or it may be, as with Marx, class struggle, the eventual outcome being absolute dominance of the proletariat and then socialism. Different though the outcome in Tocqueville's and Marx's predictions, they are the result of precisely the same method: seizing upon some seemingly dominant aspect of the present and then projecting it into the future.

Basically, futurology has not changed. All invocations of computerology, systematic, institute-based research, and econometric models to the contrary notwithstanding, what today's forecasters work from, essentially, is the same kind of identification of a trend or of trends in the present and then the extension of these into the future with whatever modifications insight and intuition may suggest.

Although many such projections in our part of the century are increasingly pessimistic for reasons I shall come to later, a surprising degree of optimism still exists. It may be remembered that the now historic *first* Club of Rome forecast, which saw a rather dismal future for the world, was resoundingly criticized; this resulted in a *second* Club of Rome prediction that was significantly more optimistic, although some of its premises, especially those relating to the have-nations' generosity to the impoverished areas of the world in the future, leave the critical reader with a sense of hollowness in the report's optimism.

In the next chapter we shall consider some of the multifold predictions of doom so far as economic growth and availability of natural resources and food supply are concerned. But it is well to bear in mind that defenses, justifications, and positive predictions of long continuing economic progress are very much in the air right now. Ernest Beckerman in his *In Defense of Economic Growth* has masterfully summarized and synthesized—and significantly added to on his own—the arguments in behalf of the solid ground on which forecasts of long-run prosperity, of continuing availability of resources and food supply, and of uninterrupted economic growth can and do rest. By no means is faith in economic progress dead! As recently as 1969, one S. Brenner wrote in *A Short History of Economic Progress*: "It appears that economic progress may well be an organic process similar to others which take place in various forms of biological development. Once started, it will grow and spread its seed in evergrowing circles over the greater parts of the earth wherever and whenever conditions are suitable." No classical economist, no publicist of Manchester in the nineteenth century could have improved upon that.

Herman Kahn in *The Next 200 Years* also presents a persuasive and sophisticated case for the high probability of continued progress in the decades ahead. He is not uncritical; he is well aware that catastrophes—including such spiritual and moral "catastrophes" as sudden failure of the will to live and work and occupation of the mind by ineradicable boredom—can make the best of predictions come out wrong. But such possible catastrophes put aside, Kahn argues that we have ample resources in sight right now, and that even more resources will be brought to use by methods of search and discovery already under way by science and technology. The partisans of economic growth will outnumber those of nongrowth, the desire for work will generally remain resistant to the temptations of leisure, and, although there will be occasional lulls, even setbacks, the prospects for continuing progress during the next two centuries at least remain excellent.

Kahn's optimism is far more widely shared by the American (and Western European) people than our intellectuals' quarterlies might suggest. Polls and surveys of the highly skilled, the professional, and the managerial classes reveal a great deal of confidence in a progressive future, with respect to economic growth, standard of living, and the advance of knowledge. The only impediment cited repeatedly is constriction (largely political) of opportunities for growth and advancement. But overall faith is there. Or, I must add at this writing, has been until quite recently!

There are still other reflections of continuing belief in progress in the twentieth century. The kind of regimentation and exercise of power in the name of some progressive ideal—which we saw in the nineteenth-century theories of Comte, Fourier, Cabet, Marx, and their followers—have their representations in our day. I refer to the large and increasing number of "communes," not very different from the utopian communities established in the last century. These may seem on first thought to signify nothing more than escapism. But they signify also—at least the serious, dedicated, and morally committed ones, leaving aside such travesties and horrors as the Manson Family and Jonestown—faith in human progress that requires only stimulation and example.

Nor has the racist philosophy of progress disappeared; or is it likely to. Faith in Anglo-Saxonism and Nordicism and also in eugenics, the means of protecting racial purity, remained strong during the early decades of this century, as witnessed by the immense popularity of Madison Grant's *Passing of the Great Race* and Lothrop Stoddard's *Rising Tide of Color*. These books were at once warnings and reaffirmations of the racial basis of progress. Of the success (and horror) of racism-as-progress in Nazi Germany, nothing need be said here.

Still another sign of the hold that the idea of progress has held upon the minds of Americans during the present century is the boundless popularity of the word "progressive." Even in our present time of troubles, with disenchantment and failure of nerve rampant, there is no evident inclination on the part of individuals to be thought "unprogressive." It is hard to think of any major sphere of American life in the twentieth century that has not seen faith in progress represented by joyous use of the word "progressive." There was the Progressive Party early in the century and the very differently constituted Independent Progressive Party of the late 1940s. But there is no party or social movement I can think of that has not often and clamantly declared itself to be more progressive—read "more in step with ongoing progress"—than all others. Who will ever forget what was so loudly hailed and worshipped by countless educationists as Progressive Education? There has been and continues to be "Progressive" music, drama, poetry, jazz, painting, architecture, and so forth. Always the implication is that what is given the honor of being progressive is in the vanguard, holding a position that the natural march of progress will bring others up to in time. The often mindless worship of the new in any sphere has behind it, whether consciously or not, a philosophy of progress that by its very nature declares the new or latest the highest in an ascending progression through time.

Futurist fiction, scientific and other, also contains a surprising amount of optimism affecting the future. We are sometimes given to thinking that Huxley's *Brave New World* and Orwell's *1984* set a pattern of melancholy and gloom which nearly all subsequent imaginative forays into the future follow. But this is far from the case. As I write, the movie *Star Wars*—which gives us a marvelous and fascinating future indeed, with romance, handsome men and beautiful women, truly lovable mechanical creatures, and even cops and robbers chasing one another in the distant stellar regions and much more that we are familiar with—is setting box office records. There are literally scores of science fiction novels and short stories appearing each year that have to be judged optimistic in high degree. As Michael Wood several years ago in a review article in *The New York Review of Books* observed: "This may not be the kind of science fiction that intellectuals like, but it is the sort that science fiction fans read." Let it be emphasized: Arthur C. Clarke has more Jules Verne in him than Orwell!

Nor has our century at any time been without its celebrants of the progress of knowledge. Sir Julian Huxley, grandson of T. H. Huxley and no less confident of inevitable progress than his forebear, attests to the quasi-autonomous nature of science. "Once a science has reached the state of having a coherent theoretical basis, it will inevitably proceed (provided it is not discouraged by authority) to make further discoveries and further extensions of its theory." With this inevitable increase in knowledge, Huxley continues, so must mastery of nature and, therefore, "effective, progressive change" in our relations to nature and among ourselves increase. Natural selection can never be halted, but, Huxley argues, with our scientific knowledge of its processes, there is nothing to prevent our guiding it, as it were, to the emergence of ever more perfect human beings.

Sir Julian Huxley is not alone in his optimism. Still another grandson of a Victorian believer in progress, Sir Charles Darwin, physicist, tells us while he looks into the future, that:

. . . there will be vast stores of learning, far beyond anything we can now imagine, and the intellectual stature of man will rise to ever higher levels. And sometimes new discoveries will for a time relieve the human race from its fears, and there will be golden ages, when many for a time may be free to create wonderful flowerings in science, philosophy, and the arts.

Even the sphere of the visual arts has been declared recently by an art historian, Suzi Gablik, in *Progress in Art,* to be the setting of demonstrable progress. She writes that just as there are three stages in the development of consciousness in the human being, so three "megaperiods of art history" are to be discerned in the European past: the ancient-medieval, the Renaissance, and the modern. The first stage, we are told, was capable only of static representations. In the second stage, the Renaissance, the artist, while significantly beyond his ancient-medieval predecessors in ability to deal with space, was limited to the world of direct perception. Only in the third, the modern stage, has it become possible at long last to deal with space and perspective through means made available by modern logic and mathematics, thus advancing visual art well beyond anything known in earlier times.

How many artists, art critics, and historians there are to concur in this argument I cannot even guess; perhaps there are none. What is of greater interest, however, apart from the Gablik thesis, is the remarkable parallel that exists between this thesis and the argument of the advocates of the Moderns in the seventeenth-century Quarrel which we have already dealt with. They too rested their case on the proposition that since art is a form of representation or interpretation of man and nature, all of the advances which have been made in knowledge of man and nature were bound to yield better art in the seventeenth century than in the Athens of Pericles.

Let us conclude this chapter with this question: Are there or have there been in this century philosophers of history for whom the progress of mankind has assumed the same positive importance it did in the writings of Comte and Spencer? That is, are there major philosophers dedicated to construction of a whole system that is pivoted on progress? The late A. J. Toynbee will come to mind at least tentatively. His monumental *A Study of History* is built around a neo-Spenglerian panorama of cyclical rises and falls of twenty-one (instead of Spengler's eight) civilizations, and written with heavy stress on the phenomena of decay and degeneration in history; nevertheless, it leaves its readers with the sense of an ascent of mankind through time, each cycle on a somewhat higher level than its predecessor, and the hope that if spiritual values will but replace current domination by materialistic compulsions, especially those of technology, further ascent into the future may be predicted. But Toynbee came to have less and less confidence (witness only his final book, *Mankind and Mother Earth: A Narrative History of the World,* with its concluding paragraphs) in such a future, and in any event his *magnum opus* will always be known best for its pluralistic, cyclical pattern of world history. Not in Toynbee will one find anything analogous to what such philosophers of linear progress as Comte, Marx, Tylor, and Spencer built their systems around.

I venture the guess that there is but one such philosopher of history in the twentieth century: the late Pierre Teilhard de Chardin. Frank Manuel is surely correct when he writes that "more and more the late Teilhard de Chardin emerges as the central figure of this twentieth century cosmic myth, with his arms outstretched to embrace humanist English biologists as well as French Marxists."

He was at once a respected scientist (paleontologist) and member of the Jesuit order. Most of his scientific work was done in China. He was party to the discovery of Peking Man, and became well known for his studies of Asia's sedimentary deposits and stratigraphical correlations with fossils. Increasingly, though, his interest turned to philosophy of history, on a cosmic scale. It is a philosophy of progress grounded in both modern science and a kind of Augustinian Catholicism. For Teilhard there was no disharmony between belief in a sovereign God and full acceptance of the data and conclusions of evolutionary geology and biology. His work is indeed a fusion of science and Christianity. His best-known work is *The Phenomenon of Man,* published in French in 1938–40 and translated into English for publication in 1959, just four years after his death. Sir Julian

Huxley was fascinated by Teilhard's ideas, and wrote a long introduction to the English edition. The following passage from Huxley's introduction is illuminating:

Once he [Teilhard de Chardin] had grasped and faced the fact of man as an evolutionary phenomenon, the way was open towards a new and comprehensive system of thought. It remained to draw the fullest conclusions from this central concept of man as the spearhead of evolution on earth, and to follow out the implications of this approach in as many fields as possible. The biologist may perhaps consider that in *The Phenomenon of Man* he paid insufficient attention to genetics and the possibilities and limitations of natural selection, the theologian that his treatment of the problems of sin and suffering was inadequate or at least unorthodox, the social scientist that he failed to take sufficient account of the facts of political and social history. But he saw that what was needed at the moment was a broad sweep and a comprehensive treatment. This is what he essayed in *The Phenomenon of Man*. In my view he achieved a remarkable success, and opened up vast territories of thought to further exploration and detailed mapping.

For Teilhard, the whole of cosmic history has been one of progress determined by the working of all evolutionary processes toward the making, and then the increasing perfection of, man. Progress began first in what he calls "the biosphere," that is, the sphere of organic life in its totality; then, with the emergence of man, it moved into "the noosphere," the domain of human intelligence. The latter for Teilhard is superimposed upon the former. It is the noosphere that serves as the arena within which the ever-accelerating "hominisation" of the world occurs: the psychosocial dominance of man over the entire evolutionary process. It is this "hominisation" that for Teilhard constitutes the certainty of an ever more perfect world and human society. I shall content myself with but a few revealing passages taken from his posthumous *The Future of Man* (1959), a book in which he sought to extend the implications of his earlier and more famous *The Phenomenon of Man*.

If we are to find a definitive answer to the question of the entitative progress of the Universe we must do so by adopting the least favorable position—that is to say, by envisaging a world whose evolutionary capacity is *concentrated upon* and *confined* to the human soul. The question of whether the Universe is still developing then becomes a matter of deciding whether the human spirit is still in process of evolution. To this I reply unhesitatingly, "Yes, it is." The nature of man is in the full flood of entitative change. But to grasp this it is necessary (a) not to overlook the *biological* (morphogenic) value of moral action, and (b) to accept the organic nature of individual relationships. We shall then see that a vast evolutionary process is in ceaseless operation around us, but that it is a situation within the *sphere of consciousness* (and collective consciousness).

The great superiority over Primitive Man which we have acquired and which will be enhanced by our descendants in a degree perhaps undreamed-of by ourselves, is in the realm of self-knowledge; in our growing capacity to situate ourselves in space and time, to the point of becoming conscious of our place and responsibility in relation to the Universe.

I make no claim to be a prophet. Moreover I know, as a scientist, how dangerous it is to extend a curve beyond the facts, that is to say, to extrapolate. Nevertheless I believe that, basing the argument upon our general knowledge of the world's history over a period of 300 million years, we can advance the following two propositions without losing ourselves in a fog of speculation:

Firstly, Mankind still shows itself to possess a *reserve*, a formidable potential of concentration, i.e., of progress. . . . If we are to judge by what history teaches us about other living groups, it [mankind] has, organically speaking, some millions of years in which to live and develop.

Everything leads us to believe that it really does dispose of the vast reservoir of time, which is necessary to the normal achievement of its evolution. The earth is far from having completed its sidereal evolution. We may envisage all kinds of mischance (disaster, disease) which might in theory put an end to evolutionary progress: but the fact remains that for 300 million years Life has paradoxically flourished in the Improbable. Does this not suggest that its advance may be sustained by *some sort of complicity on the part of the "blind" forces of the Universe*—that is to say, that it is inexorable?

It is interesting to learn that before his death Teilhard came into contact with Marxism. He seems to have read little of Marx or of the Marxians, but he knew enough about Marxism to sense, however dimly, that there was affinity between his and Marx's ideas. His interpretation of Marx has much in common with that which is popular among Western intellectuals at the present moment, one based upon Marx "the humanist" rather than Marx the determinist. In one revealing passage Teilhard declares that what gives lasting strength to Marxism is orientation not toward simple social justice but rather toward "the thirst for fuller being, the 'creation' of man on earth." He continues:

Our faith in God sublimates in us a rising tide of human aspirations, and it is into this original sap that we must plunge back if we desire to communicate with our brothers whom it is our ambition to unite. . . . Are not the two extremes, the Marxist and the Christian, destined, in spite of their antagonistic concepts, because they are both animated by an equal faith in man, to find themselves together on the same summit?

From those words alone one can understand the controversy that to this moment surrounds Teilhard de Chardin's writings. Even before he reached the point of foretelling the eventual union of Christianity and Marxism, his writings on evolution and progress had become objects of the Vatican's critical attention. He was in some degree punished for "errors," though not

315

with a severity that prevented him from continuing his work. After his death, the Vatican issued a warning to Catholics that de Chardin's ideas were not to be accepted in full or uncritically. So far as his vision of the future union of Christianity and Marxism is concerned, it is simply a reflection of his belief that Marxism has become one of the dominant religions of the world, that it too encompasses all mankind in its doctrine, and rests upon a philosophy of history that apart from nomenclature is close kin to the Christian philosophy of history—from which indeed, as we have seen, the Marxist philosophy descends. It is worth mentioning in this connection that A. J. Toynbee in his *Study of History* predicted that Marx would eventually be regarded by historians as within the great Judeo-Christian tradition; heretical, yes, but within the tradition nevertheless.

It is entirely possible that Teilhard saw himself in much the same role in the twentieth century as that of St. Augustine in the fifth: that of master synthesizer; aware of spiritual conflicts, but endowed with the mission of resolving them or at least prophesying their eventual resolution. Manichean himself in the beginning, Augustine became of course the enemy of this doctrine after his conversion to Christianity. He devoted a great deal of his time to refuting the ideas and beliefs of the Manicheans but never lost the hope of persuading them to become Christian, whether in his own time or later. So did Augustine and his successors look forward to the eventual conversion of the Jews. There is much to suggest that Teilhard de Chardin saw all the major religions of the world, Marxism included, as destined to become one, Christian at core, in the long run. And the rock on which this world religion must rest is, of course, the rock of progress. He writes: *"I am convinced that finally it is upon the idea of progress and faith in progress that Mankind, today so divided, must rely and reshape itself."**

How many millions of people in this final part of the twentieth century would not gratefully accept that conviction? There is considerable reason for believing that a major religious renascence is forming at this time in the West and other parts of the world. If so, it seems highly probable that the fusion of science and religion achieved by Teilhard de Chardin, one based upon the inexorable progress of human knowledge into the very distant future—and with this progress, the progress also of man's spirit and his estate on earth—will hold a very prominent place in it.

*Italics mine.

Chapter 9

Progress At Bay

WHILE the twentieth century is far from barren of faith in progress, there is nevertheless good ground for supposing that when the identity of our century is eventually fixed by historians, not faith but abandonment of faith in the idea of progress will be one of the major attributes. The skepticism regarding Western progress that was once confined to a very small number of intellectuals in the nineteenth century has grown and spread to not merely the large majority of intellectuals in this final quarter of the century, but to many millions of other people in the West.

The idea has been able to survive a great deal of adversity in its twenty-five hundred years: mass poverty, plagues and famines, devastating wars, economic depressions, eruptions of political and religious tyranny, and so on. But what the idea cannot survive (and this holds true for any complex idea) is *the loss of its crucial premises.*

There are at least five major premises to be found in the idea's history from the Greeks to our day: belief in the value of the past; conviction of the nobility, even superiority, of Western civilization; acceptance of the worth of economic and technological growth; faith in reason and in the kind of scientific and scholarly knowledge that can come from reason alone; and, finally, belief in the intrinsic importance, the ineffaceable *worth* of life on this earth.

Each of these premises has been severely challenged by doubt and disillusionment, even outright hostility, in the twentieth century, especially its second half. The present crisis of the idea of progress lies in the inability of a constantly growing number of people to accept as our ancestors so largely did the axiomatic truth of these premises. Either belief in these premises is restored among large elements of the population in the West, commencing with the intellectual class (an unlikely eventuality at this moment), or else faith in the once powerful idea of human progress must die altogether.

There are, to be sure, reasons for at least partial rejoicing if the idea is buried. For, as we have seen, the same idea of inexorable, unfolding, necessary progress that could provide foundation for ideas of freedom, welfare, and justice could also be made to serve the ends of absolute power—utopian, political, and racist. But there is no moral value that is not susceptible to corrupt use; we need think only of what has happened in this century in the totalitarian nations to the values of freedom, popular sovereignty, equality, and justice: a repugnant spectacle, without question, but hardly a reason for our abandoning belief in these values in the rest of the free world. It is the same, I suggest, with the idea of progress. In its oldest and broadest meaning the idea has been associated far more often with good than with evil. It is inseparable, as I have argued in these pages, from the incentives which have led Western man from the time of the Greeks to the magnificent accomplishments which give substance and historical identity to Western civilization.

The tragedy is that today there is a great deal more conviction of the reality of progress in some of the unfree nations of the world, beginning with the Soviet Union, than there is in the free Western nations. For those at least who continue to hold some kind of belief in the Marxist philosophy of history, the advancement of collectivism under the name of socialism or of popular democracy can seem, even when attended by the limitless despotism of the Soviet Union, a truimphant course of progress. In those nations faith in the past (Marxist, of course), in the nobility of their own civilizations, in the worth of economic and technological advancement, in knowledge (undergirded by Marxian writ), and in the supreme importance of life and work in this life, on this earth, reigns. Such, one must record in melancholy tones, is not the case in Western civilization at the present time. Disbelief, doubt, disillusionment, and despair have taken over—or so it would seem from our literature, art, philosophy, theology, even our scholarship and science.

Early Prophets

Very little of the current state of mind in the West is new or original so far as intellectual content is concerned. What is now so widespread in the West is a development and expansion of ideas, moods, and beliefs which came into existence in the nineteenth century but which were held then by a very small number of historians and philosophers; small in number and limited in influence. But the significance of this group has become steadily greater in the twentieth century, particularly since World War II, and there is very little written today in the way of repudiation of progress, or skepticism toward its reality in past, present, and future, that is not grounded in the ideas of Tocqueville, Burckhardt, Schopenhauer, Nietzsche, and others in the nineteenth century.

During his lifetime and for several decades after, Tocqueville was generally regarded as an optimist in his assessment of democracy and other elements of modernity. Certainly, he was hailed thus in America during the century, and cited with evident satisfaction by those in this country who made faith in America synonomous with faith in the progress of the world. But such appreciation, while not wholly without foundation in Tocqueville, failed utterly to take into consideration a very different and prominent aspect of *Democracy in America*. In the first volume he had warned of the dangers of majority tyranny and democratic obeisance to public opinion, but he was nevertheless hopeful that existing institutions would check these. In the second volume, however, what we have is an almost unrelieved succession of analyses and prophecies testifying to the destructive effects modern democratic equality could have on Western civilization. He thought philosophy, literature, science, and the arts generally would all in time languish or become seriously crippled; he saw the consequences of affluence in terms of an unstable restlessness, sense of relative deprivation, and alienation from the human community. Human beings would become diminished, degraded by division of labor in the economy; ambition and individuality would be erased or reduced to insignificance by processes leading to homogeneity and regimentation; and, he thought, under, or rather from democracy might come the most terrible form of despotism known in history. And there is a passage in his *Recollections*, written a short while before his death, in which he records his despair of mankind ever reaching the fulfillment it seeks.

Burckhardt presented his vision of the *terribles simplificateurs* ahead, those who would raze civilization, leaving only elemental tyrannies and primitivisms. "The new tyrannies will be in the hands of military commandos who will call themselves republican." The Enlightenment-derived belief in man's natural goodness would only lead to human evil on a scale never before known.

Schopenhauer wrote that history, far from evidencing progress, only alters superficial forms: "History shows on every side only the same thing under different forms. . . . The chapters of the history of nations are at bottom different only through the names and dates; the really essential content is everywhere the same." Efforts by governments to improve the lot of their populations would only create fresh and more insidious problems—among them boredom. Nietzsche was no more encouraged by what he saw around him in Western society. Progress, he wrote, "is merely a modern idea, that is, a false idea. The European today is vastly inferior to the European of the Renaissance." Nothing avails, Nietzsche writes; "One *must* go forward—step by step into further decadence."

For Kierkegaard the dominant feature of the West was the loss of all authority and the suffocation of true individuality and of community under the blanket of "leveling" and "abstraction." "The abstract, leveling process, that self-combustion of the human race, produced by the friction when the individual ceases to exist as singled out by religion, is bound to continue like a trade wind and consume everything."

Max Weber, greatest of sociologists, foresaw a bureaucratization of the human spirit—resulting from the successive conquests in the institutional spheres of society of what he called "rationalization," the "disenchantment of the world" through worship of system. It is the Iron Cage that Weber sees for the West. "Not summer's bloom lies ahead of us but rather a polar night of icy darkness and hardship." The spirit of asceticism, Weber wrote, which had originally given so much impetus to economic creativeness and to a great deal of other creativeness as well, has already become transformed into increasingly destructive hedonistic materialism. In France, Ernest Renan, reared and trained Catholic but later an apostate from the Church, foresaw "an immense moral and perhaps intellectual degeneracy." Everything will become syndicalized and regimented, and "organized egoism will replace love and devotion." Hungarian-born Max Nordau—educated in Germany, and a resident of Paris—declared in two sensationalist and widely read works, first in *The Conventional Lies of our Civilization* that Western institutions had become hopelessly corrupted, and second in *Degeneration* that Western man was already in a condition of biological regression that would lead to increasing decadence and barbarism of culture.

What began as a tiny stream in the nineteenth century widened considerably in the early twentieth century—that is, among a sector of intellectuals. Georges Sorel (already referred to in the context of the Quarrel of the Ancients and Moderns) wrote his *Illusions of Progress*, putting into ridicule the foundations of the modern idea of progress, and also his *Reflections on Violence*, seeking to prove the utter impossibility of human improvement through the cumulative processes of "progress" and the necessity of taking drastic revolutionary action if any change whatever was to be effected. His love-hate relationship with Marxism was based precisely upon his admiration for the genuinely revolutionary spirit in Marx and his disdain for the evolutionary-progressive spirit also in Marx that was currently being exploited, he thought, by Marx's heirs.

At about the same time that Sorel was reaching his conclusions on progress, across the Atlantic the Adams brothers Henry and Brooks were venting their own disgust with and renunciation of the economic and political values which had become ascendant in America and the West generally. In two books, *Mont-Saint-Michel and Chartres* and in *The Education of Henry Adams*, Henry contrasted a medieval civilization built around spirituality symbolized by the Virgin, and the modern civilization resting upon materialism and mechanism and symbolized by the dynamo. He saw the past in terms of stages which proceeded from instinct through religion, through science and, finally, an age of the supersensual that was decadent at the core. The next hundred years, he believed, would see an "ultimate, colossal, cosmic collapse." Brooks Adams in his *Law of Civilization and Decay* went back to Renaissance inspiration for a panorama of recurring cycles of genesis and decay in civilization. Theoretically, there was room in Brooks's scheme for at least some future Western progress. But in a letter to his brother, Brooks wrote: "How can we hope to see a new world, a new civilization, or life? To my mind we are at the end; and the one thing I thank God for is that we have no children."

The year 1920, which saw the publication of J. B. Bury's historiographic celebration of the idea of progress began a decade in which the literature of disillusionment also flowered. In the very year of publication of Bury's book, W. R. Inge, Dean of St. Paul's ("the gloomy dean") delivered the Romanes Lecture on the idea of progress; in it he declared the idea a "pernicious superstition," the monstrous product of Enlightenment-born, secular optimism, one that was already debasing the major intellectual disciplines and transforming Christianity into something "beyond recognition." One year after Inge's lecture, Austin Freeman published *Social Decay and Degeneration* in England. He declared that far from progressing, the West is regressing at an increasingly higher rate, the result chiefly of industrialism and its technology and the destructive effects of these upon earth, air, and sea, and above all upon the very nature of man. Even the primitive Negro in Africa, Freeman wrote, is the superior—in wit, agility, technical skill, and imagination—to the Western working man who has become a "subman" as the result of industrialism and its coercions.

The 1920s also saw the translation from the German into English of Oswald Spengler's *The Decline of the West* (1918). Spengler is unaware of the origin of his cyclical theory of civilizations and cultures in certain ancient Greek writings; indeed, he insists that the Greeks had no sense of history or development. Most of his prognoses of cultural decay, pullulation of the masses, breakdown of political institutions, and rise of military despotisms have, as we have just seen, clear roots in the nineteenth century, whether or not Spengler was aware of them. But his book was nevertheless a sensation among intellectuals and certainly influenced a few of them even in the 1920s when so much of the Western intellectual world was moving steadily toward the progress-oriented doctrines of Karl Marx. In any event, it is one of the considerable number of assaults upon the idea of progress which came out in the 1920s. Toynbee, in a later and vastly more learned multivolume work, *A Study of History*, would also deal with history cyclically and pluralistically, but concede the genuine if small ascendancy of each new civilization over its predecessor and, beyond this, declare that if the West could be liberated from its worship of technology and achieve a new spirituality, the progress of the West might well continue far into the future.

One of the most penetrating criticisms of the idea of progress was published by Frederick J. Teggart in 1925: *Theory of History*. Teggart was little interested in the moral and eudamonic aspects of the idea; even less in prophesied golden ages in the future. It was the impact and, as he demonstrated, lasting influence of the idea of progress *as a method*, a framework of presentation of past and present, that attracted his attention. Not only are conceptions of historical necessity ("historicism," in Popper's later treatment of the subject) products of the idea of progress; even the conventional historian's linear, narrative treatment of historical events is a direct offshoot of the idea; so, Teggart argued further, is the social scientist's perspective of social evolution or social development ineradicably associated with the envisagement of past and present that is inherent in the idea of progress. Not, Teggart concluded, until we have expunged the idea—along with its progeny—from the social sciences and the writing of history will a scientific, comparative, problem-oriented study of the past be possible.

Still another manifestation of rising disillusionment with faith in Western progress is to be seen in the literary works of T. S. Eliot, James Joyce, Ezra Pound, W. B. Yeats, and others who began to flourish in the 1920s. They are without exception prophets of decay and death, echoing in poem, drama, essay, and novel the indictments of the West made by Nietzsche, Schopenhauer, and others in the preceding century. In *The Wasteland, The Hollow Men*, and other works, Eliot sees little but vulgarity, decadence, and emptiness around him and continuing into the future. Yeats, in what has surely become in our day the single most quoted poem in all English literature, wrote in "The Second Coming" of a civilization become rotten and chaos-ridden; "things fall apart," "the center cannot hold," and "the

best lack all conviction, while the worst are full of passionate intensity."
Joyce in his novel *Ulysses* made a single day in Dublin—with the aimless
wanderings of Bloom and Dedalus through the city providing the action—
the symbol of the inanity, the squalor, meaninglessness, and ultimate futility of the modern West in comparison with earlier ages. Aldous Huxley
recorded his dismissal of the West and its culture in *Point Counterpoint*,
and gave us his vision of the future in *Brave New World* where everything
including one's emotions were directed and governed by technology. From
the point of view of the idea of progress, the best representation of what life
had come to seem to this group lies in some lines from T. S. Eliot's later
Four Quartets:

> It seems as one grows older,
> That the past has another pattern, and ceases to be a mere sequence—
> Or even development: the latter a partial fallacy
> Encouraged by superficial notions of evolution,
> Which becomes, in the popular mind, a means of disowning the past.

Disowning the Past

Eliot's phrase from the lines just quoted serves admirably as title and theme
of this section. There is by now no single influence greater in negative
impact upon the idea of progress than our far-flung and relentless jettisoning of the past. The past, let us remember, is sacred ground for any genuine, creative, and free civilization. Readers will not have forgotten how
crucial it was for the rulers of Orwell's society in *1984* to blot out or else
remake the past. Without the past as represented by ritual, tradition, and
memory, there can be no roots; and without roots, human beings are condemned to a form of isolation in time that easily becomes self-destructive.

The past, as I have stressed several times, is vital to the idea of progress.
It is the future that we are more likely to think of immediately when the idea
of progress is brought up. But it was only when men became conscious of a
long past, one held in common through ritual and then history and literature, that a consciousness of progressive movement from past to present
became possible, a consciousness easily extrapolated to the future.

Fundamental in all periods in which faith in progress has prospered has
been the remembered past. The ancient Greeks, even at the highest point of
their exploration of the present, were nevertheless profoundly interested in
their past, in finding or recreating its great events, in revering it in all that

was taught at home, school, and temple, and in giving it permanent representation in such structures as the Parthenon. Faith in Demeter, the goddess Athenians took for their own, was never higher than in the so-called Age of Reason in the fifth century, and she was but one of the gods the Athenians gave homage to for their gifts in the distant past to mankind. So was awareness of the past vivid in Roman civilization, and when by the fourth century belief seemed to waver in the past that had been recorded by pagan historians, there were the Christians to pick up the torch. A great deal of St. Augustine's *The City of God,* as we saw, is taken up with his construction of the past, sacred and secular, and his awareness of the utter indispensability of the past to present and future.

I think it safe to say that the past has loomed large in every age or century of Western history—that is, to the beginning of our own century. We have come to learn how passionate, unceasing, and determined were the labors of the learned during the Dark Ages in keeping the past alive through text and oral tradition. The Middle Ages, Renaissance, and Reformation were all periods of intense interest in and respect for the past. There were a few philosophes of the Enlightenment in France who may have uttered only disdain for the past, seeing it as no more than a long avenue of follies, superstitions, and tyrannies, but we nevertheless find such minds as Turgot, Condorcet, Lessing, and Herder rich in their evocations of the successive stages and epochs which led up to and made possible the present that these and other minds of their age revered and saw as the takeoff for the future.

A respect for the past, nowhere more dedicated than in the United States, continued into the twentieth century. There were the innumerable festivals, holidays, and rituals, the purpose of which was a fusing of a people into a community, and this through a kind of telescoping of past and present. There could not have been many homes in which elements of the past—political, military, and religious, preponderantly—were not frequently, even constantly, brought to the attention of the young. How else to make children love country, race or nationality, and religion except through the incessant recreation of the past and its great events, heroes, leaders, and prophets? No single subject in school or college was more honored than history, and it was not uncommon for a young American—or Englishman, Frenchman, German, or other—to be taken through the history of the Western world or the United States several times, commencing with grade school and concluding with college. Everywhere history was one of the binding requirements of graduation. Nor was it all modern history. I can testify that a mere half-century ago in a small, typical California town, not only was a full year course in ancient history given regularly—and taken in substantial numbers by pupils—but two years of Greek and four of Latin were available, in each of which, inevitably, the past was brought alive. There is no need to elaborate. Suffice it to say that few indeed were Western Europeans of however low a station in life who were not respectful, even reverential, toward the past; and there were few whose awareness of what lay around them in the present was not strongly tinctured by the sense of its continuity with the past, and, of course, the future. Customs and traditions abounded through which memory of the past was activated. And until we were well into the twentieth century, the most frequently cited reason for the emphasis in academia on the past was that if we did not know it well, we were unqualified for coping with the present and for planning the future. For many millions of pupils in the early decades of the century, the principal function of school was of conveying tools and skills drawn from the past and of committing the past to memory, as the basic requirement of citizenship.

Even the utopians, reformers, and revolutionists in the nineteenth and early twentieth centuries had their full consciousness of the past. Radical and sweeping though the utopias of Saint-Simon and Comte are, in each the past was honored in a variety of ways. Although the substance of Saint-Simon's proposed golden age in the future was industrial and technocratic, he nevertheless settled on "New Christianity" as the eventual label for his doctrines, and he was unsparing in his acknowledged obligations to the Middle Ages and its unifying, stabilizing symbols. In his proposed, re-formed Positivist calendar which consisted of thirteen months, Comte took care to identify not only each month but each week and day with the name of some great philosopher, scientist, or statesman of the past. He too enjoined upon all Positivists, present and future, the importance of gratitude to the Middle Ages.

Nor did Karl Marx think that ties with the past would be dissolved once mankind had escaped "prehistory" and taken up abode in communist society, with all alienations at last terminated as the result of abolition of private property and social class. Marx himself read widely and avidly in the classics—ancient, medieval, and modern—and he did not think that transposition of mankind to an utterly new kind of society need destroy or weaken communist man's ability to enjoy the past as reflected in its history and above all its literature, irrespective of the social and economic contexts in which this literature had been written. The past, then, could be sacred ground for even minds which were consecrated to abolition of present institutions and the establishment of a golden age in the future.

But whatever may have been true through the nineteenth and the early part of the twentieth centuries, we as a historically developed consciousness, as a civilization, stand today in a very different position toward the past. What J. H. Plumb has written in his perceptive *The Death of the Past* is instructive:

> Wherever we look, in all areas of social and personal life, the hold of the past is weakening. Rituals, myths, the need for personal roots in time are so much less strong than they were a mere hundred or even fifty years ago. In education and economic activity the past has ceased to be a guide to the present, even if bits of it still litter and hamper the development of both. In family and sexual relations the past offers little understanding and no comfort. . . .
>
> Over the centuries, however, men always turned to the past for more than a guide to the authority of the present. They thought that by its study they could discern the future, and maybe even predict it. They discovered repetitions, unfolding purpose, inevitable consequences in their study of it. . . .

Exactly! Not that in reality we ever can descry the future in any reliable way through study of trends in the past and present. The future is a proper subject for intimation, intuition, surmise, and guess, but never for prediction in any scientific sense. But, if I read Plumb correctly, this is of vastly less importance than the historic dependence of human beings upon the past as an indispensable support for living in the present and for *consciousness* of the future as a distinct and real time frame.

It should be said immediately that although Professor Plumb accurately describes our present situation with respect to the past, he does so in no spirit of lament whatever. As far as he is concerned, we don't need the past. Moreover, we are better off without it. What is wanted in place of a strong sense of the past is a clear realization of *history* as process, as change, as creative force. "The old past is dying," writes Plumb, "its force weakening, and so it should. Indeed the historian should speed it on its way, for it was compounded of bigotry, of national vanity, of class domination."

Such a characterization of the past will seem limited and ungenerous to many readers. After all, there were salutary revolutions, wars of liberation, the geneses of creative cultures, the emergence of geniuses and prophets who remain relevant to us, great literature, science, and philosophy; these too compose the past. But argument is gratuitous here. The only important point is that a distinguished historian accurately diagnoses our condition, which is one of being cut off from more and more of the past that once gave anchor to human beings.

It may be asked, why have we in the late twentieth century reached the point of disowning, forgetting, or actually killing off the past in the sense that our forefathers knew it? Stanley Hoffman has addressed himself knowledgeably to this question in a recent article in *Daedalus*. He concedes that through book, television documentary, article, and movie we retain some connection with the *recent* past "if only as a horror show, a pageant, or a pep pill." But Hoffman continues:

> What is striking is the growing disconnection with the more distant past. . . . The past is becoming an object of erudition or diversion, rather than a part of one's own being, through family or school transmission. What the French called *le passé vécu*, the experienced past, is displaced by the past as a product of specialists, a consumer product, a subject matter for scholars, or a spectacle.

Professor Hoffman offers several plausible explanations for this monumental change in our relation to the past. First, there is the sheer speed of social change, "the sweeping away of old customs and rites, the disappearance or transformation of old occupations . . . and the collapse of traditional modes of social control." It is indeed hard to retain any sense of the reality or the identity of the past amid the kind of changes Western society has known during the twentieth century. Second, Hoffman argues, there is the disappearance of the kind of historical writing that was once commonplace. "Romantic history is gone, replaced by scientific history," the latter having of course a vastly different kind of interest in the past, an interest more like that of an antiquarian, a museum keeper, or a laboratory worker. Even more important is the degradation or, rather, dissolution of the discipline of history in the schools and, increasingly, in colleges. "In the educational system the teaching of history regresses. . . . High school history is being diluted into social studies—the contemporary." Hoffman believes that the place of history is stronger in the United States than in France and other Western European countries, and he may be right, at least with respect to some of our better religious and other private schools.

But so far as the vast majority of pupils and students in America are concerned, history is virtually extinct as a discipline, as a window to our long and continuous past. What Frances Fitzgerald has written in a recent arresting volume, *America Revised*—on the basis of a voluminous and searching examination of history textbooks written for the schools—is at once illuminating and profoundly depressing. Whereas up until a few decades ago all pupils received through their required courses in American history a reasonably common, accepted view of the past, a past that could be plainly seen making its way continuously to the present and thus exciting thought of the future (Fitzgerald uses the famous David Muzzey American history text, nearly universal in American schools for more than a half-century until after World War II, as her standard for what was once accepted practice), the situation is utterly different now. There is no longer, as she points out, a common, understood, and accepted past to be found in current American histories for the schools.

Triumph of the Idea of Progress

What is to be found in these textbooks, as Frances Fitzgerald learned, is either no past, no history at all—only "social studies" and "current events" —or else, more and more typically, a congeries, a potpourri, of "pasts," each tied to some currently engrossing ideological theme such as ethnicity, sexuality, or an ideological-political framework, with disharmony inevitably the result. In these contexts any sense of relation of past to present, quite apart from respect for the past, is made virtually impossible. Or, as she learned repeatedly, the "pasts" chosen were arrived at in advance by publisher's market-analysis, with portrayal left to hack writers working to specifications contrived to meet the desires and pressures of this or that school board, this or that state textbook commission. Chiefly in parochial and a few other private schools there are distinguished exceptions, to be sure, but for the vast majority of school children today, and during the past two or three decades, the past in any meaningful sense has been almost obliterated. Once again, we may profitably turn to Stanley Hoffman for proper commentary:

> We are left then with two questions for morose or worried speculation. First, can one live forever in the economic present, comforting oneself with comparative statistics and half-cozy, half-worried enjoyment of goods, freedom, and rights? Second, to what extent are the poverty of inspiration and imagination, the concentration on the here and now, related to European nations' fall from international eminence? Are images of the past and visions of the future tied either to struggles for national identity or to the possibility of strutting on the world's stage, fighting or speaking out for a great cause, national or not?

Hoffman need not, of course, limit his commentary to European nations. There can be no question that in America at the present moment, a great deal of the moral disenchantment we discover through poll and survey, the proliferation of single-interest groups, the fragmentation of party and thus of polity, and the obsessive concern with one's self at the expense of the social bond or community, is the result of loss of the past—of having, as noted, disowned the past on the ground of its overwhelming iniquities or its irrelevance to present and future. What this loss or disowning of the past means to one distinguished literary historian, Hoxie Neale Fairchild, is well represented by the following words taken from the final volume of his *Religious Trends in English Poetry:*

> The Modern Temper. Hollow men eating their Naked Lunches in the Wasteland while awaiting Godot. Botched civilization. Sick world. *Untergang des Abendlandes.*
>
> No life beyond the grave. Loss of traditional symbols of Western culture. No integrating myths. No worship.

No reality independent of the disinterested observer. No objective, sharable truth or truths. No scale of values. No norm of human nature. . . . No boundaries between the rational and the irrational, normal or abnormal. . . . Semantic stultification: chasm between words and meaning. Solipsism. Nothing to discipline our emotions. No firm roots in domestic or civil ritual. Life patternless, purposeless, meaningless. Everything "phony."

Including, in this final part of the twentieth century, the historic idea of progress. If loss or death of the past were *only* that, as Professor Plumb has argued, matters would be different. But what T. S. Eliot pointed out in a celebrated essay more than half a century ago—to wit, the absolute necessity of a remembered past, of tradition, to the creative mind—holds as well for science and for statecraft as it does for poetry and painting. The great scientists of this century, Einstein, Planck, Bohr, and others, are all on record as to the vital importance of the past to the scientific imagination. So are Aristotle, Ptolemy, Roger Bacon, Newton, Boyle, Lavoisier, Faraday, and Maxwell. But it is very different today. The past appears to have as little meaning today in science as in the humanities and arts. What *The New York Times* science writer John Noble Wilford writes is instructive: "Everywhere we look there is tension between the past and the future, between a pessimism we cannot shake and an optimism we cannot believe in. The present is thus a turmoil of understandable nostalgia, crippling indecision, and bewildering prospect. The immediate consequence is too often malaise and negativism, a general disorientation."

The Displacement of the West

As our common past recedes into nothingness, so, it would seem, does the West. And this is hardly less crippling to the historic idea of progress than the death of the past. For, as we have had numerous opportunities to observe, the rise and development of the idea of progress has taken place within Western civilizations which were profoundly important to their members and, in different purview, to those on the outside. Progress of the arts and sciences was perceived as such by the Greeks in the light of their deep devotion to all things Greek and of their conviction that Greek culture was the best and most advanced in the world. The same holds for Rome, whose expansion north and west from Italy to England really created Western civilization. And when Rome (in the West) lost its power to govern and its institutions were in arrears, a Greco-Roman Christianity picked up the torch. Just as firmly as any pagan historian or philosopher, St. Augustine believed in the greatness of Greece and Rome and in their strategic roles in progress toward the City of God.

All of this, however, is but prologue. For observation of the truly great significance of the West and of its link with the faith in humanity's progress, we come down to the last four centuries, in which ascendancy of the West over the rest of the world was not just a matter of ethnocentric belief but a military and political reality. It was, Toynbee has written in *Mankind and Mother Earth,* between 1837 and 1897 that the West "completed its ascendancy over all the rest of the world." But, as Toynbee also observes, this was but the culmination of a trend that had begun four centuries earlier —with Columbus's voyages across the Atlantic and Vasco da Gama's around the Cape of Good Hope to the west coast of India. Toynbee adds:

> In the course of those four centuries, all but two of the non-Western countries, Afghanistan and Abyssinia (Ethiopia), had either fallen under Western domination or had salvaged their independence by voluntarily adopting the triumphant Western civilization's way of life in some degree. . . . In 1897, six of the seven existing Great Powers were Western states, and the seventh, Russia, was a Great Power in virtue of her having Westernized herself to a considerable extent in the course of the last two centuries.

Japan would of course become a Great Power in the early twentieth century, and this too was a consequence of her Westernization.

But no mere enumeration of the world's Great Powers even begins to do justice to the ascendancy the West held on a constantly increasing scale during the four centuries, reaching its all-time high point at the beginning of the twentieth century. To do this ascendancy justice we are obliged to think of Christianity and its diffusion, the spread of Western political values, the worldwide extension of the Industrial Revolution—or the conveying to all parts of the world the products of the Industrial Revolution—and, with these, innumerable other traits of the West's culture and consciousness. It is hardly surprising that even before, but especially during, the nineteenth century "world history" could be and almost universally was written in the epic pattern, one in which the growing power and ascendancy of the West could be made to seem foreordained, inevitable, and irreversible. Western supremacy and the faith in mankind's progress became circular in conceptual relation. The West, it was said, became ruler of the world by virtue of the laws of progress; and these could be of course validated by the manifest fact of Western superiority. Down until very recently, it was a cardinal article of belief by all but a small minority of skeptics and doomsayers that the Westernization (or in the United States, the Americanization) of the world was as inexorable and would be as lasting as any process in history.

But within an astonishingly short time, what had required more than two thousand years to create as condition and as belief has come to an end. Manifestly, the power and influence of Western civilization in the world have been declining ever since World War I. Every geopolitical apprehension that Sir Halford Mackinder expressed some six decades ago in his *Democratic Ideals and Reality* has been fulfilled. Perhaps in the long view, with the welfare of the whole of mankind as the criterion, this displacement of the West will prove salutary. No one can even pretend to know the answer. All we now know is that the West, still with all its flaws the major complex of reasonably free and democratic governments, has become, irreversibly, one would guess, the object of disdain, contempt, and hostility in the greater part of the world. The West is envied for its material wealth but is no longer either feared or respected, much less regarded as model, in the communist and most of the Third World countries. What Spengler referred to in the title of his famous work is already well under way. In a large number of respects America, the world's political colossus, it seemed, after World War II, has lost world respect and gained world hostility at a rate greater than that which applies to the West as a whole. What the late Christopher Dawson wrote on Europe several decades ago is relevant to both Europe and America: "Not only is Europe reduced to insignificance by the giant powers to which she has given birth, but it is difficult to find any people, however weak or backward, who will admit her claim to cultural superiority."

What is in all ways most devastating, however, is the signal decline *in America and Europe themselves* of faith in the value and promise of Western civilization. What has succeeded faith is, on the vivid and continually enlarging record, guilt, alienation, and indifference. An attitude—that we as a nation and as a Western civilization can in retrospect see ourselves as having contaminated, corrupted, and despoiled other peoples in the world, and that for having done this we should feel guilty, ashamed, and remorseful—grows and widens among Americans especially, and even more especially among young Americans of the middle class. For good reason or bad, the lay clerisy of the West—the intelligentsia that began in the eighteenth century to succeed the clergy as the dominant class so far as citizen's beliefs are concerned—devotes a great deal of its time to lament, self-flagellation, and harsh judgment upon an entire history: Western history. Inevitably, the media, television leading the way, reflect the clerisy's mood and attitudes. With excellent reason, therefore, a widening sector of the population finds itself adopting the same view of American and Western guilt. Clearly, any idea of progress must be precariously based indeed in such an environment.

Coupled with the collective sense of guilt that grows in the West is the sense of the meaninglessness and purposelessness of what we do and have done in past generations. A year or so ago there appeared in *The New York Times* a remarkable letter by the distinguished Harvard historian David Donald. It was in fact more than a letter; it was a searching, searing essay. It is almost inconceivable that anyone other than an American historian of our time could have written it. What Professor Donald declared was that for him both history as such and the teaching of history had become meaningless; even worse, potentially dangerous.

What undergraduates want from their history teachers is an understanding of how the American past relates to the present and the future. But if I teach what I believe to be the truth, I can only share with them my sense of the irrelevance of history and of the bleakness of the new age we are entering. . . . Unlike every previous American generation, we face impossible choices. . . . What, then, can a historian tell undergraduates that might help them in this new and unprecedented age? Perhaps my most useful function would be to disenthrall them from the spell of history, to help them see the irrelevance of the past. . . .

If David Donald were a lone voice, the words would not be worth quoting; but he is very far from being a lone voice in the American clerisy; he is merely a more open and candid voice. Professor Donald speaks of disenthralling students "from the spell of history." He could have said—many are saying and will continue to say—disenthrall them from "the spell of the West or of America." For that is the real, underlying message of this essay.

Behind this spreading atmosphere of guilt and loss of meaning or purpose in the West and its heritage lies a constant erosion of faith in Western institutions; not just political but social, cultural, and religious institutions. Hardly a week passes without some fresh poll or survey indicating still greater loss of respect by Americans and Europeans for government, church, school, profession, industry, the media, and other once respected institutions—and, naturally, those who in one or other degree preside over or represent these institutions. The major periods of efflorescence, growth, and diffusion of the idea of progress have been periods in which popular trust in reigning institutions—city-state, republic, empire, church, family, monarchy, democracy, and others—has been high, just as those periods in which the idea of progress languished or lay dormant have been periods of substantial popular indifference to or distrust of such institutions. In no period of Western history, not even the Dark Ages, has alienation from, lack of confidence in, and hostility toward fundamental institutions been as deep and widespread as in this final part of the twentieth century in the West. After all, in the Dark Ages there was, there *had to be,* considerable confidence in and gratitude for family, clan, kindred, and then manor and fief. And whatever lack of faith in linear progress existed during the Renaissance, when ideas of *ricorsi* appealed to intellectuals, when pessimism and occultism were widespread among many groups in society, there was, as we saw, no lack of confidence in enlightened princes, popes, and moneymen. But in our age lack of confidence seems to be the fate of *all* institutions!

What the respected foreign correspondent, Flora Lewis, of *The New York Times,* wrote in the *Times Magazine* more than a year ago about Europe is instructive:

[I]nstead of feeling a move toward a constructive culmination as the century and millennium draw to a close, Europeans have a sense of being at the beginning of a downhill slide . . .

There is a pervading sense of crisis, although it has no clear face, as it did in the days of postwar reconstruction. People are disillusioned and preoccupied. The notion of progress, once so stirring, rings hollow now. Nobody can say exactly what he fears, but neither is anyone sanguine about the future. Although the countries of the European Economic Community have never been so dependent on common efforts to solve their national problems, there is a sense that governments no longer have the wisdom or power to cope. "We are a church that is beginning to lose its faith," says Guido Brunner, a Common Market commissioner . . .

The disillusionment with other forms of political action covers all versions of Communist society. Scarcely anyone points to Moscow (or Peking) any longer as a fount of social wisdom . . .

When it does look at itself, Europe tends to throw up its hands. So it is looking at Washington once again, but without great enthusiasm or faith. There are no more prophets.

Indeed there are no prophets of hope and progress, and least of all in the United States. There is one individual who is not a Westerner but who currently lives in the United States and who may fairly be called a prophet in just about every sense of the word: Solzhenitsyn. But, as his historic commencement address at Harvard University revealed, this exile from the Soviet Union he loathes, in which he suffered imprisonment and torture for many years, who has his full share of gratitude to the free West that has given him haven, is virtually without hope so far as the future of Western civilization is concerned. He sees the West's decline as the result largely of loss of faith in its own values and of revolt, on a widening scale, against authority—the authority of culture and morality, of the values around which the West has been built or toward which it progressed. And without this kind of authority—which is the absolute opposite of power—there cannot be, Solzhenitsyn declares, stability, liberty, or creativity.

There is another, closely related kind of authority that is crucial to any thriving civilization and that the West also sorely lacks at the present time: the authority of some kind of class or elite. It may be political, economic, artistic, philosophical, religious, or other in composition. History reveals a myriad of ruling classes in culture as well as polity. It would be difficult, though, to find any class whatever today in the West that even begins to meet the requirements of leadership. Intellectuals are fast becoming as naked of these requirements as politicians and corporation executives.

In an arresting article in *The American Historical Review* several years ago entitled "The Idea of the West" the historian Loren Baritz emphasized the spell that has been cast by this idea on Westerners since the time of the early Greeks. Almost everything that could be aspired to by the Greeks, beginning with the fabled Isles of the Blest, lay west. It was not different, as Baritz notes, with the Romans or with the people of the Middle Ages (St. Augustine had claimed divine sanction for his belief in the westward course of empire). Among the most cherished of legends was that of St. Brendan whose "exploits," writes Baritz, "were told in virtually every European tongue, and which became one of the most widespread tales of adventure in the western sea in Christendom . . ." We know well the appeal of the west to Columbus and to many another navigator and explorer, an appeal that became embodied too in a great deal of literature, with Bishop Berkeley's "Westward the course of empire takes its way" the most celebrated line. In America almost from the very beginning, the west had close to hallowed significance. Thoreau wrote: "Eastward I go only by force; but westward I go free" and also "Every sunset which I witness inspires me to go to a West as distant and as fair as that into which the sun goes down." Such beliefs, sentiments, and impulsions are rare in our day.

The Attack on Economic Growth

From the very beginning there has been close relationship between belief in the general progress of mankind and belief in the necessity of economic growth and development. The Athenians of the fifth century B.C. did not suffer from any want of respect for the economic base of civilization. They knew full well that behind the art and philosophy in which they took pride lay the progress of economy and commerce. Plato in both *The Laws* and

The Statesman makes very evident his own knowledge of the vital relationshp between economy and culture, and his accounts of mankind's long ascent in time are rich in references to the practical arts—agriculture, metallurgy, and others—which could alone supply the base for progress in knowledge and culture generally. So was Lucretius vividly aware of the importance of economic progress. And high among the achievements which St. Augustine praised in his account of the material progress of mankind through the centuries are those of economic and technological character. The Puritans needed no instruction in this respect, as we saw in some detail in chapter 5. No one outdid Voltaire and Condorcet in their lauding of commerce and its economic-technological base. And so it has been down to this second half of the twentieth century, with the exceptions throughout the history of the idea of those relatively few who found their golden ages in the past rather than in the future and for whom all economic and technological developments have been symbols of social and moral decline instead of milestones of progress.

Matters are very different, however, in the second half of our own century. Within steadily enlarging sectors of Western and particularly American society, a disenchantment with or more ominously an outright hostility toward economic growth is to be discerned. There is rising fear that we and our planet are doomed unless we bring this growth to a halt, unless we drastically curtail our use of fuels and minerals, unless we renounce all nuclear power, unless we declare vast areas of land and water to be ecosystems, off-limits to any kind of economic or technological use, and so forth. Rarely has human society been without doomsday predictions based upon some kind of belief, but what we are experiencing today in the West is without precedent in kind or in volume. The appeal of what John Stuart Mill referred to as "the stationary state" widens steadily at the present time, no matter what the nomenclature may be. No one has questioned the virtues of economic growth and its impact upon morality, society, and the individual mind more influentially than E. J. Mishan. Mishan is himself an able economist, having worked in the field for more than a quarter of a century. A decade ago in his book *The Costs of Economic Growth*, he argued that the continued effort to achieve or to accelerate any kind of economic growth that rests—as most of it must rest—upon technological innovations is very likely to have such negative, destructive effects upon our total physical environment as to reduce the quality of human life.

In his more recent *The Economic Growth Debate* Mishan carries his argument farther. Here he lists carefully the various measurements or criteria of what we call the good life. Among these criteria, Mishan writes, are food, health, security, and shelter, of course; but also family, religion, tradition, and custom. Stability of morality or of a moral code conceived in whatever way is vital to man, as are his primary modes of association: friendship, love, mutual aid, and so on. What Mishan brings out in a series of arresting chapters is the profound disharmony that exists—must exist, he argues—between continued prosecution of economic progress and these constitutive moral and social values. Mishan goes so far as to declare that the very legitimacy and thus the strength of our most vital institutions is being undermined by the central, mostly technological elements of economic growth. Unlimited continuation of the kind of industrial expansion we have known for two centuries in the West must result, Mishan concludes, in a slow but inexorable disintegration of the social order, a collapse of the disciplines and authorities which are built into any social order, and a casting of individuals into a social and moral void, one that is most likely to be filled by the totalitarian state. Mishan is convinced of the reality of historical decline, one that really commenced in the Enlightenment, accelerated in the nineteenth century, and is proceeding at an increasingly faster pace today. And the cause of this decline, Mishan observes, is the very economic growth that was so widely hailed in the late eighteenth and the nineteenth and early twentieth centuries as the mainspring of progress in general—social, moral, and cultural.

In another widely read and discussed work, *Social Limits of Growth,* Fred Hirsch reaches an analogous conclusion. A visible and significant erosion is taking place in the moral values on which the modern capitalist system has been based. Despite the classical (and Marxian) economists' insistence that capitalism rests upon individual self-interest and its constant expression in the marketplace, a truer analysis, Hirsch tells us, would show that what was so easily called "self-interest" was in the beginning and indeed in the subsequent history of this economic system until a short while ago much more than that. It was self-interest, if we like, but it was inseparable from the restraints which sprang from a religious and moral atmosphere that was at the time highly influential. "Economic man" was in fact a being strongly driven by or held back by considerations which were not economic at all and which were once strongly influential in Western man's existence. These moral and spirtual values have, however, become weakened. This, it will be remembered, was the prediction that Max Weber made in his famous "iron cage" passage in *The Protestant Ethic and the Spirit of Capitalism.* And Joseph Schumpeter in his classic of 1942, *Capitalism, Socialism and Democracy,* argued somewhat along the same line, seeing the slow but inexorable decline of capitalism as the result of the "crumbling" of precapitalist social and moral supports.

Irrespective of final validity, there is freshness in Hirsch's interpretation.

Economists interested in growth for too long paid insufficient attention to the *moral* bases of growth and affluence. "Truth, trust, acceptance, restraint, obligation—these are among the social virtues grounded in religious belief" which have proved indispensable to the capitalist spirit, according to Hirsch. What we call the free market, Hirsch continues, actually has drawn more from and has had greater dependence on religious and moral coercions than did the feudal economy. But the long-run effect of our celebration of not these vital moral supports but rather the individual and his supposedly enlightened self-interest has been to weaken and at last virtually destroy the necessary moral values.

Another type of limit that Hirsch sees inevitably affecting economic growth is the rising disaffection for or boredom with the kinds of goods which present-day industrialism is making so widely available. Rather than material goods, what Hirsch calls "positional goods" are the key to the matter. As he points out, our individual enjoyment of such material goods as food, shelter, and clothing is largely unaffected by the fact that others in society are also enjoying these same material goods. However, a different situation arises when we consider the way in which our enjoyment of certain goods is instantly and often lastingly affected by others' possession of these same goods. Congested highways, teeming camp grounds, and crowded bicycle lanes will come quickly to mind. But, as Hirsch suggests, positional goods can be intellectual in nature. When everyone has a diploma, what real satisfaction can there be for the individual in having worked to acquire one?

Hirsch's conclusion is that a constantly increasing number of "positional goods" is the heritage in our day of economic growth. Indeed, it could be argued that the desire for positional goods was among the principal incentives to the work ethic or capitalist spirit in the first place. But when these proliferate so as to diminish their attraction to the average worker-consumer, a great deal of motivation to work and save is bound to disappear. The effect of decline in the attraction of positional goods is, Hirsch argues, to greatly enhance the lure of money in and for itself. We are becoming, he suggests, vastly more money-minded than our forebears for whom money was seen chiefly as the necessary means for material and positional goods. And, as social critics from Edmund Burke on have emphasized, the "cash-nexus," as Carlyle termed it, will not support a social order. Money, unlike hard property, has the effect of atomizing a population, of giving each individual that sense of self-security that allows, even encourages, his withdrawal from binding relationships with others.

Very much implicated in the spreading disillusionment with economic growth is fear of scarcity, of depletion of the resources in the earth, the seas, and the atmosphere which are crucial to economic growth. It should be remembered that one of the prime assumptions of the modern idea of progress was the invariability of nature, a nature that would be the same tomorrow as it is today and was yesterday. Such nature, the Moderns in the seventeenth-century Quarrel of the ancients and moderns said, includes *human* nature. It was no stronger or more productive in the days of Aeschylus and Sophocles than it is today and tomorrow. On such foundation of confidence in a nature that has and always will be the same, the moderns could joyfully argue that with such invariability present had to be superior to past simply by virtue of the increase in knowledge.

But in the twentieth century, and in steadily rising degree, the thought becomes obsessive that given the undeniably prodigious utilization of our resources—soil, water, air, minerals, fuels, nutrients, and so forth—and given also the often wanton destruction, especially in the United States, of what we produce but do not need in a given week, month, or year, the time may be rapidly approaching when we shall have no more resources or too few for use and abuse. I am aware of the fact that among scientists and technologists, no single view as it applies to the foreseeable future is universally accepted. There are those such as Wassily Leontieff who after careful and sober study have concluded that there are enough resources including food to take care of any predictable population on earth for a long time ahead. But when Professor Leontieff's report is read to the end, it becomes evident that in order for such plenty to exist for the world, political planning and allocation, political alliances, and the creation of centralized world agencies would be required, all of such magnitude and implication that it is very hard even for the most optimistic of minds to take very much encouragement.

Closely allied to the fear of scarcity is fear for our environment in the widest sense: physical and social. Such a book as Talbot Page's recent *Conservation and Economic Efficiency* can only have traumatic impact on many minds. His statistics on the prodigality of the United States alone (admittedly the worst offender in the world, but the most powerful and influential) with respect to scarce and nonrenewable resources make grim reading. So do the conclusions presented in the final part of his book with respect to the problems involved in reaching *criteria* for ascertaining optimal rates of depletion of resources over a period of time. Page's book can only heighten distrust of models of future consumption, so dear to econometricians, which purport to predict relationships among individual consumers, standards of living, ethical preconceptions, and natural resources.

But let us assume for the moment that all pessimistic forecasts concerning natural resources and environment will within the rest of this century be shown to be in fact baseless. Again we return not to reality but perceptions of reality. For perhaps the first time in more than two millennia there are enough intellectuals convinced of the hopelessness of our population-consumer resources problems to communicate to an even larger number of people the futility of hopes for human progress.

It would be bad enough for belief in progress if the kind of problems or fears just described could be limited to what has been briefly discussed here. But if there is indeed an Age of Scarcity coming upon us, or if belief in such an age spreads widely enough or influences enough rulers of powerful states on earth, it is not difficult in light of the history of wars involving the vying for natural resources to foresee intensification of all current tensions of the potential for war. Modernization, so long cherished by the great majority of Western intellectuals, has already manifested effects in the Third World which suggest that even if these nations are not yet wholly Westernized in their technology, arms, and aspirations, they are far enough along to make the quest for vital minerals and resources just as pressing for them as for any Western country. I doubt that it occurred to many people a generation or two ago that what the "modernization" of "backward" nations would accomplish is what is in effect a world economy with internal relationships ever more delicate, complex, even unobservable, but nevertheless powerful in impact upon human beings, and, alas, beyond the capacity of any single mind or group of minds so far discovered to manage fruitfully. What this line of attack upon progress argues in effect is that whereas the earth, sky, and sea could support a few "modernized" nations with all their demands upon nature, such support cannot be reasonably extrapolated to include all the nations now feverishly in the process of "modernization." Belief widens that there are not now, nor will there be, minds in any and all professions capable of handling the problems such universal transformation would entail.

How powerful and pervasive this state of mind is in America is attested to in a long article on America at its bicentennial in *The Economist* (October 25, 1975) by its deputy editor Norman Macrae. On the basis of nearly a year's travel through America, Macrae came up with a far from optimistic account of what he had seen and heard. Just as the British "handled the task of world leadership" from 1776 to 1876, the Americans did from 1876 to 1976. But, looking ahead insofar as it was possible, Macrae saw the high possibility of a signal recession in America's influence. "[T]he Americans on the eve of 1976 are showing the same symptoms of a drift from dynamism as the British did at the end of their century in 1876." The reasons Macrae cites are pertinent to this section on economic growth. I shall list the major ones briefly: American Fabianism and adoption of "many of the upper-class snob habits that checked Britain's economic dynamism . . . such as anti-business paternalism, a glorification of gamekeepers"; treason of the clerks—"On campuses across the continent, a peculiarly innumerate anti-growth cult is being taught to idealistic kids as if it was high moral philosophy or even a religion"; "the retreat from Mr. Edison"—that is, the bureaucratization of our technology and also business; and "the dreamy monster": "America has the right government system for running a free enterprise society; but the wrong one for running the one-third socialist society into which it has meandered." Macrae offers other reasons, including the middle-class deification of environmentalism even and especially when sharp reductions in standard of living quite apart from industrial productivity and technological achievement must result. But I shall close with Macrae's own conclusion:

There are three main questions. First, will America continue to believe in economic growth? Half the world will remain hungry if it does not, and that half-world may blow us up.

Second, should America believe in participatory producers' democracy in factory and politics, or in extended and informed consumers' freedom in both? Please God, it should believe in consumers' freedom.

Third, does the star-spangled banner still wave o'er the land of the free, and the home of the brave? The stars glitter, but no wise foreigner at this hour will rely wholly on George Washington's order of April 1777: "Put none but Americans on guard tonight."

The Degradation of Knowledge

Of all challenges to which the idea of progress is subjected in our time, none is more deadly in possibility than the present fast changing position of knowledge and of the man of knowledge. I use "knowledge" in William James's sense of "knowledge about" in contrast to "knowledge of." The first is the province of the scholar, scientist, historian, philosopher, technologist, and others whose primary function is that of advancing our knowledge about the cosmos, society, and man. The second is, as James noted, the common possession of all living beings and describes simply the habits, adjustments, and techniques we employ in the business of living.

As we have seen, the idea of progress had its origin in Greek fascination with knowledge—knowledge *about*—and in the realization that this knowledge had required long ages of slow, gradual, and continuous advancement in order to reach the level the Greeks knew. Inherent in the Greek and Roman idea of progress, then, was profound and unvarying faith in objective knowledge. With the rise of Christianity, it will be remembered, a second dimension of progress arose, one directed toward mankind's spiritual and moral improvement over time to reach fulfillment in a distant millennium. But at no point did the Church Fathers dismiss the Greek criterion of progress; that is, advancement of knowledge of world and society. Appreciation of such knowledge never flagged in the history of Christianity; not in the Middle Ages; most certainly not in the Puritan seventeenth century when the contributions Isaac Newton or Robert Boyle made toward an understanding of the laws of nature were regarded as vital steps toward attainment of the golden age on earth, of the millennium.

Nor did appreciation for the work of the scholar and the scientist and philosopher wane during the Enlightenment, the whole of the nineteenth century, and the first half of the twentieth. Not even in the medieval university or in Renaissance libraries did the professional man of knowledge rank as high as he did in Western Europe from the middle of the eighteenth to the middle of the twentieth century. If he enjoyed somewhat less status in the United States in the nineteenth and early twentieth century than in Europe, it was by no means a low status. The extraordinary speed with which not only public and private schools but also colleges were founded in the nineteenth century is sufficient evidence of American appreciation of both science and the humanities. But in our present age the scholar and the scientist and their works do not enjoy anything like the respect—even self-respect—once a staple of Western civilization.

As recently as the 1950s it would have seemed absurd had anyone predicted that the day would soon come when scientists would find themselves not only substantially reduced in popular esteem, but, far more important, beset more and more frequently by self-doubts concerning their overall worth to society on social and moral and esthetic grounds—and their capacities for extending the limits of knowledge. The hard fact is that among some of our most respected scientists at the present time there are very serious doubts as to, first, the sheer ability of scientists to proceed much farther than they have in the acquisition of important, new knowledge and, second, the social and psychological value of such acquisition even if it occurred.

In his recent book *Scientific Knowledge and its Social Problems* Jerome Ravetz explores the question of *esprit* among scientists at the present time. From Ravetz's findings one can only infer that the changed structure of science—that is, the sheer number of scientists and the increasing bureau-cratization of science—has affected significantly the morale, creative urge, and self-esteem of scientists, generally for the worse.

In the spring of 1978 an entire issue of the journal *Daedalus* was devoted to contributions of scientists on "The Limits of Scientific Inquiry." In his introduction, Robert Morison identifies some of the voices I refer to. What follows in this paragraph is direct citation or paraphrase of Morison's open-ing remarks on what he refers to as "the new anxiety." (1) The harm that may be done to individuals in the simple pursuit of knowledge; (2) the concern for the possible damaging effects of new technologies that may result from new knowledge; (3) the long-term hazards that carry some finite possibility of serious perturbations in our current ways of living—as with the possible results of genetic engineering and climatological altera-tions; (4) the possibly unsettling results of new knowledge so far as man's concept of himself or his relation to others is concerned; and (5) the possible emergence of deep anxieties about the possible limitations and bases of scientific knowledge itself. Professor Morison writes:

Finally, it may be worth noting that unease in regard to science reflects a general decline in public esteem for authority figures of all kinds. Scientists are thus sus-pect, not only as authorities in their own right, but also because the scientific establishment has become identified with the general power structure, which to some of our citizens at least appears to become ever more overbearing and untrust-worthy. We may be witnessing here the result of an exchange of roles between science and religion in relation to the stability of the prevailing political system.

In 1969, the distinguished molecular biologist Gunther Stent published under the auspices of The American Museum of Natural History an arrest-ing and widely read little volume titled: *The Coming of the Golden Age; A View of the End of Progress*. Professor Stent's golden age, as set forth in this book, is the very antithesis of the golden ages which have been cele-brated for the future from the time of Greeks and Romans such as Protago-ras and Seneca all the way to Saint-Simon, Marx, Spencer, and Charles G. Darwin. For him the Golden Age will be quite literally the culture of a Polynesia, the culture we commonly have in mind when we say *"back to the Golden Age,"* the kind of view that Rousseau is so often and so falsely accused of presenting.

Stated briefly, Professor Stent's argument is that already a withdrawal from and a waning of interest in science, technology, and economic growth is to be seen, especially among youth drawn from the middle class. This is illustrated in his view by the character type we epitomize in the words "hippie" and "beat." The continued development in currently "backward" countries will only lead in time to the same kind of disillusionment with "progress" in all of these countries that is now so vivid in the West. There will be a spreading desire all over the world for escape from the work ethic, the disciplines of technology, and the stigmata of affluence. Gradually but surely, more and more peoples will make their way along "the road to Polynesia," that is, toward a society in which simplicity, naturalness, and tranquil ease will be the highlights. Not all technology will be lost, Stent believes; at one end of the social spectrum will be a minority of people still interested in running technology that gives comfort.

In the middle of the distribution will be found a type for whom the distinction between the real and the illusory will still be meaningful and whose prototype is the beatnik. He will retain an interest in the world and seek satisfaction from sensual pleasures. At the other end of the spectrum will be a type largely unemployable, for whom the boundary of the real and the imagined will have been largely dissolved, at least to the extent compatible with his physical survival. His prototype is the hippie.

In summary: "The history of the South Sea Islands, or, more specifically, of Polynesia, can, I think, serve as a paradigm for the more general evolution toward the Golden Age."

But we should miss the larger argument of Stent's little book if we were to think that the attractions of a worldwide Polynesia came from desire to escape the disciplines and demands of *advancing* culture and society, of *progressing* arts, letters, and sciences. On the contrary, what above all else characterizes our contemporary age, Stent writes, is the visible decline, stagnation, and inertia of these areas, the arts as well as the sciences. Stent's learning is diverse, and he presents the case for the contemporary decline of the quality of the arts, ranging from literature to such areas as music and painting. Needless to say, Stent is not taking the rather more familiar argument of decline in the arts as the result of their increased licence, libertinism, and decadence. He is much subtler. The evolution of art in the modern world has been attended by greater freedom of the artist from understood canons and limits—those of a strictly esthetic nature.

However the artist's accession to near-total freedom of expression now presents very great cognitive difficulties for the appreciation of his work: The absence of recognizable canons reduces his act of creation to near-randomness for the perceiver. In other words, artistic evolution along the one-way street to freedom embodies an element of self-limitation.

Professor Stent does not exempt even his own science, molecular biology, from this *stasis*, this coming apart in which he finds music, painting, and the other arts. His argument is too detailed to make possible more than

the briefest summary here. It will suffice to say that while he is fully aware
—in his own words—that back in Sumer the invention of the wheel doubtless caused many people to say in effect, "We can't possibly go beyond this
triumph," we have nevertheless reached a level today in our study of the
human mind and nervous system beyond which any thought of further
progress is in vain. In a series of chapters, Stent describes the progress that
has been made during the past century, the ascending levels of understanding of ever more complex phenomena. He refers to this advance as having
moved from the Classic to the Romantic to the Dogmatic to the Academic,
and, now, in his words, to "the end of progress." We have reached the point
in molecular biology, Stent tells us, where the one remaining great problem
is that of the "mind-matter paradox." He asks: "Is it in fact likely that
consciousness, the unique attribute of the brain, that appears to endow its
ensemble of atoms with self-awareness will ever be explained?" His answer
is in the negative. Borrowing from the physicist Bohr's famous reflection on
the ultimate impossibility of really examining the mind because "the mental
content is invariably altered when the attention is concentrated on any
single feature of it . . .," Stent writes:

> This attitude would mean nothing less than that searching for a "molecular"
> explanation of consciousness is a waste of time, since the physiological processes
> responsible for this wholly private experience will be seen to degenerate into seem-
> ingly quite ordinary, workaday reactions, no more and no less fascinating than
> those that occur in, say, the liver long before the molecular level has been reached.
> Thus, as far as consciousness is concerned, it is possible that the quest for its
> physical nature is bringing us to the limits of human understanding, in that the
> brain may not be capable, in the last analysis, of providing explanation of itself.

But Stent's view of the very high probability of cessation of progress in
science goes well beyond the example he selects from his own field of
scientific research. Modern Western progress, he writes,

> . . . has depended on the exertions of Faustian Man, whose motivational
> mainspring is the idea of the will to power. But when progress has proceeded far
> enough to provide ambiance of economic security for Everyman, the resulting social
> ethos works against the transmission of the will to power during child rearing and
> hence aborts the development of Faustian Man. . . . Thus I reach my first general
> conclusion concerning progress: It is by its very nature, by its very dependence on
> the will to power, *self-limiting.*

Let us turn to still another renowned physical scientist who has spent
time in recent years reflecting on the place of scientific knowledge in our
time: Dr. Robert L. Sinsheimer. Dr. Sinsheimer is concerned by the possibility that while science indeed may be able to go well beyond present levels

of knowledge, the upshot of such advancement is increasingly likely to be deleterious to the human race.

He begins by observing a truth that has been implicit in philosophy and science from very earliest times: "Scientific endeavour rests upon the faith that our scientific probing and our technological ventures will not displace some key element of our protective environment and thereby collapse our ecological niche. It is a faith that nature does not set booby traps for unwary species."

In the past, as Dr. Sinsheimer continues, this faith has been justified and rewarded. But can we afford such faith at the present time, given the presence and the operation or activity of manifestations of science which contain as science did not contain a century ago innumerable possibilities for the destruction of large and vital areas of our planet, including its precious layers of life-giving ozone?

For four centuries science has progressively expanded our knowledge and re-shaped our perception of the world. In the same time technology has correspond-ingly reshaped the pattern of our lives and the world in which we live.

Most people would agree that the net consequence of these activities has been benign. But it may be that the conditions which fostered such a benign outcome of scientific advance and technological innovation are changing to a less favorable set. . . .

Can circumstances change so as to devalue the net worth of new knowledge? Might a pause or slowdown for consolidation and reflection then be more in order? Hard questions, perhaps not answerable, perhaps not the right questions, but they are not answered for 1977 by invoking Galileo or Darwin or Freud.

There are three major areas of research Dr. Sinsheimer singles out for inspection of their implications: (1) continuation of research in isotope frac-tionation; (2) the search for means of contact with extraterrestrial intelli-gence; and (3) research into the aging process. The first cannot help but so simplify the process of manufacturing nuclear bombs as to magnify hugely the condition of terror that is generated by the presence of such bombs. This applies especially to nations where the temptation to use them lethally is bound to be greater than in such relatively well-off nations as those cur-rently in possession of them.

The second area of research, that of making contact with peoples remote from our planet, also disturbs Dr. Sinsheimer. He asks us to assume that intensive effort will be rewarded someday by establishment of contact with one or more such peoples. Will this be good? Not at all, or at least not necessarily, writes Dr. Sinsheimer. "If such intelligent societies exist and if we can 'hear' them, we are almost certain to be technologically less ad-vanced and thus distinctly inferior in our development to theirs." What would be the impact upon human values? As Sinsheimer reminds us, Copernicus was a "deep cultural shock to man." So was Darwin. Humanity could no longer take quite the same pride in itself after it learned, first, that the earth is not the center of things and, second, that man, far from being *sui generis*, was in fact genetically related to and a product of speciation that included quite literally every form of life on earth. The impact of more advanced cultures on less advanced "has almost invariably been disastrous to the latter . . . . Less advanced cultures quickly become derivative, seeking technological handouts. What would happen to *our* essential tradition of self-reliance? Would we be reduced to seekers of cosmic handouts?"

As to the danger presented by possible or even probable research success in the understanding and control of aging, we need think only, Sinsheimer writes, of youth. It is from youth that virtually all creative energy comes, no matter what the sphere of activity. To contemplate a world in which by the sheer mass of the aged the proportion of youth would drop to near insignificance is to contemplate intellectual and spiritual desiccation. As Dr. Sinsheimer noted:

> The logic is inexorable. In a finite world the end of death means the end of birth. Who will be the last born? If we propose such research we must take seriously the possibility of its success. The impact of a major extension of the human life span upon our entire social order, upon the life styles, mores, and adaptations associated with "three score and ten," upon the carrying capacity of a planet already facing over-population would be devastating.

It must not be assumed from the foregoing that all or even most scientists share the views—however respected such views may be in the scientific community—expressed by Stent and Sinsheimer. Far from it! But it is difficult to believe that any serious and reflective physical or biological scientist alive today can be utterly without apprehensions from time to time about the effects of continued advancement of science and development of technology. There may still be a few who echo the enthusiasms of the nineteenth and early twentieth centuries. What the historian of science and physicist Gerald Holton has recently written is clarifying:

> Until not too long ago, the conception of science as inexorably "progressing" had been a component of thought also in the historiography of science. George Sarton went so far as to assert in 1936: "The history of science is the only history which can illustrate the progress of mankind. In fact, progress has no definite and unquestionable meaning in other fields than the field of science." Just in the last few years these progressivist assumptions have come under a variety of attacks from scholars in the history and philosophy of science.

What holds for the physical and biological sciences holds *a fortiori* for the social sciences. The depressingly broad gulf between expectations for the social sciences at the beginning of the twentieth century—expectations by the social scientists and, back in those days, by the public at large—and the reality we have to look back on for three-quarters of a century is being noted by more and more of the better minds in the social sciences. It is quite evident, quite obvious, that the contributions of the social sciences have been minimal when not actually counterproductive, and that in so many of the projects of social reconstruction designed by social scientists for government execution more harm than good has been the result—as in benignly intended but disastrous "wars" against poverty, ethnic discrimination, poor housing, slums, and crime.

Let us not forget what has happened during the past several decades to social scientists themselves. Down through the early 1950s, no stronger objective existed anywhere in the world of science than that of social scientists to become ever more scientific, to become as much like physical scientists as possible so far as success in working from data to hypotheses and principles was concerned. To attend annual meetings of social science societies was to know through the hundreds of papers delivered how far-reaching and how deep-seated was this impulse toward objectivity in the study of society and its institutions and values.

Today, however, a very different social science world prevails. The breed I have just described hasn't wholly disappeared—it remains perhaps strongest in economics—but it is outweighed in current importance by other, extremely different breeds of self-styled social scientists. The number of those for whom objectivity is either a delusion or something inherently repugnant rises constantly. There is widespread retreat to all the diverse forms of subjectivism which hold up preoccupation with and study of one's self as the beginning of true wisdom. So, too, does the number of those who see direct social action and not social observation and analysis as the true purpose of social science rise.

Whether with respect to physical or social science, or to any other form of organized, rationally motivated knowledge, there is simply no question but that public confidence has waned a great deal during the past several decades. It is not that all recognition of what the sciences, especially the physical, biological, and health sciences have accomplished has been lost. It is that in the first place, what in fact has been achieved is so much below what had been promised and guaranteed from the end of World War II on. Public expectations had been inflated by the expectations of the scientists and their publicists in the great universities and research centers. And in the second place, the immense prominence and the hugely enhanced visibility of the scientists have made prominent and visible the incessant controversies, differences of diagnosis and evaluation, increasingly shrill, even bitter (especially where political and social ideologies become attached),

347

and, far from least, outright, advertised political orientation of scientists, have inevitably diminished public respect for men of knowledge. The same erosion of status that began with the clergy in the last century is to be seen today in the ranks of scholars and scientists. With loss of public confidence in the man of knowledge there must go loss of confidence in knowledge itself. How can there be belief in the progress of knowledge and in the progress of civilization as the result of increasing knowledge when confidence in knowledge has been diminished or erased?

There is one final, ominous measure of the retreat from reason and knowledge in our time. I refer to the fast spreading preoccupation with the religiously bizarre and exotic; with the occult; and with the innumerable forms of communication which repudiate the rational and base themselves solely upon the emotional and the affective and even the physical. Here the sense of some kind of interpersonal community, at however low a level in psychological terms, crowds our respect for rationality. Perhaps most noteworthy, in scale at least, is the passion for one's self, for the avowedly egocentric and hedonistic. A mere two decades ago, all of this was espoused by the counterculture alone, and gave little evidence of becoming, as it actually has, espoused by constantly enlarging sections of the whole population. The expression "counterculture today, establishment tomorrow" has too many positive illustrations in its behalf for it to be regarded any longer as facetious exaggeration. And, finally, we must consider the number—especially in the colleges and schools—for whom the year 2000 has become the well-ensconced symbol of not any kind of millenarianism that Joachim de Fiore or the seventeenth-century Puritans knew, but the very reverse: the destruction of the world through natural or man-made catastrophe, without even a postmundane spiritual eternity to be anticipated.

Clearly, the idea of progress can breathe only with the greatest difficulty, if at all, in a civilization as bedeviled as our own Western civilization is at the present time by irrationalism and solipsism. In a powerful article, George Steiner has recently summarized the situation in the West:

There are three times as many registered astrologers in Europe and the United States as there are chemists and physicists. Charlatans, either giggly or sinister, peddle millions of copies of books about visitants from outer space. . . .

Star Trekkers and galactic warriors drug the imagination. Frightened of future wars and famines, dizzied by models of scientific and technological futurity . . . a bone-tired human species is looking toward saucers in the sky for solace and surveillance.

Where the West does not peer at the stars it looks to Asia. Or, rather, to the *kitsch* of Asia.

The children of Krishna tango along our soiled pavements. . . . The mendacities of Zen and fairground meditation, pre-packaged nirvanas . . . are big business. Neon tantras flash from the boulevards of San Francisco and Chelsea . . .

Narcotics and horoscopes, little men with pointed ears and margarine-gurus, the pitiful bullying of encounter groups and the trek to Katmandu, the orgone box and the nauseous, million-dollar industry of Satanism in the movies, on television and in magazines—all breathe and feed on the same hunger, the same solitudes, the same bewilderments.

Progress, belief in progress, amid such circumstances? The intelligent mind reels at the thought.

The Pall of Boredom

Faith or even interest in progress is hardly to be expected in a civilization where more and more groups are ravaged by boredom; boredom with world, state, society, and self. Boredom is of course no new affliction in history. We are told by legend that Alexander the Great succumbed to it when there were no more worlds to conquer. Suetonius and other historians of the Roman Empire have given us vignettes and sketches of emperors, aristocrats, and plutocrats who were seized by this malady and who sought relief through one kind of debauchery or another. The bored aristocracy is an integral part of histories of modern Europe. Quite possibly there were a few bored Americans in the nineteenth century.

But always prior to our own day boredom was restricted to the minority, to those with leisure on their hands and without the psychological capacity to endure it save through dosages of thrill and diversion. The overwhelming majority of people, engaged necessarily in the unremitting struggle for existence, had no time for or susceptibility to boredom.

But the twentieth century has brought into existence for constantly enlarging numbers of people what Denis Gabor in his *Inventing the Future* has called The Age of Leisure. There are many components of the Age: reduced work weeks, expanded holidays and vacations, earlier age of retirement, greater longevity, the social welfare rolls, unemployed youth, significant enlargement of the number of the rich who withdraw from either political or economic participation in society, unlike their forebears, and so on. What all of these highly disparate groups have in common is, in a word, leisure; much more leisure than any population in history has ever had prior to our own century. Even Rome, with its leisured ruling class and its equally leisured impoverished who depended upon free "bread and circuses," does not begin to compare, even in proportional terms, to contemporary reality.

Both Tocqueville and Schopenhauer foresaw the high probability of boredom as one of the costs of egalitarian-humanitarian democracy. Tocqueville was struck by the "restlessness amidst prosperity" among both the French and Americans, with suicide a common form of relief in France and, Tocqueville suggests, insanity in America. The reduction of cultural diversity, the loss of "lofty ambition," the leveling of the masses and the future rise of a form of despotism that would extinguish desire to either work or live, all of this Tocqueville could see ahead as a distinct probability for those living in the democracies. He was struck too, it should be noted, by the two great, contrasting forms of escape from apathy and boredom: on the one hand, indulgence by the rich in hedonistic materialism; on the other hand, by a turning to "fanatical spirituality" through which all connection with the present was severed. Schopenhauer, later, doubted in the first place any government's capacity for removing the social ills which beset people in modern society, but, in the second place, declared: "even if these evils are all removed, boredom would at once occupy the place vacated by the other evils."

Looking out on present-day Western society, there is no reason to quarrel with either Tocqueville's or Schopenhauer's prevision. Denis Gabor refers to the great "trilemma" facing mankind today: nuclear warfare of prolonged nature, gross overpopulation on the earth, and the "age of leisure." We can undoubtedly, Gabor writes, survive the first two. Even if nine-tenths of the human race were killed, the remaining tenth could be depended upon to breed in high intensity and to restore most if not all of what is vital to survival. Human beings either learn to adapt to overpopulation through inherited genetic wisdom or counteract it with sudden sharp reduction of birthrates.

But, Gabor tells us, the Age of Leisure is very different. There has been nothing in our evolution—physical or social—to prepare humanity, or crucial segments of it, for leisure. How could there have been, given the necessity of constant struggle for life throughout the evolution of our species—that is, until very recently? Granted that some individuals learn to cope with leisure in some degree at least; many more do not. Gabor suggests possible programs of conditioning which if maintained for several generations might offset the neurological heritage of millions of years. But he is not convincing in his proposals. His quotation from the philosopher C. E. M. Joad is all too apposite: "Work is the only occupation yet invented which mankind has been able to endure in any but the smallest possible doses." The folk wisdom of all peoples is strewn with warnings of what must befall the individual with idle hands.

Only the unthinking could fail to note the nature of the behavior that springs from boredom and its pains. Violence as its own end steadily increases, on the streets and in our homes. For most of those who initiate it sadism is the generator, the kind of sadism that can come only from leisure become intolerable and with no other avenues of escape available. But there is also to be seen, in much greater volume, vicarious indulgence in violence in movies; television programs; the major sports (where, as we know, the violence factor becomes steadily larger, the consequence of spectator-craving); in drugs, of course, as evidenced by rising usage and narcotic intensity; the spread of orgiastic or perverted sex; the sheer inundation of pornography; the turning to the occult and the bizarre; the mind- or self-escaping by increasing numbers of people for whom once-hallowed middle-class norms and values have become objects of derision or contempt; and, following from all of this, the unmistakable if not always fully voiced longing for some kind of secular redeemer, the Caesar, the Napoleon, even the Hitler or Stalin. *Anything* to liberate one's self from the boredom which today lies associated with politics, culture, even life itself.

The late Harlow Shapley, eminent Harvard scientist, two or three decades ago listed the five afflictions which are most likely to destroy Western civilization. Boredom ranked third in his list—which included nuclear warfare, overpopulation, climatic or topographical catastrophe, and invincible plague. It might be remembered too that Aldous Huxley in his *Brave New World*, fully aware of the boredom that must be expected in utopia, conceived as one final adornment of the technology that gave leisure to all, the drug Soma, free to all those suffering unusually intense attacks of boredom or leisure-related anxiety. Orwell in *1984* did not feel it necessary to go beyond unlimited handouts of gin for the masses to thus spare them the pains of boredom and to offset possible eruptions of revolt spawned by boredom. Anthony Burgess in his *1985* has very recently shown how much worse the future may prove to be; Burgess, after all, has had the opportunity denied Orwell to witness the past two decades.

We have not reached that point; perhaps we never will. But we very clearly have reached approximations of it. Leaving the neurology and psychology of boredom to one side, what this state of mind means in social and cultural terms is increasingly widespread and chronic indifference to ordinary values, pursuits, freedoms, and obligations. The present becomes a scene composed of the absurd, the irrelevant, the demonic. So, necessarily, does the past and of course, the future. All that matters is what lies within the Me—its pains and release from pains. As G. K. Chesterton wrote (and I paraphrase), the result of ceasing to believe in God is not that one will then believe nothing; it is that one will believe anything.

Clearly, any faith, belief, or interest in progress is utterly impossible under such circumstances.

Epilogue: Progress and Providence

WHAT is the future of the idea of progress in the West? Any answer to that question requires answer to a prior question: what is the future of Judeo-Christianity in the West? For if there is one generalization that can be made confidently about the history of the idea of progress, it is that throughout its history the idea has been closely linked with, has depended upon, religion or upon intellectual constructs derived from religion.

The Greeks, even during their Age of Rationalism, never abandoned the gods, as the seminal statements on progress by Hesiod, Aeschylus, Plato, and others make clear. The same holds true largely for the Romans. It was within Christianity, as a result of the fateful union of Judaic and Greek thought, that the idea attained the form and content which were to reach the modern world: the vision of all humanity in necessary advancement, stage-by-stage, from a remote and primitive past to a distant and glorious future, the whole process an unfolding of initial Providential design. This vision reached its high point in Christianity during the seventeenth-century Puritan efflorescence in the arts and sciences.

Even during the Enlightenment, a few Condorcets excepted, the idea of progress continued to be closely and deeply united with Christianity, as the important works of Lessing, Kant, Herder, Priestley, and others emphasize. It is much the same in the nineteenth century. For every Marx among prophets of progress, dozens lived and wrote who made Christianity or some religious substitute for Christianity the cornerstone of faith in progress. The mature writings of Saint-Simon and Comte, both preeminent in the history of the idea of progress, bear this out. Even Mill, apparent atheist through much of his life, came in his final years to declare the indispensability of Christianity to both progress and order. Spencer scorned atheism and endowed his First Cause with divine essence. Marx may have repudiated all manifest religions, but his Dialectic is Augustinian in ultimate origin, and the concept has a providential role in the Marxian theory of progress. In sum, it is evident beyond reasonable challenge that from Hesiod to Toynbee, Schweitzer, and Teilhard de Chardin the relationship between religion and the concept of progress has been organic in character.

Our own century provides much negative evidence to this conclusion. For just as the century especially in its second half is almost barren of faith in progress, so is it almost barren of widespread and life-permeating religious faith. No prior age in the West's history comes even close to our own age in this respect. The Renaissance humanists detested much of the ecclesiastical structure of Christianity in their day, but they were profoundly concerned with Christian creed. True atheists were few and far between in the Enlightenment, though this takes nothing away from the philosophes' assault on Christianity as a power in society.

In our day, however, religion is a spent force. If God is not dead, he is ebbing away, and has been since the early part of the century. We have, in Jonathan Swift's coruscating words, "just enough religion to make us hate but not enough to make us love one another"—or, enough to make us see the flaws and cankers of the society around us but not enough to generate hope for the future. Just as religion has seriously waned, so have most of the systems of thought which for a time served intellectuals as surrogates. There aren't many today who find either Spencer's First Cause or Marx's Dialectic convincing. Already in the West Freudianism and Marxism have lost most of the status each enjoyed a century ago. The same acids which weakened the fabric of religious belief beginning in the late nineteenth century have remained on the scene long enough to weaken the fabrics of secular faiths.

The acids I refer to have taken a large toll in the twentieth century. Philosophy, the sovereign discipline in Western thought for two and a half millennia, scarcely exists today in any sense that would be recognizable by our ancestors. It remained strong for three or four decades in this century. Royce, James, Dewey, and Russell were household names. We have none such today. Who at this moment would have the slightest interest in what a living philosopher had to say on any subject, cosmological, moral, political, or social? Philosophers have been dislodged by other influences just as theologians at the beginning of our century were being dislodged by philosophers.

The question is, who has succeeded the philosophers? There is no ready answer. We appear to be destitute of any reigning intellectual class. Intellectuals and artists have gone the way of business and political titans, of clergy and philosophers, of scholars and scientists. When has literature been held in as low estate as it is today in the West? Never has the gulf between creative writer and the public been as wide as it is now. Even in the Dark Ages those who could read—and even many of those who couldn't—revered such classics as they could put their hands on or listen to, and out of this age came some of the greatest of medieval epics and romances. How far we have fallen during the past century; where are the Goethes, Tolstoys, and Dickenses, even the Manns, Pasternaks, and Hardys?—those, that is, who could combine genius, or high talent at least, with the status of culture heroes, of being household names. Dickens was not only a great novelist; he is one of the most widely read writers in history. Our writers today are divided unequally between the so-called serious group whose fame lies for the most part in coteries, and the popular writers whose shoddy works sell in the millions of copies but earn no respect. There isn't a true culture hero in the lot; nothing to compare with what we knew a mere half-century ago.

The reason for this condition, this debasement of literature and estrangement of writer and public, is our lack of a true culture. And fundamental to this lack is the disappearance of the sacred, always at the heart of any genuine culture—from ancient Athens to Victorian England. For some time we thought we could live off the yield of the sacred, even though it was gone or passing away. Then it was easy to maintain belief in progress and, so believing, to seek to add to what a cherished past had contributed. It is no longer easy, for behind the death of the past, the displacement of Western pride of civilization, the waning faith in economic growth and in the works of reason lies the moribundity of religious conviction, of belief and faith in something greater than the life immediately around us. Many years ago Lord Bryce, who greatly admired American civilization, wondered: "What might befall this huge yet delicate fabric [if Americans ceased to believe] that there is any power above them, any future before them, anything in heaven or earth but what their senses told them of . . . ?"

Earlier, in his *Democracy in America,* Tocqueville had put the matter more descriptively and prophetically.

In ages of faith the final aim of life is placed beyond life. The men of these ages, therefore, naturally and almost involuntarily accustom themselves to fix their gaze for many years on some immovable object towards which they are continually tending, and they learn by insensible degrees to repress a multitude of petty, passing desires in order to be able to content that great and lasting desire which possesses . . .

This explains why religious nations have so often achieved such lasting results; for while they were thinking only of the other world, they found out the great secret of success in this . . .

But in proportion as the light of faith grows dim, the range of man's sight is circumscribed. . . . When men have once allowed themselves to think no more of what is to befall them after life, they lapse readily into that complete and brutal indifference to futurity which is but too conformable to some propensities of mankind.

It was belief in the sacred and the mythological that in the beginning of Western history made possible belief in and assimilation of ideas of time, history, development, and either progress or regress. Only on the basis of confidence in the existence of a divine power was confidence possible with respect to design or pattern in the world and in the history of the world. In the beginning all knowledge was sacred by virtue of its content—the divine, the mythological. It was persistence of this sense of the sacredness of knowledge that accorded the arts and sciences high status in Western civilization long after they had ceased to be concerned solely with the gods. Drama emerged from ritual, in ancient Greece and in post-medieval Europe; so of course did innumerable other arts emerge from their religious matrices—and in time also philosophy and the sciences. The aura of the sacred remained with the arts and sciences until well into the twentieth century.

But it is absent now, whether ever to be recovered, we cannot know. And with absence of the sense of sacredness of knowledge there is now to be seen in more and more areas absence of respect for or confidence in knowledge— that is, the kind of knowledge that proceeds from reason and its intrinsic disciplines. From the Enlightenment on, an increasing number of people came to believe that reason and its works could maintain momentum and could preserve their status in society with no influence save that which they themselves generated. But the present age of the revolt against reason, of crusading irrationalism, of the almost exponential development and diffusion of the occult, and the constant spread of narcissism and solipsism make evident enough how fallible were and are the secular foundations of modern thought. It is inconceivable that faith in either progress as a historical reality or in progress as a possibility can exist for long, to the degree that either concept does exist at the present moment, amid such alien and hostile intellectual forces.

I return to the question that began this final section of the book: what is the future of the idea of progress? Any logical answer must be that the idea has no future whatever if we assume the indefinite, prolonged continuation of the kind of culture that has become almost universal in the West in the late twentieth century. If the roots are dying, as they would appear to be at the present time, how can there be shrub and foliage?

But is this contemporary Western culture likely to continue for long? The answer, it seems to me, must be in the negative—if we take any stock in the lessons of the human past. One cannot be certain, of course; there is no sure way of catapulting ourselves into the future; no way of being confident that even the hardiest or most promising of current trends will continue indefinitely. But we can take some reasonable guidance, I believe, first from the fact that never in history have periods of culture such as our own lasted for very long. They are destroyed by all the forces which constitute their essence. How can any society or age last very long if it lacks or is steadily losing the minimal requirements for a society—such requirements being the very opposite of the egocentric and hedonistic elements which dominate Western culture today?

Second, it is impossible to overlook at the present time a phenomenon that as recently as the 1940s we thought so improbable as to be unworthy of serious thought or discussion. I refer to the faint, possibly illusory, signs of the beginning of a religious renewal in Western civilization, notably in America. Whatever their future, the signs are present—visible in the currents of fundamentalism, pentecostalism, even millennialism found in certain sectors of Judaism and Christianity. Even the spread of the occult and the cult in the West could well be one of the signs of a religious renascence, for, as is well known, the birth of Christianity or rather its genesis as a world religion in Rome during and after the preaching of Paul was surrounded by a myriad of bizarre faiths and devotions.

The signs I speak of lie amid other, very different signs which even though negative in implication are pertinent. By every serious reckoning the spell of politics and the political, strong since at least the seventeenth century, is fading. It is not simply a matter of growing disillusionment with government and bureaucracy; fundamentally, it is declining faith in politics as a way of mind and life. If such apparent decline be real and lasting, the case is all the stronger for a recrudescence of religion. For politics and religion are and will always be adversaries; this, be it noted, by virtue of what they have in common as much as by what separates them. They are the only major areas of life in which charismatic leaders, prophets, followings, rituals, feast days, creed, and calling have a commanding place. Only in these two areas do human beings exist who are not only willing but eager to sacrifice—worldly possessions, even life itself. Only in the mass followings of the Caesars and Napoleons of history are we able to find phenomena comparable to the mass followings of Jesus and Mohammed. But what makes them analogous also makes them adverse. When religion is powerful, as it was in the Middle Ages, the political tie is weak, raddled, and confused. But when the political tie becomes powerful, as in the modern totalitarian state, the role of religion is diminished—in large measure as the result of calculated political repression but also as the result of the sheer lure of the political-ideological "church." Today, certainly in the West and possibly in other areas of the earth also, including the Soviet Union, the appeal of the political diminishes visibly year by year. The Church of Politics began to lose communicants during World War I, but that was only a small apostacy by comparison with what the polls and surveys reveal at the present time. And in the ancient world, it is possible to measure the progress of Christianity in the very terms of the decline of the Roman Empire.

Such may well prove to be the case during the decades ahead in Western (and many non-Western) nations: on the one hand, there could be a continuing erosion of political values and commitments, while on the other, there might be a continuing enlargement of the religious, of the sacred, in the realm of human devotion and loyalty. Of course, we can only speculate. In spite of the current proliferation of religious consecrations and enthusiasms, it is always possible that these will have been decimated and put to rout before we reach the year 2000. But I do not think this will happen. Much more probable, I believe, is the appearance of yet another full-blown "awakening," even a major religious reformation. For some time now we have been witnessing what might properly be called the beginnings of such a transformation, beginnings which range from the popular to the scholarly, from eruptions of fundamentalism, pentecostalism—and, even within the Jewish, Roman Catholic and Protestant establishments, millennialism —all the way to what has to be regarded as a true efflorescence of formal theology. This efflorescence is manifested in books and articles of an intellectual quality not seen in such sudden abundance for many decades in the West. In Yeats's words, "Surely some revelation is at hand?"

Perhaps yes, perhaps no. We shall know before very much more time passes. What is really germane here is not the possibility of revelation and reformation, fascinating as these are in contemplation, but rather the future of the idea or dogma of progress. Here, too, genuine prediction is impossible. But one conclusion seems to me inescapable. This idea or dogma is bound to remain moribund, likely indeed to go all the way over the brink, so long as, citing Yeats again, "Mere anarchy is loosed upon the world." Only, it seems evident from the historical record, in the context of a true culture in which the core is a deep and wide sense of the *sacred* are we likely to regain the vital conditions of progress itself and of faith in progress— past, present, and future.

INDEX

Index

Index

Index

Index

Index